Politics, work, and daily life in the USSR

Data for this study were produced by the Soviet Interview Project. The Project was supported by Contract No. 701 from the National Council for Soviet and East European Research to the University of Illinois at Urbana-Champaign, James R. Millar, Principal Investigator. The analysis and interpretations in this study are those of the authors, not necessarily of the sponsors.

Politics, work, and daily life in the USSR

A survey of former Soviet citizens

Edited by

JAMES R. MILLAR

University of Illinois at Urbana-Champaign

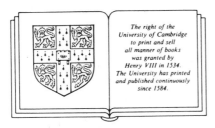

The right of the
University of Cambridge
to print and sell
all manner of books
was granted by
Henry VIII in 1534.
The University has printed
and published continuously
since 1584.

CAMBRIDGE UNIVERSITY PRESS

CAMBRIDGE

NEW YORK   NEW ROCHELLE   MELBOURNE   SYDNEY

Published by the Press Syndicate of the University of Cambridge
The Pitt Building, Trumpington Street, Cambridge CB2 1RP
32 East 57th Street, New York, NY 10022, USA
10 Stamford Road, Oakleigh, Melbourne 3166, Australia

First published 1987
Reprinted 1988 (twice)

Printed in the United States of America

Library of Congress Cataloging-in-Publication Data
Politics, work, and daily life in the USSR.
Includes index.
1. Soviet Union – Social conditions – 1970–
2. Soviet Union – Politics and government – 1953–
3. Soviet Union – Economic conditions – 1976–
4. Quality of life – Soviet Union.   I. Millar, James R.,
1936–
HN523.5.P63   1987   306'.0947   87-10855

British Library Cataloguing in Publication Data
Politics, work, and daily life in the USSR:
a survey of former Soviet citizens.
1. Soviet Union – Social conditions –
1970–
I. Millar, James R.
947.085'4   HN523.5

ISBN 0 521 33476 4 hard covers
ISBN 0 521 34890 0 paperback

Contents

Foreword

American scholarship on the USSR expanded rapidly after World War II. The critical obstacle to research at the time was the paucity of data, particularly reliable data, on Soviet society. The publication of a national statistical abstract had been discontinued in the midthirties, and the last full population census dated back to 1926. Few foreigners were admitted to the country for purposes of observation, study, or research. Under those circumstances the several million former Soviet citizens living in the West were an invaluable source of information about the society that they had left during the turbulence of the war. They provided the raw data gathered by the Harvard Refugee Interview Project, which produced a set of publications that greatly enriched Western understanding of Soviet society in those years.

The volume of data available on Soviet society today is vastly greater than in those lean years. In 1956 the publication of an annual statistical abstract resumed, and three decennial population censuses have been published since then. Hundreds of foreign students and scholars have lived and worked in Soviet universities, institutes, libraries, and archives under various cultural and scientific exchange programs. Journalists and businessmen have established relationships that have enabled them to penetrate fairly intimately into parts of the society. A large volume of social and economic research by Soviet scholars on Soviet society is available in the West, as are the unofficial research and data published as *samizdat*.

Then, with detente, came a new large wave of emigration from the USSR during the 1970s. In the light of the greatly expanded volume of data available on the USSR, the question for the scholarly community was whether a large-scale survey research project on the new emigrants was worth the effort and expense. After a period of extensive discussion in government and academic circles, the answer was clear. Although the volume of Soviet data and other information is far greater than in the dark postwar years, it is still very much less than that which is available on most Western societies. It also contains large gaps on matters that Western scholars regard as interesting aspects of societies in general and of the USSR in particular. It was that view that led to the organization of the Soviet Interview Project (SIP), from which this collection of papers has emerged as a first installment.

vii

The differences between the Harvard Project and SIP reflect the remarkable change in the state of Soviet studies in the quarter-century between them. In the young field of the late 1940s, for example, there were very few professors and many graduate students; in the mature field of today there are many professors and relatively fewer graduate students. Consequently, a great deal of the work of the Harvard Project was conducted by graduate students gathering material for dissertations, under the direction of a few senior scholars. Virtually all the work of SIP, by contrast, was conducted by experienced scholars, many with substantial records of published research. The difference mirrors the change in the state of the Soviet studies, from one in which the incremental contribution of Ph.D. dissertations was substantial to one in which it is now relatively modest.

The two projects also span the period that Soviet writers used to call the scientific-technical revolution. The Harvard Project prided itself in using state-of-the-art data-processing technology, which consisted of a shiny new IBM card sorter housed in an office called the "shop." Chi-squares and correlation coefficients were produced by fast new Monroe calculators with what seemed like machine-gun speed. A quarter-century later, survey research data collection and management had become so technical a business that SIP decided to employ the services of a specialized research service organization: the National Opinion Research Center. The new computer technology made it possible for SIP analysts, like contemporary quantitative analysts generally, to employ methods that were infeasible in the past. Multivariate regression techniques, for example, which are widely employed in the papers in this volume, were far beyond the capacity of even the fastest Monroe calculators of that time.

Survey research itself was a young discipline in the postwar years, and the Harvard Project was at the cutting edge of the art, through both its own personnel and the consultants upon whom it drew for counsel and criticism. That edge has done a lot of cutting in the intervening years, however, and is far less accessible to the nonspecialist than in the past. The training of the graduate student interviewers (it was my good fortune to be one of them) occupied a considerable number of sessions and produced interviewers who regarded themselves as quite sophisticated in the art. That training time, however, was but a fraction of that which NORC requires today to produce interviewers competent in the art as it has developed to this time.

One major difference involves not the passage of time but the logistics of interviewing. Most of the postwar emigrants had been living for some time in temporary "displaced persons camps" in Germany and neighboring countries. They were easy to locate, and they had a surfeit of time on their hands. The opportunity to tell the story of their lives to a sympathetic outsider was a welcome diversion. In contrast, the SIP respondents were scattered all over the United States. Most of them were living active lives and holding full-time jobs, and did not regard it as a great privilege to give up a couple of nights for the sake of science. Consequently, the time and cost of locating respondents and persuading them to be interviewed were much greater. The Harvard interviewers were able to spend two to three days with each respondent, whereas the SIP interviews consisted on average of one three-hour session. SIP, however, conducted personal interviews with a much larger number of respondents.

In one dominating respect, however, the two projects are quite similar, despite the passage of time. Both had to confront the crucial question of whether reliable knowledge about Soviet society can be obtained from the testimony of people who must be regarded as hostile to the political system.

The Harvard Project had a somewhat easier task. Many of its respondents had not left the USSR voluntarily because of disaffection with the system; some had been prisoners of war, and some had been seized by the German authorities in occupied Soviet territory and shipped to Germany or Austria as involuntary laborers. Almost all the SIP respondents, however, had left voluntarily, and some had faced harsh sanctions for having announced their wish to emigrate. Second, the Harvard Project respondents were almost all Slavic, mostly Great Russian by nationality. The SIP respondents, in contrast, come predominantly from the Jewish nationality, which is a small minority in the USSR that suffers from discrimination. Fortunately, there is a sufficient number of respondents of other nationalities to provide a basis for assessing the extent to which the responses and experiences of the Jewish respondents may differ from those of other nationalities.

Both projects devoted a massive effort to the detection of bias of various sorts in the testimony of the respondents. The wide acceptance of the findings of the Harvard Project signified that the scholarly community by and large was persuaded that their testimony, as analyzed by researchers sensitized to the problem of bias, did provide an acceptable basis for drawing inferences about the parent Soviet society. SIP had available the accumulated experience of several additional decades of survey research in dealing with bias, which will be evident in the papers in this volume. The Harvard Project, for example, devoted considerable attention to the precision of the translation of its interview questions from English into Russian, but it did not have available the "double-blind translation" method employed here. With the care and ingenuity with which the SIP researchers dealt with the bias problem, as set forth in these essays, they have good reason to expect that their data will be regarded as a reasonable basis for the inferences they have presented here about Soviet society.

Perhaps more important than the inferences that are drawn about Soviet society are the inferences that are deliberately not drawn. The proportion of respondents who accept regime norms, for example, provides no basis for an estimate of the proportion of the parent Soviet population that accepts regime norms. However, the finding that older people in the sample are more likely than younger people to accept regime norms, other things equal, does support the inference that a similar relation between age and acceptance of regime norms is to be found in the Soviet population. That is an important finding about Soviet society, although it tells us far less than could be learned if it were possible to survey the Soviet population itself.

The findings in any research project reflect the questions that the analysts seek to answer. Those questions emerge from the state of knowledge and the research agenda at the time. In the postwar years Western views were heavily influenced by Soviet claims about the nature of their own society. Those claims were challenged by critics abroad, but the research base for assessing the controversies was very small, because of both the paucity of reliable data and the small number of researchers with the requisite language and analytic skills. The Harvard Project provided a unique opportunity to develop a body of data for illuminating that debate.

A central question at the time was the extent to which the abolition of private ownership of the means of production had eliminated the basis of the division of society into social classes, as Marx predicted and as the Soviets claimed. Was it in fact a society of a new kind, unlike those with which we are familiar, in which social class is the predominant predictor of life chances, lifestyle, attitudes, and so forth? A major thrust of the project was the exploration of that issue, and the conclusion was strikingly clear. On question after question the variable that best explained the distribution of responses was social class – not nationality, not age or sex, but social class. In most respects Soviet society reflected the characteristics of a class society of the Western industrial kind. That conclusion is perhaps the principal contribution of the Harvard Project to the advance of knowledge at the time.

It is therefore worthy of note that social class does not emerge in this volume as a major analytic variable. The largest differences among groups in the SIP sample are those between the younger and the older. Education, occupation, income, sex, and nationality distinctions also show up, but it is age differences that dominate the social fabric.

Like the dog that didn't bark, the variable that does not appear may provide the clue to an interesting difference in the state of knowledge at that time and now. Several conjectures may be offered. First, the Harvard Project contributed decisively to the advancement of knowledge by settling the question that occupied center stage at the time; the class nature of Soviet society became the conventional wisdom, and the question disappeared from the agenda of subsequent research. It is simply no longer an interesting question. Second, the subject of social class, which occupied so central a role in general sociological theory and research a few decades ago, is perhaps no longer at the core of disciplinary interest. Third, contemporary data-processing power may have diminished the usefulness for social research of so aggregative a concept as social class. Traditional measures of social class like socioeconomic status scales consisted of a set of scores on such underlying variables as education, income, occupation, and so forth. It is now so easy and inexpensive to investigate the separate effects of those variables that little is gained by the use of the composite measure (I am indebted to Paul Gregory for this interpretation). It is a mark of the passage of time and of the advance of knowledge that a curiosity about the influence of social class on Soviet society reveals not one's knowledge but one's age.

The Harvard Project researchers enjoyed some of the advantages and excitement of pioneering; one did not have to be particularly ingenious to discover or explore a new terrain at that time. The age of pioneering, however, has long been over. As in all developed fields of endeavor, genuinely new contributions are rare, and it takes greater talent and training to find an important new property of a society that so many earlier researchers had overlooked. Therefore, one should not read this book in the expectation of finding startling new insights into Soviet society that had somehow escaped the microscopes of several generations of dissertation and monographic research. One should expect rather to find those kinds of insights that could not be obtained or verified by any methods other than the surveying of substantial numbers of people who have been members of the society. The Harvard Project and SIP are the only two bodies of data in the world (excluding the USSR, though possibly including it as well) to have produced the kind of data that could support those insights.

The finding that will perhaps attract the greatest attention, as reported by James R. Millar in his introduction, is the remarkable reversal in the relation between age and support for the regime that occurred between 1940 and 1980 (the years on which the two projects focused attention). In the earlier period it was the younger who were most supportive and the older who were most hostile. In 1980 it was the other way around. Another striking finding is the extent to which education level has come to dominate the factors determining social position and attitudes. In question after question, education level emerges as the variable that explains the largest proportion of the variation in responses. Education, of course, was a major component of the social class variable that occupied a similar dominant role in the Harvard Project study, so that there may not have been so great a change in this respect. However, the gradual attenuation of the significance of such characteristics as one's social origin, which played an important role before the war, may well have elevated education to the dominating position that this study finds it to occupy today.

The political significance of this finding is that education, like age, bears a strong negative relation to support for the regime. As Brian Silver's analysis reveals, however, given the level of education, support for the regime *increases* with income level. Coming at a time when a new leader has undertaken to transform Soviet society, these and other SIP findings will provide a valuable basis for the assessment of the prospects for that program of reform.

What counts as a contribution to knowledge is to a great degree a matter of taste. For scholars of a more intuitive disposition, many of the findings will be regarded as not interesting because they are not new. The intuitionist needs no survey research project to inform him that Soviet youth are hostile to the regime; any reader of Soviet novels, or even *Pravda*, knows that is true, as does anyone who has lived in the society. Well, says the survey researcher, maybe it is, and maybe it isn't. And if it is, is it as true of female youth as of male youth? And is it as true of highly educated male youth as of less educated? And among the more highly educated male youth, is it more true of those who earn higher income than of those who earn less? The intuitionist may find something of interest in questions like these that are explored in this volume, but he may be more interested in the second set of SIP studies, which are based on in-depth interviews with emigrants with particular experiences, such as factory management or the law. The results of those studies will begin to appear shortly.

Twenty-five years elapsed between the first emigrant interview project and the second. Will there be a third, sometime in the next millennium? If Secretary General Gorbachev's policy of *glasnost'*, of openness, plays itself out, there may never be a third. If the time comes when Soviet scholars are free to design their own research projects, there is no doubt that they would undertake to look into the social structure of their own society as scholars around the world look into their own. If that research were published, there would be no need for foreign scholars to do that work, much less with such unrepresentative respondents as emigrants. Extracting valid results from a biased sample is an intriguing exercise, but no one would mourn if it never needed to be done again.

JOSEPH S. BERLINER

Contributors

BARBARA A. ANDERSON is professor of sociology and a research scientist at the Population Studies Center of the University of Michigan.

DONNA BAHRY is professor of political science at New York University.

CAROLYN S. BREDA is a research assistant to Michael Swafford at Vanderbilt University.

BRADLEY P. BULLOCK is a research assistant to Michael Swafford at Vanderbilt University.

ELIZABETH CLAYTON is professor of economics at the University of Missouri–St. Louis.

PAUL R. GREGORY is professor of economics at the University of Houston–University Park.

RASMA KARKLINS is professor of political science at the University of Illinois–Chicago.

LINDA L. LUBRANO is professor of political science in the School of International Service at American University.

JAMES R. MILLAR is the director of International Programs and Studies and professor of economics at the University of Illinois at Urbana-Champaign.

GUR OFER is professor of economics at the Hebrew University of Jerusalem, Israel.

BRIAN D. SILVER is professor of political science at Michigan State University and a research affiliate of the Population Studies Center at the University of Michigan.

MICHAEL SWAFFORD is professor of sociology at Vanderbilt University.

AARON VINOKUR is professor of sociology at the University of Haifa, Israel.

Carol A. Zeiss is research assistant to Michael Swafford at Vanderbilt University.

William Zimmerman is professor of political science at the University of Michigan.

PART I

Introduction

CHAPTER 1

History, method, and the problem of bias

JAMES R. MILLAR

The Soviet Interview Project (SIP) has interviewed thousands of recent emigrants from the Soviet Union as a means of learning about politics, work, and daily life in the contemporary USSR. The project was designed by a team of Soviet specialists as a study of everyday life in the USSR with the expectation that the results will contribute not only to Sovietology but also to general theories in the basic disciplines represented by the research team – notably political science, economics, and sociology.[1] The initial phase of the project has involved administering highly structured question-naires covering a wide range of topics bearing on life, work, and politics in contemporary Soviet society to a probability sample of eligible Soviet emigrants currently residing in the United States. As the principal aim has been to learn about life in the Soviet Union, the absorption process has been of interest for validation purposes only. The essays collected in this volume represent a first strike from the data set.[2]

The purpose of this chapter is to provide a brief history of the Soviet Interview Project, a description of the methods and procedures that have guided the SIP General Survey I, and an overview of first findings.

History

On August 3, 1979, a meeting was held at the Kennan Institute to promote a project to interview recent Soviet emigrants to the United States. The meeting's organizers were senior academic scholars and interested U.S.

[1] The team for the General Survey consisted of James R. Millar, Project Director, University of Illinois at Urbana-Champaign; Barbara A. Anderson, University of Michigan; Donna Bahry, New York University; John Garrard, University of Arizona; Paul R. Gregory, University of Houston – University Park; Rasma Karklins, University of Illinois – Chicago; Norman Nie, University of Chicago; Brian D. Silver, Michigan State University; Michael Swafford, Vanderbilt University; William Zimmerman, University of Michigan; Aaron Vinokur, University of Haifa; Linda Lubrano, Senior Research Associate, American University; Marjorie Balzer, Senior Research Associate, Columbia University.
[2] The data set has been deposited with the Inter-university Consortium for Political and Social Research, Institute for Social Research, P.O. Box 1248, Ann Arbor, MI 48106. The tape has 2,739 records, one for each respondent, and each record contains 1,446 variables. The tape also contains an SPSS-X export file.

government specialists, some of whom had been involved in the Harvard Project on the Soviet Social System of the early 1950s.[3] The Harvard Project was a pioneering survey effort that sought to assay the "strengths and vulnerabilities of the Soviet social system" by interviewing expatriate Russians in displaced-person camps in Allied-occupied Europe following World War II.[4]

Despite the seemingly unpromising character of its sample, the Harvard study is widely regarded today as a success. With funding from the U.S. Air Force, principal investigators Clyde Kluckhohn, Alex Inkeles, and Raymond Bauer of the Harvard Russian Research Center sought to learn about life under Stalin by interviewing former citizens of the USSR who had elected not to return home after the war. Most of them had had their lives in the Soviet Union disrupted ten years or so earlier by the war, and all hoped to be allowed to stay in the West.

The results of the Harvard study have withstood the test of time, including the unanticipated release of large quantities of new data on Soviet society and the opening of Russia's borders to foreign visitors by Khrushchev after he consolidated power in the mid-1950s. Moreover, as any Soviet specialist may confirm, the Harvard Project established paradigms for the study of Soviet society that, to a surprising extent, still inform research in the West to this day.

When, in the 1970s, tens of thousands of Soviet citizens were allowed to leave the Soviet Union for West Germany and Israel, it did not take long for Western specialists to recognize the potential for Soviet studies. Between 1968 and 1984 (inclusive), approximately 265,000 persons left the Soviet Union with Israeli visas, and some 90,000 Soviet citizens of German extraction left for West Germany. Another 20,000 or so left under other auspices, including some Russian, Ukrainian, and Baltic nationalities and more than 10,000 Armenians who came almost exclusively to the United States. As time passed, an increasing proportion of those who initially were slated for Israel decided, once they were out of the USSR, to come to the United States instead. By 1986, more than 100,000 had arrived in the United

---

[3] Attendees included: James R. Millar, University of Illinois at Urbana-Champaign; Jeremy Azrael, University of Chicago; Paul Cook, Department of State; Alex Dallin, Stanford University; Maurice Friedberg, University of Illinois at Urbana-Champaign; Fred Giessler, Office of Net Assessment, Department of Defense; Gregory Grossman, University of California–Berkeley; William Manthorpe, Office of Net Assessment, Department of Defense; Norman Nie, University of Chicago; Vladimir Toumanoff, National Council for Soviet and East European Research; William Zimmerman, University of Michigan; S. Frederick Starr, Kennan Institute.

[4] Some of the interviews were conducted in New York City, too. See Inkeles and Bauer 1959 (Part 1) for a more detailed description of the Harvard Project.

States, with 35,000 former Soviet citizens arriving in 1979 alone, the largest inflow of any year. Since 1979, the rate of immigration to this country has declined sharply and in recent years has not exceeded 1,000 per year.[5]

Development of a major research program on the order of the Harvard Project in this country faced a number of obstacles, not least of which was the difficulty of locating financial support. The Ford Foundation had recently lowered the priority of Soviet area studies. U.S. government funds were also restricted by what was known as the Kissinger rule, after the secretary of state during the Nixon administration, who had established a personal policy against the use of federal funds for academic or government studies of recent emigrants from the Soviet Union. (He was concerned, presumably, about potential adverse effects upon the migration itself as well as with possible repercussions upon U.S.–Israeli and U.S.–Soviet relations.)

The August 1979 meeting was called following a successful lobbying effort to revise the Kissinger rule, which had remained effective policy during the first three years of the Carter administration. Some form of government funding was considered essential because survey research on the scale anticipated is very expensive and requires assured long-term financing. The agenda focused on a series of obstacles that would have to be overcome and decisions that would have to be taken to get the project under way.

First, there was the question of methodology. The Harvard Project had utilized a variety of methods, including life histories, expert testimony, and a lengthy, closed, "paper and pencil questionnaire" administered to almost 3,000 respondents. Feelings have run high ever since the Harvard Project in the Soviet field, especially among political scientists, with respect to the validity of the various methods. Disagreement over the relative merits of quantitative and qualitative research and over various survey procedures was clearly evident at this first meeting. A related, subsidiary issue involved whether or not to employ the services of a professional survey research organization.

Second, there was the question of what disciplines to include in the research team. The principal investigators of the Harvard Project included an anthropologist, a psychologist, and a sociologist. Economics, political science, and other disciplines such as history were represented either by graduate students, who served initially as interviewers and subsequently as analysts while developing dissertations with the data, or by senior consultants. In 1979, there were few anthropologists or social psychologists in the field and only a small number of trained sociologists. It was clear that

---

[5] Sources of data: telephone communication with the staff of the Conference on Soviet Jewry, New York City, and unclassified figures from U.S. Department of State (courtesy Paul Cook).

political science and economics would play more significant roles in the current project. The Harvard study had relied primarily upon the faculty and graduate students associated with the Russian Research Center. It was presumed that the current project would be broadly based, drawing members from a variety of academic institutions.

Third, would it be possible to locate a reasonable sample? Compiling a list for the sample frame and locating the sample would depend heavily upon cooperation from resettlement agencies. Moreover, because such a high proportion of the immigrants to this country were Jewish (by some definition), cooperation was also necessary from a variety of Jewish organizations that had become involved in the outmigration of Jews from the Soviet Union and in their absorption here or in Israel. Various emigré organizations were potentially important to the success of the project also.

Fourth, even with success in the development and location of a reasonable sample of recent Soviet emigrants, would they respond freely and candidly? Many of our consultants believed that they would not or that their innocence of survey research as Soviet citizens would make them poor subjects. There were still others who asserted that former Soviet citizens would, as respondents, fear penetration of the project by the KGB or by American intelligence agencies. It was obvious, therefore, that confidentiality would be a key factor.

Fifth, how was the project to be funded? It was understood that the federal government would be the principal funder and that the Department of Defense (DOD) would play a very substantial role as a funder. The meeting was assured "not to worry about what the sponsor was interested in." The sponsor was prepared "to trust academic judgment" regarding both methodology and substance. The general aim of the Office of Net Assessment in the Pentagon, which at that time represented the prime potential funder, was described as support for basic research into the "underlying factors and dynamics of contemporary Soviet society that will determine the future power and development of the USSR." This was a sufficiently broad and fundamental objective to pose no serious constraint upon academic formulation of the research agenda.

The real question was how to insure that the profession, the emigrants themselves, resettlement workers, and others whose cooperation was essential would perceive the project as an academic exercise and not as merely a front for official intelligence. The Harvard Project had been funded by the U.S. Air Force directly, but concerns about possible Soviet reaction to direct DOD funding for SIP and about possible adverse effects upon potential respondents made a search for alternatives desirable. The newly created National Council for Soviet and East European Research offered a promising vehicle for the provision of oversight for the project and a buffer between the project and the ultimate government funders.[6]

Finally, what should the aims of the project be? It was agreed that, regardless of the source of funding, the research agenda should be determined by academics and that the aim should be basic rather than applied research on the Soviet social system. The most fundamental question, however, was what we could and should seek to learn from what was viewed by all of us as an extremely valuable "living archive" on contemporary Soviet society but one that was at the same time badly flawed because unrepresentative of the USSR taken as a whole. It was also a highly perishable archive that needed utilization as soon as possible.

A design phase proposal was funded by the National Council for Soviet and East European Research in November 1979. During the design stage of the study, more than 100 scholars specializing in Soviet studies or in survey methodology participated in seminars on the ideal substance and survey methodology of such a project. The seminars were held all over the country during the first half of 1980 in an attempt to involve the maximum number of scholars in a variety of disciplines.[7] Concentrated work on the topics that could and should be treated and on the various methods available to obtain reliable information on them was conducted at the University of Illinois during the summer of 1980. The written statements that were produced at that time later formed the basis for development of the General Survey questionnaire.

To a considerable extent the research team was self-selected, for it composed itself primarily of those scholars who participated the most actively in the feasibility design seminars and who were also willing to commit themselves to a five-year project. Selection was constrained, of course, by the need to have various methodological and disciplinary skills represented and by the requirement that a variety of academic institutions be represented. The research team ultimately consisted of two economists, five political scientists, three sociologists, and one Russian literature specialist. A number of other individual scholars also contributed questions and participated in questionnaire development during formulation of the General Survey protocol.

[6] The National Council for Soviet and East European Research was founded in 1978 by the presidents of twelve institutions: University of California–Berkeley, University of Chicago, Columbia University, Duke University, Harvard University, University of Illinois, Indiana University, University of Michigan, University of Pennsylvania, Stanford University, American Association for the Advancement of Soviet Studies, and Kennan Institute.

[7] For a list of attendees, see Exhibit 3-A of *The Soviet Interview Project General Survey Codebook* 1986.

8   James R. Millar

Feasibility issues

The two most critical issues governing feasibility were (1) whether or not we could identify and locate a sample worth interviewing, and (2) whether or not Soviet emigrants in this country would participate freely and candidly. The sample design our methodologists recommended called for maximizing analyzable heterogeneity within the sample and stratifying to reduce anomalies produced by the constraints that shaped the migration of former Soviet citizens to this country. This meant that it was essential to develop a sample frame that would be as close to a census as possible of the most recent immigrants to the United States. It followed, therefore, that we would have to have the active cooperation of the various resettlement agencies in this country that had received, placed, and continued to keep contact with the sample we required. Use of U.S. government official sources was, of course, out of the question.

We discovered that participation and candor hinged upon our ability to guarantee very strict confidentiality. Indeed, the most frequent reason given by emigrants who refused to be interviewed was the fear of adverse effect upon relatives still in the USSR and upon their chances of emigrating subsequently. In general, given assurances of confidentiality, most of our respondents were eager to participate precisely because they believed that they had valuable information on the Soviet system, which was needed to correct American misimpressions, both official and unofficial, about life in the Soviet Union.

Very rigorous confidentiality procedures were worked out with the assistance of the National Opinion Research Center (NORC) of the University of Chicago. The system SIP used was derived from – and more stringent than – procedures that had previously been used in survey projects to protect the identities of persons who had been interviewed about serious criminal activities, such as drug dealing, where candid participation could expose the respondent to felony criminal charges. In brief, the system involved use of a "Canadian link file" to separate name and address from case number and encryption of various case and interviewer "links." The face sheet and all materials conveying information that might identify the respondent were separated from the questionnaire in the presence of the respondent and placed in a separate envelope for immediate mailing to the Canadian link. The questionnaire was placed in another envelope addressed to NORC. These procedures, plus rigorous training of our interviewers about the significance of confidentiality measures, were successful in generating a response rate of almost 80 percent.

Once we were confident that we could achieve a satisfactorily high response rate, it was necessary to persuade the various resettlement agencies,

Jewish organizations, various emigrant groups, and other interested parties that the very existence of an interview project of this magnitude would not – in and of itself – provide Soviet authorities with a pretext to terminate outmigration altogether. The historical record shows that the Jewish and German-Russian emigrations from the USSR had been tied to major foreign policy issues, particularly to international economic issues (Millar 1985). On the individual level, Soviet authorities clearly exercise discretion over those who wish to leave. People whom they do not want "debriefed" by Western intelligence agencies or interviewed by the press or scholarly organizations are simply not allowed as individuals to emigrate. It was our best judgment, therefore, that SIP would not precipitate a change in Soviet policy, and most of those who were experienced with the Jewish emigration from the USSR agreed. Subsequent events substantiated this view.

Although we were ready to begin work on the questionnaire by the end of the summer of 1980 and had established the feasibility of the project, political events in Washington, D.C., put the project on ice until the fall of 1981. The principal reason for the delay was the change in national administrations, which required persuading a new set of government officials of the desirability and feasibility of the project. Thus, it was not until September 1981 that the Soviet Interview Project got under way in earnest.

Funding

Fortunately, during the summer of 1981 an arrangement was made by the DOD, the Central Intelligence Agency, and the State Department, with the blessings of a number of other federal departments and agencies, to fund the Soviet Interview Project through the National Council for Soviet and East European Research. The National Council was charged with oversight and quality assurance for the project as it had been proposed June 20, 1980.

The contract specified three principal goals for the Soviet Interview Project. The first was to conduct a study of contemporary Soviet society based upon interviews with recent emigrants from the Soviet Union who now live in the United States. The second was to promote the involvement of young scholars and thus to serve as a means for development of the field of Soviet studies. The third aim was to make the data and research products collected by SIP available to all interested scholars in the field simultaneously with the delivery of any and all research products to the National Council and government sponsors.

The study as proposed in June 1980 called for two complementary types of interviews. One was to be a general survey of a relatively large sample of respondents, based upon a questionnaire that would be developed in advance and would, therefore, be as "closed-ended" as possible and amenable to statistical analysis. The other involved a set of "expert" or special knowledge interviews, each of which would involve a limited number of "informants" who would be able to report on the way certain institutions of Soviet society are organized and how they really work. Examples of the latter are enterprise managers, jurists, and camp returnees. The studies that are reported in this volume pertain only to the SIP General Survey.

Questionnaire development

Thus, in September 1981, after almost exactly a year's hiatus, the research team began drafting the questionnaire for the General Survey. Two aspects of this process proved particularly challenging. First, the team sought to develop a truly interdisciplinary questionnaire in which, for example, political scientists' questions would serve economists and vice versa. This was not merely a desirable goal but a necessity, because the number of questions that members of each discipline wanted to ask far exceeded the space available. The task was analogous to designing the payload of a satellite. Each experiment must be compatible with all the rest, and only so many experiments can be accommodated on board. We were forced to share variables wherever possible, therefore, which meant "selling" one's own discipline's variables to other team members. Space in the questionnaire was not merely allotted to team members, who would be free to use the space as they saw fit. Rather, all questions were treated as though they belonged to everybody, a policy that generated considerable interdisciplinary give-and-take.

Just as challenging was the task of paring down the list of questions suggested by the various disciplinary subcommittees of the research team and their consultants – a list that would have required interviews lasting more than a dozen hours instead of the targeted average length of three hours. Team members were obliged to write "passports" explaining the utility of each question, or set of questions, they wished to place in the questionnaire. Passports had to be quite specific, detailing the hypothesis to be tested, the relevant literature, and the frequency distributions expected for each question, and they served as a basis for discussion and decision making by the questionnaire "editing committee."

Technical assistance in developing the questionnaire was provided by NORC. NORC staff formatted questions in accordance with established survey principles and organized the questionnaire to facilitate the flow of questions and answers. In August and October of 1982, NORC conducted two English pretests of the questionnaire with 54 English-speaking Soviet emigrants. After each pretest, the questionnaire was revised under the direction of the research team to take into account the reactions of respondents and the impressions of the NORC staff as to which questions were "not working." The pretests were also used to close as many open-ended questions as possible, because open-ended questions cost so much more to administer and process than do questions offering fixed response categories.

In keeping with standard practice, the questionnaire was written in English because that was to be the language of analysis. After a satisfactory English questionnaire was developed, it was translated into Russian by three recent Soviet emigrants. Translation was supervised and edited by Aaron Vinokur, a research team member who is himself a member of the Third Emigration.

The preliminary Russian questionnaire then underwent blind back-translation into English by an independent professional Russian-to-English translator (who was himself a native speaker of English). Substantive, measurement, and linguistic equivalence of the original English version and the back-translation was checked both by the NORC staff and by appropriate members of the research team. Substantive and measurement equivalence was treated as controlling where conflicts emerged with linguistic equivalence. Differences were resolved in November 1982 at a meeting of the translators, the back-translator, the NORC staff, and the research team's special editing committee. The Russian questionnaire was pretested with 12 emigrants during the next two months. Further corrections and refinements were introduced on the basis of these pretests.

The content and structure of the questionnaire

The research team chose to focus on everyday life in the Soviet Union, not on emigrants' experiences in attempting to leave their homeland or on their adjustment to life in the United States. Emigration and absorption are interesting and worthy topics, and we would have liked to study them as well, but dealing with them seriously would have occupied valuable questionnaire space and thus detracted substantially from the team's ability to study many aspects of life in the USSR.

The concept of the last normal period of life in the USSR

To insure that respondents would report on their normal preemigration lives, the team adopted a strategy initially employed by Gur Ofer and Aaron Vinokur in their research on Soviet emigrants in Israel: leading respondents to define and talk about their last period of normal life in the USSR (Ofer, Vinokur, and Bar-Chaim 1979). Because applying to emigrate usually brings marked changes in Soviet citizens' lives, respondents were asked to

Table 1.1. *Temporal structure of the general questionnaire*

Life history	Last normal period	At interview
Respondent		
Migration	Residence	Residence
Education	Highest educational attainment	
Employment (unemployment) and military service	Employment	Employment
	Income/wealth	Income
Evaluation of nationality policy and ethnic conflict	Nationality	Ethnic self-identification
Marriage, fertility	Marital status	
	Languages, religion	
	Cultural preferences	
Political participation	Political participation	Religion
Evaluation of changing economic conditions	Economic/social status	
	Job satisfaction	
	Quality of life	
Evaluation of changing political and social freedoms	Evaluations of regime and leaders, economic attainment	
	Values	
Spouse		
Marriage and fertility	Marital status	Marital status
Migration	Nationality/ethnic self-identification	
Selected education history	Educational attainment	
	Religion	
Job interruptions		Family roster
Household		
Family migration history	Income/wealth	Income
	Decision making	

pinpoint the month and year in which they applied to emigrate. They were also asked whether plans to emigrate significantly changed their lives even before that date and, if so, to specify the month and year in which their lives changed. The five years leading up to the earlier of these two dates were defined as the last normal period (abbreviated "LNP"), and the prior month was defined as the end of the last normal period ("end LNP"). Interviewers explained the terms and, in full view of respondents, clearly marked the LNP on the life history charts, which had been filled out using information from respondents. Interviewers were instructed to refer to the chart as often as necessary during the rest of the interview to make certain that respondents focused on the correct period when questions referred to the LNP.

The frequency distribution of respondents' LNPs reveals that 2,562 of the 2,793 respondents specified the end of their LNP between 1978 and 1981. Inasmuch as the vast majority of interviews took place in 1983, it follows that most respondents were asked to answer questions about events from two to five years prior to the interview (*SIP General Survey Codebook* 1986).

The function of the LNP concept is revealed more fully in Table 1.1, which gives the temporal structure of the General Survey questionnaire. (Disregard the lower two sections of the table for the time being.) Note the column pertaining to the LNP. It shows that respondents were asked a wide range of questions about the LNP, from straightforward questions about their place of residence to subjective questions about job satisfaction and regime performance. As the life history column indicates, respondents were also asked to recall facts about the years leading up to their LNP. These questions developed a series of educational, marital, employment, migration, and military histories, which allow analyses that escape the usual shortcomings of cross-sectional data. Finally, as the right-hand column shows, respondents were asked a few questions about their status at the time of the interview. For the most part, these questions were raised to allow the team to test whether or not emigrants' status at the time of the interview might have affected their perceptions of the past.

Table 1.1 reveals another important aspect of the questionnaire. Most questions pertained to the respondents' own lives, not to their households. Nevertheless, since household events were expected to bear on respondents' lives, questions about spouses and households were raised. As the lower part of the exhibit indicates, special attention was devoted to household fertility, migration decision making, and budgets.

Partitioning of the questionnaire

To reduce the burden on respondents while retaining as many questions as possible, the research team decided to break interviews into two components – a two-hour core to be administered to all respondents; and three one-hour supplements, each of which was randomly assigned to one-third of the respondents. This tack allowed the team to retain five hours of questions while demanding, on the average, only three hours from each respondent. The thematic, modular structure of the questionnaire is shown in Table 1.2. Note that the core contained biographical questions as well as questions about employment, education, fertility, mobility, language and ethnicity, household structure, political participation, and opinions. Each of the supplements, on the other hand, offered a more narrow range of related questions: One supplement focused on politics; another on socioeconomic and demographic topics; and a third on a potpourri of topics such as leisure

Table 1.2. *Disciplinary structure of the general questionnaire*

Core ($N = 2{,}793$)	
Mod A: Biography, parentage	Mod H: Household structure, standard of living
Mod B: Education	Mod I: Bureaucratic encounters
Mod C: Early employment	Mod J: Opinions (e.g., sex role attitudes)
Mod D: Life history	Mod K: Spouse
Mod E: Fertility	Mod L: Institutional evaluations
Mod F: Emigration, LNP employment	Mod M: Military experience
Mod G: Language, ethnicity, religion	Mod N: Emigration and current status

Supplements		
Green ($N = 922$)	Orange ($N = 926$)	Blue ($N = 933$)[a]
Religious practices	Politics	Employment
Media	Crime	Income
Nationality	Foreign policy	Standard of living
Science views	Evaluations	Birth control
Leisure activities	Sex roles	Soviet census

[a] The sum of the Ns for the three supplements equals 12 less than the N for the core because 12 respondents did not complete a supplement.

activities, media preferences, attitudes toward science, and the like.

Splitting the questionnaire in this way, of course, reduced the number of cases for questions in the supplements to about one-third of the sample each and rendered it impossible to calculate correlations between variables covered in different supplements. These disadvantages were minimized, however, by making certain that key control variables were covered in the core and by putting questions requiring a large number of cases in the core also. Furthermore, questions in the supplements were grouped by themes to maximize the probability that interesting correlates would appear in the same supplement, if not in the core.

Recruiting and training interviewers

From the outset, it was clear that recruiting good interviewers would be uncommonly challenging: They would have to be fluent in Russian and able to administer a long, complex questionnaire in accordance with the demanding standards set by academic survey organizations. And they would also have to be willing to do the interviewing wherever the emigrants lived. Interviewers would have to be trained from scratch also, because the language requirement precluded using NORC's pool of trained interviewers.

The large population of Soviet emigrants presented itself as a potential source of interviewers, and some consultants argued for employing emigrants on grounds that they would be more likely to catch subtleties in answers given in Russian. Others, however, were concerned that respondents – having spent their lives in the USSR avoiding sensitive topics with potential informers – would not be candid with emigrant interviewers with whom they were unacquainted. Still others wondered whether emigrant interviewers could refrain entirely from imposing their views on responses they considered wrong. Taking all arguments into consideration, applications from emigrants were disallowed only for those who fell into the sample frame (that is, those who had arrived in the United States after 1978). Applications from other qualified emigrants who were U.S. citizens were judged against the same standards as other applicants. All interviewers were obliged, of course, to have proficiency in the English language.

Applicants were evaluated on the basis of three criteria: (1) "interviewing personality," that is, the ability to establish rapport with respondents, to elicit responses without reflecting judgments, and to follow directions in questionnaires; (2) knowledge of Russian (and of English, in the case of emigrant applicants); and (3) proximity to areas in which respondents lived. Performance on the first criterion was evaluated by NORC's field managers using normal hiring procedures. The second was evaluated by means of two Russian-language tests administered by the field managers and graded by faculty members at two participating universities.

On the basis of the screening process, 95 applicants were invited to the training sessions. Fifty-eight percent were women, and 66 percent were under age 30. About one-quarter had earned, or were in the process of earning, doctorates; another quarter, master's degrees. The remainder all had bachelor's degrees. The language tests were highly successful in identifying the necessary level of language skills. Much to the delight of the research team, almost 90 percent had spent time in the USSR; 75 percent had spent four or more months in the USSR. Of the 26 who were foreign born, 13 had immigrated to the United States prior to 1952; 21, prior to 1967. Seventy-six percent of all applicants had majored in Russian or Russian area studies, and 61 percent held jobs that made direct use of such knowledge (*SIP General Survey Codebook* 1986).

Those selected attended six-day training sessions that included NORC standard procedures and a program designed specifically to meet the needs of SIP. Extensive use of Russian was emphasized.[8]

The sample

Ideally, the questionnaire would have been administered to a probability sample of Soviet citizens. But even Soviet sociologists studying politically innocuous topics have seldom managed to administer surveys to a probability sample of the general population. Obviously, the SIP General Survey is based on a unique population: adults who have succeeded in emigrating from the Soviet Union and settling in the United States. The implications of this fact were explored at length in the methodological sessions mentioned earlier. It became clear to all participants that formal statistical inference to the Soviet population would be unwarranted.

To state the point in more concrete terms: The frequency distributions presented in sections 6 through 9 of *The Soviet Interview Project General Survey Codebook* cannot be taken as estimates of the frequency distributions that would be obtained from a probability sample of Soviet citizens. Simple-minded attempts to use the distributions in such a manner will be likely to yield misleading results. Extraordinary measures are necessary, therefore, to deal with problems of bias when it comes to the analysis of SIP General Survey data.

With this orientation, the team set out to enumerate all adult emigrants who had arrived between January 1, 1979, and April 30, 1982. These dates represented a compromise that took into account both the demand for very recent emigrants with fresh recollections and the demand for a large enough sample frame so that certain sparsely populated categories of emigrants, such as those from Central Asia, could be studied as groups.

Fortunately, the vast majority of Soviet emigrants had found their way into American society through domestic resettlement agencies, and these agencies were persuaded by our stringent confidentiality procedures and by a dedication to education and scholarly research to cooperate in the process of building a list and, subsequently, in locating the sample. NORC's staff was, therefore, able to build a list of 37,156 Soviet emigrants, of whom 33,618 met the eligibility criteria: adults who arrived in the United States between the dates given above and who were between the ages of 21 and 70 inclusive at the time of arrival. An initial sample size of 3,750 was planned, with the expectation of an 80 percent response rate, or 3,000 completed questionnaires. The effective sample turned out to be 3,551, with 2,793

---

[8] For a description of the training program, see Edwards 1983.

completed interviews, for a response rate of 79 percent.[9]

A more detailed description of the General Survey sample is provided by Barbara A. Anderson and Brian D. Silver in Appendix A.

Field work

Well before interviewing commenced, NORC began locating members of the sample. Working from each person's last known address, NORC utilized all standard procedures to establish a current address. As part of this process, a letter (in Russian and in English) was sent to all members of the sample informing them of their selection. In some cases, the resettlement agency took letters supplied by NORC and, at NORC's expense, had its own staff supply addresses and mail letters without divulging the addresses to NORC.

Interviewing began in March 1983. The work of each interviewer was checked after two interviews; any errors in procedures were brought to their attention before they were allowed to proceed. Thereafter, each tenth interview underwent a quality check.

An important feature of NORC's field procedures was its policy of handling multiple respondents in households in such a way that respondents could not discuss the interviews of other household members before they were themselves interviewed. In most survey research, this does not present a problem because the selection rate is so low that two respondents from the same household are rarely chosen. However, since this survey selected 3,750 people from a sample frame of 33,618 and because of certain stratification constraints, the problem was fairly common. NORC's policy was to arrange either simultaneous or consecutive interviews.

By August 27, a total of 2,408 interviews had been conducted, yielding a response of 65 percent. As would be expected in a survey of this sort, NORC found itself facing problems in achieving the targeted 80 percent response rate. An unusual number of respondents were difficult to locate by virtue of their relatively high geographic mobility as recent immigrants. Many also initially declined to participate because (1) they were concerned for the safety of relatives in the USSR, (2) they did not want to dredge up painful memories, and (3) they feared that they knew too little to discuss worldly issues. Several sorts of remedial action were taken to raise the response rate. Interviewers were trained in converting "soft" refusals and in field locating, and resettlement agencies were asked to verify for respondents that reliable and effective confidentiality and security measures were being taken on their behalf by NORC. In addition, arrangements were made to use other

9 The number of valid completed interviews was 2,793. When the sample size ($N = 3,738$) is lowered to take into account 187 members who were deceased or out of scope, the calculated response rate is .79; that is, $2,793/(3,738 - 187)$.

languages in interviewing ten people who did not know Russian.

By January 31, 1984, a total of 2,824 interviews had been conducted. Of these, 31 were discarded for one of two reasons: (1) The interviewers reported that, despite their best efforts, another person in the room where the interview was conducted answered most of the questions; or (2) the person was incompetent for purposes of interviewing (senile or deaf, for example). These cases were discarded, of course, without regard to the opinions the respondents had expressed.

Confidentiality

Confidentiality is virtually always a concern in survey research; it has been a special concern in this project. Many respondents, fearing for relatives in the USSR or for their own well-being, requested assurance that confidentiality would be maintained. Some even sought and received assurance from their resettlement agencies. The research team is strongly committed to maintaining confidentiality, and it has taken steps to insure confidentiality, not only to protect SIP respondents against possible Soviet intrusion but also to protect them against possible intrusion by federal, state, or local authorities in this country.

As with all survey research conducted under the aegis of universities, all aspects of this project have been reviewed by a "human subjects committee" – in this case, the Institutional Review Board of the University of Illinois at Urbana-Champaign. The research team is bound by measures agreed upon in negotiations with that committee.

The research team has taken extraordinary measures to maintain confidentiality. The use of a Canadian link file has already been described. Among the other measures are: (1) All team members, assistants, coders, interviewers, and NORC staff members have signed confidentiality pledges; (2) the link between names and data will ultimately be destroyed, and no list of participants will ever be made available; (3) in keeping with standard survey practice, answers have been aggregated when they might uniquely identify respondents. Special care has been taken to aggregate answers when the questions pertained to matters that might be documented in the USSR or the United States (such as dates, unusual occupations, some locations).

It is encouraging that not a single respondent has complained during or since the interview about the conduct of SIP interviewers or about any failure to maintain the highest degree of confidentiality and professionalism.

The problem of bias

The SIP sample obviously was not a random, probability sample of the general population of the Soviet Union. In addition, our respondents voted with their feet and have faced the trauma of relocation in the United States. Any bias raises a question about the reliability and generalizability of survey results. Given the potential sources of bias in any survey – such as sampling errors, faulty recall, desire to please the interviewer, and refusal to participate or to answer questions considered sensitive or confidential – and given that the SIP survey offered more opportunities for bias than most surveys, the reliability and usability of our data and findings are critical issues.

It should perhaps be stressed at the outset, however, that the problem of bias in the SIP General Survey is shared by any attempt to use recent Soviet emigrants as sources of information about their lives in the mother country. The hard facts remain for all who seek to use this source of information that the individuals being interviewed are, with few exceptions, self-selected, that they have been exposed to life outside the Soviet Union for an extended period, that they are required to recall their past, and that some degree of risk is perceived to attach to complete candor.

Survey research offers no sure method as proof against bias in such cases. Although the nature, type, and risk of bias differ for different methods of interviewing recent Soviet emigrants, none is bias free, and this includes conversing with a Soviet emigrant colleague over brandy. It is obvious, however, that students of contemporary Soviet life cannot refuse to exploit this source. It is simply too valuable, and there is no alternative. It is not clear, in fact, that a survey conducted in the USSR on topics that involved political issues would be answered candidly even if a representative sample could be interviewed. The only question is how best to use emigrant respondents and what safeguards to employ.

Self-selection (emigration) bias

Because a very high proportion of the members of the sample frame elected to leave the Soviet Union voluntarily, it is generally assumed on first consideration that our respondents would be uniformly hostile to the Soviet social system. Members of the research team and most others who have had extensive contact with this emigration have learned, however, that the stereotype of emigrants as Soviet dissidents is wrong. Although a small proportion certainly do count themselves as dissidents, the emigrants taken as a whole have left their homeland for a variety of reasons, with only a minority reporting ideological motives.

When asked an open-ended question, for example, about why they emigrated, 923 respondents volunteered that they emigrated because other family members were emigrating. Counting multiple answers, the reasons most often cited were family or friends, 48 percent; "religious" or ethnic, 46 percent; political, 43 percent; and economic, 27 percent. Thus, political reasons did not predominate as the motive to emigrate. Moreover, only a tiny fraction of our respondents indicated that they had ever participated in any kind of overt unconventional political activity during the last normal period of their lives in the Soviet Union. Only 20 percent, for example, reported having attended an unofficial art show. Participation in more politically sensitive activities, such as job actions or public protests, was reported by less than 2 percent of the respondents, and the fraction reporting that they had been "activists" in any unconventional activity was well under 1 percent.

The point is that the former Soviet citizens who have migrated to the United States are not uniformly hostile to the Soviet system, nor are they a homogeneous population. A principal purpose of stratification of the sample was, in fact, to maximize heterogeneity precisely because our main interest is in differences among diverse groups within the sample.

Moreover, most emigrants seemed to exercise considerable objectivity in assessing their experiences in the Soviet Union. They were quite willing to list ways in which the United States could learn from the Soviet Union, and even the 18 percent who stated that the United States could "learn nothing" revealed in response to questions elsewhere in the questionnaire that a substantial proportion had no quarrel with such fundamental institutions of Soviet society as state ownership of the means of production or public provision of medical care. Respondents were also quite willing to list ways in which they were disappointed with life in the United States. Because the variation in respondents' reasons for emigrating was measured, analysts can determine which questions were most susceptible to bias correlated with emigration. An extensive test of response effects has also been conducted by the SIP Data Management Center (DMC). The results suggest minimal problems on these dimensions.[10]

Bias as a limit

Where the direction of the bias is known a priori, the frequencies obtained can be useful in setting conservative limits on the distributions that would be found in the USSR itself. Given, for example, that less than 30 percent of respondents reported ever having read *samizdat* (illegal, underground literature) during their last normal period in the Soviet Union (indeed, some respondents had to request definitions of the word), it is easy to believe that even less of the general population had read any forbidden material during those years.

[10] See Appendix B by Michael Swafford et al.

Ethnic bias

Being "Jewish" has offered the best ticket out of the Soviet Union since 1970 for emigrants likely to come to the United States. Thus, ethnic bias is, for all intents and purposes, a principal manifestation of self-selection bias. Bias matters, of course, only when it affects the questions one wants answered. Where an ethnic bias could be established in advance, such as in the consumption of alcohol, which is cross-nationally relatively low for Jewish communities, potential ethnic bias was avoided by avoiding the question. In this instance, respondents were used exclusively as "observers" of the effects, for example, of alcohol consumption in the workplace. Stratification and weighting of the sample were used to reduce the bias toward, for example, higher education in a "mostly Jewish" sample.

Where one cannot be sure of the existence or direction of ethnic bias, it is necessary to test for it. Team member Donna Bahry has shown that ethnic bias is selective and can ordinarily be identified. In the SIP General Survey it clearly comes into play on issues related to ethnicity or nationality policy but not systematically on general social, economic, or political questions (Bahry 1985).

Professor Bahry divided the respondents to the General Survey into five categories. The majority (2,137) fell into the category labeled "intense identifiers," defined as "those who saw themselves as Jewish only, and who felt that they belonged to no other nationality."

The other categories included "moderate identifiers" (262), "who saw themselves both as Jewish and as belonging to one or more other nationalities of the USSR." A third category represents "non-identifiers" (66), "individuals whose parent(s) was Jewish but who claimed another nationality" exclusively. "Spouses" (183), "non-Jewish respondents married to a Jewish spouse in the USSR," composed the fourth category; and the fifth and last category, "other", consisted mostly of the nationality Russian.

Bahry discovered that the responses of these five groups to questions related to ethnicity or nationality differ in significant ways that reflect ethnic bias. Answers to more general questions, however, revealed little or no variation by category. When asked, for example, whether they would desire to have a relative seek a Jewish spouse, the more intense the respondent's self-identification as Jewish, the more likely that response would be in the affirmative.

Similar significant gradations in responses are found in the respondents' answers to other questions dealing with ethnicity or nationality, such as their opinions about the role of ethnic discrimination in access to education or in job advancement. When asked, however, whether agricultural or medical care should be private, there was no significant variation by ethnic category.

All categories of respondents were heavily in favor of private agriculture. And all categories favored public provision of medical care just as strongly. There is no significant variation in either instance by category of respondent.

Thus, although the SIP General Survey is clearly subject to ethnic bias, the questionnaire was designed so that investigators would be able to test for bias that could not be eliminated on a priori grounds.

Memory decay, contamination and interviewer effects

As was indicated earlier, 2,562 of the 2,793 respondents on the SIP General Survey defined the end of their LNPs as falling between 1978 and 1981. As almost all interviews took place in 1983, most respondents were answering questions about events or attitudes that had occurred two to five years earlier. Evidence that they were in fact able to respond with reliability has been adduced by research team members Barbara A. Anderson and Brian D. Silver (1986a).

Largely because the sample design called for maximizing the number of non-Jews drawn, the sample included 192 cases of related individuals who had shared the same household both during their last normal periods of life in the USSR and at the time interviews were undertaken in this country. Most of these individuals were interviewed separately and simultaneously (or consecutively), which has allowed Anderson and Silver to evaluate the impact of memory decay and contamination.

The results have been quite encouraging. Anderson and Silver found a very high degree of agreement on such objective questions about life in the USSR as square meters of living space in their residence, household wealth, monthly household expenditures in total and in composition, spouse's monthly income from main job, and the like.

Interestingly, spouses' responses to subjective questions were also strikingly similar. Where one spouse reported satisfaction with housing in the LNP in the Soviet Union, the probability was very high that the other would report a similar degree of satisfaction. Moreover, the answers provided by married couples about satisfaction with housing, jobs, medical care, and consumer goods are closely correlated without regard to whether the pairs were interviewed separately and simultaneously, separately at different times, or with others present at the time of the interview.

Tests of selected "response effects" were conducted by the SIP Data Management Center. The effects tested were: (1) time lapse between the respondent's departure from the USSR and the date of interview; (2) disparities between "willing" and "reluctant" respondents; (3) differences between Jewish and non-Jewish respondents; (4) influences associated with country of origin of interviewers (i.e., Russian-born or not); and (5) interviewer sex effects. The results were reassuringly negative. For an extended treatment, see Appendix B.

Stratification and the "referent population"

The General Survey is based upon a stratified random sample. Stratification was based upon characteristics of members of the sample frame while Soviet citizens. The criteria used to stratify the sample were educational attainment, nationality, size of city, and region from which they emigrated. Limits on the characteristics offered by the sample frame limited the referent population to the European population of large and medium-sized cities of the Soviet Union (Anderson and Silver 1986b). The desire to analyze major life events led the team to restrict the sample frame to adults, defined as persons who were between 21 and 70 years of age inclusively at time of arrival in the United States. To minimize memory decay and contamination, the sample frame was restricted to the most recent emigrants, those who arrived between January 1, 1979, and March 30, 1982. (For more detail, see Appendix A.)

Limitation of the referent population to adult Europeans from large and medium-sized cities of the USSR is not sufficient to assure the validity of generalizations. And this holds for weighted results as well. As Anderson and Silver state in Appendix A: "it is ... important to establish that survey respondents with specific sociodemographic backgrounds are similar to persons with the same backgrounds who did not emigrate from the USSR or who were not Jewish." Although far from complete, there are Soviet data that can be used for comparison with the distributions being analyzed by SIP team members.

Consider, for example, the economic data developed by team member Paul Gregory in an analysis of the earnings of Soviet workers (Gregory and Kohlhase 1986). He found "striking similarities between the SIP sample means and referent population means of economic and demographic variables ... not used to stratify the sample." The official figure for square meters of urban housing space per capita for the 1978 urban population is 12.9. The SIP sample for approximately the same data is 13.5. Hours worked per week is given officially as 40.6, and for the SIP sample it is 40.0. Family size, respectively, is 3.2 and 3.4. Finally, the percentage employed of the SIP sample is 69.5, whereas it was 71.0 percent in 1979, according to official figures. Where this kind of correspondence is found for aggregates or means, one can have considerable confidence in the finer breakdowns that SIP data permit, breakdowns that are not available in any form in Soviet official publications.

Again quoting from Anderson and Silver, Appendix A: "The concept of a referent Soviet population is relevant not because it represents the population from which the sample is drawn and against which the sampling error could be determined in precise statistical terms but, rather, because it provides a referent population of Soviet society whose experiences and behavior the SIP General Survey respondents are most likely to represent."

Analysis of the data

The SIP study is expected to be useful primarily in examining multivariate relationships. In other words, the point of the study is not to describe the univariate distributions of, say, income, education, and political conservatism. These distributions are very likely unrepresentative of Soviet reality. The point instead is to explore the relationship between such variables under the kinds of controls all too seldom employed in Soviet studies. Are, for example, the monetary returns to higher education less for women than for men, as is the case in most of the world? Is political conservatism inversely correlated with education attainment? What accounts for the fact that women earn less than men? Note that such relationships may well be properly reflected in a survey of Soviet emigrants even though univariate distributions are skewed.

Regrettably, until Soviet social scientists administer questionnaires to a probability sample in an environment conducive to frank responses, Soviet and Western social scientists alike will have to settle for less certainty and more cautions than are considered normal or desirable in Western research. For the time being, if the findings of the SIP General Survey are used prudently as pieces of a puzzle to be put into the context of related Soviet findings and firsthand experiences in the USSR, they can substantially fill out our picture of everyday life in the USSR.

First findings

The essays that compose this volume represent first findings of the SIP General Survey. Much remains to be analyzed, and subsequent analyses will be published in various formats, depending upon the author. Only after the data have been more thoroughly analyzed will it be possible to produce a truly synthetic overview of the results. Even so, the essays collected here point to a number of general findings about the dynamics of the contemporary Soviet social system.

At the most general level the General Survey raises a perennial issue in Soviet studies: Is the Soviet socialist system fundamentally different from the industrial and postindustrial societies of the West? Does it represent a different genus of social, political, and economic system? Or is it instead merely a different species of the Western systems that we know much more about because they are more open societies? This issue has troubled Western social science from the origins of Soviet studies. At stake is whether standard tools of analysis of the various social science disciplines are appropriate for study of Soviet society. If not, new and quite different methods would have to be applied in its analysis.

Systemic similarities and differences

The SIP General Survey protocol was designed on the hypothesis that the Soviet social system *is* amenable to analysis with standard Western disciplinary tools. The assumption is that the obstacle to standard disciplinary analysis has been the absence of data, not the intractability of the system to standard types of analyses. The SIP General Survey constitutes, therefore, a test of this hypothesis. Nonsense results, or routinely extreme values for the variables, would constitute falsification, other things equal. The essays collected here demonstrate unequivocally that Soviet society differs in quite specific ways from other societies but that the differences are in degree rather than in kind. This is, perhaps, our most fundamental finding.

Max Weber's explanation of class, or social stratification, as a function of wealth, power, and prestige, for example, seems to offer a better explanation of actual prestige rankings in the Soviet Union than does Karl Marx's analysis, which viewed social class as derived from relationship to the means of production. What is more, despite heavy advertising for the dignity of manual labor and championing of the blue-collar worker, members of the working class do not fare better in prestige ranking than in the West. Status is conferred instead on the basis of attainments such as occupational level, party membership, and education, with the highest status ascribed to lawyers, doctors, writers, professors, engineers, and army officers, in that order.

Similarly, the distribution of income and wealth in the Soviet socialist system may be more equal than in most Western mixed economies, but the difference is not radical. It appears more as a moderate outlier than as an observation associated with a different distribution. The distribution fluctuates also, as it does elsewhere, according to social policy. Poverty is still widespread, and the data indicate a trend toward the feminization of poverty in the USSR, much as has been noted in the United States and in other mixed economies.

Members of the research team are frequently asked what our most surprising findings are. There have been some surprising findings, such as the relatively high degree of satisfaction with housing that two-thirds of our respondents reported for their last period of normal life in the USSR, or the differential impact of unconventional behavior on white- and blue-collar workers. In general, however, our aggregate findings confirm theories or predictions that some scholar somewhere in the West or East has offered at some time. This is not unexpected given the intensity with which Soviet society has been studied in the West over the last three decades. As Joseph Berliner put it at a conference at Airlie House, reviewing SIP first findings, if there were to be major "surprises" in SIP's findings, Soviet specialists in this country "ought to be fired." Confirmation of results or discrimination among hypotheses put forward by other methods and using other sources is no mean feat even if it were the only result of SIP.

Fortunately, it is not. Perhaps the single most significant "surprising" finding at the macro level that emerges from the General Survey is what appears to be a transformation in the structure of support for the Soviet regime since the Harvard Project. Harvard interviewers found the young and well educated to be the most supportive, relatively, of the Soviet system. The older and less well-educated were by far the more critical. Those who had benefited the most from the Bolshevik Revolution were, therefore, the least alienated of the refugees interviewed (Inkeles and Bauer 1959). The SIP General Survey has yielded exactly the opposite result, for the younger, more educated members of the sample are the most alienated from some of the fundamental characteristics of the system. They are much less likely to have been satisfied with the quality of their lives, and they are more likely to have been critical of the system's economic performance during their LNP. This was true despite the fact that, by their own admission, the younger and better educated were disproportionately reaping the material benefits of Soviet socialist society in the 1970s.

Where SIP findings are most generally surprising, however, is along dimensions about which we have had little or no information, as, for example, at the micro level of Soviet society. It has been essentially impossible to analyze the impact of gender, generation, education, income, class, unconventional behavior, size of city, and so forth, upon behavior and attitudes in Soviet society because of the absence of sufficient well-defined data in adequate detail. As one reviews the essays that follow, several factors stand out as crucial for an understanding of the structure and dynamics of contemporary Soviet society. Most significant at this stage appear to be generation, educational attainment, material incentives, and political conventionality.

The generational factor

SIP findings indicate clearly that there are significant elements of regime support among the older generation, among blue-collar workers, and among the less educated. The strength and direction of generational differences may be the single most significant finding to date. Generational differences surface in almost all analyses, and the differences being found are true generational differences and not merely life-cycle effects. The older generation is unforgiving of Stalinism and correspondingly more forgiving of contemporary problems. Thus, the older generation regards Stalin's era as the "worst" and Khrushchev's as the best, with the Brezhnev period somewhere in between. The young agree that Khrushchev's era was the best, but they regard Brezhnev's as the worst. They are completely unimpressed, it would appear, with the economic progress that has been achieved since Stalin and impatient with the economic slowdown of the late 1970s. The generational factor offers, then, a challenge for Soviet leadership and one that is likely to increase over time.

The General Survey reveals relatively higher rates of criticism among the young at all educational levels. Significantly, as their educational attainment increases, the young tend to become more critical and more inclined toward unconventional activities. The pattern that emerges is that the young, much more so than those who are older, judge the regime on the basis of its current performance. They are generally more critical and less inclined to accept present conditions just because they are an improvement over the past.

The older generation, which experienced one or more of the many traumatic events in Soviet history, is apparently more philosophical about current failings of the Soviet economy. After all, taken as a whole, the years since Stalin have been peaceful and relatively prosperous also. The young and successful are clearly less philosophical about the recent stagnation of the economy. They may also be victims of the rewriting of Soviet history. Having never experienced Stalinism, and having been taught only a sanitized version of the Stalin era, the realities of Stalinism carry much less weight with them than with the older members of Soviet society. Thus it is that if there are neo-Stalinists today they are among the young.

The educational factor

Perhaps as important as the generational factor is the educational factor. The General Survey reveals an unambiguous and negative relationship between the level of educational attainment and the level of support for various political and economic institutions of the Soviet system, other things equal. The level of support for state control and management of major sectors of the system declines with each increase in the level of education attained, and this is true even for attainments in primary and secondary school. The same pattern is evident in responses to questions that juxtapose individual rights and the power of the state, such as the provision of civil liberties. As education increases, support for state power relative to individual rights decreases.

This is not to suggest that material rewards do not matter, for they do. Other things equal, support for regime values and for the institutional structure of the Soviet social system increases with increases in material rewards. The problem, however, is that material benefits do not keep pace. As the young are also, relatively speaking, the best educated, generational and education effects reinforce one another. Hence the significance of providing adequate material rewards for education and hard work. Hence also the importance of getting the Soviet economy moving again. This conclusion is underscored by the fact that workers on the shop floor indict the system of material incentives as explanation for the poor productivity performance of Soviet industry. Widespread "time theft" from employment supports this conclusion also.

The participation factor

It is equally significant to note that the fact that SIP respondents endorsed strongly some key features of the Soviet system while sharply criticizing others enhances confidence in their candor and in the reliability of the survey's findings generally. Even those who were extremely hostile to the regime (to judge from their responses to other questions on the survey) did not reject everything about the system. Those who believed, for example, that the United States can learn nothing from the USSR still strongly favored, for example, state-provided medical care (48 percent), and nearly three out of ten reported that they favored state ownership of heavy industry.

Ironically, the young, successful generation reported itself as the most highly "mobilized" of any generation ever in the formal sense of the word. They reported belonging to the correct social and political organizations, and they participated at higher rates than did less successful and less well-educated members of their cohort. Yet this same group of "the best and the brightest" also was the most likely to be involved in "unconventional" behavior – refusing to vote, listening to BBC and other foreign broadcasts, reading and distributing *samizdat*, reading foreign fiction and nonfiction, and participating in other unsanctioned activities.

There is also evidence to suggest that a gradual "privatization" of personal life has been taking place since Stalin. The use of *blat* (connections and influence) to avoid undesirable activities such as military service or to obtain advantageous choices, such as a good job, has increased steadily and significantly over time. A long-term trend toward privatization is evident, which shows up not only in the evasion of mobilization efforts by state agencies but also in the economic realm. The study reaffirms the pervasiveness of illegal as well as legal private economic activity.

The early findings of the Soviet Interview Project suggest a strategy that the Soviet leadership might develop to regenerate and strengthen popular support. Because support is weakest among the best educated and the young, it follows that educational opportunity could be manipulated to constrain educational attainment more closely to employment possibilities. Greater effort would need to be made to validate the differentiation of incomes; that is, goods and services would have to be made available to those who have worked hardest to earn higher incomes. And the young would have to be cultivated especially intensively – partly by linking the current regime to the progressive aspects of the Khrushchev period. This would have to be done, of course, without calling up memories of Khrushchev's often boorish public behavior. Pressures for economic progress, for access to Western culture, for "private," quiet lives, and, thus, for reform are therefore likely to grow as the "best and brightest" of the young generation replace generations with indelible memories of Stalin and his time.

Future research

The Soviet Interview Project has recently launched three additional projects. One involves recoding available materials from the Harvard Project. A second involves systematic interviews with a probability sample of Soviet emigrants who have arrived in the United States since the first General Survey was conducted, that is, since May 1982. The purpose of the second General Survey is to investigate change over time in contemporary Soviet society. The second survey will also permit the clarification and amplification of certain findings of the first. The second survey is shorter, and the questionnaire is not partitioned. With few exceptions, questions are stated exactly as they were in the first survey.

The third survey being fielded is devoted to an investigation of the Soviet military and focuses upon the "human face" of the Soviet military system and upon a comparison of civilian and military sectors of the Soviet social system. The instrument is being administered to a probability sample drawn from the sample frame from which the first General Survey was drawn.

Additional publications on the SIP General Survey I and reports on these new initiatives will appear in the future, and the data and associated materials will be placed in the public domain for the benefit of all scholars in the field. In planning the Soviet Interview Project, we discovered to our

great disappointment that the Harvard Project data cards had been lost.[11]
We decided that every effort should be made to insure that SIP materials are
properly archived for the benefit of current and future scholars. We have
even made an effort to recover what we could from the Harvard Project. All
of these materials will be carefully archived both at the University of Illinois
at Urbana-Champaign and, where appropriate, with the Inter-university
Consortium for Political and Social Research.

References

Anderson, Barbara A., and Brian D. Silver. 1986a. "The Validity of Survey
    Responses: Insights from Interviews of Multiple Respondents in a Household in
    a Survey of Soviet Emigrants." Soviet Interview Project Working Paper no. 14,
    University of Illinois at Urbana-Champaign.
    1986b. "Descriptive Statistics for the Sampling Frame Population: The Eligible
    Population for the Soviet Interview Project General Survey." Soviet Interview
    Project Working Paper no. 2, University of Illinois at Urbana-Champaign.
Bahry, Donna. 1985. Oral presentation, Soviet Interview Project Report to
    Sponsors, Airlie House, Airlie, Va., October 27.
Balzer, Marjorie. 1980. "Guide to Materials for the Project on the Soviet Social
    System (Harvard Project/Soviet Refugee Interview and Questionnaire Data,
    1950–53)." Soviet Interview Project Working Paper no. 1, University of
    Illinois at Urbana-Champaign.
Edwards, W. Sherman. 1983. "Interviewer Training for the Soviet Interview Project
    General Survey." Soviet Interview Project Working Paper no. 3, University of
    Illinois at Urbana-Champaign.
Gregory, Paul R., and Janet Kohlhase. 1986. "The Earnings of Soviet Workers:
    Human Capital, Loyalty, and Privilege." Soviet Interview Project Working
    Paper no. 13, University of Illinois at Urbana-Champaign.
Inkeles, Alex, and Raymond A. Bauer. 1959. *The Soviet Citizen.* Cambridge, Mass.:
    Harvard University Press.
Millar, James R. 1985. "The Impact of Trade Interruption and Trade Denial on the
    U.S. Economy." In Bruce Parrott (ed.), *Trade, Technology, and Soviet-American
    Relations*, pp. 324–50. Bloomington: Indiana University Press.
Ofer, Gur, Aaron Vinokur, and Yechiel Bar-Chaim. 1979. "Family Budget Survey of
    Soviet Emigrants in the Soviet Union." Rand Paper P-6015. Santa Monica,
    Calif.: Rand Corporation.
The Soviet Interview Project General Survey Codebook. 1986. University of Illinois at
    Urbana-Champaign.

---

[11] For a description of what materials remain of the Harvard Project, see Balzer
    1980.

CHAPTER 2

Quality of life: subjective measures of relative satisfaction

JAMES R. MILLAR and ELIZABETH CLAYTON

In both the United States and Europe, people's subjective perception of life's overall quality is not wholly reflected by their objective conditions: Riches do not necessarily bring satisfaction, nor are the poor always dissatisfied. In this chapter, we explore the recollections of recent Soviet emigrants about how satisfied they felt about their lives in the Soviet Union. We then identify the groups among whom satisfaction levels differed significantly.

The first goal is to discover how Soviet emigrants rated the quality of their lives in the Soviet Union during their last normal period of life in the Soviet Union (LNP).[1] The data sought are the individual respondents' own assessments of the quality of their lives. The respondents' answers had a normative reference that is unique in Soviet studies, for it was the individuals' own expectations, values, and experiences that shaped their judgments. In order to minimize psychological weighting, they were asked to evaluate not Soviet society in general but their own life events.

Quality of life differs, of course, among different people. It also varies over time in an individual's life. There is a difference to be noted between an index of "happiness" (or "misery"), which assesses a momentary, fleeting state of one's feelings, and an index of satisfaction (or dissatisfaction), where reality is judged more soberly against one's expectations.[2] It would be impossible to obtain a reliable index of happiness from Soviet emigrants

The authors thank Marianne Ferber and Joe Spaeth for helpful comments on an earlier draft, Thomas Richardson and Chong-Ook Rhee for their excellent research assistance, and Mary Cummings for editorial help.

[1] For most Soviets, the decision to emigrate is irrevocable, and the complex effects of emigration itself upon the respondents' subjective judgments are the subject of this volume's methodological appendixes. Briefly put, the problems are memory decay, contamination, and "psychological weighting." The last is defined as a subjective tendency to romanticize or denigrate conditions irrevocably left behind. It can only be inferred from the comparison of objective and subjective indicators and will be considered in the text. To deal with memory decay and contamination the interviewers asked respondents to focus on the last normal period (LNP) before the decision to emigrate (or some other earlier event related to emigration) caused their lives to change. This device put the respondent into a historical ambience as close as possible to yesterday's reality.

[2] Campbell 1981: 22.

31

because so much time has elapsed since the respondents lived in the Soviet Union. Results based on an index of satisfaction, however, are more reliable because the elapsed time and new environment actually enhance judgmental reflection and contribute to validity.

As people evaluate the overall quality of their lives, they are aware that some aspects of it are more satisfactory than others and that not all aspects are weighted equally. In this chapter we use an operational concept of quality of life that separates the respondents' satisfaction in the domains of job, housing, goods, and medical care, plus a summary measure of satisfaction, the standard of living. When analyzed by factor analysis, the domains were strongly associated with one another, except for job satisfaction. The association between job satisfaction and other domains of life satisfaction has also been weak in U.S. data, although it is somewhat stronger in European data.[3]

Just as respondents differed in the satisfaction they experienced in different domains, they also differed among each other. In order to differentiate between the more and less satisfied groups of Soviet society, we consider differences between groups in the community with different demographic characteristics. Men who were married when they lived in the Soviet Union, for example, were more satisfied with their lives than divorced men, which indicates that marital status contributed somehow to overall satisfaction. Other demographic variables we shall consider are sex, income, age, and education.

Standard of living

To discover how Soviet emigrants felt about the overall quality of their lives in the Soviet Union, we asked them: "How satisfied [udovletvoreny] or dissatisfied [ne udovletvoreny] were you with your standard of living [uroven' zhizni]?" The same form of question was asked about respondents' jobs, housing, medical care, and access to material goods. Their answers were scored in categories ranked from 1 to 4: very satisfied (= 1), somewhat satisfied (= 2), somewhat dissatisfied (= 3), or very dissatisfied (= 4). Thus, *the higher the numerical score, the less the satisfaction.* Respondents' scores are shown in Tables 2.1–2.7, in total and according to demographic and economic categories.

Our respondents reported themselves as relatively satisfied with certain aspects of the quality of their lives during their last normal periods in the Soviet Union. When asked to score satisfaction with standard of living, a

---

[3] Near, Smith, Rice, and Hunt (1984: 184) find a weak association in U.S. data; Andrews and Inglehart (1979: 85) find that the association is stronger in European data than in U.S. data.

Quality of life: relative satisfaction

Table 2.1. *Self-assessed satisfaction among Soviet emigrants*

	Standard of living	Housing	Goods	Job	Medical care
Very satisfied					
N	310	645	139	711	518
%	11.1	23.1	5.0	25.5	18.5
Somewhat satisfied					
N	1,343	1,213	488	1,054	1,142
%	48.1	43.4	17.5	37.7	40.9
Somewhat dissatisfied					
N	694	379	634	303	570
%	24.8	13.6	22.7	10.8	20.4
Very dissatisfied					
N	403	533	1,477	170	450
%	14.4	19.1	52.9	6.1	16.1
Missing values					
N	43	23	55	555	113
%	1.5	0.9	1.9	19.9	4.0
Total N	2,793	2,793	2,793	2,793	2,793

Table 2.2. *Average satisfaction scores among Soviet emigrants, by age in LNP (quartiles)*

	Standard of living	Housing	Goods	Job	Medical care
Under 31 years	2.59	2.56	3.44	2.08	2.48
N	662	663	657	544	644
%	23.70	23.74	23.54	19.48	23.06
31–40 years	2.48	2.30	3.40	1.98	2.54
N	720	722	717	680	692
%	25.78	25.85	25.67	24.35	24.78
41–54 years	2.38	2.17	3.20	1.93	2.31
N	715	718	710	646	694
%	25.60	25.71	25.42	23.13	24.85
Over 54 years	2.28	2.14	2.99	1.84	2.07
N	653	667	654	368	650
%	23.38	23.88	23.42	13.18	23.27

Table 2.2. (*contd.*)

	Standard of living	Housing	Goods	Job	Medical care
Average score	2.43	2.29	3.26	1.97	2.36
Missing values					
N	43	23	55	555	113
%	1.54	0.82	1.95	19.86	4.04
Total N	2,793	2,793	2,793	2,793	2,793

Table 2.3. *Average satisfaction scores among Soviet emigrants, by sex*

	Standard of living	Housing	Goods	Job	Medical care
Men	2.46	2.35	3.28	2.04	2.45
N	1,200	1,205	1,197	1,083	1,149
%	42.96	43.14	42.86	38.78	41.14
Women	2.41	2.24	3.24	1.91	2.29
N	1,550	1,565	1,541	1,155	1,531
%	55.50	56.03	55.17	41.35	54.82
Average score	2.43	2.29	3.26	1.97	2.36
Missing values					
N	43	23	55	555	113
%	1.54	0.82	1.95	19.86	4.04
Total N	2,793	2,793	2,793	2,793	2,793

Table 2.4. *Average satisfaction scores among Soviet emigrants, by marital status*

	Standard of living	Housing	Goods	Job	Medical care
Married	2.40	2.26	3.27	1.94	2.37
N	2,148	2,158	2,146	1,802	2,105
%	76.91	77.26	76.83	64.52	75.37
Widowed	2.45	2.20	2.95	1.97	2.05
N	213	220	211	120	211
%	7.63	7.88	7.55	4.30	7.55

Table 2.4. (*contd.*)

	Standard of living	Housing	Goods	Job	Medical care
Single[a]	2.61	2.49	3.39	2.13	2.46
N	389	392	381	316	364
%	13.93	14.04	13.64	11.31	13.03
Average score	2.43	2.29	3.26	1.97	2.36
Missing values					
N	43	23	55	555	113
%	1.54	0.82	1.95	19.86	4.04
Total N	2,793	2,793	2,793	2,793	2,793

[a]Includes divorced (D), separated (S), and never married (NM).

Table 2.5. *Average satisfaction scores among Soviet emigrants, by city size*

	Standard of living	Housing	Goods	Job	Medical care
More than 1 million	2.44	2.27	3.29	2.00	2.44
N	1,977	1,995	1,971	1,605	1,928
%	70.78	71.43	70.57	57.47	69.03
0.5–1 million	2.54	2.51	3.30	1.92	2.28
N	229	228	227	185	220
%	8.20	8.16	8.13	6.62	7.88
100,000–0.5 million	2.34	2.28	3.12	1.87	2.05
N	468	471	468	390	459
%	16.76	16.86	16.76	13.96	16.43
Less than 100,000	2.43	2.27	3.08	2.05	2.17
N	75	75	71	58	72
%	2.69	2.69	2.54	2.08	2.58
Average score	2.43	2.29	3.26	1.97	2.34
Missing values					
N	44	24	56	555	114
%	1.57	0.86	2.00	19.87	4.08
Total N	2,793	2,793	2,793	2,793	2,793

Table 2.6. *Average satisfaction scores among Soviet emigrants, by occupational status*

	Standard of living	Housing	Goods	Job	Medical care
Professional	2.47	2.30	3.38	1.98	2.49
N	1,540	1,550	1,533	1,330	1,487
%	55.14	55.50	54.89	47.62	53.24
White collar	2.38	2.31	3.11	1.98	2.22
N	434	441	434	326	426
%	15.54	15.79	15.54	11.67	15.25
Blue collar	2.38	2.25	3.07	1.93	2.15
N	699	701	694	572	690
%	25.03	25.1	24.85	20.48	24.70
Average score	2.43	2.29	3.26	1.97	2.36
Missing values					
N	120	101	132	565	190
%	4.29	3.61	4.72	20.23	6.81
Total N	2,793	2,793	2,793	2,793	2,793

majority were either "very" or "somewhat satisfied" (59.2 percent). Only a minority were "very dissatisfied" (14.4 percent). A midpoint score would be 2.5. The average (mean) score for our respondents was 2.43, somewhat better than mid scale.[4]

As has been found to be true for other countries and other surveys, our respondents' satisfaction with their standard of living varied over the life span and from place to place. Older people were more satisfied than younger people. Married people were more satisfied with their standard of living than those who were widowed, divorced, separated, or never married. People who lived in cities with less than 100,000 population were more satisfied than those who lived in very large cities of more than one million population (except for young people, who were more satisfied in very large cities).[5]

We were surprised that so many respondents expressed themselves as relatively satisfied with their standard of living. It was not expected from people who had chosen to leave their country. The degree of satisfaction

[4] For consistency and following standard practice in describing quality-of-life statistics, we shall refer to degrees of "satisfaction" rather than degrees of "dissatisfaction." Readers should keep this in mind in reading our description so that they do not draw false or confusing conclusions. After all, most of our respondents judged their LNP lives unsatisfactory on an overall basis – else they would not have left.

[5] All statistical tests are significant at a level of 95 percent or higher unless otherwise noted.

Table 2.7. *Average satisfaction scores among Soviet emigrants, by respondent's highest education*

	Standard of living	Housing	Goods	Job	Medical care
Less than 4 years	2.04	1.89	2.38	1.59	1.61
N	25	26	26	12	26
%	0.90	0.93	0.93	0.43	0.93
4–6 years	2.23	2.18	2.75	1.66	1.77
N	108	108	105	58	112
%	3.87	3.87	3.76	2.08	4.01
7–8 years	2.25	2.11	2.83	1.76	1.93
N	216	222	223	154	216
%	7.73	7.95	8.00	5.51	7.73
Incomplete sec.	2.30	2.23	3.07	1.82	2.17
N	88	91	86	61	89
%	3.15	3.23	3.08	2.19	3.19
Trade school	2.12	1.77	3.04	1.85	2.00
N	26	26	25	20	26
%	0.93	0.93	0.90	0.72	0.93
Attestat	2.43	2.39	3.12	1.89	2.20
N	455	458	452	360	440
%	16.30	16.40	16.18	12.90	15.75
Complete sec. specialized	2.37	2.26	3.15	1.85	2.25
N	671	673	669	558	651
%	24.02	24.10	23.95	20.00	23.31
Incomplete higher	2.54	2.39	3.51	2.20	2.70
N	160	160	158	111	154
%	5.73	5.73	5.66	4.00	5.51
Complete higher	2.55	2.33	3.55	2.12	2.65
N	1,001	1,006	994	904	966
%	35.84	36.02	35.59	32.37	34.59
Average score	2.43	2.29	3.26	1.97	2.36
Missing values					
N	43	23	55	555	113
%	1.54	0.82	1.95	19.86	4.04
Total N	2,793	2,793	2,793	2,793	2,793

Table 2.8. *Average satisfaction scores among Soviet emigrants, by role in the decision to emigrate*

	Standard of living	Housing	Goods	Job	Medical care
Decision maker	2.51	2.36	3.29	2.05	2.42
N	897	901	895	753	859
%	32.12	32.26	32.04	26.96	30.76
Shared decision	2.42	2.27	3.28	1.96	2.36
N	1,633	1,646	1,624	1,324	1,601
%	58.47	58.93	58.15	47.40	57.32
Follower	2.20	2.11	3.02	1.72	2.05
N	207	209	206	151	206
%	7.41	7.48	7.38	5.41	7.38
Average score	2.44	2.29	3.26	1.97	2.36
Missing values					
N	56	37	68	565	127
%	2.00	1.33	2.43	20.23	4.54
Total N	2,793	2,793	2,793	2,793	2,793

expressed varied with the extent to which the respondent participated in the decision to emigrate. The actual decision maker varied within families. Most members shared in the decision, but some families had a single decision maker and a follower or two. In single-decision-maker families, the leader and the followers differed, as might be expected, in reported satisfaction. Those respondents who themselves made the decision to leave the Soviet Union were significantly less satisfied with their lives in the Soviet Union than were those who simply followed along. Those who shared in the decision to leave fell somewhere in between (see Table 2.8).

Emigrants who participated in the survey originated in different Soviet regions and republics, and their responses show some regional variation. The Soviet Union's dominant republic, the Russian Soviet Federated Socialist Republic (RSFSR), is believed by many to be the regime's favorite, but those of our respondents who came from the RSFSR (46 percent) were less satisfied with their standard of living than were the people who lived in western or southern republics.

When respondents scored both their satisfaction and their actual standard of living, some regional divergences appeared.[6] Most satisfied with their

[6] Respondents were asked both to score their satisfaction with their standard of living and to rank their standard of living against other Soviet people.

standard of living were the ethnic Ukrainian respondents who lived in the Ukraine, and they also estimated their standard of living there as relatively high. Ethnic Russians from the RSFSR reported their standard of living as higher than others, but they rated their satisfaction with it lowest of all. Jewish respondents estimated their actual standard of living as below average, but they reported themselves to be fairly satisfied with it. The results offer some evidence of ethnic variation and suggest that the highest standards of living may not yield comparable satisfaction and that respondents compared themselves to different standards.

Standard of living has many individual domains. In the next section, we focus on the domain of housing, which is most closely related to reported satisfaction with standard of living among our respondents.

Satisfaction with housing

The strongest impact on our respondents' overall satisfaction with their standard of living in the USSR was made by the evaluation of their housing during the LNP. As is also true for Western Europe, a favorable evaluation of standard of living was most highly correlated with a positive rating of LNP housing, and a negative evaluation with a poor rating. In general, our respondents were more satisfied with their housing than with their standard of living. Only one-third expressed any dissatisfaction.

Most Soviet citizens rent apartments very cheaply in buildings owned by municipalities or enterprises. A few become homeowners by buying (or inheriting) an apartment in a cooperatively owned building or a detached house located on public land. Half of the respondents in our sample lived in state-owned separate apartments, and one-fifth rented rooms in those apartments or lived in public dormitories. The remainder owned privately either a cooperative apartment (22 percent) or a free-standing house (9 percent). See Figures 2.1 and 2.2.

As might be expected, homeowners were the most satisfied with their housing. Cooperative apartment owners were only slightly less satisfied than house owners. Apartment renters, the majority of our respondents, were fairly satisfied with their housing. A minority, however, who lived in rented rooms in others' apartments or who sublet apartments or who lived in dormitory rooms were highly dissatisfied.

As Soviet citizens are obliged to invest a considerable amount of time and energy to obtain and maintain housing, reported satisfaction with housing is significant. We asked respondents who had received new quarters in their LNP about the quality of service they received from local government in searching for housing or for housing improvements. When a large sample ($N = 2,793$) were asked about *any* contacts they may have had with govern-

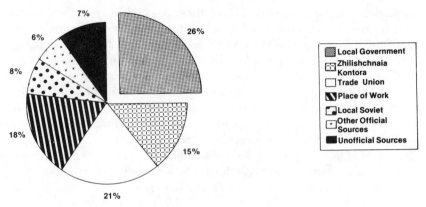

Figure 2.1. Sources of housing

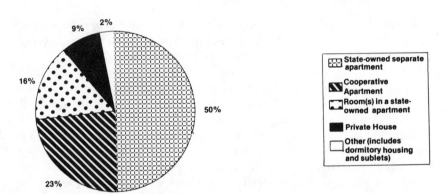

Figure 2.2. Respondents' housing type

ment officials, over half of their reported contacts concerned housing, for themselves and for others, for acquisition or repair. More than half of these respondents also replied that government officials had satisfied their requests. When a smaller sample ($N = 933$) were asked in greater detail about the service they received when searching for housing, official bureaus were described as slow, discourteous, and incompetent. The result seems to be the judgment that when government officials did respond to respondents' requests relating to housing they were insulting.

Younger respondents in our sample (those under the age of 30) were the least satisfied with housing. The burden of queuing for housing does in fact fall predominantly on the young, and most of their dissatisfaction clearly derived from the poor quality of the housing they were able to find. By and large, younger people in our sample lived in dormitories or had to sublet apartments. Dormitories are sparse in conveniences and creature comforts, and apartments are expensive to sublet.

The desire for space of one's own was felt by respondents of all ages. As in most Western countries, the difference in satisfaction between those who owned and those who rented is evident.[7] Owners are, as usual, more satisfied. For our Soviet respondents, however, the difference between shared living space and separate living space was a more significant distinction. Whether their housing was state-owned or owner-occupied, our respondents unambiguously rejected communal life. Soviet citizens obviously do not want to share kitchens, bathrooms, or space with other families. See Figure 2.3.

Satisfaction with housing in the LNP was highly sensitive to the qualitative attributes of housing. Most important to reported satisfaction was sheer space: square meters. Our respondents had very precise knowledge about housing space. The people who were most satisfied with their housing during the LNP occupied, on average, 86 percent more total space and 80 percent more space per person.[8]

Although Soviet state-owned apartments dominate Soviet housing, about one-third of our respondents owned a home in the Soviet Union: a house, a cooperative apartment, and/or a dacha. Most of these respondents were married or widowed, and family size was somewhat smaller than average. As

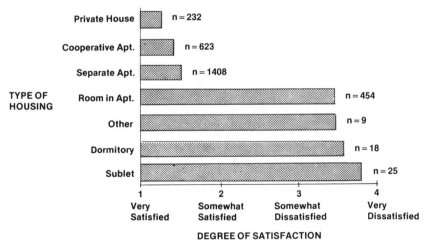

Figure 2.3. Satisfaction with housing by type of housing

[7] Davis, Fine-Davis, and Meehan 1982: 348.
[8] This close relationship between space and space per person indicates how successfully Soviet housing was allocated on the basis of family size. Accordingly, housing satisfaction differed not at all among families of different sizes.

Table 2.9. *Average satisfaction scores among Soviet emigrants, by capital city and other cities*

	Standard of living	Housing	Goods	Job	Medical care
Capital cities	2.45	2.27	3.27	1.99	2.42
N	2,076	2,090	2,069	1,689	2,020
%	74.3	74.8	74.0	60.5	72.3
Other cities	2.37	2.34	3.20	2.00	2.12
N	673	679	668	549	659
%	24.1	24.3	23.9	19.6	23.6
Average score	2.43	2.29	3.26	1.97	2.36
Missing values					
N	44	24	56	555	114
%	1.60	0.86	2.01	19.87	4.08
Total N	2,793	2,793	2,793	2,793	2,793

might be expected, the owners of houses and dachas tended to live in smaller cities (population less than 100,000), whereas owners of cooperative apartments tended to live in larger cities (more than one million). Many received their dwellings by inheritance. Very few owned more than one housing unit (which is the legal maximum). Owners generally tended more than other respondents to have witnessed an improvement in general housing conditions during their last five years in the Soviet Union. Insofar as the results of our survey can be extrapolated to the Soviet urban population, they indicate a reservoir of middle-class stability among homeowners that has seldom before been noted.

Satisfaction with goods

The strongest negative impact on respondents' satisfaction with standard of living was made by their recollection of Soviet goods shortages and their dissatisfaction with daily queues, inferior quality, and sporadic supply. The score on goods satisfaction is almost a full point lower than any other satisfaction score (see Table 2.1).

Although this response is not surprising, some related aspects are striking. One unexpected finding is that respondents who lived outside the capital cities were less dissatisfied with goods supply than those who lived in capital cities, where the supply is certainly better (Table 2.9). According to official Soviet statistics, for example, large cities are so superior to small towns in their supply of goods that the rural population buys a significant share of its goods in large cities.[9] The daytime population of major cities vastly exceeds their permanent population because of commuting shoppers. Moscow, for example, is estimated to have one million transient shoppers on any given day. The relatively greater goods dissatisfaction of the inhabitants of the largest cities must, therefore, be based upon something other than comparison with life elsewhere in the USSR.

A possible explanation for the greater goods dissatisfaction in the large cities is that their citizens have more knowledge of what goods are available to consumers outside the Soviet Union. Thus, our respondents are reporting dissatisfaction because of an unfavorable international comparison.[10] Some evidence for this view is found in the fact that the more satisfied respondents listened much less frequently to foreign broadcasts than did the more dissatisfied.

Although all of our respondents were dissatisfied with Soviet goods shortages, differences can be found among them. Dissatisfaction with goods availability rises sharply with household income and against the household savings rate. Better-off respondents were earning more and saving less in the LNP, and shortages clearly aggravated them more than the others. The potential adverse effect upon incentives to work is clear and supported by the frequency with which this group of respondents reported the unauthorized use of working time for personal shopping.

The sources of dissatisfaction with goods availability can be examined more closely in our respondents' experience with the distribution of food. Most respondents agreed that meat was in deficit supply in state stores most of the time, but this did not mean that meat was always and everywhere unavailable. When asked to estimate how frequently they ate meat in the LNP, the majority (62 percent) answered "daily," and only a very few ate meat as infrequently as several times a month. The majority of respondents also reported cheese, kefir (fermented milk), milk, and eggs in their daily diets (Table 2.10). The coexistence of fairly frequent meat consumption and complaints about deficits emphasizes the effects of price distortion and of the distribution of meat and other premium products outside the state retail network.

In general, our respondents' criticisms did not focus directly on the food distribution system. When respondents were asked to give reasons for meat

[9] *Narodnoe khoziaistvo SSSR v 1983 g. 1984*: 461. (Moscow: Tsentral'noe statisticheskoe upravlenie).
[10] The "Easterlin paradox" states that people usually compare themselves to citizens of their own country and only rarely to citizens of other countries. The paradox has received some rather general empirical support, but apparently not from our respondents. (Easterlin 1974; Duncan 1975: 273).

Table 2.10. *Dietary frequencies: meat, cheese, kefir, milk, and eggs*

	Meat	Cheese	Kefir	Milk	Eggs
Daily					
N	575	738	635	672	514
%	62.4	80.0	68.9	72.9	55.7
Several times per week					
N	265	144	220	155	319
%	28.7	15.6	23.9	16.8	34.6
Several times per month					
N	16	14	21	25	40
%	1.7	1.5	2.3	2.7	4.3
Several times per year					
N	1	0	1	1	6
%	0	0	0	0	0.6
Missing values					
N	6.5	26	45	69	43
%	7.1	1.8	4.9	7.5	4.7
Total N	922	922	922	922	922

shortages they criticized the producers, not the distribution system. They believed that deficits were caused by the system of farming, or because farm labor productivity was too low. They also saw little relationship between the low price of subsidized meat in state stores and supply shortages. They seemed to want low (below cost of production) prices and perfectly elastic supply at those prices.

Meat and other foods are, of course, normally available at higher prices on the legal private market, the *rynok*. Two groups spent much more than average in the *rynok*: those who reported themselves very satisfied with goods availability and those who reported themselves very dissatisfied. Both groups received more household income than average and spent more than average, but the *rynok* served as a safety valve only for those few who were satisfied. It is probable that this difference between groups marks a shift of demand from food to nonfood items, for the dissatisfied bought much more on the unofficial (*na levo*) market also.

In contrast to the *rynok*, which attracted both satisfied and dissatisfied urbanites, the *na levo* market attracted primarily the dissatisfied, and dissatisfaction rose steadily with expenditures *na levo*. It is probable that the dissatisfaction arose not only from the higher prices but from the inconvenience, for dissatisfied shoppers spent far more time shopping and were much more likely to take time off from work for personal business such as shopping. The dissatisfied were more pessimistic too: They saw a significant change for the worse in the supply of goods, and almost all of them believed that the Soviet Union would never be able to solve its goods shortages.

Another distribution system outside regular state retail stores is the network of shops that are closed to all but specially privileged shoppers. Only a few of our respondents had access to closed shops. Interestingly, they were only slightly more satisfied than average with the goods available to them when they lived in the Soviet Union. The prevailing system of food distribution is clearly a major source of dissatisfaction for essentially all income classes, even the best off and even the most privileged of these.

The Soviet Union takes pride in its facilities for sports, the arts, and other leisure-time activities. Since these activities are often subsidized and supplied primarily by the public sector, they are a possible additional source of goods satisfaction. There was, however, no spillover effect between goods satisfaction and a respondent's attendance at spectator sports or cultural events. For what it is worth, the dissatisfied were much more likely than the satisfied to read in their leisure time.

Satisfied and dissatisfied consumers differed in their attitudes toward poverty. When respondents were asked to estimate a minimum poverty level of family income, those who were dissatisfied specified a relatively high minimum (393 rubles per month), whereas respondents who were satisfied chose a relatively low figure (324 rubles per month). Correspondingly, the dissatisfied estimate that a much larger number of people live in poverty than do the satisfied. These results are consistent with the notion that Soviet consumers, as they divert their expenditures into the *rynok* and *na levo* channels, perceive a sharp discontinuity between official prices and open market prices, which amplifies the difference between their expectations and reality. It makes the actual market prices seem unrealistic and the state retail prices seem realistic. It frustrates consumers (and thus workers).

Job satisfaction

Job satisfaction looms large in what satisfaction our respondents recalled about their former lives in the Soviet Union. See Figures 2.4A–2.4D. Jobs were reported as the most satisfying aspect of life in the Soviet Union. The women in our sample were especially enthusiastic about their LNP jobs, and they ranked job satisfaction even higher than did the men. As with the other satisfaction measures, the older people were again more satisfied than the younger. But even the young people were more satisfied with their jobs than with any other aspect of their lives.

Following the tenets of economic rationality, one might expect

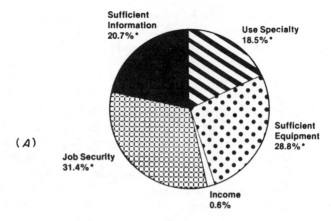

(A)

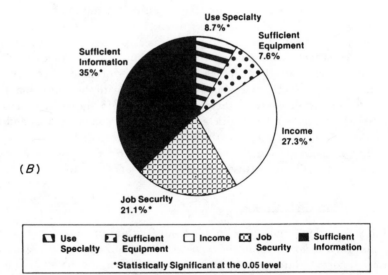

(B)

Figure 2.4. Sources of job satisfaction: *A*, all workers; *B*, professional workers; *C*, white-collar workers; *D*, blue-collar workers

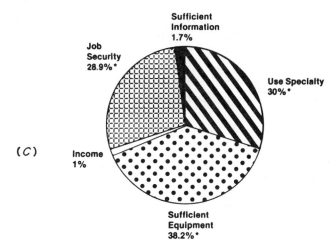

Sufficient
Information
1.7%

Job
Security
28.9%*

Use Specialty
30%*

(C)

Income
1%

Sufficient
Equipment
38.2%*

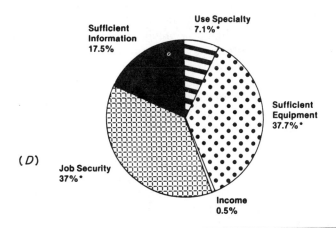

Use Specialty
7.1%*

Sufficient
Information
17.5%

Sufficient
Equipment
37.7%*

(D)

Job Security
37%*

Income
0.5%

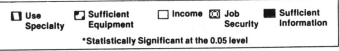

Use Specialty | Sufficient Equipment | Income | Job Security | Sufficient Information

*Statistically Significant at the 0.05 level

that – other things equal – the people who earned more would be more satisfied with their jobs, and, indeed, the respondents who earned the highest incomes ranked job satisfaction higher than the people who earned less, but the relationship is weak and only the gap between the *very* satisfied and *very* dissatisfied is statistically significant. A major part of job satisfaction must be attributed, therefore, to noneconomic factors.

Working conditions on the job contributed to job satisfaction for all income groups. Most of all, however, job satisfaction is associated with whether respondents were able to work in the specialties for which they had been trained. It was also associated with the job holder's feeling that working conditions allowed him or her to do the job well, that both enough information and suitable equipment were available. Strikingly, the people who were most satisfied with their jobs – and this is the majority – felt that trade unions, and even the Communist party (CPSU), did not worsen working conditions. Many of them, in fact, felt that these institutions served to improve conditions.

In contrast, the minority of people who were dissatisfied with jobs were more likely to support certain commonly held Western perceptions about Soviet working conditions. They felt that they often were not able to use their skills or to receive enough information or equipment. They usually believed that the trade union and CPSU worsened their working conditions and that *blat* or *protektsiia* was the main source of job advancement. They were more likely to criticize Soviet enterprises for low productivity.

It is important to note that the people whose jobs gave them little or no satisfaction were not working at menial, repetitive tasks. They were among the well educated, often having completed college. They felt secure in their jobs, fearing being fired less than others for any reason. But they still felt highly alienated. They scored themselves relatively low in "influence" and "privilege." They felt that they had been held back more than anyone else by their nationality and/or political beliefs (but, interestingly, not by their religious beliefs). They were alienated not only from their work but from their coworkers. They were not tolerant, being, for example, much less willing to accept a Buriat or an Uzbek as a coworker or supervisor than were less alienated workers.

There is a modicum of evidence for cognitive dissonance here: Despite confidence in job security, the dissatisfied were much more likely than average to have experienced unemployment. Despite their belief that fewer workers could accomplish the same job tasks, they were much more likely than others to spend work time on personal business, a problem that differs from sheer redundancy.

As might be expected, the workers who were dissatisfied with their jobs in the Soviet Union played leading roles in the decisions of their families to emigrate. Interestingly, they are more satisfied than average with their lives in the United States and more optimistic about their future here. The alienation that pervaded their lives in the Soviet Union has almost disappeared in the new environment. Were these alienated workers a majority in the Soviet Union? Are their reports about jobs and enterprise conditions more accurate than those of the less alienated, or had alienation spread from other dimensions to color perception of job and work station? The evidence of the Soviet Interview Project indicates they were a well-educated, critical minority.

Health and medical care

When our respondents were asked to name what the United States could learn from the Soviet Union, they often pointed to its health care system. When they were asked if they preferred financing for health care that was private or public, they overwhelmingly reinforced their approval of the Soviet medical system and chose public financing.

Despite a ringing endorsement of socialized medicine, our respondents were not as satisfied with Soviet medical care as they were, say, with their housing or their jobs. The main reason is a differentiation of respondents by educational level. Although a clear majority of respondents declared themselves satisfied or very satisfied with medical care, the best educated – the people who had completed higher education – were highly dissatisfied, and their responses brought down the average score (see Figure 2.5).

Respondents who were satisfied with Soviet medical care did not, however, avoid private doctors or private clinics. On the contrary, they were much more likely to have used a private clinic or physician during the LNP than were the people who were more dissatisfied. The people who were satisfied with Soviet medical care also were more pleased with the promptness, courtesy, and quality of private medical services than with those of public services. But they regarded their encounter with private medicine ambivalently. Paid clinics scored very high, but paid doctors gave little satisfaction.

The satisfied users of official Soviet medical care included the elderly, and association between satisfaction and age is strong. Older people were more satisfied than younger, and retired people were more satisfied than working people or students. The older group was generally less educated, but even when their scores were adjusted for education they were more satisfied with medical care. The elderly, of course, suffered from poorer health, for the scores on a measure of self-assessed health in the LNP diminish steadily with age. Presumably, this group had more experience with the health care system than did other respondents.

James R. Millar and Elizabeth Clayton

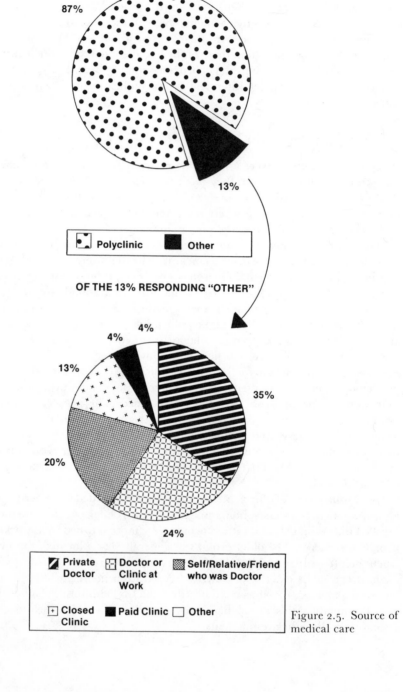

Figure 2.5. Source of medical care

Although a large majority of respondents received medical care at public polyclinics, a small number obtained it at work, and an even smaller number had access to closed clinics. Both the workplace clinics and the closed clinics satisfied their users more than did the polyclinic. The main reason seems to be that clients were treated more promptly.

An important economic reason for endorsing socialized medicine is its low user cost, and the support for publicly provided health care was indeed strongest among low-income respondents. As with goods satisfaction, support was also stronger among people who lived outside capital cities, where medical services are in fact assumed by most Western observers to be relatively poor. It was also stronger among women, who earn less. The demographic group most satisfied of all with medical care was composed of older widows who lived in cities with less than one million population.

Conclusions

Certain subgroups of our respondents have been identified with different degrees of reported satisfaction or dissatisfaction. Sex, age, and educational differences stand out with particular strength. It will be useful also to compare our emigrant groups with the citizens of other countries to see if Soviet experience is unique or typical of broader social phenomena.

Sex differences

The women in our sample were more satisfied with all measured aspects of their Soviet lives except goods, where there was no significant difference between the sexes. They were more satisfied with medical care than were men, despite (or perhaps because of) reporting themselves as in poorer health. They were slightly more satisfied with housing and significantly more satisfied with their jobs.

Yet, it is interesting to note that both men and women ranked women's life as the more difficult in the USSR. Our respondents were asked: "Taking everything into account, who has the better life in the Soviet Union – men or women?" Overwhelmingly, they responded that men had a better life. Only 3 percent of men and 2 percent of women answered "women." Furthermore, when people were asked to evaluate their actual standard of living, women ranked themselves consistently lower than men, but their satisfaction with that standard of living was not appreciably different from men's.

Most striking of all is the very strong degree of women's satisfaction with their jobs, and this in the face of high male job satisfaction too. Whatever the reason, wage discrimination and job segregation, which have been shown to prevail in the USSR as elsewhere in the industrialized world, do not seem to have taken the satisfaction out of women's jobs in the USSR. One reason may be an association between satisfaction and job security. The analysis by Paul Gregory in this volume suggests strongly that the levels of employment that pay higher wages and impose greater responsibilities are the least secure. The most security is found in unskilled and blue-collar jobs. Women would benefit in job satisfaction (other things being equal) from the security that comes with holding lower-status jobs.

Women, especially if they were elderly, also expressed much more satisfaction than men with socialized medical service. This phenomenon has been found also in Italy and Ireland.[11] In commenting on the cross-national difference between women's attitudes toward health care, Fine-Davis and Davis (1982) hypothesize that greater satisfaction with health care occurs among lower-income and lower-status women because their relative powerlessness in society limits their expectations. The evidence is that women are much more dissatisfied with health care when their status improves, as in Denmark. This interpretation suggests that Soviet women, as they lighten their home burdens and improve their status, will emerge more articulate *and* more dissatisfied.

Age differences

A second group whose satisfaction stands out from others is made up of older people. They were more satisfied with health care than the young, despite (or perhaps because of) their poorer health. They were more satisfied with their housing, jobs, and standard of living too. In contrast, the younger members of society in Western Europe recently reported themselves among the most satisfied.[12] (The British represented a notable exception in that study, and Americans have also been exceptions.)

Memories of World War II and the 1930s and the ability to gauge the great changes that have taken place since Stalin's death in 1953 may be relevant. Comparatively speaking, these long-term improvements swamp any reversals in material well-being and political liberties in the late 1970s. Access to free medical care seems to be an important determinant of well-being for the aged, too. The satisfaction of older citizens is potentially significant in a larger sense, for the USSR is passing through a transition from older to younger leaders. Donna Bahry's analysis in this volume

[11] Fine-Davis and Davis 1982: 353. Marianne Ferber has suggested in a private communication that Soviet women may have been more satisfied with Soviet medical care than men because the primary care physicians are mainly women in the USSR.
[12] Fine-Davis and Davis 1982: 351.

(Chapter 3) expands upon the political significance of this generational difference.

The prospect of future reform brings us to examine the sentiments of the younger generation among those who immigrated to the United States. This group expressed more disaffection than any other with life in the USSR. They were more dissatisfied with their jobs and the goods that they could (or could not) buy. They were more likely to slip away from work to attend to personal matters or to buy goods *na levo*. More often than other respondents, they felt that the United States could learn nothing from the Soviet Union and that a large number of Soviet citizens live in poverty.

Educational differences

The dissatisfaction of youth is, however, confounded by the effects of education. College-educated emigrants formed the most consistently dissatisfied group. They were much the most dissatisfied with their jobs and goods availability. They were only diffident about their housing. But they ranked their standard of living and their relative privileges fairly high. The dissatisfaction of this group is critical for understanding the Soviet Union today, for these dissatisfied people by and large are both young and well trained.

The two demographic elements that are common to all measures of satisfaction are age and educational level, which are themselves highly correlated. The demographic components can be aggregated, along with other components, into one composite indicator of satisfaction by weighting each component by a standardized beta coefficient that represents its contribution to satisfaction. The method that estimates the beta coefficient is a path analysis, or two-stage least squares, one of which is shown for each satisfaction measure in Figures 2.6–2.9. In order to clarify the diagrams, paths whose coefficients were less than 0.04, or which were not statistically significant, have been deleted.

In the path analysis we assume that satisfaction with standard of living (SATSOL) is a composite built from the satisfaction that people gained from their jobs (SATJOB), medical care (SATMEDC), housing (SATHOUSE), and goods availability (SATGOODS). Our assumption is based on a factor analysis, which showed that all satisfaction variables clustered together and can be considered as one entity. We have adopted the intuitively plausible assumption that the cluster centers around the most general satisfaction, that of "standard of living." The cluster will be useful in further, more aggregated analyses, but the cluster's components still have some particular characteristics of interest in themselves. These are shown in the path analysis diagrams, and several may be mentioned explicitly.

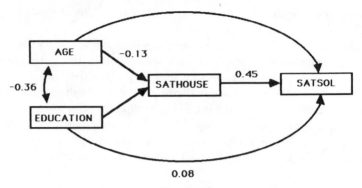

Figure 2.6. Path analysis of satisfaction with housing: indirect effect of age through SATHOUSE = − 0.06

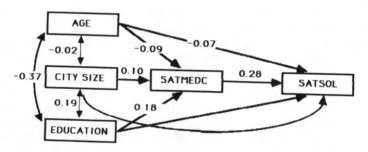

Figure 2.7. Path analysis of satisfaction with medical care: indirect effect of city size on SATSOL = 0.03; indirect effect of age on SATSOL = − 0.027; indirect effect of education on SATSOL = 0.05

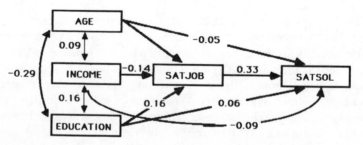

Figure 2.8. Path analysis of satisfaction with job: indirect effect of income on SATSOL = − 0.048; indirect effect of education on SATSOL = 0.055

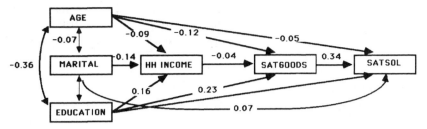

Figure 2.9. Path analysis of satisfaction with availability of goods; indirect effect of marital on SATGOODS = 0.006; indirect effect of education on SATGOODS = 0.007; indirect effect of age on SATGOODS = 0.004; indirect effect of marital on SATSOL = 0.002; indirect effect of education on SATSOL = − 0.0024; indirect effect of age on SATSOL = 0.001

1. As noted, age and education were negatively correlated: Younger people were better educated. The correlation was lowest in the path analysis for job satisfaction, which includes only those respondents who had jobs. This indicates that the age–education correlation is probably disappearing from the population, however slowly.

When the correlated effects of age and education were removed, housing satisfaction was affected only by age: Older people were more satisfied with their housing. Put in other words, the people who were well educated were as satisfied with their housing as those who were less educated.

In other analyses, educational level had an impact that was independent of age. Less-educated people were more satisfied with medical care, goods availability, and jobs. Although older people were similarly more satisfied with medical care and goods availability, they were as satisfied with their jobs as younger people. Thus, the effects of age and education on people's satisfaction with medical care and goods availability were the same, but on satisfaction with housing and jobs they differed.

2. Marital status affected goods satisfaction in that married people were more satisfied, but its primary effect was to increase household income (HH INCOME), which mildly increased satisfaction.

3. High-income respondents were overall more satisfied with their jobs, but well-educated people were not, and the effects of education were somewhat stronger than the effects of income.

4. Satisfaction with standard of living was captured best by jobs, goods, and housing. Medical care played a lesser role.

The data collected by SIP do not permit us to determine unambiguously just how satisfied or dissatisfied the referent population is on an absolute scale. These results do, however, provide a view of differentiation within the referent population – differentiation primarily by sex, age, education, income, and city size. For the first time it is possible to see the general contours of social satisfaction (or dissatisfaction). What is striking is the discovery that those who were disproportionately reaping the material benefits of Soviet socialist society in the late 1970s were, in general, the least satisfied members of that society. Those who lived in the most desirable cities, had the highest educational attainment, held the most skilled jobs, earned the top-level incomes, occupied the best housing, and dominated consumption in all markets reported themselves the least satisfied. This is in sharp contrast with the findings of the Harvard Project of the early 1950s, in which those who had been the most successful materially expressed the least dissatisfaction with Soviet society.[13]

Finally, although our respondents have demonstrated their negative overall evaluation of Soviet society by having left the USSR, our findings show that there were nonetheless certain aspects of Soviet society that generated satisfaction and thus presumably support from the urban population. Comparisons based upon their subsequent lives in the United States have undoubtedly affected their judgments, but in most cases the effect would have been to clarify or improve the accuracy of such qualitative judgments. This is clearly the case, for example, for evaluations of medical care, goods availability, job satisfaction, and the like. The view from the bottom upward, from the household sector toward the top, shows considerable heterogeneity and variety.

References

Andrews, Frank M., and Ronald F. Inglehart. 1979. "The Structure of Subjective Well-being in Nine Western Societies," *Social Indicators Research*, 6: 73–90.
Campbell, Angus. 1981. *The Sense of Well-being in America*. New York: McGraw-Hill.
Davis, E. E., M. Fine-Davis, and G. Meehan. 1982. "Demographic Determinants of Perceived Well-being in 8 European Countries," *Social Indicators Research*, 10: 341–58.
Duncan, Otis Dudley. 1975. "Does Money Buy Satisfaction?" *Social Indicators Research*, 2: 267–74.
Easterlin, R. A. 1974. "Does Economic Growth Improve the Human Lot?" In P.A. David and M. W. Reder (eds.), *Nations and Households in Economic Growth*. New York: Academic Press, pp. 89–125.
Fine-Davis, M., and E. E. Davis. 1982. "Predictors of Satisfaction with Environmental Quality in 8 European Countries," *Social Indicators Research*, 11: 341–62.
Inkeles, Alex, and Raymond Bauer. 1959. *The Soviet Citizen*. Cambridge, Mass.: Harvard University Press.

[13] Inkeles and Bauer 1959: 260.

Near, Janet P., C. Ann Smith, Robert W. Rice, and R. G. Hunt. 1984. "A Comparison of Work and Nonwork Predictors of Life Satisfaction," *Academy of Management Journal*, 27: 184–90.

PART II

Politics: sources of regime support

Politics, generations, and change in the USSR

DONNA BAHRY

Given the turbulence of Soviet history since 1917, students of Soviet politics have looked to the rise of new generations as a key source of change in the USSR. Upheavals from the Revolution and civil war, through collectivization to World War II and de-Stalinization, all created markedly divergent conditions in which succeeding generations have come of age. Life experiences and opportunities vary so much that new generations – among the leadership and the population alike – should have different political values and expectations of the Soviet system. If formative experiences shape adult political orientations, the terror of the 1930s should have left its mark on the Stalin generation, just as the thaw of the post-Stalin era should have created a less fearful and more critical cohort. Thus, the process of generational replacement could give a different cast to the Soviet political landscape. To borrow Karl Mannheim's (1972) phrase, generational differences may be fundamental guideposts for understanding social and political change in the USSR.

Yet we have little empirical evidence on how the members of succeeding age groups vary in their relationship to the Soviet system – how the regime engages the members of each generation, or how they respond. Nor has it been possible to disentangle the political impact of rising educational levels and occupational attainments from the effects of generational replacement.

This chapter is a first attempt to explore the political "generation gap" at the individual level, using interviews with recent emigrants conducted by the Soviet Interview Project to assess age cleavages in political involvement. How does behavior vary among those who came of age in the purge era, during World War II, in the postwar and in the post-Stalin eras? Are there measurable differences in the willingness to conform to official expectations of political activism or to engage in unconventional behavior? The SIP

I would like to thank Joe Berliner, Thane Gustafson, Bogdan Harasymiw, David Lane, James Millar, and Brian Silver for comments on an earlier version of this chapter. I would also like to thank Gary King, Bert Holland, and George Sharrard for assistance with the analysis, and Nasrin Abdolali for help in preparing the manuscript.

survey, with its 2,667 voting-age respondents,[1] allows us to assess potential age cleavages by examining each individual's involvement in Soviet elections, public organizations, and contacts with public officials, as well as in unsanctioned activities such as study groups, protests and strikes.

Behavioral differences are especially important, for several reasons. First, asking people what they actually did helps to minimize possible recall problems. Interviews centered on an individual's life in the last five years before it was disrupted by plans to emigrate (in the survey, this was referred to as the "last normal period" or LNP); and given the lag between the time of emigration and the time of the interview, respondents should find it easier to recall specific activities than to recall more general reactions to the Soviet system.[2] In fact, focusing on behavior strengthens the case for the accuracy of recall on subjective questions. If a compelling pattern emerges in the data on individual behavior, and if it corresponds to a similar pattern in attitudes, then we can have more confidence in items tapping a respondent's subjective evaluations.

Second, concentrating on behavior offers a stringent test of generational differences. Any individual may dislike some or all aspects of the system, but since the regime expects public conformity, the *willingness to act* in nonapproved ways offers stronger evidence of deviations from the Soviet model of an active but compliant citizen. And, given the costs of nonconformity, we should expect to find relatively few differences in unconventional activity among generations. Therefore, to the extent that we do find a generation gap in public behavior, it offers more powerful evidence of a fundamental cleavage.

To assess the degree of individual political involvement, the questionnaire included items about a range of activities from voting and election work, participation in public organizations, and contacting to strikes and protest. The survey thus asked about behaviors requiring varied political resources,

---

[1] In all, the SIP sample included 2,793 respondents, who ranged in age from 13 to 74 at the end of their "last normal period" (LNP) of life in the USSR. For purposes of analyzing political activity, I chose to focus on respondents who were at least 18 at the start of their LNP. The distinction yields an effective sample of 2,667 and excludes 126 individuals between 8 and 17 at the start of their LNP.

[2] The accuracy of recall can in fact be tested, since the sample included 227 pairs of respondents (454 individuals) who had lived in the same household in the USSR at the end of their LNP. A comparison of their responses (Anderson and Silver 1986) shows substantial agreement on many key household characteristics, such as square meters of housing shared by the family and household expenditures. The level of agreement is only slightly lower on subjective items, such as a respondent's reported degree of satisfaction with the family's housing, standard of living, or access to consumer goods.

imposing different costs on the participants, and in some cases (e.g., contacting the authorities) offering benefits as well.[3]

However, certain types of behavior cluster together, and this suggests an underlying pattern of activity that spans only a few basic modes of political involvement. Respondents who were active in public organizations were also likely to work in an election campaign; those who engaged in nonconformist political acts were also likely to avoid voting, work privately, and attend religious services; those who contacted a party or government official were also more likely to write to the media; and those who expressed an interest in politics were also more inclined to listen to Western radio broadcasts. The different activities, when subjected to a factor analysis, thus yield four basic political roles:[4]

> _compliant_: people engaged in what Brzezinski and Huntington (1965) labeled "mobilized participation," or involvement in public organizations such as housing commissions, voluntary police and fire protection, trade union committees, the Komsomol, and other communal groups
>
> _spectator_: people with a self-defined high degree of interest in politics and public affairs
>
> _parochial_: people whose activity focuses on gaining individual benefits or redress by contacting public officials or the media (Di Francesco and Gitelman's [1984] "covert participation in policy implementation")
>
> _nonconformist_: people who took part in protests, strikes, unsanctioned study or discussion groups, or other unconventional political acts as defined by the respondent.[5]

---

3 Given the political sensitivity of the question of party membership for Soviet immigrants to the United States, we asked respondents in the pretests whether others they knew would admit to membership, or whether the question would disrupt the interview (e.g., respondents might break off the interview altogether or answer subsequent questions less openly). The reactions in the pretest (and advice from consultants to the project) all indicated that a direct question about party membership would not yield accurate information and would likely undermine the rest of the interview as well. Consequently, the questionnaire did not ask if the respondent was ever a member of the CPSU.

4 For a fuller description of the factor analysis, the variables, and the questions used to construct them, see Bahry 1986.

5 I have purposely avoided using the terms "dissent" and "dissident," because they connote active, programmatic opposition. I wanted instead to examine the distinction at the individual level between those who fit the model of a compliant citizen and those who turned to unorthodox political activity, programmatic or not. I also avoided the term "dissident" because many respondents would not so describe themselves. One other point should be noted about the definition of

Political involvement can best be conceptualized not along a single dimension but along several, each with a distinct focus and each with a potentially different clientele. In light of the distinctions, my analysis will deal with these four dimensions separately.

The validity of emigrant responses

None of the discussion thus far is meant to argue that the level of either conventional or unconventional activity in the sample can be taken to represent the actual levels in the Soviet Union as a whole. Respondents are more educated and more urban than the average Soviet citizen; they are far from representative of the Soviet ethnic mix; and, of course, they quit the USSR. Yet their responses say a great deal about the *structure* of generational differences – about the gaps between the highly educated and the less educated, between men and women, and so on. If the goal of social science is to discover the patterns in behavior and attitudes, a carefully balanced sample with carefully constructed questions can speak volumes about the connections among age and education, political activity, and a host of other fundamental political issues. And it is the structure of such political relationships that concerns us here.

The critical question is whether the patterns of behavior and attitudes among emigrant respondents allow us to make inferences about political activity in the USSR. How valid is it to generalize back to the Soviet system? The data can be judged by three separate criteria: the logic and coherence of responses within the survey, the fit between SIP and Soviet survey results, and the conformity of the results with empirical theory on political behavior. The first standard is internal, relying on the biases we would predict in an emigrant sample as a baseline for measuring political behavior in the Soviet Union. We would expect respondents to be negative toward the system and nonconformist in their behavior. If respondents report a relatively high degree of compliant activism and little nonconformity, then conventional activity is likely to be even greater, and nonconformity even less, in the USSR. A second, external criterion for assessing the data is the degree to which responses correspond to Soviet findings. If the patterns match, in spite of the differences in sample selection and in the conditions under which

nonconformity used here. The series of items in the questionnaire that touch on unsanctioned activities also included attendance at any "unofficial art show, poetry reading, or concert" during the LNP. But comments from interviewers suggested that some respondents did not pick up on the word "unofficial" and answered instead in terms of the regular cultural events they had attended. Thus, it was impossible to tell how many of the responses to this question actually referred to *unsanctioned* activity.

interviews took place, then the data support inferences about behavior in the USSR. Finally, the third critical standard for evaluating the responses is how well they correspond to established theories of political action. Data that fit not only what we know of the Soviet system but also what we would predict from the empirical study of political behavior make the case for validity even stronger.

The responses are encouraging on all three counts. In spite of the unrepresentativeness of the sample and the fact that each individual "voted with his feet," the picture of individual activity that emerges from these respondents is far more conventional than unconventional. Nearly 20 percent served as leaders or activists in public organizations ranging from housing and parents' committees to *druzhinniki* to the Komsomol during the years just before they applied to emigrate.[6] Another 30 percent were among the rank and file of such conventional political groups. In contrast, only 2 percent took any leading role in protests or other overt noncon-formity; and 10 percent more engaged in at least one such activity during their LNP.[7]

However, behavior varied among individuals with different ethnic backgrounds. Political nonconformity was much less common among Jewish respondents than it was among the other nationalities represented in the sample (chiefly Russians). This may simply reflect an ethnic distinction in conventional political behavior – as exemplified by the fact that the Soviet Jewish population had the highest party saturation rate of any ethnic group through the mid-1970s (Jacobs 1976, 1978, 1980). But the ethnic split here more likely reflects the fact that Third Wave emigrants had essentially only two tickets out of the USSR, one based on nationality and one based on political dissidence. In either case, the potential for ethnic bias must be considered in any assessment of respondents' political activities and

---

6 Except for Komsomol membership, all such questions on compliant political activity refer to a respondent's LNP. In the case of the Komsomol, the questionnaire asked if a respondent had *ever* belonged. I therefore counted a Komsomol member as a "compliant" during the LNP only if he/she was 28 or younger at that time.

7 The relatively low incidence of unconventional behavior is all the more persuasive since respondents might be expected to exaggerate their antiregime activities to impress American interviewers. If respondents offered answers they thought Americans would want to hear, the real proportion of political nonconformists could be even lower than our survey indicates. To control for this possibility, the survey included several items to measure the propensity to flatter the interviewer. Nonconformists turned out to have the lowest flattery scores; they showed the least inclination to give answers that would please American interviewers. They would therefore seem to be little disposed to overstate (or, for that matter, to understate) the extent of their unconventional political behavior.

attitudes, and all of the results below are presented with an eye to such biases.[8]

The responses also reveal another important distinction in nonconformist behavior, related to the decision to emigrate. Individuals who engaged in unconventional activities were more likely than others to make the decision to emigrate themselves, whereas "compliant" respondents typically shared in or played no part in the family's decision to leave the USSR.[9] Thus, the number of nonconformists in the sample could be influenced by a selectivity bias: It may include a disproportionate share of a relatively small, disgruntled group – people who actively wanted to emigrate. And respondents who did not themselves make the decision may therefore be more similar to the population that remained in the USSR. If so, then a respondent's role in the family's decision to leave should be an important variable in assessing the biases within the sample.

Validation through external sources is more difficult, given the dearth of comparable Soviet surveys. Yet, the available data confirm the basic patterns in SIP responses. Thus, for example, Soviet analysts reveal a gap in political participation, with college graduates far more heavily engaged in compliant political activism (*obshchestvennaia rabota*) than are individuals who had only primary or secondary schooling (see Figure 3.1). SIP data yield much the same conclusion: The highly educated turn out to be nearly twice as active as are respondents with a general secondary education or less.[10] Both Soviet findings and SIP data also reveal a connection between higher occupational status and greater compliant activism (Ikonnikova and Lisovskii 1969).

Even more important for our purposes, Soviet results confirm the levels of Komsomol saturation reported by different generations in the sample. Thus, according to Kogan and Pavlov's (1976) study of two generations of workers in heavy industry (one group 30 years old or younger, and a second group 50 and over), the young had a higher rate of Komsomol membership than the old did decades earlier. The same age gap emerges among SIP respondents – especially among the men, as we would expect since Kogan and Pavlov's sample was drawn from a predominantly male industry (see

---

[8] For an assessment of the degree of ethnic bias on different types of questions, see Bahry 1987.

[9] Among nonconformist leaders, 48.4 percent made the decision to emigrate themselves; among others engaged in unconventional political activities, the percentage is 45.3. In contrast, only 30.9 percent of other respondents decided themselves to leave the USSR. The correlation (gamma) between nonconformist activity and role in the emigration decision is .30.

[10] The same connection between education and political activity emerges in a Belorussian study by N. N. Beliakovich (1978).

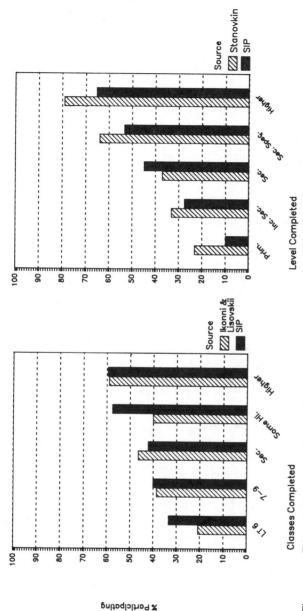

Figure 3.1. Education and compliant political activism: a comparison of responses among Soviet surveys and SIP. *Sources*: Ikonnikova and Lisovskii 1969: 64 (data based on a sample of respondents aged 30 or under in the early 1960s; corresponding SIP data in Part *A* cover the same age group); Stanovkin 1981: 73 (data cover multiple generations; no adjustment in SIP data was necessary)

Table 3.1. *Komsomol membership by generation* (%)

Study	Older generation (began work in early 1930s)	Younger generation (30 or under in 1970)
Kogan and Pavlov	51.6	70.9[a]
SIP		
Men	55.6	76.1
Women	30.0	79.8

	Intelligentsia/white collar		Blue collar	
Study	36–45	Under 35	36–45	Under 35
Harvard Project (Rossi)	26.0	54.0	21.0	31.0
SIP[b]	29.2	52.3	21.7	32.1

[a] Includes young workers who were party members.
[b] Age at time of Harvard Project interview.
Sources: Soviet Interview Project; Rossi 1957:331; Kogan and Pavlov 1976: 149–50.

Table 3.1). Both sets of data also match Fainsod's (1964) account of the Komsomol's evolution from an elite organization to one with broader mass membership. Soviet survey results should of course be interpreted with care, because procedures for drawing the samples and conducting the interviews are not always clear. Yet, the variation in Soviet procedures makes SIP responses all the more compelling: The patterns basically match, even in the face of divergent methods, the different political atmosphere in which interviews were conducted, and the difference in samples between citizens who left and those who stayed.

One other external source can also be brought to bear in assessing the data: the interviews conducted by the Harvard Project shortly after World War II. Although they did not include all of the same questions on what we have labeled as compliant and nonconformist activity, they did ask about Komsomol membership, allowing us to compare individuals from the same generations interviewed more than 30 years apart. The samples, of course, are much different; the Harvard Project respondents were primarily Russian and Ukrainian, as likely to come from rural as from urban areas, and most of the interviews were conducted in displaced persons camps after the war, whereas SIP respondents, predominantly Jewish and urban, were interviewed in their homes in the United States. Once again, however, these differences turn into an advantage, for the levels of Komsomol saturation as reported by the two different samples are nearly identical[11] (see Table 3.1).

The third criterion for judging the data, conformity with theory, adds still more evidence on the basic validity of the responses. The most careful cross-national studies show that political involvement covers a broad spectrum of activities, each demanding different resources from participants and each with different implications for the political system (Verba and Nie 1972; Verba, Nie, and Kim 1978; Barnes and Kaase et al. 1979). Voting, for example, demands few resources (e.g., little commitment of time or funds) from any one participant but conveys only a diffuse message about the voter's policy preferences to candidates and parties. Compared to individuals who go to government to appeal or complain, work in campaigns, or take part in community groups (among other political activities), voters incur fewer costs but also have fewer opportunities to articulate individual concerns or demands to political elites. At the other end of the spectrum, protest imposes greater costs and is less frequent than either voting, work in political organizations, or contacting. The pattern proves to be a common one, resembling the curve for West Germany presented in Figure 3.2.

The incidence or distribution of these political activities among SIP respondents proves to be very similar.[12] Voting, which requires the fewest resources, is far more common than engaging in an election campaign, taking an active role in a public organization, or contacting the authorities; and unconventional activity is even less common (see Figure 3.2).

Not only does the relative frequency of different acts correspond to theory about political involvement; so, too, does the structure of political action. Comparative research on participation reveals consistently that diverse

[11] Alice Rossi (1957) reports, however, that the Harvard Project results on Komsomol membership were lower in the written questionnaire (WQ), which was self-administered, than in the life history interviews administered personally by Harvard Project researchers. Because these latter data correspond more closely to Soviet data for the period, they are the ones cited here.

[12] It is possible that exposure to the West might somehow contaminate responses and thus account for the frequency of different activities. However, most if not all respondents in the survey had arrived too recently to gain citizenship by the time of the interview and thus were not in a position to vote. And the likelihood of respondents in the United States being contaminated by patterns of West German political activism is remote. A second question might be raised about the nonequivalence of such political activities for West German versus Soviet citizens: Can voting in competitive elections and noncompetitive elections, or contacting of Soviet versus Western officials, be legitimately compared? If we are concerned primarily with the outcomes of elections, then the issue is a formidable one. But if we are concerned with the structure of political activity in each system, and the within-nation comparison of costs and benefits associated with different behaviors, then the data in each case reveal something similar about the nature of political involvement.

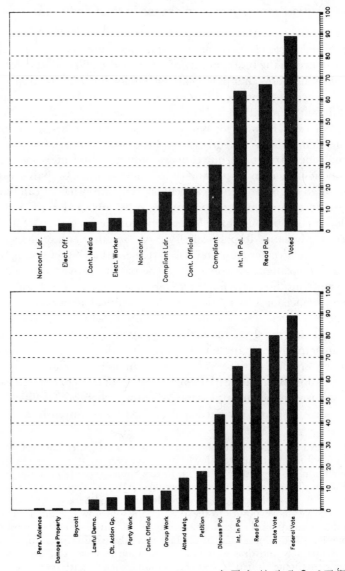

Figure 3.2. Frequency distribution of political acts: West Germany and USSR (West German data from a survey conducted in 1980; SIP data refer to respondent's LNP, which primarily fell during latter half of Brezhnev era). *Source:* Dalton 1984: 272

political activities basically represent only a few underlying types of involvement, which impose different demands on the participant and on the political system and appeal to different clienteles: voting, campaign activity, collective but nonpartisan action, individual contacting of political authorities, and protest (Welch 1975; Verba et al. 1978; Barnes et al. 1979). The factor analysis described above yields a very similar picture among SIP respondents, with four modes of political involvement: compliant, spectator, parochial, and nonconformist. In the Soviet case, election work does not constitute a separate factor, since elections serve as extensions of more general mobilized participation. And since it takes some initiative *not* to vote, nonvoting (or allowing someone else to cast the ballot) clusters with other forms of unconventional behavior.

Needless to say, the many other questions in the survey require similar tests before we can accept them as legitimate measures of individual behavior and attitudes. For our purposes, the relatively conventional nature of the sample, the conformity with external data from the Harvard Project and from Soviet surveys, and the close fit with empirical theories of political behavior all help to increase confidence in responses on political activity.

The concept of generational change

The problem of generations, as Mannheim called it, has come to be a controversial issue for Western and Soviet scholars alike. All concede the distinctiveness of different age groups, but there is little consensus on the nature or political implications of the generation gap. Among Western researchers, much of the discussion of Soviet generations focuses on elites and on their distinctive formative experiences. Jerry Hough (1980) argues, for example, that fundamental changes in both the educational system and the political climate produced different experiences and career opportunities for each successive age group. Thus, the "Brezhnev generation," born between 1900 and 1909, benefited from dizzying career mobility during the purges, often with formal but hardly rigorous schooling. In contrast, the purge generation, born between 1910 and 1918, entered the schools in time to face the more stringent and rigorous demands of the educational system during Stalin's "Great Retreat" but began their careers too late to benefit from the political dislocations of the purges. Those who came of age during World War II (born between 1919 and 1925) experienced both the wartime sacrifices and the limited opportunities for education they caused. Finally, the postwar generation (born between 1925 and 1940) entered school and began their careers not only in a freer political atmosphere but also in a system where education had been upgraded and had become more rigorous. As Hough concludes, it is the joint impact of age and specific educational experiences that sets generations apart. Seweryn Bialer (1980) offers a similar typology, distinguishing among the purge generation (who came of age in the 1930s), the wartime generation (who entered the political arena during World War II), and the post-Stalin generation (who came of age after the war.) And Jeremy Azrael (1966) begins with an earlier cohort but suggests a comparable fourfold categorization of political generations among industrial specialists and managers.

If formative experiences do influence each generation's political orientations, we should find similar cleavages in the mass population. The political terror, the dislocations of World War II, and the attacks on Stalinism that set elite generations apart also shaped the political environment, education, and career opportunities for nonelites.

However, few researchers agree on the political implications of the generation gap among the mass public. Jonathan Harris (1971) suggests, for example, that willingness to criticize the regime divides into those with firsthand experience of Stalinism versus those for whom the Stalin era is only history. Other authors (Brzezinski and Huntington 1965; Connor 1975) focus on the divergence between young and old with respect to lifestyle – traditional preferences versus Western music, clothing, and pop culture. Generational differences might thus be expected to embody little or no *political* content.

Even if they did, the impact should be minimized by pervasive mobilizing institutions such as the schools and the Komsomol, dedicated to insuring public conformity and keeping the younger generation compliant (Kassof 1965). As Connor (1975: 21–22) explains,

The combined machinery of tightly controlled youth organizations and a traditional, non-permissive educational system focused on the "adult" concern of preparation for the world of work . . . has had its effect. The social space in which Soviet youth might develop its own group consciousness, its own set of political orientations, has been tightly circumscribed by that machinery.

In addition, the regime has been able to blunt potential discontent with slow but steady improvements in the standard of living, buying acquiescence, and managing popular expectations. Bialer (1980: 163–64) sums up the argument by noting that "for the average Soviet consumer [the] reference point is neither the West nor even Eastern Europe but his own past. . . . Comparison with this past can only heighten approval of ongoing improvements and temper expectations." From this perspective, as Bialer suggests, the record of the Brezhnev era can be considered a success.

For Soviet authors, the political implications of the age gap raise a similar controversy. That generations are distinctive is virtually a foregone conclusion, with many researchers treating the rise of new cohorts as the driving force behind social progress. Formative experiences early in life are viewed as critical, as sociologist Iu. E. Volkov (1972: 336–37) explains:

The period of youth is the period of forming a new member of society and of a specific class – a citizen, a worker. Social activism created in youth, as a rule, remains during one's whole life, creating an active builder of communism through all successive stages of one's life.

Yet, Soviet studies of aging and politics are contradictory. Researchers describe new generations as more politically active and aware than their fathers and grandfathers, but also as less committed and less active than previous generations. Volkov (1972), for example, contends that contemporary young people exhibit a higher than average level of political commitment. And N.M. Blinov (1983: 6) takes the argument even further, contending that "contemporary Soviet youth" are characterized by an increasing social activism. But virtually every study also emphasizes shortcomings in the political socialization of new generations, castigating the young for narrowness, putting selfish interests ahead of the collective, and preferring petty consumerism over work for society at large. Komsomol members participating in one Soviet survey (Blinov 1983) reported that their contemporaries within the Komsomol are ideologically shallow, and Leonid Brezhnev (1981), in his remarks to the Twenty-sixth Party Congress, lamented the political naivete and less than professional attitude toward work that characterize "some young people." More recently, a Central Committee decree complained that Soviet youth were preoccupied with Western fashions and politically apathetic (Tolz 1984).

Thus, Soviet research leads to the conclusion that the young are both more mobilized and less mobilized than their fathers and grandfathers. However, empirical evidence to support either view is limited. Most Soviet studies of age differences focus exclusively on youth, with little attention to the attitudes or behavior of older cohorts. Survey samples typically encompass only respondents aged 30 or younger, precluding any direct evaluation of intergenerational cleavages (see, e.g., Ikonnikova and Lisovskii 1969; Vershlovskaia and Lesokhina 1975; Gorshkov and Sheregi 1979). And though Soviet assessments offer some intriguing evidence on the political activities of young people, they seldom explore in depth the causes behind different levels of activism or the attitudes that distinguish the active from the nonactive.

There is, then, a consensus among both Soviet and Western researchers that age matters, but there is substantial disagreement over the content of the generation gap and its impact on the political system. The literature leaves us with two basic questions: (1) How and how much do age groups differ? And (2) what is the political content of the generation gap?

Defining generations

To speak of a generation gap implies a definition of where each cohort begins and ends, a set of specific age groups that are sufficiently similar in their behavior and sufficiently unlike previous or successive ones to warrant the use of the term "generation." Yet defining the cut points is never an easy task. As Mannheim emphasized, in the absence of major changes in the social or political environment, not every cohort emerges with a distinctive outlook; and even when one does, the exact boundaries between generations may still be difficult to identify without a well-defined theory.

In the Soviet case, political upheavals have been so pronounced that researchers are in substantial agreement on the basic cut points, diverging chiefly on the *number* of age groups they identify and the group with which they begin. For our purposes, the first cohort in the sample is a given, since the sample includes respondents up to age 74. The oldest individuals in the sample thus belong to the "Brezhnev generation" that Hough (1980) identifies. As for the number of generations to be analyzed, the best scheme empirically is the one with the greatest number of categories, since it allows us to test for more potential cleavages. I therefore rely on Hough's cut points to define age groups, with a fifth category added to incorporate respondents born after 1940. My generational scheme and the corresponding frequencies are as follows:[13]

Age group	Frequency
Brezhnev generation, born 1900–09	34
Purge generation, born 1910–18	396
Wartime generation, born 1919–25	301
Postwar generation, born 1925–40	879
Post-Stalin generation, born 1941–60	1,057

Assessing the differences among these five groups also raises a fundamental question about how to interpret generational cleavages. Almost any survey sample will exhibit differences based on the age of the respondent, but an interview conducted at only one point in time makes it difficult to separate generational versus life-cycle effects. The distinction is crucial, as Converse (1976) argues, for it bears not only on the explanation for age differences but also on our ability to predict the consequences of generational replacement.

---

[13] To test the appropriateness of these categories, I plotted residuals from the regression analysis in Table 3.2 against a respondent's year of birth. If the categories were inappropriate, they would yield out-liers (i.e., standardized residuals with an absolute value greater than 2) clustered in certain years. However, there were few out-liers and little systematic pattern in their distribution.

If a life-cycle process dominates, and the activities and attitudes of the young gradually come to resemble those of older generations, the entrance of new cohorts into political life and the disengagement of the old should balance each other out. Replacement alone will have little net effect on mass activism and beliefs. On the other hand, if each generation has a unique political profile that endures with age, then replacement can lead to a transformation of mass politics.

The problem of distinguishing between the two explanations has stimulated a lively debate in the social sciences, and the results suggest that it would be inaccurate to single out only one explanation for age-related political differences. Work by Abramson and Inglehart (1984), Jennings and Niemi (1981), Verba and Nie (1972), and others reveals that generational change is a complex process that involves *both components*. Each age group takes on some new roles at different stages in the life cycle, but each one also diverges markedly from younger and older groups in other ways, because of the era in which it came of age. Age differences grow out of the combination of life-cycle and cohort or generational effects, which come into play differently depending on the type of political activity or value in question (Jennings 1976).

Verba, Nie, and Kim (1978) demonstrate, for example, that conventional involvement in seven nations follows an inverted U-shaped curve: The very young and the very old participate least. The young have yet to assume the adult roles that generate political activity; the old experience a slowdown in participation because of declining health, disengagement from the work force, and limited mobility.

Yet, though some types of activity follow the life cycle, other political characteristics tend to be relatively stable with age. Each new generation in the United States, for example, has come into the electorate with a distinctive profile of party identification and has continued to be distinctive through successive elections and successive stages in the life cycle (Converse 1976; Markus 1983; Jennings and Markus 1984). The old stereotype of younger voters turning increasingly to Republicanism (and, by implication, to conservatism) as they age has proved to be a myth.

In similar fashion, panel or two-wave studies of political nonconformity from the 1960s onward reveal that young civil rights activists interviewed again after several years continued to hold distinctive political views in spite of the aging process and in spite of passage through different stages of the life cycle. Compared to other members of their generation, individuals who protested in the 1960s were still radical and still active in both conventional and unconventional politics years later (Fendrich 1974; Jennings and Niemi 1981).

We need not, however, rely solely on findings from Western systems to judge trends in the USSR. SIP data allow us to test for life-cycle versus generational effects directly, by comparing the activities of different cohorts when they were the same age and by assessing the impact of various roles – such as employment, marriage, having children – that correspond to different stages in the life cycle. If a life cycle process dominates, each generation's behavior should match the activities of others at the same age. Levels of political activity should also change with each individual's passage through various adult roles. On the other hand, if formative experiences shape political activism, then there ought to be no smooth progression in activity from young to old; assumption of different adult roles should have little impact; and generations should exhibit different levels of activity even at the same age.

The paradox of generations

Plots of the different political roles among the five age groups (Figure 3.3) reveal that the Soviet generation gap is indeed political, with the five groups diverging substantially in compliant behavior, nonconformity, and political interest. In each case, the postwar and post-Stalin generations prove to be the most active: the most interested in public affairs, the most heavily engaged in "mobilized participation," but at the same time taking a greater part in unsanctioned study groups, protests, strikes, and other unconventional activities. Soviet ambivalence about the young would thus appear to be well founded. The last two cohorts are both more compliant and more unorthodox than are older groups. Only contacting of public authorities and media (parochial activity) proves to be unrelated to age.

Compliant behavior

In one sense, the responses indicate that the system has worked well to insure that it mobilizes ever greater numbers of new entrants into political life. The postwar and post-Stalin cohorts are almost twice as likely to belong to at least one group and twice as likely to take a leading role than are their fathers and grandfathers. There is, however, a degree of specialization by age, with the two youngest generations heavily engaged in the Komsomol but less involved in other organizations. One reason appears to be that many other organizations are geared to specific adult roles: Parents' committees attract people with school-age children; housing or repair commissions include citizens who have their own rooms or apartment. There is also something of a trade-off between joining the Komsomol and joining other organizations: for someone aged 14 to 28 who wants to demonstrate political trustworthiness, the Komsomol is simply more accessible – and, for many, unavoidable.

SPECTATORS

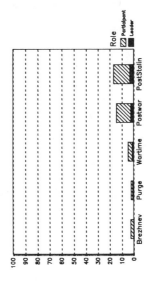

COMPLIANTS

NONCONFORMISTS

PAROCHIALS

Figure 3.3. Generation and political involvement. *Compliants*: those who led or participated in conventional communal organizations, as defined in text. *Spectators*: those who reported being "very" or "somewhat" interested in politics. *Parochials*: those who reported contacting a government or party official or the media. *Nonconformists*: those who led or participated in unconventional political activity, as defined in text.

Yet the trade-offs among different organizations do not explain why the total level of compliant activism differs so radically between young and old. We might hypothesize that the gap stems from the life cycle, where the younger the individual, the fewer the obligations of family and work – and, perhaps, the greater the optimism about political life. Aging might thus produce some erosion of political activity. The responses, however, suggest a very different process, because the postwar and post-Stalin generations are also more highly mobilized than their fathers and grandfathers were *at the same age*. As Figure 3.4 shows, only a small percentage of the older generations (chiefly men with higher education) joined the Komsomol in their youth, whereas nearly three-fourths of the postwar and post-Stalin cohorts joined. And, as noted above, Soviet and Harvard Project findings yield a similar picture. Komsomol saturation among the young has thus deepened since the early days of the Soviet regime, with the greatest expansion among groups that were underrepresented earlier: the less educated, the blue-collar workers, and women. It appears, too, to be relatively evenly distributed among the nationalities represented in the sample, with few differences in Komsomol membership among these ethnic groups. The age gap, then, is not simply a product of maturation or of changing adult roles; it reflects basic differences in the level of each generation's early mobilization. Moreover, for older generations, there is a strong connection between early mobilization in the Komsomol and political activism during the LNP.[14] Few of the non-Komsomol members turned active in later life.

Figure 3.4 also indicates that the generation gap persists even when education, occupational status, and gender are controlled. This conclusion is confirmed by the multiple regression analysis presented below. When other characteristics – basic socioeconomic status (education, income, employment), self-defined levels of personal influence and interest in politics, and fear of the authorities – are factored in, the postwar and post-Stalin cohorts still prove to be the most active (see Table 3.2). And there is little evidence that the assumption of different adult roles through the life cycle has any significant impact. Thus, for example, neither marriage nor having a family influences an individual's average level of activity.[15] Retirement seems to be

[14] Among those past the age of Komsomol membership during their LNP, having been an activist early on is a strong predictor of later involvement in other compliant organizations. The unstandardized regression coefficient is .415, which is significant at ($p \leq 0.1$).

[15] Gordon and Klopov (cited in Friedgut 1979: 282) report, though, that people at different stages of the life cycle devote different amounts of time to compliant organizations and that there are further differences between men and women. Given the limited data presented in their study, it is difficult to tell how much of the difference is a result of varied levels of education, type of job, or other factors that are controlled for in Table 3.2.

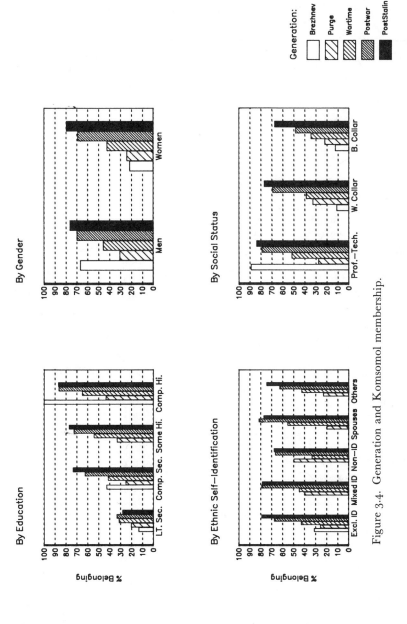

Figure 3.4. Generation and Komsomol membership.

Table 3.2. *Explaining compliant activism and nonconformity: multiple regression results*

Independent variables	Dependent variables	
	Compliant activism	Nonconformity
Purge generation	.006	− .084*
Wartime generation	.002	− .028
Postwar generation	.222*	.024
Post-Stalin generation	.564*	.000
Purge generation* some higher education	.490*	− .007
Wartime generation* complete higher education	.297*	− .011
Postwar generation* complete higher education	.215*	.032
Post-Stalin generation* some higher education	.013	.184*
Post-Stalin generation* complete higher education	.012	.060*
Completed secondary education	.012	− .017
Some higher education	·003	− .025
Completed higher education	.014	.019
Majored in humanities, natural or social sciences	− .173*	.193*
Interest in politics	.055*	.053*
Sense of personal influence	.048*	.040
Self-ranked sense of personal privilege	.017	.019
Access to material privileges	.133*	.042
Felt privilege gap widest under Brezhnev	.034	.041*
Mixed ethnic identity (Jewish and non-Jewish)	.043	.044
Jewish nonidentifier	.014	.002
Jewish spouse	− .012	.117*
Non-Jewish	.038	.352*
Working	.106*	.008
Job on all-union party *nomenklatura*	.012	− .015
Job on republic party *nomenklatura*	.021	.022
Job on local party *nomenklatura*	.361*	− .025
Job on ministry *nomenklatura*	.292*	.000
Male	− .010	.078*
Prior arrest of family member	.002	.106*
Made decision to emigrate	.004	.054*
Shared in family decision to emigrate	.017	.035
Married in USSR	− .031	− .034
Had children in USSR	− .023	− .030
Household income	.013	.036
Some higher education* median income	.249*	.016
Completed higher education* high income	.194*	.033

Table 3.2. (*contd.*)

Independent variables	Dependent variables	
	Compliant activism	Nonconformity
Felt greater ease in avoiding KGB	.016	.031
Ranked KGB influence high	.020	− .012
Felt KGB most powerful under Brezhnev	.026	− .009
R^2 (adjusted)	.172	.141

Note: The numbers are unstandardized regression coefficients, with those significant at ($p \leqslant .01$) denoted by an asterisk. Additional interaction terms measuring the joint effects of variables listed here were also included in the models but did not prove to be significant.

Compliant activism: participation during the LNP in a housing, sanitary, or repair commission, parents' committee, *druzhina*, comrades' court, local party or Soviet commission, committee commission at work, Komsomol, or any other public organization; also includes holding an office in a trade union (but simple trade union membership is excluded). Leaders are coded 1, participants, 2, and nonparticipants, 3.

Nonconformity: participation during the LNP in an unsanctioned study or discussion group, protest, or strike; distributing *samizdat/tamizdat*, or participating in any other such activity as defined by the respondent. Leaders received a code of 1, participants, 2, and nonparticipants, 3.

Generations: see definitions in text; the four generations are denoted by dummy variables; the fifth category is represented in the intercept.

Ethnic identification: respondents were divided into five categories: (1) exclusive Jewish identifiers, who reported their nationality in the USSR as "Jewish" only; (2) mixed identifiers, who felt they belonged to at least two different nationalities, one of them Jewish; (3) nonidentifiers, whose parent or parents were Jewish but who felt they belonged to a different or to no nationality; (4) spouses, those who were not Jewish but whose spouse in LNP was; and (5) others, chiefly Russians.

Household income: a decile ranking, based on total household expenditures in the end of LNP. Expenditures are used because they prove to be more reliable than data on total household income.

Variables for generation, education, educational major, privilege gap under Brezhnev, ethnic identity, work force participation, type of job, gender, prior arrest of family member, decision to emigrate, marital status, children, and KGB power under Brezhnev are all dummy variables, with the residual category counted in the intercept.

a different matter, as pensioners were less involved in compliant groups than were others still in the labor force; but both the employed and the nonemployed were less active than younger generations.

In addition to generation, several other important sources of compliant behavior also stand out: Activism is associated with an interest in politics and public affairs, a greater sense of personal influence, access to material privileges, and a job in the public sector – especially one on a local party's or ministry's *nomenklatura*. Given the data presented in Figure 3.1, we would also expect education to weigh heavily. But, once other variables are included, it has little direct impact, and then only for the college-educated members of the three middle generations – purge, wartime, and postwar. Thus generation and schooling interact, as Hough (1980) and Silver (1986) contend, lowering mobilized participation for the older and less-educated groups in the sample and increasing it among the younger and more highly educated.

Not all of the college educated are equally active, however. Table 3.2 reveals a split between majors in the natural and social sciences and humanities versus those who specialized in engineering law, medicine, teaching, and other applied professions. The "physicists and lyricists," to borrow Azrael's (1966) phrase, devote significantly less energy to conventional political organizations – and, as we shall see, engage far more in behaviors the regime would like to curb.

The results also show that some of the most unrepresentative characteristics of the sample, such as ethnic identification and the decision to emigrate, have little effect on reported levels of involvement. Jewish and non-Jewish respondents were engaged about equally in compliant organizations. And activism differed little between those who were simply "co-migrants" – who came to the United States because other family members decided to leave the USSR – and those who decided themselves to emigrate. As Table 3.2 demonstrates, dummy variables included to capture both these sources of potential bias turn out to be nonsignificant. Neither ethnicity nor selectivity would seem to distort the findings on age and compliant behavior.

Compliant participation, then, appears to be rooted in a combination of job expectations, personal motivation and sense of influence, generation, and, for certain generations, education. Pressures at work lead to political activism, especially among those with responsible posts; the importance of the workplace as a key socializing device is reaffirmed among SIP respondents. So, too, is the importance of material privileges as an incentive for compliant behavior. Yet external pressure and material rewards are not the only motives. Personal interest and perceptions of the organizations themselves also figure prominently. Thus, despite the image of depoliticization that surrounds conventional mass organizations in the USSR, the active members are the most interested in politics and public affairs. And despite the image of passivity that characterizes such groups, many participants felt that members like themselves could have a degree of influence over the organization's activities. Those respondents who attended the meetings were asked if "people like you, who regularly [or sometimes] went to meetings, had influence over the adoption of the group's decisions about its activities." Their answers are surprisingly positive; in fact, for some organizations (see Table 3.3), an absolute majority felt that individual

Table 3.3. *Members' perceptions that they could influence the activity of compliant organizations* (%)

	Leader	Attended regularly	Attended occasionally
Trade union	42.7	31.0	20.6
Housing commission	64.0	64.7	50.0
Parents' commission	83.6	64.7	57.1
Local soviet or party commission	50.0	57.1	12.5
Druzhina/comrades' court	58.8	20.6	21.4
Commissions at workplace	66.3	54.4	43.1
Other organizations attended regularly	81.1	37.0	—

Note: Question about influence was asked only of people who attended the meetings of any of the listed organizations.

members could influence the group's activities. This question does not, of course, ask whether individuals can influence "policy" or help to shape the decisions of the top leadership; surely, the answers in that case would be far more negative. And not all of those who engaged in compliant organizations were equally positive: Predictably, members who also participated in nonconformist activities felt much more negative about the influence of individuals. Yet, among most "compliants," the perception of even modest influence suggests that there is more behind compliant activism than either political pressure or pure career or material calculations.

Compliant behavior also hinges on age and thus highlights the efforts to expand mass political involvement after Stalin. For earlier generations, proof of political conformity seems to have primarily meant voting. Figure 3.5 illustrates, for example, that the overwhelming majority of the Brezhnev, purge, and wartime generations, and especially the less educated among them, rarely failed to cast their ballots in Soviet elections during their last years in the USSR – although they had been less involved in the Komsomol during their youth and were also less politically active in later life. For the postwar and post-Stalin generations, voting seems less important, whereas compliant activism in public organizations seems more so – a product, apparently, of the various campaigns to revitalize mass political involvement after 1953. Membership in compliant organizations became more inclusive, and in this sense the reforms of the post-Stalin era succeeded in widening the net of mobilized participation. But they had very different effects on different age groups.

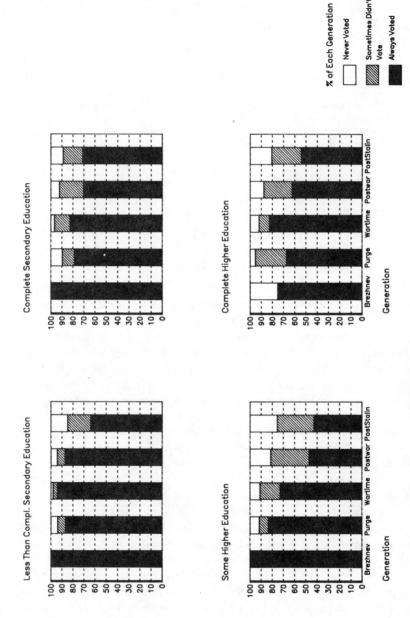

Figure 3.5. Generation and voting behavior

Unconventional participation

Paradoxically, the most highly mobilized generations are also the most unconventional. Whatever the activity, from unsanctioned study groups to distribution of *samizdat* or *tamizdat*, from open protests and strikes to nonvoting, respondents who came of age after the war and especially after Stalin are twice as likely as their elders to be involved. In contrast, the generations that experienced the purge era firsthand seem to have learned the lessons of Stalinism all too well.

However, the generation gap proves to be more subtle than a simple dichotomy between young and old. Once other variables are included in the model (see Table 3.2), the seemingly linear decrease in unconventional behavior with age disappears, and only two age groups emerge as distinctive. One is the purge generation, which stands out as significantly less nonconformist than either older or younger respondents; the men and women who had reached their teens or early twenties at the time of the Great Purge were the most likely to avoid political risk 40 years later. At the other end of the spectrum, those members of the post-Stalin generation with a higher education were significantly more unorthodox than any other age or educational group.

One could argue that political disaffection among the youngest generation is only to be expected, that their fathers and grandfathers were surely just as unorthodox in their day but grew more compliant as they aged. Yet, the uneven age pattern suggests that this gap cannot be attributed to the aging process itself. After adjustment for differences in education, gender, ethnic identification, income, and other variables, nonconformity does not decrease proportionately from young to old. Or, to put the argument another way, there is little reason to suppose that respondents belonging to the Brezhnev or wartime generations were more unconventional in their youth than they were just before leaving the USSR.

Other evidence in the survey bears out this conclusion. Respondents were asked, for example, if they had any personal contact with the KGB while in the USSR and, if so, when and why the last contact took place. The question allows us to determine the age at which each person had his last political trouble with the KGB/NKVD before deciding to apply for emigration (excluding contacts for administrative reasons such as permission to travel or for KGB investigations of some other person). If individuals simply grow out of unconventional behavior as they mature, then their last political trouble should be at a relatively early age; and the proportion of each generation's last contacts should drop as the members age (the percentages in Table 3.4 should therefore drop from left to right).[16] Yet, as Table 3.4 reveals, the

[16] Some of the contacts, of course, were most likely not prompted by anything a respondent did, and we should not necessarily equate a KGB encounter with

Table 3.4. *Generation and timing of contacts with the KGB*

Generation	Age at last political contact (%)					N
	15–24	25–34	35–44	45–54	55–70	
Brezhnev	—	—	—	—	—	0
Purge	14.3	14.3	0.0	28.6	42.9	7
Wartime	0.0	0.0	16.7	33.3	50.0	6
Postwar	12.9	25.8	61.3	—[a]	—[a]	31
Post-Stalin	38.8	61.2	—[a]	—[a]	—[a]	49
Total N						93

Note: Excludes contacts related to investigations of other people or to administrative issues such as permission to travel.

[a] Respondents emigrated before reaching the upper age limit in the category.

proportions *increase* with age among the older generations.[17] In no case does any generation display a pattern of youthful or adolescent trouble with the KGB that slowly diminished as the years passed.

Similarly, variables included to capture the effects of the life cycle have no significant impact. Neither marriage and family responsibilities nor retirement moderate the level of unorthodox behavior. These results, coupled with the distinctiveness of the purge and post-Stalin generations, emphasize that a life-cycle explanation alone cannot account for the age gap in unorthodox politics. Formative experiences appear to carry greater weight.

In addition, several other critical variables emerge from Table 3.4 as predictors of unconventional behavior. One is gender: Nonconformity is predominantly a male activity, even among men and women with the same levels of education and of the same age. A second factor is the arrest of a close relative. Respondents with a family history of political arrests are more likely to be nonconformist themselves.[18] This hints at the impact of both political socialization within the family and the punishment by association that

political nonconformity. Yet, to judge from Table 3.4, this does not seem to be a problem – unless we want to argue that only older respondents were contacted without cause.

[17] The age pattern in Table 3.4 may, however, be shaped in part by the impact of the purges in the sense that, among the older generations, those whose last contact was at an early age (during the 1930s) did not survive to be interviewed. Yet, though this possibility must be borne in mind, it cannot explain the age pattern among the *survivors*; nor can it explain the similar age pattern among younger generations who did not experience the purges.

[18] By "family history" I mean arrests prior to the first one that a respondent himself may have experienced.

affects family members after an arrest. Political disaffection gets handed down from fathers to sons.

As in the case of compliant activism, education has only a limited effect, and then only in conjunction with generation and specialty. Members of the post-Stalin generation who attended a university or institute emerge as significantly more unorthodox than other age groups or others with higher education. And, among the highly educated, nonconformity is the province of the "physicists and lyricists," the natural scientists and the humanists (Azrael 1966: 156; Shatz 1980: 139–56). The doctors, teachers, economists, and engineers are less likely to stray from officially approved political activism. As Shatz (1980) argues, the split reflects the fact that political controls – restrictions on information and travel – fall more heavily on researchers, artists, and writers. It may also reflect a degree of self-selection: Individuals already disposed to unconventional politics may be more likely to choose academic or creative fields (Fendrich 1974).

The variables that prove insignificant for predicting nonconformity are also noteworthy. We would expect, for example, that high job status would inhibit unorthodox activity; but Table 3.2 reveals that individuals with *nomenklaturnye* positions are neither more nor less likely to stray from compliant behavior. The effect of the workplace would seem to be asymmetric, prompting compliant activism but not necessarily preventing nonconformity. Nor do a respondent's material privileges, either real or perceived, appear to influence political deviance.

Finally, it is important to note that the relationships in Table 3.2 hold even when we account for the sample's uneven ethnic makeup and for the differences between those who actively decided to emigrate and "co-migrants." Unorthodox behavior is more common among non-Jewish respondents, suggesting once again that the most common ticket out of the USSR for non-Jews was political dissent (see Table 3.2). And it is significantly higher among those who decided themselves to leave the USSR. These results are important, for they emphasize the need to consider the potential biases in emigrant responses. Yet they also encourage some confidence in the findings, since the fundamental relationships between unconventional activity and age, socioeconomic status, interest, education, and gender hold among Jewish and non-Jewish respondents alike, among those who actively tried to leave and those who did not.

Thus, both personal circumstances (interest in politics, arrests of family members) and political environment help to shape unconventional political behavior. Given the political environment when the purge generation came of age, few of its members were willing to challenge conventional political norms even decades after the 1930s. The contrast with the post-Stalin generation could not be greater, especially with the most highly educated.

Unorthodox activity grows out of a combination of different formative experiences and certain political resources, such as information and abstract reasoning skills, that come with higher education (Connor 1975: 28).

Information and abstract reasoning, in turn, contribute to a more critical stance toward fundamental political orthodoxies about the role of the state in Soviet society. As Brian Silver shows elsewhere in this volume (Chapter 4), the greater the education, the less the support for the Soviet model of state control in heavy industry, agriculture, and medical care, and the less support for the dominance of society's needs over the rights of the individual. Thus, the connections would seem to be straightforward: Education breeds a less conformist set of political values, and these should prompt overt unconventional behavior.

Yet, if we add attitudes toward state control and toward individual rights into our model of nonconformist activity (in Table 3.2), the relationship turns out to be more complex.[19] Although some members of each generation favor greater private control of the economy, the issue prompted overt nonconformity only among the youngest – the post-Stalin generation. Similarly, some members of every generation believe in greater protection of individual rights, but among them concern for the individual turned only the postwar generation to unconventional politics.[20] Part of each generation rejects the old orthodoxies about the role of the state; but the old are much less disposed to act on their objections. Moreover, the results suggest that not only behavior but the salience of certain values may be tied to generational cleavages, with individual rights ranking higher for those who came of age in the public ferment of de-Stalinization and with economic issues receiving higher priority for those who began their careers in the stagnating economy of the Brezhnev era.

Interest in politics

In addition to higher levels of compliant and unorthodox activity, the young also rank higher as "spectators," with a greater degree of interest in politics. However, in this case, generational differences disappear once other characteristics are added into the equation. Interest is more heavily influenced by level of education, gender (women report substantially less

[19] These two measures are based on those used by Silver (1986).
[20] These are results based on a regression model of nonconformity that includes measures on rights and control (see Silver 1986) and that also includes dummy variables measuring the interaction between these two attitudes and generation. Of all these variables, only two interaction terms, for *postwar generation* rights* and for *post-Stalin generation* state control* have any significant effect in predicting unorthodox behavior. The unstandardized regression coefficients are .017 and .028, respectively, both significant at ($p \leq .01$).

interest), and other factors than by the era in which individuals came of age. Generation proves more important in an individual's choice of media: Although a majority of all generations listened to both Soviet and Western radio during their LNP, the younger the individual, the greater the attentiveness to Western sources.[21]

Interpreting the generation gap

The generation gap, then, embodies far more than a difference over Western music or clothes: It reflects a real divergence in the willingness to engage in overt unorthodox political activity. And it has grown up in the face of increased mobilization among younger cohorts. In spite of ambitious efforts to mold new generations into "active builders of communism," one key target – the post-Stalin generation – ranks first in both mobilized participation and unconventional politics. In fact, the younger the individual, the more likely he or she is to engage in both regime-supporting and nonconformist activities. After all, both draw on the same basic resources of social status and education (Jennings and Niemi 1981; Abramson and Inglehart 1984). Mobilization succeeds in drawing participants into compliant organizations, but it may also create expectations about wider citizen influence that conventional organizations cannot satisfy.

If mobilized participation has failed to prevent nonconformity among new generations, then other key regime strategies must also be called into question. The higher degree of political deviance suggests that the post-Stalin generation either has less fear of the authorities or different expectations of the regime.

The evidence in the survey suggests both. The post-Stalin generation felt the most optimistic about the possibility of avoiding trouble with the KGB; and the college educated among them rated their ability even higher (see Figure 3.6). Those who came of age after Stalin also felt slightly less constraint in talking with people outside the immediate family about sensitive issues, for example, criticizing a government official. At the same time, the post-Stalin generation found it no easier than other age groups to tell who might be a KGB agent or an informer; and they would feel more nervous in the USSR about talking with a teacher if they were treated unfairly or disagreed with something the teacher said. They reflect the political ambivalence of the post-Stalin era: Partial relaxation of controls has made them somewhat more confident about their own ability to stay out of

[21] For example, over 70 percent of the older age groups listened daily to Soviet radio, compared to 65 percent of the post-Stalin generation. In contrast, 90 percent of the post-Stalin group listened to Western radio broadcasts, whereas only 70 percent of the purge generation and 40 percent of the Brezhnev generation did so.

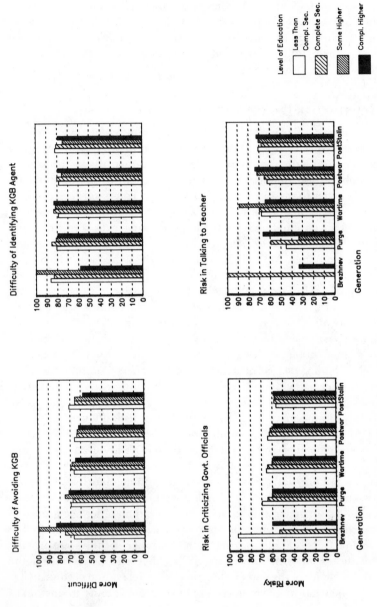

Figure 3.6. Perceptions of political risk by generation and education

trouble with the KGB, yet they are still uncertain about exactly which people and activities are "safe" (see Figure 3.6).

When the question turns to the broader role of the police in contemporary Soviet society, the burnishing of the KGB's image under Andropov appears to have had its effect: The youngest generation ranks the influence of the secret police in contemporary Soviet society higher than do their fathers and grandfathers, and the young and less educated rank it even higher. They also have a distinctive view of the KGB's role in Soviet history. When asked in which era – Stalin's, Khrushchev's, or Brezhnev's – the KGB was most influential, the majority of all ages agree on Stalin; yet a small but surprising number of respondents who came of age after Stalin choose *the Brezhnev years* (see Figure 3.7). They are more inclined to see their own era as the worst, even in comparison with Stalin's time. Some members of the last generation also hold a more idealized image of Stalin himself: The less educated among the post-Stalin cohort give him the highest marks as a leader.

This perception gap among Soviet generations is even more pronounced on issues of material well-being and privilege (see Figure 3.8). *The younger the respondent, the more likely he is to condemn the Brezhnev era as the most unequal, with a privilege gap wider than in Khrushchev's or even Stalin's time.* More than half of the post-Stalin generation believes that inequality reached its peak under Brezhnev, whereas only a third of respondents among the oldest generations felt the same. Moreover, the sense of material inequality is so strong that it figures prominently in predicting who will engage in political nonconformity (see Table 3.2).

If different age groups have disparate perceptions, then the regime's strategy of managing expectations can only yield diminishing returns. Appeals to the past may succeed with the generations who survived the terror and the material deprivation; but, for those who came of age after Stalin, the standard for judging the regime is how the system currently performs rather than how far it has come. They are more critical than their elders and less inclined to be satisfied with a backward look at the Soviet past to judge their own well-being. New generations seem little disposed to measure the regime against a distant past they only dimly recognize.

This conclusion bears out the findings of the Harvard Project in the 1950s. As Bauer, Inkeles, and Kluckhohn (1956) and Rossi (1957) discovered, the generations born after the Revolution had no memory of the old Russia and reacted to the Soviet system primarily on its current performance, whereas the older generations viewed it from the perspective of the old regime. *But there is one striking difference: In Stalin's time, it was the young and highly educated who responded most positively to the Soviet system – to government control over light industry, to welfare state programs, and to Soviet achievements in general.* They felt relatively satisfied with their jobs in the USSR and less fearful than did older cohorts,

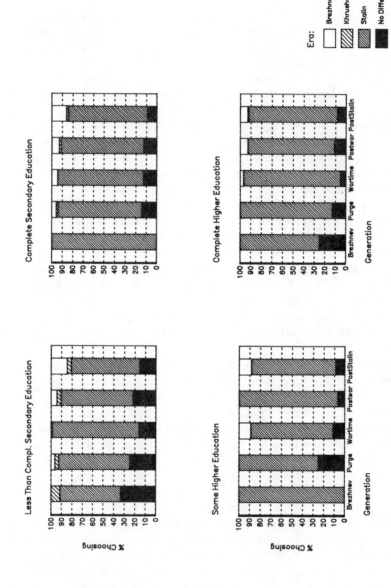

Figure 3.7. Perceptions of when the KGB had most power, by generation and education

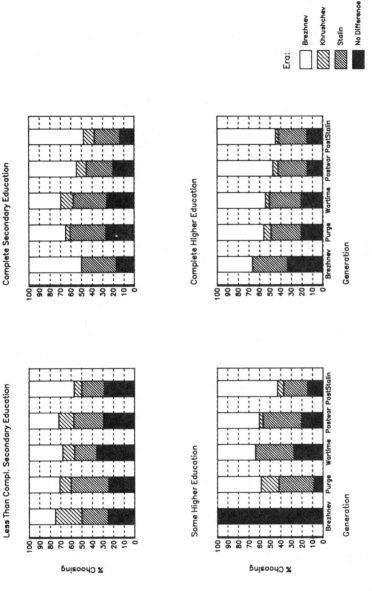

Figure 3.8. Perceptions of when privilege gap was greatest, by generation and education

although they ranked the regime's use of terror as one of the major reasons for emigrating. Even so, a majority of respondents born after the revolution reported that they had not wanted to leave the USSR in 1940; and when they did leave, it was most likely to be because exposure to the West during the war highlighted the poverty of living standards at home. All told, they evaluated the system largely in instrumental and material terms, by what they had gained from it. And, comparatively speaking, they *had* gained; they were the beneficiaries of Stalin's Big Deal, with its rapid social mobility and its ambitious plans for a new social order. It tended to disappoint them chiefly when they found an external yardstick by which to measure the regime's material successes.

In contrast, the prerevolutionary generation, especially those with less education, evaluated the USSR in terms of principle and in comparison with the past. They were more convinced that nothing of the Soviet system should be kept in the event of a change in regime; they found the old system preferable to the sacrifices and the upheaval created by the new; and they were more likely to have left on grounds of opposition to or disillusionment with communism. They were more inclined to say that they had always opposed the regime. They had paid the price for the transformations of the 1920s and 1930s, and they proved to be far less positive toward Soviet leaders, institutions, and policies.[22]

In contemporary Soviet society, the generation gap revealed by the Harvard Project has been reversed. Younger respondents still evaluate the regime in terms of the present, as their counterparts did decades ago. In both cases, the focus falls on current system performance, with few backward looks at the past record. The difference is that, for the youth of the purge era, "system performance" yielded more dramatic gains.

Conclusions

Our data suggest that the turbulence of Soviet history has created divergent political values, levels of activism, and evaluations of the regime among successive generations. Age cleavages extend beyond cultural tastes and preferences; they reflect different orientations to political life.

However, the generation gap is far more complex than a simple split between young and old. There is no smooth pattern, no simple progression from one generation to the next. This fact, along with the other data presented here, highlights the role that formative experiences play in

---

[22] A more elaborate comparison of the responses between SIP and the Harvard Project (HP) was not possible at this writing: Some of the HP data, such as the written questionnaires, have been lost; the life history interviews were preserved but must be recoded.

shaping both behavior and perceptions. It also implies that the aging process itself does not necessarily close the gap; progression through the life cycle does not bring a convergence among disparate age groups. The conclusions of the Harvard Project would seem to bear this out: Younger generations then did not begin their adult life less supportive of the system, nor were the old necessarily more favorable toward it.

The Harvard Project results led Bauer and his colleagues (1956) and Rossi (1957) to conclude that the young under Stalin wanted both improved living standards and a measure of political peace – and that, if the regime delivered, it might increase public support among new generations. Yet a careful examination of contemporary age cleavages leads to the opposite conclusion. The decline of terror and the real improvements in living standards may appeal to the age groups with the longest memories; but for those with only "appropriated memories" – that is, with no firsthand experience – expectations would seem to have outpaced regime performance. History can work as a baseline for tempering expectations only if all see it in the same light; but our results say they do not.

If neither mobilized participation nor containment of material aspirations has sufficed to prevent political deviance among the post-Stalin generation, what does seem to work to the regime's advantage are the countervailing perceptions that divide this last age group. The least educated prove to be slightly less negative toward the Brezhnev record on privilege and inequality, which suggests less disaffection with the regime's material performance. Even so, more than 40 percent still feel that the Brezhnev era was the most unequal. But they are also twice as likely as the college educated to see Brezhnev's KGB as more influential than either Khrushchev's or Stalin's, whether they had themselves been picked up by the police or not.[23]

To judge from other results in the survey, their perceptions mirror the regime's selectivity in dealing with political deviance. Reprisals were more than twice as likely for "blue-collar" deviance as for "white-collar." Thus, for example, 18.8 percent of those who led an unofficial study group, and 4.2 percent of those who simply participated in one, experienced some reprisal; so, too, did 23.1 percent of those who played a leading role in distributing *samizdat/tamizdat* and 8.8 percent of those who simply transmitted it. But over half of those who led a strike and 13 percent of those who participated in one were punished, as were all of those who led a protest and 23.1 percent of the

[23] Fifteen percent of the members of the post-Stalin generation with less than a secondary education said that the KGB was most powerful in the Brezhnev era, and another 15 percent felt there was no difference in the KGB's power under Stalin, Khrushchev, or Brezhnev. Among those with higher education in this same age group, 7 percent replied with "Brezhnev," and 8 percent replied that there was no difference.

other protestors. The different perceptions among the college educated and the less educated mirror a real difference in political cues about when and where coercion will come into play.

Thus, the generation gap is not simply one cleavage but two, and this goes far in explaining the discrepancy between the negative evaluations of the regime's performance and the still low level of overt political deviance. Across the board, the last generation proves to be more disenchanted with the performance of the system in their own time. But those with less education, whose sheer numbers could prove the most threatening to the regime, also remain more aware of the heavy hand of the state.

References

Abramson, Paul. 1974. "Generational Change in American Electoral Behavior," *American Political Science Review*, 68: 93–105.

Abramson, Paul, and Ronald Inglehart. 1984. "Generational Replacement and Value Change in Six West European Societies." Paper presented at the Annual Meeting of the American Political Science Association, Washington, D.C.

Agnello, Thomas. 1973. "Aging and the Sense of Political Powerlessness," *Public Opinion Quarterly*, 37: 251–59.

Anderson, Barbara, and Brian Silver. 1986. "The Validity of Survey Responses: Insights from Interviews of Multiple Respondents in a Household in a Survey of Soviet Emigrants." Soviet Interview Project Working Paper.

Azrael, Jeremy. 1966. *Managerial Power and Soviet Politics*. Cambridge, Mass.: Harvard University Press.

Bahry, Donna. 1986. "Mass Politics and Structure of Participation in USSR: A Comparative Perspective." Mimeographed.

——— 1987. "Surveying Soviet Emigrants: Political Attitudes and Ethnic Biases," mimeo.

Barnes, Samuel, Max Kaase, et al. 1979. *Political Action: Mass Participation in Five Western Democracies*. Beverly Hills, Calif.: Sage.

Bauer, Raymond, Alex Inkeles, and Clyde Kluckhohn. 1956. *How the Soviet System Works*. New York: Vintage Books.

Beliakovich, N. N. 1978. *Sotsial'naia aktivnost' rabochego klassa*. Minsk: Izd-vo BGU.

Bialer, Seweryn. 1980. *Stalin's Successors: Leadership, Stability, and Change in the Soviet Union*. New York: Cambridge University Press.

Blinov, N. M. 1983. "The Sociology of Youth: Achievements and Problems," *Soviet Sociology*, 21: 3–19. Translated from "Sotsiologiia molodezhi: dostizheniia, problemy," *Sotsiologicheskie issledovaniia*, no. 2 (1982): 7–15.

Boriaz, V. N. 1973. *Molodezh: metodologicheskie problemy issledovaniia*. Leningrad: Nauka.

Breslauer, George. 1984. "Is There a Generation Gap in the Soviet Political Establishment? Demand Articulation by RSFSR Provincial Party First Secretaries," *Soviet Studies*, 36: 1–2.

Brezhnev, Leonid. 1981. "Otchet TsK KPSS XXVI s"ezdu," *XXVI s"ezd KPSS. Stenograficheskii otchet.* Moscow: Politicheskaia literatura, vol. 1.

Brzezinski, Zbigniew, and Samuel Huntington. 1965. *Political Power: USA/USSR.* New York: Vintage Books.

Bushnell, John. 1979. "The New Soviet Man Turns Pessimist," *Survey,* 24: 1–18.

Callaghan, Tim. 1960. "Studying the Students: Between Conformity and Dissent," *Survey,* no. 33: 12–19.

Connor, Walter. 1973. "Dissent in a Complex Society," *Problems of Communism,* 22: 40–52.

  1975. "Generations and Politics in the USSR," *Problems of Communism,* 24: 20–31.

Converse, Philip. 1976. *The Dynamics of Party Support: Cohort-Analyzing Party Identification.* Beverly Hills, Calif.: Sage.

Cutler, Neal. 1969–70. "Generation, Maturation, and Party Affiliation: A Cohort Analysis," *Public Opinion Quarterly,* 33: 583–88.

Dalton, Russell J. 1977. "Was There a Revolution? A Note on Generational versus Life Cycle Explanations of Value Differences," *Comparative Political Studies,* 9: 459–73.

  1984. "Politics in West Germany." In Gabriel Almond and G. Bingham Powell (eds.), *Comparative Politics Today: A Worldview.* Boston: Little, Brown.

Di Franceisco, Wayne, and Zvi Gitelman. 1984. "Soviet Political Culture and 'Covert Participation' in Policy Implementation," *American Political Science Review,* 78: 603–21.

Efimov, V. I. 1977. "Obrazovanie i sotsial'no-professional'noe prodvizhenie molodikh rabochikh," *Sotsiologicheskie issledovaniia,* no. 1: 47–51.

Fainsod, Merle. 1964. *How Russia Is Ruled.* Cambridge, Mass.: Harvard University Press.

Fendrich, James. 1974. "Activists Ten Years Later: A Test of Generational Unit Continuity," *Journal of Social Issues,* 30: 95–118.

Flanagan, Scott C. 1982. "Changing Values in Advanced Industrial Societies: Inglehart's Silent Revolution from the Perspective of Japanese Findings," *Comparative Political Studies,* 14: 403–44.

Foner, Anne. 1974. "Age Stratification and Age Conflict in Political Life," *American Sociological Review,* 39: 187–96.

Friedgut, Theodore. 1979. *Political Participation in the USSR.* Princeton, N.J.: Princeton University Press.

Glenn, Norval D., and Michael Grimes. 1968. "Aging, Voting, and Political Interest," *American Sociological Review,* 33: 563–75.

Glenn, Norval, and Ted Hefner. 1972. "Further Evidence on Aging and Party Identification," *Public Opinion Quarterly,* 35: 31–47.

Gorshkov, M. K., and F. E. Sheregi. 1979. "Dinamika obshchestvennogo mneniia molodezhi," *Sotsiologicheskie issledovaniia,* no. 4: 33–40.

Harris, Jonathan. 1971. "The Dilemma of Dissidence," *Survey,* 68: 107–22.

Hough, Jerry F. 1980. *Soviet Leadership in Transition.* Washington, D.C.: Brookings Institution.

Huntington, Samuel, and Joan Nelson. 1976. *No Easy Choice: Political Participation in Developing Countries.* Cambridge, Mass.: Harvard University Press.

Iaroshenko, T. M. 1977. "Vozrast v sotsiologicheskom issledovanii," *Sotsiologicheskie issledovaniia*, no. 1: 133–39.

Ikonnikova, S. N., and V. T. Lisovskii. 1969. *Molodezh: o sebe, o svoikh sverstvakh.* Leningard: Lenizdat.

Inglehart, Ronald. 1971. "The Silent Revolution in Europe: Intergenerational Change in Post-industrial Societies," *American Political Science Review*, 65: 991–1017.

——— 1985. "Aggregate Stability and Individual-Level Flux in Mass Belief Systems: The Level of Analysis Paradox," *American Political Science Review*, 79: 97–117.

Inkeles, Alex, and Raymond Bauer. 1961. *The Soviet Citizen: Daily Life in a Totalitarian Society.* Cambridge, Mass.: Harvard University Press.

Jacobs, Everett. 1976. "A Note on Membership of the Soviet Communist Party," *Soviet Jewish Affairs*, 6: 114–15.

——— 1978. "Further Considerations on Jewish Representation in Local Soviets and in the CPSU," *Soviet Jewish Affairs*, 8: 26–3.

——— 1980. "A Note on Jewish Membership of the Belorussian Communist Party," *Soviet Jewish Affairs*, 10: 51–57.

Jennings, M. Kent, and Gregory Markus. 1984. "Partisan Orientations over the Long Haul: Results from the Three-Wave Political Socialization Panel Study," *American Political Science Review*, 78: 1000–18.

Jennings, M. Kent, and Richard Niemi. 1981. *Generations and Politics: A Panel Study of Young Adults and Their Parents.* Princeton, N.J.: Princeton University Press.

Juviler, Peter. 1961. "Communist Morality and Soviet Youth," *Problems of Communism*, no. 3: 16–24.

Kassof, Allen. 1965. *The Soviet Youth Program.* Cambridge, Mass.: Harvard University Press.

Khudushin, F. S. 1977. "Marksizm-Leninizm i problema preemstvennosti pokoleniia," *Sotsiologicheskie issledovaniia*, no. 3: 35–41.

Klecka, William. 1971. "Applying Political Generations to the Study of Political Behavior: A Cohort Analysis," *Public Opinion Quarterly*, 34: 358–73.

Kogan, L. N., and B. S. Pavlov. 1976. *Molodoi rabochi: vchera, segodnia.* Sverdlovsk: Sredne-Ural'skoe knizhnoe izdatel'stvo.

Kon, I. S. "Vozrastnye kategorii v naukakh o cheloveke i obshchestve," *Sotsiologicheskie issledovaniia*, no. 3: 76–86.

Mannheim, Karl. 1972. "The Problem of Generations." In Philip Altback and Robert Lanfer (eds.), *The New Pilgrims: Youth Protest in Transition.* New York: McKay, pp. 101–36.

Markus, Gregory. 1983. "Dynamic Modeling of Cohort Change: The Case of Political Partisanship," *Political Methodology*, 27: 717–48.

Marsh, Alan. 1977. *Protest and Political Consciousness.* Beverly Hills, Calif.: Sage.

Molodezh: ee interesy, stremleniia, idealy. 1969. Moscow: Molodaia gvardiia.

Moshniaga, V. P. 1978. "Molodezhnye organizatsii i sovremennoe sotsial'noe razvitie," *Sotsiologicheskie issledovaniia*, no. 4: 64–72.

Nie, Norman, Sidney Verba, and Jae-on Kim. 1974. "Political Participation and the Life Cycle," *Comparative Politics*, 6: 319–40.

Reddaway, Peter. 1983. "Dissent in the Soviet Union," *Problems of Communism*, no. 6.

Rossi, Alice. 1957. "Generational Differences in the Soviet Union." Ph.D. dissertation, Columbia University. Mimeographed.

Shatz, Marshall. 1980. *Soviet Dissent in Historical Perspective*. Cambridge: Cambridge University Press.

Silver, Brian. 1986. "Political Beliefs of the Soviet Citizen: Sources of Support for Regime Norms." Soviet Interview Project Working Paper.

Smirnov, V. A. 1978. "Problema formirovaniia u rabochei molodezhi soznatel'nogo otnosheniia k trudu," *Sotsiologicheskie issledovaniia*, no. 4: 80–86.

Sokolov, V. M. 1976. "Formirovanie kommunisticheskogo mirovozzreniia molodezhi," *Sotsiologicheskie issledovaniia*, no. 2: 29–37.

Speranskii, V. I. 1975. "Eksperimental'naia proverka pokazatelei effektivnosti raboty komsomol'skikh organizatsii," *Sotsiologicheskie issledovaniia*, no. 2: 110–17.

Stanovkin, S. K. 1981. "Obshchestvenno-politicheskaia aktivnost' trudiashchikhsia i nekotorye faktory ee razvitiia," *Problemy nauchnogo kommunizma*, vol. 15.

Tolz, Vladimir. 1984. "The Party and Youth: Old Remedies and New Problems," *Radio Liberty Research*, no. 335/84.

Verba, Sidney, and Norman Nie. 1972. *Participation in America: Political Democracy and Social Equality*. New York: Harper and Row.

Verba, Sidney, Norman Nie, and Jae-on Kim. 1978. *Participation and Political Equality: A Seven-Nation Comparison*. Cambridge: Cambridge University Press.

Vershlovskaia, S. G., and L. N. Lesokhina. 1975. "Rabochaia molodezh i obrazovanie," *Sotsiologicheskie issledovaniia*, no. 2: 90–99.

Volkov, Iu. E. 1972. "Razvitie obshchestvennoi aktivnosti molodezhi i sotsial'nyi progress." In *Ekonomicheskie i sotsial'no-politicheskie problemy kommunisticheskogo stroitel'stva*. Moscow: Mysl', pp. 332–49.

Welch, Susan. 1975. "Dimensions of Political Participation in a Canadian Sample," *Canadian Journal of Political Science*, 8, no. 4: 553–59.

Zhitenev, V. A. 1978. "Issledovanie problem molodezhi: sostoianie i zadachi," *Sotsiologicheskie issledovaniia*, no. 2: 12–20.

Zuckerman, Alan S., and Darrell M. West. 1985. "The Political Bases of Citizen Contacting: A Cross-National Analysis," *American Political Science Review*, 79: 117–32.

CHAPTER 4

Political beliefs of the Soviet citizen: Sources of support for regime norms

BRIAN D. SILVER

Students of Soviet affairs have long been concerned with how the Soviet political elite generates popular support. The conventional view of the Soviet system before the death of Stalin is summed up in a chapter in Merle Fainsod's *How Russia Is Ruled* entitled: "Terror as a System of Power." That chapter's first sentence is, "Terror is the linchpin of modern totalitarianism" (Fainsod 1961: 354). Seweryn Bialer's later formulation, describing the Stalinist period, is similar: "[T]error functioned principally not as a tool of social *change*, but as a normal method of rule and *governance*" (Bialer 1980: 12).

If it is true that "totalitarian dictatorship may be regarded as a substitute for other forms of coordination with a stronger groundwork in popular consensus" (Moore 1954), then the critical question is: What has been the method of achieving consensus, or support, for the established political order in the Soviet Union, once terror was no longer the main instrument of control? It is worth recalling Vera Dunham's observation that "In Stalin's time – and even in Stalin's worst times – the regime was supported by more than simple terror, a truism still overlooked from time to time" (Dunham 1976: 13). But the balance of methods of generating mass support is said to have shifted in the post-Stalin era (by Dunham's account, in the *late* Stalin era).

Two main methods of generating mass support for the Soviet system in the post-Stalin era have been emphasized in the scholarly literature: (*a*) agitation, propaganda, or, more generally, education; and (*b*) the manipulation of material rewards. I believe each should be regarded as a possible means of generating political support, the efficacy of which must be determined empirically. I shall outline briefly how the impact of these factors has been described in the scholarly literature on Soviet politics.

I would like to thank Paul R. Abramson, Barbara A. Anderson, Jeremy R. Azrael, Donna Bahry, Robert W. Jackman, and James W. Tong for their comments on earlier drafts of this chapter; Harriet Dhanak for programming assistance; Mike Coble, Kathleen Duke, and Amy Hsu for preparing the graphs; and Cynthia Buckley and Victoria Velkoff for research assistance.

Education

One method by which the government is said to generate political support is the invocation of patriotic feelings and the indoctrination of a common world view through both formal education and the day-to-day manipulation of information through the mass media.

The conventional interpretation of the efficacy of the methods used by Soviet leaders to control political thought and action was expressed many years ago by Fainsod: "The power of the regime to bombard the minds of the young is perhaps its most formidable weapon. While loyalties may erode with experience and maturity, each new generation offers the ruling group a fresh opportunity to rebuild its mass support and to renew its life energies" (Fainsod 1961: 494). Jeremy Azrael has described the goals of the Soviet school curriculum as follows:

The ultimate goal of the educational system has been to render terror superfluous by establishing a *totalitarian* consensus in society and creating a "new man" characterized by the sort of self-control and self-mobilization that would permit the establishment of a wholly "consensual" or "popular" totalitarianism. [Azrael 1965: 267]

The implicit hypothesis is, then, that people's level of educational attainment is positively related to their support for the regime.

Three processes could produce such a relationship. The first is an *exposure effect*. People with higher levels of formal educational attainment have had much more extended exposure to formal instruction and indoctrination in the officially prescribed outlook. Organized *extra*curricular activities in the schools are also designed to reinforce an appropriate outlook.

The second is a *selection effect*. Educational institutions tend to select those who are more committed to working within the system, so that at each stage in the educational process the survivors are more likely to be the conformists.

The third is a *credentials effect*. Educational credentials are often critical requirements for access to the most remunerative jobs. Those who succeed in the system are therefore likely to look favorably on that system and its operating norms. This kind of process seems to be responsible for the fact that, in the United States, the higher one's education, the more likely one is to support such regime norms as individual political efficacy and tolerance toward minorities (Wright 1976; Abramson 1983: ch. 10; Jackman and Muha 1984).

In contrast to these effects, however, one could argue that advanced education is likely to be intellectually liberating and to induce a more critical stance toward official dogma, even where, as in the Soviet Union, the curriculum is aimed toward training specialists in technical fields (Dobson 1980). If education works in this way, then it is likely to weaken rather than strengthen the acceptance of established ways of doing things. Moreover, since the more educated in the Soviet Union are attentive to a wider variety of mass media and other sources of information, including foreign sources (Mickiewicz 1981: ch. 9), they are likely to be more aware of alternatives to established practices.

Thus, under some models of behavior we have reason to expect education to be positively related to support for the regime, but under other models we have reason to expect education to be negatively related to support for the regime.

Material incentives

The second major factor that is said to affect popular support for the Soviet regime is the distribution of material incentives. But does change in the material welfare of society as a whole generate a payoff in the form of popular support for the government? It is widely assumed in the scholarly literature on Soviet politics that there is such a payoff.

For example, what Vera Dunham describes as the "Big Deal" assumes such a payoff. In the period of post–World War II reconstruction, the Big Deal offered to the middle class the promise of a comfortable material life and a modicum of freedom in the conduct of their private lives in exchange for hard work *and* support for the established political order.

Similarly, what George Breslauer has called the "social contract" of "welfare-state authoritarianism," which he says originated when Brezhnev came into office in 1964, also involved an exchange: granting "a considerable measure of physical security and privatism for the politically conformist" (Breslauer 1978: 4).

It has been common for analysts to evaluate the prospects for political stability and for reform in the USSR in terms of the strength of popular support for the political system generated by the satisfaction of material wants. Bialer argues:

[T]o gauge the regime's stability, the only legitimate vantage point is that of Soviet citizens themselves. And here the crucial sphere is the domestic economy, and the point of reference for judging performance is the comparison with the immediate Soviet past. By this standard the regime's performance in the Brezhnev era can be judged a success. [Bialer 1980: 149]

John Bushnell (1980) also claims that the increasing supply of consumer goods in the late 1950s and the 1960s generated substantial support for the regime, particularly within the middle class. He claims that the current perception of shortages of goods has weakened that support.

More recently, Timothy Colton has argued that the Soviet regime's solidity rests also on a record of positive achievements.... Cradle-to-grave social services and safeguards...give Soviet citizens a security few would happily surrender.... All told, the regime's accomplishments represent a store of political capital on which it can draw for some time. [Colton 1984: 27]

All of these arguments depend on the strong assumption that citizens' material satisfaction leads to support for the political system. But how valid is that assumption? How large is the "store of political capital" that has been generated by cradle-to-grave social services? Does the ever-increasing educational level of the population raise expectations for the provision of goods and services more rapidly than they can be met?[1] Is there a viable strategy by which the leaders of the Communist party can maintain political support – the store of political capital needed to undertake major reform of economic institutions – by appeasing the population's demand for material goods? The answer to the last question is Yes, but the strategy would need to be complex.

Emigrants as sources of information on political beliefs

The answers to all of these questions require information about the states of mind of the Soviet population. Most scholars who have referred to the critical importance of subjective popular evaluations for the stability of the Soviet political system have not studied those evaluations empirically.

Few studies, even those based on Soviet emigrants, have generated evidence about what Soviet citizens *think* about politics.[2] Most have focused on political *behavior*. Even studies based on Soviet public opinion polls have little to say about political attitudes.[3] In contrast, the SIP General Survey probed into many aspects of both the life experience and the subjective perceptions and evaluations of recent emigrants from the Soviet Union.

[1] I assume that the greater people's support for the procedures or practices by which decisions are made, then the greater the legitimacy of established practices and hence also the greater the government's "credit" or "store of capital." Easton's concept of "diffuse support" is useful here. Diffuse support is a "reservoir of credit upon which a system may draw in times when things are going badly from the point of view of providing satisfactions to the members of the system" (Easton 1965: 249). This is essentially what Colton (1984) refers to as a "store of political capital."

[2] In addition to the Harvard Project study (see Inkeles and Bauer 1968), one notable exception is Gitelman 1977.

[3] Andrei Amalrik was probably correct in asserting that "no one, not even the bureaucratic elite, knows exactly what attitudes prevail among the wider sections of the population (Amalrik 1970: 32). However, an intelligent analyst of Soviet public opinion polling can learn a great deal about factors that shape many attitudes and behaviors of the Soviet public. The best example of such an analysis is that by Mickiewicz (1981).

That the respondents to the SIP General Survey are mostly highly educated Jews from big cities, and that they are emigrants, might prompt the premature conclusion that little can be learned about *Soviet* political attitudes and behavior from these people. Thus, in addition to the normal concerns about the validity of survey responses, two concerns are special to this study.

The first can be termed "emigrant bias." This involves several components: (*a*) the social and economic backgrounds of the emigrants differ substantially from those of the Soviet population as a whole; (*b*) the political experiences of the emigrants in the Soviet Union may not be representative even of people from otherwise similar backgrounds who did not emigrate from the USSR; and (*c*) the very experience of emigration and of living outside the USSR may have traumatized or in other ways affected the respondents' memories and evaluations of life in the USSR.

The second threat to validity can be termed "ethnic bias." Various aspects of the ethnic and religious orientation and experience of the respondents might make their outlook peculiar even if they were perfectly matched with the Soviet population with respect to socioeconomic background.

Detailed discussion of the methods of testing and adjusting for possible bias is beyond the range of this chapter.[4] But it is important to discuss briefly methods of dealing with potential bias that are especially relevant to the study of political beliefs.

First, the results of the SIP General Survey were not intended to be generalized to the Soviet population as a whole. At most, the results can be generalized to what has been termed a "Soviet referent population" of European-background residents of large and medium-sized cities.[5] Hence, I avoid representing the overall frequency distributions and averages from the respondents as those of the Soviet population. A more conservative approach is to focus on the *relationships* among variables. Although the strength of the relations among variables in the emigrant survey cannot be assumed to match those in the Soviet population, the basic direction of the statistical relationships is likely to be similar.[6]

Second, at some points in the analysis, I take information about the

---

[4] For a discussion of many of the issues involved, see Chapter 1, herein, and Bahry 1985.

[5] See Anderson and Silver 1986a; Anderson, Silver, and Lewis 1986; and Appendix A, herein.

[6] This is essentially the argument presented by Inkeles and Bauer (1968: 260) and Gitelman (1977: 547). A concomitant of this argument is that using measures of association that are dependent on the amount of variance in the sample is likely to be misleading. For this reason, in regression analyses my main concern is with the size of the unstandardized, not the standardized, regression coefficients. For further discussion of this issue, see Blalock 1967.

respondents' emigration experience and ethnic background directly into account; that is, I test whether these factors make any difference in the analytic results.

Third, evidence from the survey results can be marshaled to show that the respondents as a whole do not fit any stereotype of the refugees as embittered expatriates who are unable to say positive things about the country they have left or who are trying to report only what they think the interviewers would like to hear.[7] It is helpful to review some evidence concerning this issue.

Satisfaction with life in the USSR

The first type of evidence deals with the respondents' reported satisfaction with the material aspects of their lives in the USSR. When asked how satisfied they had been with various aspects of life during their "last normal period of life"[8] in the USSR, over two-thirds of the respondents said that they were somewhat satisfied or very satisfied with their standard of living, their job, their housing, and public medical care. Only in response to a question on the availability of goods was less than a majority either somewhat satisfied or very satisfied; less than one-fourth said they were somewhat satisfied or were very satisfied with the availability of goods.[9]

Moreover, on three of these dimensions the respondents reported that the situation had improved during their last five years of normal life in the USSR; only in their assessment of public medical care and the availability of goods did a majority of respondents report a deterioration of the situation.

This response pattern runs strongly against the presumed bias of the respondents as emigrants. The pattern does not mean that there is no response bias on the aggregate or individual level, but it is strong counterevidence for the common assumption that the very fact that the respondents left the Soviet Union indicates their total rejection of it.[10]

[7] This is the basic approach to the bias question taken by Di Franceisco and Gitelman (1984).

[8] The "last normal period" (LNP) refers to the five years preceding the month before the emigrants' life was seriously disrupted in connection with their decision to emigrate. For most respondents, the LNP ended in the month before they applied to OVIR for an exit visa.

[9] For further analysis, see Chapter 2, herein.

[10] When applied categorically, such an assumption is contradicted by considerable evidence generated in surveys of Soviet emigrants. For example, Mickiewicz (1981: 2) asserts that "The problem here [with surveys based on former Soviet citizens] is that though their testimony is dramatic, interesting, and often profound, it is, again, unrepresentative; that is, one cannot say anything about what forms attitudes for broad segments of Russian society. The reasons are well

Emigration as family decision

Although there is no question that uprooting a family and moving permanently to a foreign country is a dramatic and difficult event for most people, the impact of the move on most of the respondents is probably ameliorated by the fact that few respondents migrated alone (see Appendix A of this volume), and the vast majority felt that they played at least some role in the decision to emigrate.

Motivations for emigration

Another useful kind of evidence is reported motivation for emigration. The respondents were asked the question, "What were your reasons for leaving the Soviet Union?" The responses were coded into more than 80 categories, which I have reduced to four broad headings: political, economic, religious-ethnic, and family-friends.[11] There are many ways to look at this kind of evidence. Given the common image of the emigrants as seekers of religious and political freedom, it is especially important to determine whether religious and political motivations actually do predominate among SIP respondents.

Table 4.1 shows the percentage of respondents who stated a motive for emigration that falls into one of the four broad categories, cross-tabulated by a number of respondent background characteristics.[12] The cell entries are the percentage of respondents with the given background characteristic who reported the given motivation. For example, 49.5 percent of the men reported a religious or ethnic reason for emigrating. The percentages add to more than 100 across the rows because most respondents gave more than one

known. People who leave that society are not only those who are able to do so (a small minority of the population), but also those who have already formed negative opinions about the society."

[11] This was an open-ended question. Up to three answers were coded for each respondent. On average, the respondents gave two reasons for leaving. It is not possible to classify all responses unambiguously. I count "anti-Semitism" as a religious-cultural reason. However, respondents who report anti-Semitism as their reason for leaving the USSR could have left for material reasons if they suffered from discrimination in school or work.

[12] Five percent of all responses did not fall into one of these categories. These include references to the respondent's desire "for adventure" or "to see the world" as well as statements that the respondent emigrated to avoid military service by himself or another family member. I exclude cases where the respondent did not answer the question or where the answer did not fall into one of the four categories described above. Because multiple responses were coded, although about 5 percent of all *responses* did not fall into one of the four categories, only 2 percent of all *respondents* are not classified into one of the groups described here.

Table 4.1. *Percentage of respondents who reported given reason for emigration, by sex, education, year of birth, ethnicity, and role in emigration decision*

	Religious, ethnic	Family, friends	Economic	Political	Base N
All	45.8	48.0	26.9	43.3	2,763[a]
Sex					
Men	49.5	39.2	28.1	52.3	1,201
Women	43.0	54.8	26.1	36.3	1,562
Education					
Advanced education	45.2	26.9	29.0	68.8	93
Complete higher	45.9	38.6	26.0	58.1	907
Some higher	47.2	31.4	30.2	57.9	159
Complete secondary	46.4	51.7	29.7	37.1	1,124
Less than comp. sec.	44.2	66.9	20.6	19.8	480
Year of birth					
1905–10	43.3	64.2	11.9	16.4	67
1911–15	44.2	74.4	16.3	22.9	258
1916–20	46.4	71.1	18.7	21.1	166
1921–25	48.7	64.2	22.4	28.4	232
1926–30	44.6	55.4	19.2	37.5	224
1931–35	46.2	49.3	23.3	51.6	223
1936–40	49.6	38.0	27.8	48.9	421
1941–45	41.1	41.9	28.6	46.8	248
1946–50	45.6	35.3	34.2	54.4	476
1951–55	46.0	37.1	36.4	54.3	291
1956–60	42.9	32.7	37.8	54.5	156
Nationality[b]					
Religious Jew	55.4	52.6	20.7	29.8	523
Nonreligious Jew	50.7	47.7	29.0	42.7	1,749
Parents Jewish	22.7	35.2	31.3	66.4	128
Spouse Jewish[c]	21.8	48.9	29.3	55.5	229
No Jewish connection	7.5	45.5	16.4	60.4	134
Role in decision to emigrate					
Made the decision	45.7	38.8	27.3	52.9	905
Shared in decision	48.3	50.0	27.6	40.4	1,642
No significant role	28.0	71.5	19.8	24.2	207

[a] Cell entries add to more than 100 across the rows because up to three reasons were coded for each respondent.
[b] The "Nationality" variable used here is a composite of self-designated nationality, religion, and religiosity, as well as the respondent's report of nationality and religion of parents, spouse, and spouse's parents.
[c] Includes 17 cases where the spouse's *parents* were Jewish but spouse was identified by the respondent as non-Jewish.

answer, and a respondent's different answers could fall into different categories.

As shown in the top row of numbers in Table 4.1, religious-ethnic, family-friends, and political reasons are mentioned with almost equal frequency as a motivation for emigration. Not surprisingly, those who were Jewish in self-identification ("Religious Jew" and "Nonreligious Jew" in the table) were more likely to name a religious or ethnic motivation. And those who had "No Jewish connection" were very unlikely to mention a religious or ethnic motivation for emigrating.

Family reasons were most commonly stated by those who were passive migrants, who played "No significant role" in the decision to emigrate. Women and older people were also likely to state family reasons for leaving the USSR.

The respondent characteristic that is related most strongly to whether the respondent mentioned economic reasons is age ("Year of birth"). The higher salience of economic reasons to younger respondents is not surprising, since it is they whose lifetime career paths are potentially most affected by emigration.

Political motivations are much more common among younger emigrants than among older emigrants, among men than among women, and among those with no Jewish connection or whose only Jewish connection was through the family than among self-identified Jews.

The relationship between ethnicity and whether respondents mentioned political motivations reflects the fact that about a third of the non-Jews in the sample came as political refugees who were not part of the Jewish emigration, and almost 90 percent of those with no Jewish connection are political refugees. Over 80 percent of the respondents, however, are either religious Jews or nonreligious Jews. For neither of the latter two groups was politics the most frequently cited motivation for emigration.

To summarize the evidence on the bias issue, most of the respondents to the SIP General Survey were not dissatisfied with all aspects of life in the USSR, nor were they motivated to emigrate primarily for political reasons. On the contrary, the respondents on net claim to have been satisfied with many major aspects of life in the USSR and to have had a great variety of motives for leaving it.

Patterns of support for regime norms

I turn now to the main subject of this analysis: patterns of popular support for regime norms. The proper balance between social planning and control, on the one hand, and the workings of private markets, private decisions, and private interests, on the other hand, is at the heart of most discussions of political reform in the USSR. Thus, it is reasonable to characterize the Soviet political system and many public policy alternatives in terms of the balance between public and private control or choice.[13]

Accordingly, I examine the patterns of popular support for several key organizing principles of the Soviet political order that reflect the balance between public and private control. I refer to these principles as *regime norms*.[14] Six survey questions were designed to measure the extent of support for fundamental norms of the Soviet regime: state ownership of heavy industry, state control of agricultural production and distribution, state provision of free medical care for all citizens, denial of the right to strike, the requirement that citizens have residence permits to live in large cities, and protection of the rights of society over the rights of persons accused of crimes. The wording of the questions is given in the Technical Appendix to this chapter.

Each question gave the respondent a choice between an argument and a counterargument. For example: "Some people in the Soviet Union say that the state should own all heavy industry. Others say that all heavy industry should be owned privately. Where would you have placed yourself on this issue in [the end of your last normal period of life in the USSR]?"

For each question, respondents were asked to locate their own position on a seven-point scale. At one end of each scale was the most extreme "state" or "collective" position (e.g., "State should own all heavy industry," "Workers should not be able to strike"). At the opposite end was the most extreme "private" or "individual rights" position ("Heavy industry should be owned privately," "All workers should have a right to strike"). Thus, answers could range between 7 (state-collective) and 1 (private-individual), with 4 representing the midpoint.

We did not try to make the arguments and counterarguments equally attractive on each question. Such a goal would have been unrealistic for some of the questions. Instead, the counterarguments were designed primarily to increase the variance in responses on each issue. Balance was sought by asking about a range of issues.

I equate the "state-collective" end of each scale with the regime norm or established institutional practice on that issue. The higher the score, the greater the respondent's support for the regime norm; the lower the score,

---

[13] For an informative discussion of this theme, see Osborn 1970: ch. 3.
[14] I use the term "regime norms" to refer to the goals and norms of political behavior, in particular those related to the balance of control between the state and society. These goals and norms are not necessarily "legal" or "constitutional." For a similar usage of the term, see Easton and Dennis 1967. Thus, I do not use the term "regime" as synonymous with "leaders" or "ruling group," which are common uses of the term.

Table 4.2. *Percentage distribution of responses to questions on institutional norms*

	Private-individual						State-collective			
	1	2	3	4	5	6	7	Pct.	Mean	N
State–private control										
Medical care	6.7	2.7	5.7	19.0	8.2	5.2	52.3	99.8	5.45	2,730
Heavy industry	20.1	5.7	7.4	17.6	7.0	4.4	37.9	100.1	4.51	2,489
Agriculture	59.1	9.5	7.3	10.7	2.5	1.2	9.7	100.0	2.30	2,652
Collective–individual rights										
Rights of accused	25.1	8.4	10.4	27.1	7.0	4.8	17.2	100.0	3.66	2,436
Right to strike	42.9	11.5	10.3	15.9	4.8	3.1	11.5	100.0	2.84	2,504
Residence permits	76.2	5.1	2.5	5.2	1.8	1.7	7.6	100.1	1.87	2,688

Note: See the Technical Appendix for wording of the questions. Answers coded as "don't know," "refused," "not ascertained," or "never thought about it then" are treated as missing. The answers to the "rights of accused" question were inverted to conform with the arrangement of the other items from high state/collective support to low state/collective support.

the greater the respondent's preference for a more private or individualistic norm. Thus, I assume that people's preference for state or collective control indicates support for the established political order.

These institutionalized practices are indicators of a form of government that has variously been termed a "totalitarian dictatorship," an "organizational society" (Rigby 1964), or an "administered society" that constitutes a form of "totalitarianism without terror" (Kassof 1964). As de facto norms, these practices are not necessarily endorsed in the Constitution of the USSR or the Communist party program. But they have been readily identifiable as aspects of the established political order for at least the last 60 years. They are part of a basic commitment to plan, to organize, and to mobilize the population to serve collective rather than private or individual interests.

A factor analysis of the six measures of support for regime norms was performed to determine whether the questions tapped into one or more underlying attitudinal dimensions. This analysis revealed two distinct dimensions.[15] The first includes the items on state ownership of industry, state control of agriculture, and state provision of free medical care. I call this the *state–private control* dimension. The second includes the items on the rights of the accused, the right to strike, and the requirement of residence permits. I call this the *collective–individual rights* dimension.

The distributions of responses to the six questions are shown in Table 4.2

[15] See the Technical Appendix for information about the factor analysis.

and Figure 4.1. In Table 4.2, within each dimension the items are listed in descending order of the percentage of respondents who chose the most extreme pro-state position, code 7. This is identical to the ascending order of support for the most extreme antistate position, code 1, as well as to the ascending order of the mean scores for the items. The same pattern is observed among all six items, as shown in Figure 4.1. This consistency of the orderings suggests that relying on the means will not misrepresent the response patterns.

State versus private control

Strongest support for established practice is given to the provision of free public medical care. Fifty-two percent of all respondents state the strongest possible concurrence with the statement that "the state should provide free medical care for all citizens." The survey also asked the following question: "Think for a moment about the Soviet system with its good and bad points. Suppose you could create a system of government in the Soviet Union that is different from the one which currently exists. What things in the present Soviet system would you want to keep in the new one?" Twenty-four percent of all responses mentioned that the system of health care should be kept. This was the second most frequent response after education, which comprised 28 percent of all responses.[16] Mention of the system of health care placed well ahead of the third most common response, "Keep nothing" (11 percent of the responses), and the fourth most common response, crime control (7 percent). It is important to note that in response to a similar question, the refugee respondents to the Harvard Project study in the early 1950s also named education and medical care as the leading two features of the Soviet system that should be kept if the Bolshevik government were to be replaced by another type of government (Inkeles and Bauer 1968: 236).[17]

Of the six regime-norm questions, the institutional practice that garnered the second strongest support among SIP respondents is that "the state should own all heavy industry." Thirty-eight percent of the respondents gave the strongest possible endorsement of this practice, whereas 20 percent

---

[16] This is the distribution of *responses*, not the distribution of *respondents*. Up to three answers were coded per respondent.

[17] Complementary evidence is found in the answers to another open-ended question: "In what ways do you think that the United States could learn from the Soviet Union?" The five most frequent responses were: (1) dealing better with crime; (2) improving the educational system; (3) the United States could "learn nothing"; (4) improving the system of health care; and (5) improving the national defense.

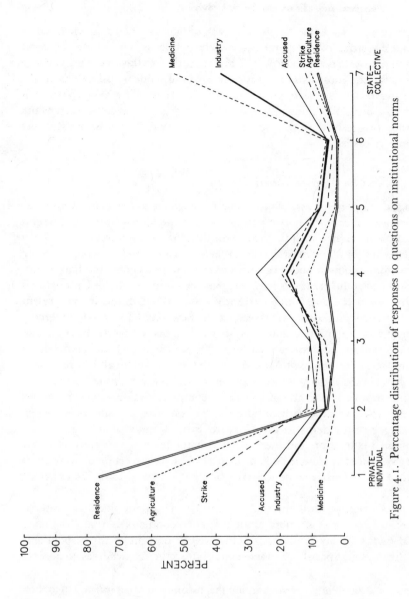

Figure 4.1. Percentage distribution of responses to questions on institutional norms

preferred the opposite extreme: that "all heavy industry should be owned privately." The strong support for state ownership of heavy industry is also consistent with the findings in the Harvard Project study (Inkeles and Bauer 1968: 243).

The endorsement of state control does not extend to agriculture. Fifty-nine percent of the respondents give the strongest possible endorsement to the position that "all agricultural production and distribution should be private." Although respondents who are positively disposed toward state ownership of heavy industry are more likely than other respondents to prefer state control of agriculture, the support for state control of heavy industry is far greater than the support for state control of agriculture. This relative ranking of support for state control of industry and agriculture also closely parallels the findings of the Harvard Project (Inkeles and Bauer 1968: 244–45).

It is reassuring for the validity of our survey results that the respondents are willing to give strong endorsements to certain key features of the Soviet regime while sharply criticizing other Soviet institutions. The consistency between these results and those of the Harvard Project further supports the conclusion that the respondents on the whole are giving answers that reflect their actual opinions. This consistency is especially important for two reasons. First, the respondents in the Harvard Project interviews had very different backgrounds from those in the Soviet Interview Project. Whereas more than 90 percent of the SIP respondents are Jews or are married to a Jew (see Table 4.1), the respondents to the Harvard Project were almost all Russians or Ukrainians. Second, the respondents to the Harvard Project were mostly refugees and displaced persons who last lived in the USSR in the 1930s and 1940s. The consistency in responses in the two surveys testifies both to the continuity of the socialization to regime norms over time and to the robustness of the survey results.

Collective versus individual rights

The respondents are less supportive of the regime norms on the three questions that deal with collective–individual rights than on the three state–private control questions. But there is considerable variation in their answers. Seventeen percent of the respondents adopt the most extreme position in favor of protection of "the rights of society, even if an innocent person [accused of a crime] sometimes goes to prison." Eleven percent adopt the most extreme position against the right of workers to strike. But only 8 percent give the strongest possible endorsement of the requirement that citizens have residence permits to live in large cities.

Systemic hostility and regime support

Even though a majority of the respondents report that they were satisfied
with several aspects of their material quality of life in the USSR, 21 percent
were so hostile to the USSR that when asked "What would you keep?"
in the present Soviet system if a new system of government were created,
they reported, "Keep nothing."[18] In addition, when asked "What would
you change?" in the Soviet system if a new government were created,
8 percent answered that they would "change everything." And when asked,
"In what ways do you think that the United States could learn from the
Soviet Union?" 18 percent answered that "the U.S. could learn nothing from
the Soviet Union."

Inkeles and Bauer interpreted these kinds of answers from the Harvard
Project refugees as indicators of hostility to the USSR, of fundamental
antipathy to the system as a whole. But they did not interpret this hostility to
mean that the emigrants rejected everything from their Soviet experience.

Table 4.3 reports the percentage distribution of support for the six regime
norms among respondents who were hostile to the USSR, using each of the
three measures of hostility. Hostile respondents are substantially less
supportive of the regime norms than the respondents as a whole (compare
with Table 4.2).

But despite the apparent conclusiveness of such phrases as "Keep nothing"
and "Change everything" there is a residue of support for parts of the system
even among those who are strongly antipathetic to the whole.[19] For
example, among those who volunteered that "the U.S. can learn nothing
from the USSR," 48 percent give the strongest possible endorsement to state
ownership of heavy industry. This may testify to how people's historical
experience, that is, their socialization within a given political system, has
shaped their fundamental beliefs about how the government *ought* to
organize its work. In particular, support for collective control is not
substantially lower among those hostile to the system than among the
respondents as a whole.

Explaining individual variation in regime support

The main objective of this study is to answer the questions: Is the variation
in the level of regime support systematically related to differences in

---

[18] This question was asked of a random one-third of the respondents. The number
who answered the question (not coded "don't know," "refused," or "not
ascertained") was 809. The percentages are calculated on this base number.
[19] For similar results, see Gitelman 1977.

Table 4.3. *Percentage distribution of support for regime norms among respondents who are "hostile" to the Soviet system*

	Private-individual						State-collective			
	1	2	3	4	5	6	7	Pct.	Mean	N
Respondents who said:										
Keep nothing in USSR										
Medical care	17.7	4.9	9.1	22.6	9.8	4.9	31.1	100.1	4.41	164
Heavy industry	38.6	3.9	8.5	19.0	5.2	3.9	20.9	100.0	3.44	153
Agriculture	70.8	9.3	7.5	5.6	0.6	2.5	3.7	100.1	1.78	161
Rights of accused	30.8	8.3	5.8	26.3	3.2	5.8	19.9	100.1	3.60	156
Right to strike	53.1	13.1	5.0	12.5	4.4	1.9	10.0	100.0	2.75	160
Residence permits	87.6	4.3	1.9	0.6	0.6	0.0	5.0	100.0	1.42	161
Respondents who said:										
Change everything in USSR										
Medical care	15.3	3.4	8.5	22.0	6.8	6.8	37.3	100.1	4.71	59
Heavy industry	30.9	7.3	5.5	18.2	1.8	3.6	32.7	100.0	3.94	55
Agriculture	65.0	10.0	10.0	5.0	0.0	1.7	8.3	100.0	3.03	60
Rights of accused	34.5	6.9	6.9	22.4	3.4	3.4	22.4	99.9	3.53	58
Right to strike	48.3	6.9	8.6	20.7	5.2	1.7	8.6	100.0	2.67	58
Residence permits	86.7	1.7	1.7	3.3	1.7	0.0	5.0	100.1	1.52	60
Respondents who said:										
US can learn nothing from USSR										
Medical care	11.4	4.0	3.8	19.2	6.9	6.5	48.2	100.0	5.18	448
Heavy industry	28.7	6.9	7.4	18.0	5.6	4.6	28.9	100.1	3.94	394
Agriculture	64.0	10.2	6.5	8.6	1.9	1.4	7.4	100.0	2.08	431
Rights of accused	31.0	9.2	12.1	25.9	4.9	3.3	13.6	100.0	3.29	390
Right to strike	47.6	11.7	9.7	13.3	3.2	2.4	12.1	100.0	2.69	412
Residence permits	79.2	3.8	1.6	3.8	1.1	1.8	8.6	99.9	1.83	443

Note: The "What would you keep" and "What would you change" questions were addressed to a third of the respondents. Of those who responded, 21 percent said they would "keep nothing," and 8 percent said they would "change everything." The "What could the U.S. learn" question was addressed to all respondents. Of those who answered, 18 percent said, "Nothing."

characteristics of the respondents? Who are the regime supporters? Who are the supporters of private interests and of individuals?

Answering these questions issue by issue is not the most fruitful approach. Considerations of measurement theory suggest that combining the items into multi-item indexes or measures is likely to provide more reliable and valid indicators of the theoretical concepts of interest. There are also technical reasons for combining the items, having to do with the heaping in the distribution of responses on the individual seven-point scales at the extreme and the middle positions.[20]

In the remainder of this analysis I use, therefore, two three-item indexes: state–private control and collective–individual rights. Each is a summated scale that is an average of the responses on the appropriate three items. Like the answers to the individual questions, the multi-item scale scores range from a high of 7 (state/collective) to a low of 1 (private/individual), and 4 is the midpoint. However, the scores on the scales are continuous rather than being whole integers. For each scale, the higher the score, the greater the support for regime norms. Further information about the scales is reported in the Technical Appendix. Some evidence concerning the validity of the scales is provided in an Addendum to this chapter.

Effects of education

Panel A of Table 4.4 summarizes the bivariate relationships between level of education and the two measures of regime support. This evidence shows that education is *negatively* related to the level of regime support. The same pattern occurs on the collective–individual rights measure: As education increases, the scores on the collective–individual rights scale decrease. This contradicts the expectation by some observers that education would be positively associated with support for the regime.

That support for the regime declines with *each* step up in education suggests that possession of a critical frame of mind is not restricted to those with higher education. The decrease in support for regime norms associated with moving from less than complete secondary education to having complete secondary education is about as large as the decrease associated

---

[20] Many respondents preferred an extreme position (1 or 7) and found it difficult to take a middle position or one that shaded toward the middle but was not exactly at the midpoint of 4. Hence, these variables assume the properties of dichotomous or trichotomous variables. For analyzing answers to individual items, it would be more appropriate to use probit or logit models rather than ordinary-least-squares regression (Aldrich and Nelson 1984). When the answers are combined into multi-item scales, however, the distributions appear as continuous variables with little heaping of responses at the extreme or middle positions.

Table 4.4. *Mean scores on state control and individual rights, by education and year of birth ($I = private/individual$, $7 = state/collective$)*

	State control		Individual rights	
	Mean	N	Mean	N
A. All respondents				
Less than comp. secondary	4.75	468	3.13	452
Complete secondary	4.20	1,125	2.78	1,118
Some higher education	3.85	161	2.65	160
Complete higher	3.81	913	2.62	908
Advanced education	3.62	95	2.26	95
All cases	4.13	2,762	2.76	2,733
B. Born 1905–15				
Less than comp. secondary	4.66	146	3.56	140
Complete secondary	4.44	107	2.95	103
Some higher education	4.47	13	3.33	13
Complete higher	3.84	50	3.00	50
Advanced education	5.00	3	3.33	3
All born 1905–15	4.45	319	3.26	309
C. Born 1916–25				
Less than comp. secondary	4.80	148	2.98	140
Complete secondary	4.33	159	3.01	157
Some higher	3.79	11	3.05	11
Complete higher	4.20	72	2.65	71
Advanced	3.94	6	2.61	6
All born 1916–25	4.46	396	2.93	385
D. Born 1926–35				
Less than comp. secondary	4.58	100	2.80	98
Complete secondary	4.40	146	2.82	145
Some higher	4.19	18	2.63	17
Complete higher	4.14	162	2.78	160
Advanced	4.00	22	2.36	22
All born 1926–35	4.32	448	2.77	442
E. Born 1936–45				
Less than comp. secondary	5.21	53	3.16	53
Complete secondary	4.34	261	2.82	260
Some higher	3.85	30	2.72	30
Complete higher	3.81	284	2.58	282
Advanced	3.62	45	2.19	45
All born 1936–45	4.11	673	2.70	670
F. Born 1946–60				
Less than comp. secondary	4.62	21	2.74	21
Complete secondary	4.01	452	2.64	453
Some higher	3.70	89	2.49	89

Table 4.4. (*contd.*)

	State control		Individual rights	
	Mean	N	Mean	N
Complete higher	3.59	344	2.53	344
Advanced	2.86	19	2.00	19
All born 1946–60	3.81	925	2.57	926

with moving from complete secondary education to having higher education. Moreover, support does not level off once a person obtains higher education; those with postgraduate education are even less supportive of the regime than are those with only completed higher education.

Because younger cohorts have advanced considerably in educational attainment over the older cohorts, it is important to determine whether the relations between education and regime support shown in Panel A are an artifact of cohort differences.[21] Panels B through F of Table 4.4 (also Figures 4.2 and 4.3) show that the education effects are not an artifact of cohort differences: On the contrary, *within* every cohort, increasing education is associated with declining political support.[22]

This does not mean that cohort effects are totally absent. A comparison of levels of regime support across the cohorts within the same education category in Table 4.4 suggests that the youngest cohort, born 1946–60, is distinctly less supportive of the regime than older cohorts. An appropriate method to test for cohort effects is to use multiple regression analysis, with each of the two regime norms measures taken in turn as dependent variables, and with each of the cohorts and educational levels entered into the equation as binary or dummy independent variables.

It is important to bear in mind, however, that many respondents in the post–World War II cohort left the USSR before completing what would otherwise have been their highest level of education. To the extent that beliefs and attitudes are likely to reflect these respondents' *expected* level of education rather than simply their *achieved* level, the political beliefs of members of recent cohorts who had only secondary education or incomplete

---

[21] Differences among cohorts are not necessarily what are understood in the technical social-scientific literature as cohort or generational effects rather than life-cycle or aging effects. With cross-sectional data, one cannot choose definitively between these two interpretations of trends from one cohort to the next. But it is possible to determine whether differences among cohorts in the level of political support are artifactual; for example, they might result from differences in educational level among cohorts.

[22] The few exceptions occur where the number of cases is very small.

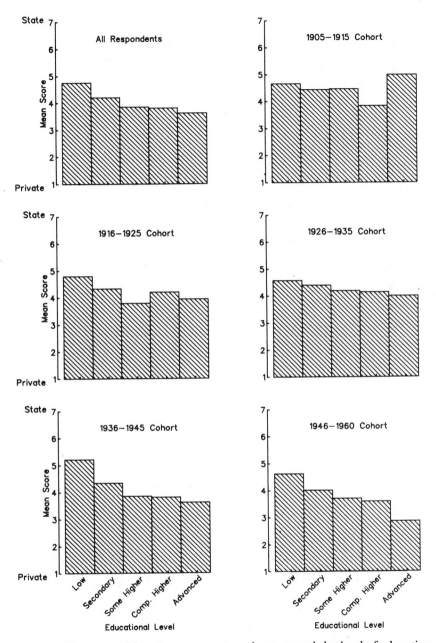

Figure 4.2. Mean scores on state–private control, by level of education and year of birth

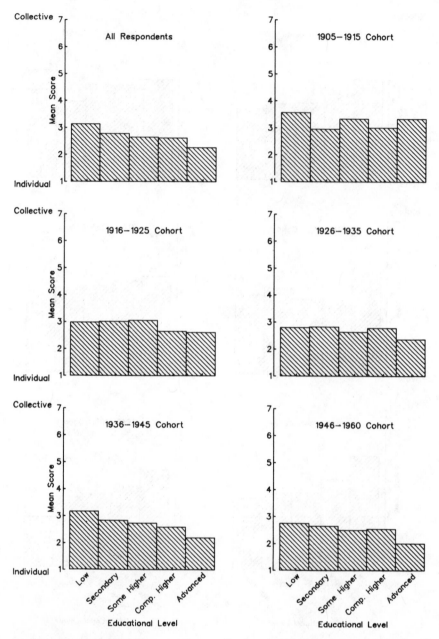

Figure 4.3. Mean scores on collective–individual rights, by level of education and year of birth

Table 4.5. *Regression of regime support onto education and year of birth*
($1 = private/individual$, $7 = state/collective$)

	State–private control				Collective–indiv. rights			
	(1)		(2)		(3)		(4)	
	b	(Sig.)	b	(Sig.)	b	(Sig.)	b	(Sig.)
Education dummy variables								
Complete secondary	−.38	(<.001)	−.37	(<.001)	−.18	(<.028)	−.19	(.036)
Some higher	−.69	(<.001)	−.69	(<.001)	−.28	(.037)	−.21	(.238)
Complete higher	−.79	(<.001)	−.77	(<.001)	−.32	(<.001)	−.35	(<.001)
Advanced	−1.04	(<.001)	−.90	(<.001)	−.71	(<.001)	−.68	(<.001)
Cohort dummy variables								
Born 1916–25	.05	(.665)	.05	(.677)	−.31	(.004)	−.31	(.004)
Born 1926–35	.07	(.557)	.06	(.614)	−.39	(<.001)	−.39	(<.001)
Born 1936–45	−.05	(.681)	−.06	(.597)	−.43	(<.001)	−.42	(<.001)
Born 1946–60	−.36	(<.001)	−.11	(.749)	−.57	(<.001)	−.65	(.039)
Cohort–educ. interaction terms								
Born 1946–60* Comp. secondary			−.24	(.490)			.08	(.795)
Born 1946–60* Some higher			−.23	(.583)			−.04	(.918)
Born 1946–60* Comp. higher			−.27	(.458)			.14	(.665)
Born 1946–60* Advanced			−.85	(.101)			−.05	(.908)
Constant	4.74	(<.001)	4.73	(<.001)	3.39	(<.001)	3.39	(<.001)
Adjusted R^2	.055		.055		.029		.028	
Number of cases	2,761		2,761		2,732		2,732	

Note: The omitted categories (reflected in the constant) are "less than complete secondary education" and "born 1905–15."

higher education might be more like those of people with higher levels of education – namely, less supportive of the regime.

I tested for these special affects in the regression analysis. I include in the regression equations terms that reflect joint effects (interaction effects) between cohort and the four highest educational levels. If these interaction effects are large and statistically significant, then at least part of the distinctive attitudes of the postwar generation could be due to frustration related to the inability to complete higher education or to obtain other benefits associated with attaining higher levels of education.

Table 4.5 presents the results of these tests. Column 1 shows the equation for the additive model with state–private control as the dependent variable; column 2 shows the model for the same dependent variable with the interaction terms. Columns 3 and 4 show the analogous results with collective–individual rights as the dependent variable. For neither dependent variable does the inclusion of the interaction effects increase the amount of variance accounted for; similarly, for neither are the b's (regression coefficients) for the interaction effects statistically significant (see columns 2 and 4). Thus, the additive models (in columns 1 and 3) appear to represent best the relationships among cohort, education, and support for regime norms. Moreover, further analysis eliminates the remaining cohort effects on support for state control but not the cohort effects on support for collective rights.[23]

The relationships among cohort, education, and support for regime norms are summarized in Figure 4.4. Panel A depicts the relationships with "state–private control" as the dependent variable; Panel B, with "collective–individual rights" as the dependent variable. For both dependent variables, the negative sign on the arrow leading from "education" reflects the fact that increases in education are associated with declining support for regime norms, independently of the cohort a person belongs to.

In addition, Panel A shows that there is no distinctive cohort effect on support for state control of the economy. In contrast, Panel B shows that support for collective rights increases with age, even after differences in educational attainment are taken into account. This pattern could result from either a life cycle (aging) or a generational effect. Regardless of the explanation, the youngest cohorts are less supportive of the rights of the collective and more supportive of the rights of the individual than the older cohorts, even after taking educational differences into account.

Effects of material satisfaction

The conventional scholarly wisdom holds that satisfaction of people's material needs generates support for the regime. If this were true, one should find a positive relationship between a respondent's income and his or her support for regime norms, even after adjusting for the effects of other factors that impinge on the level of regime support. On the other hand,

---

[23] That inclusion of the nonadditive terms in equation 2 raises the standard error of the main coefficient for the 1946–60 birth cohort so much that the coefficient is not statistically significant (the same does not occur for the analogous coefficient in equation 4) could mean that the cohort difference is an artifact of the special emigration-related experiences of that cohort. Respecifying equation 2, omitting the "main effect" dummy variable for the cohort, but including the terms expressing the joint effects with education results in the coefficients for all three interaction terms being statistically significant. Moreover, later analysis (see Table 4.6) eliminates evidence for a cohort effect on state–private control.

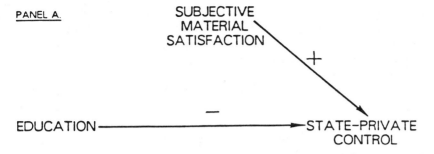

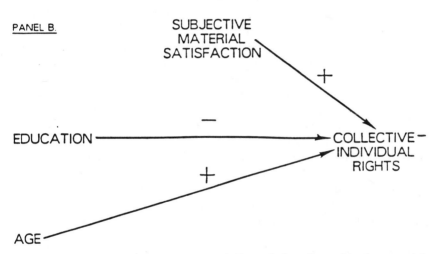

Figure 4.4. Schematic diagram of effects of education, subjective material satisfaction, and age on regime support

based on the results of the analysis to this point, one might suppose that, since education is inversely related to regime support, then income would also be inversely related to regime support, for income is positively related to education.

It would be straightforward to adopt measures of a person's individual or family income or wealth as indicators of material well-being. But, to judge from the theoretical literature about the sources of regime support, these are not the most appropriate measures to use. Rather than *objective* measures of *material welfare*, *subjective* measures of *material satisfaction* seem more appropriate, for it is the satisfaction of people's *perceived* wants, not merely the objective improvement of their material condition, that is said to generate support for the regime. Although there is usually a positive correlation between objective and subjective indicators of material well-being, the relationship is far from perfect.[24]

Therefore, I use as my measure of perceived material well-being the "satisfaction" indicators discussed earlier.[25] In the following analysis, four material satisfaction variables are included. Each variable is a four-point numeric scale, which I have recoded so that "very dissatisfied" is scored 1, and "very satisfied" is scored 4. Thus, the higher the score, the greater the reported satisfaction.[26] I will interpret the effects of the variables as a set, but I will not discuss why some of the satisfaction items do better than others in accounting for regime support.

Table 4.6 presents regression equations with the measures of material satisfaction included. Inclusion of the material satisfaction measures increases the proportion of variance in state–private control accounted for by 13 percentage points. All of the material satisfaction indicators have the expected sign (though the coefficient for the housing variable is not statistically significant): The greater the material satisfaction, the greater the support for state control. This is strong evidence for the hypothesis that the subjective satisfaction of material wants generates support for the established political order – even while increases in the level of education tend to weaken such support.

At the same time, material satisfaction has only a modest effect on support for collective or individual rights. Only an additional 2.5 percent of the variance in collective–individual rights is accounted for by the level of material satisfaction. Instead, support for individual rights is affected more strongly by the level of education and by differences between generations

[24] For a discussion of the issues involved, see Campbell, Converse, and Rodgers 1976; and Andrews and Withey 1976.
[25] A factor analysis of the responses to the five items revealed a single underlying dimension to the responses (see the Technical Appendix). A composite measure constructed from these items should be a more reliable measure of overall satisfaction than the individual indicators. I use it in analyses with "material satisfaction" as a dependent variable. However, preliminary analysis showed that, for measuring material satisfaction as an explanatory variable, the separate indicators provided a much better fit in the regression model than did the composite measure. The "satisfaction with job" variable is omitted because it was not answered by over 500 of the respondents – by respondents who were not working in their last normal period of life in the USSR.
[26] Preliminary analysis showed that it made little difference whether the variables were treated as interval-level variables (scored 1 to 4) or were broken into dummy variables representing the different levels of agreement.

Table 4.6. *Regression of regime support onto level of material satisfaction, education, and year of birth* ($1 = private/individual$, $7 = state/collective$)

	State–private control		Collective–indiv. rights	
	(1)		(2)	
	b	(Sig.)	b	(Sig.)
Education dummy variables				
Complete secondary	−.20	(.018)	−.08	(.358)
Some higher	−.24	(.086)	−.08	(.611)
Complete higher	−.37	(<.001)	−.11	(.220)
Advanced	−.41	(.016)	−.46	(.005)
Cohort dummy variables				
Born 1916–25	.00	(.970)	−.39	(<.001)
Born 1926–35	.12	(.282)	−.45	(<.001)
Born 1936–45	.13	(.206)	−.42	(<.001)
Born 1946–60	−.15	(.139)	−.54	(<.001)
Material satisfaction variables				
Medical care	.39	(<.001)	.09	(<.003)
Goods	.28	(<.001)	.16	(<.001)
Standard of living	.13	(<.001)	.06	(.091)
Housing	.04	(.233)	.03	(.280)
Constant	2.41	(<.001)	2.50	(<.001)
Adjusted R^2	.188		.054	
Number of cases	2,595		2,574	

Note: The omitted categories from the dummy variables (reflected in the constant) are "less than complete secondary education" and "born 1905–15."

or cohorts. But, for both measures of regime support, the initial hypothesis that there would be a payoff in regime support from satisfying people's material wants finds some corroboration.

The differences in the cohort effects on support for the two kinds of regime norm are more sharply defined in Table 4.6 than in Table 4.5. For the state–private control measure, none of the cohort effects is significantly different from zero, using the conventional .05 significance level as a criterion. Thus, the low support for state control in the postwar cohort noted in Table 4.5 appears to be a consequence of its comparatively low level of material satisfaction relative to other respondents with the same levels of education. Hence, the comparatively weak support for state control found in the youngest cohort is probably an artifact of emigration experience (e.g., frustration over educational and early career aspirations), not a result of a preference for private control in and of itself.

Implications

The analysis to this point supports two conclusions. First, increases in education are linked to weakening of support for regime norms. Second, increases in material satisfaction are associated with greater support for regime norms. The implications of these results merit further attention.

That the inverse relation between education and support for regime norms occurs among all cohorts, even among people who were at the end of their working lives in the USSR at the time of emigration, suggests that it is not an artifact of the emigration experience. But whether this relation is a result of education per se, rather than of other factors that are correlated with education, is difficult to determine.

Education is not a simple surrogate for other measures of social status, such as income, occupation, or privilege. For this reason, characterizing the respondents by a composite socioeconomic status or social class measure would obscure more than it would reveal.

In addition, one should not infer that the disaffection with regime norms that is associated with high education is shared by the Soviet political elite. Even though a large proportion of the SIP respondents were highly educated members of the professions, few were members of any kind of political elite. Hence, most were not subject to the special selection or socialization linked to elite membership.

It is instructive to examine another survey result. The respondents were asked to rank themselves on a ten-point ladder, with the most privileged person in the Soviet Union at the top (ranked 10) and the person with the least privilege at the bottom (ranked 1). The 1,236 respondents (over 40 percent of all respondents) who reported that they had the least privilege had a mean score on the state–private control measure of 4.05, slightly below the mean for all respondents. At the same time, the 21 respondents (less than 1 percent of the total) who ranked themselves on the top rung of the privilege ladder had a mean state–private control score of 5.36.

Thus, those few respondents who considered themselves the most privileged were substantially more supportive of the regime than those who considered themselves the least privileged. Because of the small number of cases, this result is speculative. But, assuming that the respondents' self-rankings on the privilege ladder correspond to their relative privilege in the Soviet Union, then the select set of highly privileged people among the SIP respondents provides evidence that highly privileged members of Soviet society are likely to be far more supportive of the regime than is the much larger "educated class" in which they are embedded.[27]

[27] The data do not support the expectation that respondents who had been military officers would be more supportive of regime norms than those who had not. Regardless of whether or not they had served on active duty, officers were *less*

7

Table 4.7. *Mean scores on state control (1 = private, 7 = state) and individual rights (1 = individual, 7 = collective), by education and level of political interest*

	A. Mean on state–private control, by education					
	Less than comp. sec.	Comp. sec.	Some higher	Comp. higher	Advanced	N
Interested in politics?[a]						
Not at all	5.02	4.70	4.25[b]	4.39	5.11[c]	521
Slightly	4.58	4.50	3.83	3.99	3.83[d]	439
Somewhat	4.51	4.07	4.03	3.99	4.07[e]	1,048
Very	4.25	3.76	3.49	3.47	3.17	745
N	464	1,122	161	911	95	2,753
	B. Mean on collective–individual rights, by education					
	Less than comp. sec.	Comp. sec.	Some higher	Comp. higher	Advanced	N
Interested in politics?[a]						
Not at all	3.42	3.16	2.38[b]	3.01	2.56[c]	498
Slightly	2.98	2.90	2.70	2.87	2.60[d]	438
Somewhat	2.83	2.69	2.90	2.63	2.47[e]	1,045
Very	2.88	2.51	2.40	2.49	2.01	744
N	447	1,116	160	907	95	2,725

[a] "During your last normal period [of life in the USSR], how interested were you in politics and public affairs – were you very interested, somewhat interested, only slightly interested, or not at all interested?"
[b] Base N in cell: 19 cases in Panel A, and 18 cases in Panel B.
[c] Base N in cell: 3 cases.
[d] Base N in cell: 12 cases.
[e] Base N in cell: 32 cases.

Nonetheless, the apparent disaffection of the educated class as a whole presents a challenge for Soviet leaders. This is the middle class for whom the Big Deal was arranged. This class is growing in size and importance to the Soviet economy, but with its increasing political sophistication comes increasing disaffection.

Additional evidence for this interpretation can be found in the relation between the respondents' reported level of interest in politics and their support for regime norms. Table 4.7 presents the mean scores on the two

supportive of regime norms than noncommissioned officers, corporals, privates, and ordinary seamen.

measures of support for regime norms as a function of both education and level of interest in politics. In Panel A, as one scans from the upper left toward the lower right – from persons who were "not at all interested" in politics and who had not completed secondary school toward persons who were "very interested" in politics and had graduate education – support for state control of the economy declines sharply.

Both education and level of interest contribute to the decline. Within each educational stratum, those with great interest in politics favor private control more often than those with little interest in politics. The same pattern of decreasing support for regime norms with increasing political sophistication appears in Panel B, which reports the means on the collective–individual rights measure, but it is much weaker.

That persons with higher levels of material satisfaction are more supportive of the regime, even after the effects of increasing education and political sophistication are taken into account, suggests that at least one strategy followed by the party leaders to garner support has a measurable payoff. The Big Deal may be necessary to counter the disaffection associated with increasing education. It appears to work. But to understand how it works, further investigation is needed into the factors that influence people's subjective sense of material well-being.

An obvious thing to look at is the relation between objective material welfare and subjective material satisfaction. There is no simple equation between improvement in people's objective material welfare and their subjective perception of their welfare. But there is some structure to this relationship. A preliminary predictive model is shown in Table 4.8. This model is restricted to respondents who were married at the end of the last normal period in the USSR to facilitate the interpretation of the measures of family income and household size.

The model uses a summary measure of material satisfaction as the dependent variable (see the Technical Appendix). This variable ranges from + 2.0 (most satisfied) to − 2.0 (least satisfied). For independent variables, it includes dummy variables for the educational levels and birth cohorts. It also includes several measures of objective material well-being: the number of rubles per month earned by both spouses combined at the end of the last normal period; whether the respondent was working for pay during that time; the number of square meters of housing space the respondent had; and the number of people in the household.[28]

In addition, three dummy variables represent whether the person lived in

[28] The last variable is included as a method of per capitizing both the housing space variable and the family income variable. The model is restricted to married couples because the measures of respondent's and spouse's income are more reliable than reports of gross family income. See Anderson and Silver 1987.

Table 4.8. *Regression of material satisfaction on education, family income, housing space, and residence in closed cities among married couples (2.0 = maximum material satisfaction; − 2.0 = minimum material satisfaction)*

	Material satisfaction	
	b	(Sig.)
Education dummy variables		
Complete secondary	− .21	(< .001)
Some higher	− .54	(< .001)
Complete higher	− .58	(< .001)
Advanced	− .80	(< .001)
Cohort dummy variables		
Born 1916–25	.03	(.779)
Born 1926–35	.03	(.774)
Born 1936–45	− .15	(.104)
Born 1946–60	− .28	(.003)
Objective material status in LNP		
Family income (rubles per mo.)[a]	.0011	(< .001)
Was person working?[b]	.17	(< .001)
Square meters of housing space[a]	.0029	(< .001)
Number of people in household	− .041	(.019)
Lived in closed city: dummy variables		
Moscow	− .46	(< .001)
Leningrad	− .58	(< .001)
Kiev	− .19	(.176)
Moscow* square meters	.0112	(.001)
Leningrad* square meters	.0109	(< .001)
Kiev* square meters	.0030	(.387)
Constant	.164	(.142)
Adjusted R^2	.144	(< .001)
Number of cases	1,952	

[a] "Family income" is sum of husband's and wife's incomes from main jobs at end of their LNP. Respondents were also asked about their spouse's income. In cases where both spouses were respondents to the survey but one of them did not answer the question on his/her own or spouse's income, the spouse's report was used if available. The same procedure was used to estimate missing data on housing space.

[b] Those who worked at any time during five years leading up to the end of their LNP are counted as working (coded 1). Those who never worked in that period or who never worked at all in the USSR are counted as not working (coded 0).

one of the cities closed to immigration at the end of their last normal period: Moscow, Leningrad, or Kiev.[29] One would expect people who lived in those cities to be more satisfied than those who did not. Interaction terms between the closed-city dummy variables and the housing space measure are included because the average amount of housing space is lower in the closed cities than in other cities; hence, differences in the amount of housing space may have a different effect on people's sense of material satisfaction in those cities than elsewhere.[30]

Table 4.8 shows that younger people are less satisfied with material conditions than older people, even after differences in educational attainment are taken into account. This result is consistent with the results of a study of the quality of life of the American population (Campbell, Converse, and Rodgers 1976: ch. 5) In addition, among SIP respondents, the higher their education, the less satisfied people are with their material conditions. This result is also consistent with American studies and suggests that the higher people's aspirations, the lower their sense of material well-being.

Other factors, on the other hand, increase material satisfaction. Some of these are conditions over which the government has some control. For example, family income from the main state job and the amount of housing space a person has are positively correlated with material satisfaction. Although this finding is not surprising, it is important to have it confirmed empirically.[31]

But residence in one of the closed cities, which one might expect to improve people's sense of material satisfaction, appears to work in the opposite direction. Even after adjusting for the effects of education, income, and age (birth cohort), Muscovites and Leningraders are distinctly *less* satisfied with their material conditions than are others. (The coefficient for Kiev is also negative, but it is not statistically significant.) This is ameliorated by the special premium that residents in Moscow and Leningrad place on

[29] Twenty-one percent of the respondents are from Leningrad, 21 percent from Moscow, and 12 percent from Kiev.

[30] For respondents who were married during the LNP, the average number of square meters of housing space for Muscovites, Leningraders, and Kievans was 37 (virtually identical for the three cities). For married respondents who were *not* living in one of those three cities, the average was 46 square meters.

[31] Respondents who earned income in the private sector were *less* satisfied with their material quality of life than those who did not have private income, even after taking into account the effects of education, cohort, and level of income from the main job. It seems plausible that lower material satisfaction causes people to seek private work to supplement their income. I also tested for bias in the material satisfaction measure caused by the level of satisfaction the respondents had with the quality of life in the United States. I found a negligible effect of this source. See the Technical Appendix for details.

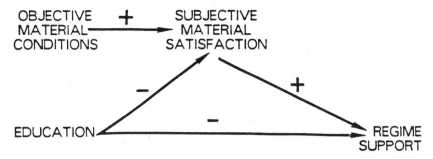

Figure 4.5. Schematic diagram of factors affecting regime support

obtaining additional housing space. For those from Moscow and Leningrad, each additional 20 square meters of housing space increases the satisfaction score by an average of .28, whereas the same additional 20 square meters for people not living in Moscow or Leningrad would increase the score by .06.[32]

Figure 4.5 summarizes the relations among the main variables of interest in this analysis. For simplicity, the diagram omits the effects of age differences and of residence in Moscow or Leningrad, as well as the weak, but positive, relation between education and objective material satisfaction.

The diagram shows the positive relation between objective material conditions and subjective material satisfaction, as well as the positive relation between subjective material satisfaction and regime support. Figure 4.5 does not show a *direct* effect of objective material conditions on regime support because further statistical tests revealed that the effects of objective material conditions on regime support are completely mediated through subjective material satisfaction.

The negative sign on the arrow leading from "education" to "regime support" reflects the fact that increases in education are directly associated with declines in support for regime norms. The negative sign on the arrow leading from "education" to "subjective material satisfaction" suggests that increasing education reduces people's sense of material well-being. As a consequence of this, increases in education work through both direct and indirect paths to reduce political support.

Thus, subjective material satisfaction appears to act as a cognitive filter that transforms the effects of both objective material conditions and education on regime support. How that filter works merits further study.

[32] From the results reported in Table 4.8, the payoff per square-meter increase in housing space is .0029 if the person does not live in Moscow or Leningrad but is .0029 + .112 for Muscovites and .0029 + .109 for Leningraders.

Conclusion

This study provides empirical evidence for an interpretation of
government–society relations in the Soviet Union based on an exchange:
from the government to the society, a supply of material goods to satisfy
people's wants; from the society to the government, a store of political capital
in the form of support for the established political order. These are not the
only items in the exchange, but they are important ones.[33]

At the same time, the long-term growth of educational attainments works
to undermine support for established institutional practices, both in the area
of state control of the economy and in the area of individual rights. The
younger generation also appears to be substantially more supportive of
individual rights, independently of levels of education.

The increase in education and the replacement of generations are dynamic
phenomena that are likely to force continual renewal of the exchange
agreement between society and the state. This is a very different process from
that described by Fainsod (1961). It is not just that "each new generation
offers the ruling group a fresh opportunity to rebuild its mass support and to
renew its life energies" but that each new generation offers the ruling group a
new challenge: Can it keep the old arrangements intact?

This study suggests that there may be a workable strategy but that it is
complex. It involves not just the manipulation of objective opportunities and
material rewards, which are heavily discounted by a population with rising
material aspirations, but also the manipulation of perceptions. For example,
Moscow and Leningrad are very desirable places to live. The great variety
of stratagems Soviet citizens use to obtain residency permits testifies to this
(Zaslavsky 1982: ch. 6). But former residents of Moscow and Leningrad
were less satisfied with their material conditions than those who lived
elsewhere.[34] This is probably due to their higher expectations.

A recently published report from a study of the subjective quality of life in
Soviet cities also confirms that Muscovites and Leningraders are less satisfied
with many aspects of their lives. On a wide range of objects of evaluation,
Muscovites and Leningraders "working in leading sectors of the economy"
appear to be less satisfied than Kievans and less satisfied than a cross-section
of respondents from 27 large Soviet cities. This includes their satisfaction
with housing, medical services, work, and "life as a whole." It even includes

[33] The notion of a contract between state and society has also been discussed by
Breslauer (1978, 1982), Zaslavsky (1982: ch. 6), and Cohen (1985: ch. 5).
[34] Respondents who had "no Jewish connection," most of whom were political
refugees, disproportionately resided in Moscow and Leningrad in the last normal
period. I reestimated the equation in Table 4.8 excluding cases with "no Jewish
connection." This did not substantially affect the pattern of relationships.

the evaluation of cultural services: 39 percent of the respondents from the 27 large cities thought those services were good, whereas 27 percent of the Muscovites, 25 percent of the Leningraders, and 44 percent of the Kievans held the same positive judgment (Bozhkov and Golofast 1985).

Further analysis of the SIP General Survey data shows that, even after their levels of subjective material satisfaction are taken into account, Muscovites and Leningraders are less supportive of established regime norms than are people from other large Soviet cities. Consistent with this finding, the proportion of respondents who reported that they "sometimes did not vote" or "never voted" during their last normal period in the USSR is substantially higher among Muscovites and Leningraders than among respondents who lived in other cities.[35] This evidence also alerts us to why an understanding of the bases of support for the Soviet regime requires study of the relations between state and society outside the dual capital cities.

Finally, understanding the sources of support for the regime requires serious empirical study of the relationship between objective conditions and subjective evaluations of the quality of material life as well as how people's evaluations of their material conditions affect their assessment of the political system as a whole. By relying on emigrants not just as reporters or informants about life in the Soviet Union but also as *respondents* whose individual experiences and political beliefs provide a clue to how the Soviet system works, we have been able to subject some of the common speculation about Soviet politics to empirical test.

Addendum: A note on the behavioral correlates of regime support

The measures of regime support used in this analysis are subjective. Analysis of the behavioral correlates of these attitudes is beyond the scope of this chapter. But an examination of the relationship between the measures of regime support and a few reported political behaviors helps to confirm that the subjective measures represent authentic attitudes.

One should not expect to find perfect congruence between attitudes and behavior. Moreover, a lack of congruence between beliefs and behavior does not mean that the subjective measures are invalid. The main reason for this is that the levels and types of political activity in which people engage are constrained by the institutional setting and by many factors in the

---

35 Among the respondents who lived outside one of the closed cities in the Soviet Union, 77 percent report that they "always voted" during their last normal period. Among Muscovites, the corresponding percentage is 62; among Leningraders, 55; among Kievans, 80.

individual's background or immediate circumstance.

Nonetheless, examination of the bivariate relationships between reported political behavior and the regime support measures that I have used provides some confirmation of the validity of the latter measures. I have focused on political activities that are indicators of regime support or of the avoidance of mobilized participation (see Chapters 3 and 11, herein). I present summary statistics in Table 4.9 without further comment.[36]

Technical appendix: construction of composite measures

Regime support: The measures of regime support are based on six questions. Respondents were asked to locate their own position on each question on a seven-point scale, which was shown on a card. A full illustration of one of the questions is presented here.

[READ ALOUD BY INTERVIEWER]

Some people in the Soviet Union say that the state should provide free medical care for all citizens.

Others believe that medical care should be provided and paid for privately.

Please look at this card and tell me where you would have placed yourself on this issue in [end of LNP]. You may have been at number 1, at number 7, or at any of the numbers in between.

[Explain: Those strongly in favor of the state providing medical care are at number 1, and those strongly in favor of medical care being provided and paid for privately are at number 7. People who aren't sure how they feel or who don't feel strongly on this issue are somewhere in the middle. Where would you have placed yourself in (end of LNP)?]

[CARD SHOWN TO RESPONDENT]

1	2	3	4	5	6	7

STATE
SHOULD PROVIDE
MEDICAL CARE

MEDICAL
CARE SHOULD
BE PROVIDED
AND PAID
FOR PRIVATELY

---

[36] Ideally, one would like to have an external standard for evaluating the validity of survey responses. This is rarely possible. Studies of American political behavior show that survey respondents commonly exaggerate how often they vote because of a propensity to give socially desirable responses to the interviewer (see Anderson and Silver 1986b; and Silver, Anderson, and Abramson 1986). Whether an analogous pattern of misreporting occurred among SIP respondents cannot be determined.

Table 4.9. *Mean scores on state–private control and collective–individual rights, by reported political behavior (1 = private/individual, 7 = state/ collective)*

	State–private control	Collective–indiv. rights
Did respondent always vote in LNP?		
Always voted	4.4	2.9
Sometimes did not vote	3.7	2.5
Never voted	3.3	2.4
Was respondent a Komsomol activist?		
Yes	3.1	2.7
No	3.9	2.7
Attended an unofficial art show?		
Yes	3.6	2.5
No	4.3	2.8
Took part in unsanctioned study group?		
Yes	3.5	2.4
No	4.2	2.8
Read samizdat/tamizdat?		
Yes	3.5	2.5
No	4.4	2.9
Distributed samizdat/tamizdat?		
Yes	3.1	2.1
No	4.2	2.8
Took part in open protest?		
Yes	3.3	2.4
No	4.1	2.8
Took part in strike at work?		
Yes	3.7	2.4
No	4.1	2.8
Listened to foreign radio?		
Yes	4.0	2.7
No	5.0	3.3
Tried to avoid military service?		
Yes	3.4	2.3
No	4.0	2.7

The other five questions are:

Some people in the Soviet Union say that the state should own all heavy industry. Others say that all heavy industry should be owned privately.

Some people in the Soviet Union believe that the state should control production and distribution of all agricultural products.
Others believe that all agricultural production and distribution should be private.

Some people in the Soviet Union say that the rights of individuals accused of crimes must be protected, even if a guilty person sometimes goes free.
Others say that the rights of society must be protected, even if an innocent person sometimes goes to prison.

Some people in the Soviet Union believe that workers should not be able to strike, because strikes are costly.
Other people feel that all workers should have a right to strike, even if it means that certain services may be interrupted.

Some people in the Soviet Union believe that people should be required to have residence permits to live in the large cities so that the authorities can plan public services.
Others think that people should be completely free to live where they want.

Partly because of the length of the interviews, the interviewers were instructed not to pressure the respondents if they did not respond after a repetition of the question. The interviewers were also instructed to record as an answer, "I never thought about this in the Soviet Union," if the respondent did not answer the question for this reason. This is similar in intent to the use of a filter question. About 40 percent of all nonanswers (including "don't know," "refuse," and "never thought about this") were of this type.

The response categories were recoded so that the high end of the scale corresponded with support for the state or collective position (coded 7) and the low end corresponded with the private or individual position (coded 1). A principal-components factor analysis of the six items revealed two distinct dimensions. The factor loadings, based on an oblimin rotation, are:[37]

[37] Since the scales used in the analysis are Likert scales rather than being based on the factor loadings, the choice of solutions is not critical. However, my method of scale construction permits the two regime norms measures to be correlated with one another ($r = .22$). For a discussion of summated, or Likert, scales, see Anderson, Basilevsky, and Hum 1983.

	Factor 1 State–private control	Factor 2 Collective–individual rights
State industry	.751	.103
State agriculture	.706	.256
State medical care	.595	.016
Right to strike	.259	.669
Rights of accused	− .185	.646
Residence permits	.412	.587

The two factors account for 47.8 percent of the total variance. The correlation between the factors is .154.

To facilitate interpretation, I constructed two three-item summated scales corresponding to the two factors rather than developing measures directly from factor scores. Answers coded "DK," "refused," "not applicable," "not ascertained," and (volunteered) "never thought about it then" were scored as missing on the given item. The numerical answers were then summed across the three items identified from the factor analysis as belonging to each scale, yielding a maximum possible value of 21 and a minimum of 3. Dividing the sum by the number of valid answers for the items in the given scale yields an average for the items answered, with a maximum possible of 7 and a minimum possible of 1.

The distribution of respondents by the number of state–private control questions that they answered is: three questions, 2,434 (87.1 percent of the respondents); two questions, 241 respondents (8.6 percent); one question, 87 respondents (3.1 percent); zero questions, 31 respondents (1.1 percent). The distribution for the collective–individual rights questions is: three questions, 2,279 (81.6 percent); two questions, 337 (12.1 percent); one question, 117 (4.2 percent); zero questions, 60 (2.1 percent). Cases are included in the analysis using a given scale if the respondent gave at least one valid answer to the items in that scale. Analyses using more restrictive criteria for keeping the cases in the analysis produced results that were very similar to those based on the more inclusive rule.

Descriptive statistics:

State–private control	*Collective–individual rights*
Mean: 4.133	Mean: 2.762
Std. dev.: 1.569	Std. dev.: 1.407
Minimum: 1.000 (private)	Minimum: 1.000 (individual)
Maximum: 7.000 (state)	Maximum: 7.000 (collective)
N of valid cases: 2,762	N of valid cases: 2,733

Material satisfaction: The "material satisfaction" measure is based on answers to the following questions:

In [end of LNP], how satisfied or dissatisfied were you with...
(*a*) your housing?
(*b*) (your/your family's) standard of living?
(*c*) public medical care?
(*d*) your job?
(*e*) the availability of consumer goods in your town?

Respondents were shown a card with the following answer categories: "very satisfied," "somewhat satisfied," "somewhat dissatisfied," and "very dissatisfied."

A factor analysis of the responses to these five items revealed a single underlying dimension to the responses. To simplify interpretation, the measure of material satisfaction is a summated scale.[38] For each item, answers of "very satisfied" were scored 2; "somewhat satisfied," 1; "somewhat dissatisfied," − 1; and "very dissatisfied," − 2. Answers coded as "DK," "refused," "not applicable," or "not ascertained" were scored as missing on that item. Summing the valid answers over the five items yields a maximum possible score of 10 and a minimum possible of − 10. Dividing this sum by the number of valid answers yields an average for the items answered, with a maximum possible of 2 and a minimum possible of − 2.

The distribution of respondents by the number of questions that they answered is: five questions, 2,127 (76.2 percent of respondents); four questions, 588 (21.1 percent); three questions, 55 (2.0 percent); two questions, 9 (0.3 percent); one question, 7 (0.2 percent); zero questions, 8 (0.3 percent). Cases are included in the analysis if the respondent gave at least one valid answer. Analyses using more restrictive criteria produced results that are very similar to those based on a more inclusive rule.

Descriptive statistics for the constructed measure:

Mean: 0.098
Std. dev.: .919
Minimum: − 2.000 (dissatisfied)
Maximum: + 2.000 (satisfied)
N of valid cases: 2,785

A test for response bias: It is important to know whether the respondents' evaluation of life in the USSR is colored by their assessment of their current situation in the United States. One might expect that emigrants who are

[38] An alternative measure, using the factor loadings to generate a factor score, performed almost identically to the summated scale in the analysis.

dissatisfied with their current conditions would take a more positive view of life in the Soviet Union, whereas those who are satisfied with life now will tend to denigrate conditions in the USSR. SIP respondents were asked:

Here is a [ten-point] scale representing the quality of life. At the top of the ladder is the best possible life, and at the bottom of the ladder is the worst possible life. Where on this scale would you put your life now?

They were then asked:

Where on the scale do you expect your life to be five years from now?

The mean answer to the first question is 5.4; the mean answer to the second question, 7.4. On average, then, people were optimistic about the next five years. Consistent with expectations, the bivariate correlations between the two measures of the quality of life in the United States and the composite measure of material satisfaction with life in the USSR are negative: − .05 and − .07. Respondents who are more favorable about conditions in the United States are likely to be less favorable about conditions in the USSR. But the correlations are very low.

When the subjective measures of quality of life in the United States now and expected *change* in the quality of life in the next five years are added to the regression equation in Table 4.8, the coefficient for the variable measuring expected change is not statistically significant.[39] The coefficient for the "life now" question is statistically significant but very small ($b = -.026$). Moreover, the coefficients for the other variables in the equation are changed only slightly.

Thus, if any bias to the respondents' assessment of the quality of life in the USSR is caused by their feelings about their quality of life in the United States, it is that positive feelings about life in the United States tend to deflate people's assessment of life in the USSR. But the amount of bias from this source is negligible. To illustrate, if respondents' assessment of life in the United States increased by an amount equal to one standard deviation (2.14) on the "life now" ladder, their score on the material satisfaction measure would decline by just .05, which is extremely small when compared with the standard deviation of .92 on this measure. An analogous test for the effects of "life now" on the respondents' support for Soviet regime norms produced a similar result.

[39] The expected change is the difference between where the respondents expect their lives to be five years from now and where they place themselves now.

140   **Brian D. Silver**

References

Abramson, Paul R. 1983. *Political Attitudes in America: Formation and Change.* San Francisco: Freeman.
Aldrich, John H., and Forrest D. Nelson. 1984. *Linear Probability, Logit, and Probit Models.* Beverly Hills; Calif.: Sage.
Amalrik, Andrei. 1970. *Will the Soviet Union Survive until 1984?* New York: Harper.
Anderson, Andy B., Alexander Basilevsky, and Derek P. J. Hum. 1983. "Measurement: Theory, and Techniques." Pp. 231–87 in Peter H. Rossi, James D. Wright, and Andy B. Anderson (eds.), *Handbook of Survey Research.* New York: Academic Press.
Anderson, Barbara A., and Brian D. Silver. 1986a. "Descriptive Statistics for the Sampling Frame Population." Soviet Interview Project Working Papers, no. 2.
    1986b. "Measurement and Mismeasurement of the Validity of the Self-Reported Vote," *American Journal of Political Science,* 30: 771–772.
    1987. "The Validity of Survey Responses: Insights from Interviews of Married Couples in a Survey of Soviet Emigrants." *Social Forces, 65:* forthcoming.
Anderson, Barbara A., Brian D. Silver, and Robert A. Lewis. 1986. "Demographic Estimates for the Post-Sampling Weights of the SIP General Survey." Soviet Interview Project, Working Papers, no. 4.
Andrews, Frank M., and Stephen B. Withey. 1976. *Social Indicators of Well Being: Americans' Perceptions of Life Quality.* New York: Plenum.
Azrael, Jeremy R. 1965. "Soviet Union." Pp. 233–72 in James S. Coleman (ed.), *Education and Political Development.* Princeton N.J.: Princeton University Press.
Bahry, Donna. 1987. "Surveying Soviet Emigrants: Political Attitudes and Ethnic Bias." Manuscript, New York University.
Bialer, Seweryn. 1980. *Stalin's Successors: Leadership, Stability, and Change in the Soviet Union.* Cambridge: Cambridge University Press.
Blalock, Hubert M., Jr. 1967. "Causal Inferences, Closed Populations, and Measures of Association," *American Political Science Review,* 61: 130–36.
Bozhkov, Oleg B., and Valerii B. Golofast. 1985. "Otsenka naseleniem uslovii zhizni v krupnykh gorodakh," *Sotsiologicheskie issledovaniia,* no. 3: 95–100.
Breslauer, George W. 1978. "On the Adaptability of Soviet Welfare-State Authoritarianism." Pp. 3–25 in Karl W. Ryavec (ed.), *Soviet Society and the Communist Party.* Amherst: University of Massachusetts Press.
    1982. *Khrushchev and Brezhnev as Leaders: Building Authority in Soviet Politics.* London: Allen and Unwin.
Bushnell, John. 1980. "The 'New Soviet Man' Turns Pessimist." Pp. 179–99 in Stephen F. Cohen, Alexander Rabinowitch, and Robert Sharlet (eds.), *The Soviet Union since Stalin.* Bloomington: Indiana University Press.
Campbell, Angus, Philip E. Converse, and Willard L. Rodgers. 1976. *The Quality of American Life: Perceptions, Evaluations, and Satisfactions.* New York: Russell Sage Foundation.
Cohen, Stephen F. 1985. *Rethinking the Soviet Experience: Politics and History since 1917.* New York: Oxford University Press.

Colton, Timothy E. 1984. *The Dilemma of Reform in the Soviet Union*. New York: Council on Foreign Relations.

Di Franceisco, Wayne, and Zvi Gitelman. 1984. "Soviet Political Culture and 'Covert Participation' in Policy Implementation," *American Political Science Review*, 78: 603–21.

Dobson, Richard B. 1980. "Education and Opportunity." Pp. 115–37 in Jerry G. Pankhurst and Michael Paul Sacks (eds.), *Contemporary Soviet Society: Sociological Perspectives*. New York: Praeger.

Dunham, Vera S. 1976. *In Stalin's Time: Middleclass Values in Soviet Fiction*. Cambridge: Cambridge University Press.

Easton, David. 1965. *A Systems Analysis of Political Life*. New York: Wiley.

Easton, David, and Jack Dennis. 1967. "The Child's Acquisition of Regime Norms: Political Efficacy," *American Political Science Review*, 61: 25–38.

Fainsod, Merle. 1961. *How Russia Is Ruled*. Cambridge; Mass.: Harvard University Press.

Gitelman, Zvi. 1977. "Soviet Political Culture: Insights from Jewish Emigres," *Soviet Studies*, 29: 543–64.

Inkeles, Alex, and Raymond Bauer. 1968. *The Soviet Citizen: Daily Life in a Totalitarian Society*. New York: Atheneum.

Jackman, Mary R., and Michael J. Muha. 1984. "Education and Intergroup Attitudes: Moral Enlightenment, Superficial Democratic Commitment, or Ideological Refinement?" *American Sociological Review*, 49: 751–69.

Kassof, Allen. 1964. "The Administered Society: Totalitarianism without Terror," *World Politics*, 16: 558–75.

Mickiewicz, Ellen Propper. 1981. *Media and the Russian Public*. New York: Praeger.

Moore, Barrington, Jr. 1954. *Terror and Progress USSR: Some Sources of Change and Stability in the Soviet Dictatorship*. New York: Harper and Row.

Osborn, Robert J. 1970. *Soviet Social Policies: Welfare, Equality, and Community*. Homewood, Ill.: Dorsey Press.

Rigby, T.H. 1964. "Traditional, Market, and Organizational Societies and the USSR," *World Politics*, 16: 539–57.

Silver, Brian D., Barbara A. Anderson, and Paul R. Abramson. 1986. "Who Over-Reports Voting?" *American Political Science Review*, 80: 613–24.

Wright, James D. 1976. *The Dissent of the Governed: Alienation and Democracy in America*. New York: Academic Press.

Zaslavsky, Victor. 1982. *The Neo-Stalinist State: Class, Ethnicity, and Consensus in Soviet Society*. Armonk, N. Y.: Sharpe.

CHAPTER 5

The attentive public for Soviet science and technology

LINDA L. LUBRANO

With the recognition of scientific and technological change as central components of national and international policies, scholars, policy makers, and public opinion specialists in the United States have studied the views of the American public toward science and technology since the late 1950s.[1] There have been no comparable studies of the Soviet public, despite the fact that science and technology play a prominent role in the official view of Soviet historical development. Soviet leaders have promoted the idea of a scientific-technical revolution and the importance of science as a key to the Communist future. Yet, we do not know whether the regime's message has had the desired impact on citizen attitudes toward science, technology, and public policy. The Soviet Interview Project (SIP) has provided us with the first opportunity to see if there is an attentive public for Soviet science and technology, at least among a small but significant segment of the Soviet population.

American research on citizen attitudes in the United States demonstrates that different issues generate different levels of attentiveness on the part of the general public. People who are more educated tend to have a broader range of issue awareness, and they tend to be more attentive (than the less educated) to issues that are perceived as specialized or less directly relevant to one's daily life. The "attentive public" for science and technology – that is, the portion of the population interested in, and knowledgeable about, science and technology issues – provides a potential base for informed support and criticism of regime policy.[2] In this chapter, we shall identify the

The author expresses her thanks to Robert Pearson, Janet Schwartz, and Susan Gross Solomon for their comments on an earlier draft and to Jim Porter, Jim Roberts, and Carol Zeiss for their technical assistance. The preparation of this paper was made possible by a Faculty Summer Research Grant from The American University. The author also acknowledges the support of the Hoover Institution at Stanford University, where she was a National Fellow in 1981–82.

[1] For a review of these studies, see Pion and Lipsey 1981: 303–16.
[2] The concept of the attentive public for science and technology is adapted from Gabriel Almond's model of policy making in *The American People and Foreign Policy* (New York: Harcourt, Brace, 1950), as developed by Miller, Suchner, and Voelker (1980).

attentive public for science and technology among recent Soviet emigrants, and we shall see whether attentiveness is a factor in determining attitudes toward Soviet science, scientists, and science policy.

At first glance, it might appear that the concept of an attentive public is less salient in the Soviet Union than in the United States, since public opinion plays a smaller role in the formation of Kremlin policy. Upon closer study, however, we find that the concept is extremely useful in assessing how broad a base of support the Soviet government has for implementing policies that have already been adopted. No regime operates in a vacuum. The support and criticism of the attentive public, along with the indifference of the nonattentive public, can have a profound impact on the long-term effectiveness of national policies. This chapter is a first step at identifying the extent to which the Soviet population may be attentive to the regime's high profile of science and technology and the degree to which the population may share the regime's proclaimed faith in science and technology to solve social problems.[3]

It is true, as with other studies from the SIP data, that the attentiveness and attitudes of the emigrant sample are not representative of the Soviet public as a whole. In the area of science and technology policy, moreover, we do not have Soviet surveys of public attitudes to serve as comparative reference points. Nonetheless, I feel confident that cross-tabulations of the characteristics of the emigrant population are valid, and the results suggest relationships that may exist also in the USSR. In addition to limitations of the sample, this study is limited further by the fact that the questions used in the Soviet Interview Project are not the same as those used in studies of the American public. Because of this, we cannot measure attentiveness to science and technology in the same way, nor can we establish a direct cor- respondence between American and Soviet perceptions of science and technology issues. However, there will be some comparative commentary in the analysis wherever meaningful comparisons are possible.

Characteristics of the attentive public among Soviet emigrants

Studies of American citizens emphasize the importance of one's educational level in developing attentiveness to organized science.[4] People who are more

---

[3] In their studies of the American public, scholars make a distinction between science and technology. See, for example, LaPorte 1980: 439–48. Different results for each are reported in Miller, Suchner, and Voelker 1980: 93–98, 125–33, and *passim*. This distinction was not made in the Soviet Interview Project.

[4] The concept of "organized science" as used by Miller et al. (1980) refers to the institutional practice of both science and technology. That is the way the term will be used in this chapter.

highly educated tend to be more attentive to science and technology than are those with less education.[5] One would expect similar findings for Soviet citizens. Unless they can see its direct impact on their daily lives, most people perceive scientific and technical information as relatively abstract. Scientists and technicians themselves, however, come into regular contact with the regime's science and technology policies and, presumably, are more attentive to them. In fact, people working in the science and technology sector may try to influence government policies through their institutions of employment. One could hypothesize that as Soviet society becomes more dependent on high-level technology the status of technical specialists will rise and the size of this potentially influential public will continue to expand.

Who has the best chance of receiving higher education and obtaining employment in scientific, technical, or other high-status occupations in the USSR?[6] The single most important factor, based on our analysis of the SIP data and corroborated by other studies,[7] is the social-educational status of the respondent's parents. Family background is an important aspect of social stratification in most countries, but it is particularly salient in the USSR where access to higher education often depends on family connections and place of residence. Children of the Soviet urban intelligentsia, for example, have a better chance of entering a major university than do children of the rural peasantry, not only because the quality of the preuniversity education is better in the larger cities but also because the Soviet urban intelligentsia is in many ways a self-generating elite. Living in an urban environment is also important in the development of one's employment opportunities and in general exposure to scientific and technical information.[8]

Three other factors that may affect the attentiveness of the emigrant population to organized science are religion, age, and gender. Religious practice in the Soviet Union tends to be more prevalent among the peasantry, the less educated, and those living in rural areas. Religion is not necessarily incompatible with science, but American studies have found that those who are less religious are more likely to be attentive to science and technology. This appears to be a characteristic that accompanies high educational attainment and urbanization and thus affects attentiveness to

5 See, for example, Miller, Prewitt, and Pearson 1980: 28–34, 50–53.
6 My analysis of high-status occupations includes people who were coded as leaders, managers, military, high-level engineering technicians, and other professionals. See Linda L. Lubrano, "The Attentive Public for Soviet Science and Technology," SIP Working Paper No. 32, pp. 54–56.
7 See Dobson 1980: 115–37; Yanowitch 1977: 58–133.
8 Almost one-half (48.9 percent) of the emigrants who were interviewed in the SIP came from very large cities (cities with populations of more than one million people). See Lubrano, "Attentive Public," p. 57.

organized science indirectly. In the United States, younger people and males are more interested in, and more knowledgeable about, science and technology. The impact of age is a consequence of rising levels of education for the adult population and the inclusion of recent scientific and technical information in school programs. The impact of gender is a result of differentiation in sex roles from early childhood development through adult life.[9] We shall see if the same is true for the Soviet Union.

The following set of hypotheses summarizes the above discussion and the relationships I expect to find:

> The higher the respondent's level of education, the more attention the respondent gave to science and technology in the USSR.
> The more closely related the respondent's occupation was to the science sector, the more attention the respondent gave to science and technology in the USSR.
> The respondents who are male, younger, and/or less religious were more likely to have been attentive to science and technology in the USSR than were the respondents who are female, older, and/or more religious.

Each hypothesis will be tested through cross-tabulations of background characteristics with responses in the questionnaire's green supplement, which was administered to a random one-third of the SIP General Survey sample and where the maximum number of respondents was 922.

Hypothesis 1
The higher the respondent's level of education, the more attention the respondent gave to science and technology in the USSR.

The attention people give to science and technology, and to other areas of public policy, can be observed in several ways. One method is to look at the respondents' reading habits. Another is to ask the respondents how closely they follow certain types of public issues. Both methods were used in the Soviet Interview Project. These differ from the measures of attentiveness developed by American scholars for surveys on science and technology. The three measures of attentiveness used in surveys of American citizens are: interest in science and technology, knowledge about science and technology,

---

9 For the impact of religion, age, and gender on attentiveness to organized science in the United States, see Miller, Suchner, and Voelker 1980: 185–89, and Miller, Prewitt, and Pearson 1980: 47–59. One variable from the American studies that I have not included in the analysis is the respondents' political activity, which accounted for 6 percent of the variance in attentiveness to organized science in the United States. Miller, Prewitt, and Pearson 1980: 51.

and the acquisition of information on science and technology issues.[10] Although there was no attempt to measure scientific or technical knowledge among Soviet emigrants, there are two variables in the Soviet Interview Project that can serve as partial indicators of interest and information acquisition, respectively, namely, the reading of science fiction and the reading of scientific-technical nonfiction. I shall examine both aspects of the emigrants' reading habits as partial objective measures of attentiveness to science and technology. Then I shall discuss the subjective measure of attentiveness obtained from the respondents' own statements on how closely they followed Soviet scientific achievements.

Soviet emigrants were asked to identify the kinds of nonfiction books they had read during their last normal period in the USSR (LNP).[11] Almost 30 percent said they had read books on science and technology.[12] This was the largest category of nonfiction responses except for books on foreign culture (read by 36.4 percent). Interest in foreign culture may have been linked to the respondents' decisions to emigrate, and they may have read scientific-technical nonfiction in anticipation of new jobs outside the USSR. Respondents were also asked what kinds of fiction they had read during their last normal period in the USSR. Almost 28 percent mentioned science fiction. This is lower than the percentage who had read classical literature, detective stories, and other types of fiction, but it is still a significant proportion. General interest in science fiction is widespread in the Soviet Union, particularly because it is a genre that allows for imaginative fantasies as well as for critical social commentary. If we use the reading of scientific literature (that is, science fiction and/or scientific-technical nonfiction) as an indicator of attentiveness, then 45.3 percent of the sample could be classified as members of the attentive public for Soviet science and technology.[13]

[10] Jon Miller and his colleagues observed "interest" by asking respondents which of 32 headlines they might read about. They observed "knowledge" by asking respondents to answer substantive questions about science and technology. And they observed "acquisition of information" by asking respondents about their reading habits, including the reading of science magazines (Miller, Suchner, and Voelker 1980: 73–118; Miller, Prewitt, and Pearson 1980: 17–45).

[11] The "last normal period" is defined as the five-year period usually preceding the emigrant's application for an exit visa. That is the reference point for SIP questions on Soviet science and technology.

[12] The number of people reading scientific-technical nonfiction may have been higher if technical journals, newspapers, and documents had been included in the response options.

[13] The range in the size of the attentive public in the United States is from 4 percent of the population to 55 percent depending on the level of education (Miller, Prewitt, and Pearson 1980: v). Almost 45 percent of the emigrants in the Soviet Interview Project are highly educated, which probably helps to account for the relatively large size of the attentive public in this study.

In testing hypothesis 1, I expected to find that the more highly educated respondents would be more likely to read scientific literature. This was true when the two types of literature were combined (see columns 1 and 4 in Table 5.1). I then separated respondents who read *only* science fiction from those who read *only* scientific-technical nonfiction. Whereas the latter remained correlated with higher levels of education, the former were distributed more evenly throughout the subsample. Compare, for example, the 19.2 percent of emigrants with seven or eight years of general education who had read science fiction to the 19.7 percent of those with some higher education who had read science fiction. This further substantiated the general popularity of science fiction, as distinct from the desire of the more educated emigrants to read scientific-technical nonfiction in connection with their jobs. The emigrant's specialty in school was also highly significant in influencing reading preferences. Respondents who had studied medicine or the natural sciences, for example, were the most likely to read scientific-technical nonfiction, whereas engineering graduates were most likely to read science fiction.[14]

If the more educated members of the sample were most likely to read scientific literature, were they also most likely to follow Soviet scientific achievements? Are these the people whom we could identify as the "attentive public" for science and technology? Based on the subjective indicator of attentiveness, 32.8 percent of the emigrants (who answered the green supplement) were attentive, and approximately two-thirds were nonattentive. (For the full frequency distribution, see the column totals in Table 5.2.) When asked how closely they had followed Soviet scientific achievements and programs, those who had completed higher education were more likely to answer "very closely" or "fairly closely," whereas those with less than four years of school were more likely to answer "not at all." Hypothesis 1 is therefore true.

Education does not guarantee a high degree of attentiveness to organized science, however. A majority (53.4 percent) of those who had completed higher education said either that they did not follow science very closely or that they did not follow science at all. In a rough comparison to the attentiveness of the American public, the SIP sample appeared to be more attentive to science and technology at all educational levels except the highest. Without similar measures of attentiveness, of course, an exact

---

[14] The chi-squares are statistically significant at the 0.00015 level for the correlation between education and science fiction, at the 0.00005 level for the correlations between education/education specialty and scientific-technical nonfiction, and at the 0.0213 level for correlations between education specialty and science fiction.

Table 5.1. *Respondents' education and reading scientific literature*

	Read neither scifi/ST	Read only scifi	Read only scitech	Read both scifi/ST	Row total
Less than 4 yrs. gen. educ.	9^a				9
	100.0^b				1.0^c
	1.8^d				
4–6 yrs. gen. educ.	35	2	1		38
	92.1	5.3	2.6		4.2
	7.0	1.4	0.6		
Either 7–8 yrs. gen. educ. or 1 yr. trade sch.	39.0	10	3		52
	75.0	19.2	5.8		5.7
	7.8	7.2	1.9		
More than 8 yrs. gen. educ. or 1 yr. spec. sec.	15	2	1	1	19
	78.9	10.5	5.3	5.3	2.1
	3.0	1.4	0.6	0.9	
Either 2 yrs. trade sch. (diploma) or 3 yrs. (no diploma)	3	1		1	5
	60.0	20.0		20.0	0.6
	0.6	0.7		0.9	
Sec. sch. diploma w/wo 2 yrs. trade/ 1 yr. spec. sec.	112	31	11	10	164
	68.3	18.9	6.7	6.1	18.1
	22.5	22.5	7.0	8.6	
Comp. spec. sec. sch.	129	29	32	25	215
	60.0	13.5	14.9	11.6	23.7
	26.0	21.0	20.4	21.6	
Higher educ. w/o degree	31	14	15	11	71
	43.7	19.7	21.1	15.5	7.8
	6.2	10.1	9.6	9.5	
Comp. higher educ. or grad. study	124	49	94	68	335
	37.0	14.6	28.1	20.3	36.9
	24.9	35.5	59.9	58.6	
Column total	497	138	157	116	908^e
	54.7^f	15.2	17.3	12.8	100.0

Note: Chi-square = 136.12359; D.F. = 24; sig. = 0.00. Given the distribution of the sample along the marginals (see row and column totals), the reader should look at the relative proportion of each row total that falls in each column. For example, compare the 37 percent of the people with a complete higher education who read neither science fiction nor scientific-technical nonfiction and the 20.3 percent who read both to the 78.9 percent of the people with one year of secondary school who read neither and the 5.3 percent who read both. (This applies to other tables as well.)
[a] N (number of respondents with less than four years of general education who read neither science fiction nor scientific-technical nonfiction).
[b] Percentage of the total number of respondents in that row who read neither science fiction nor scientific-technical nonfiction.

Notes to Table 5.1. (*contd.*)

[c] The row total (9) is 1.0 percent of total N (908).
[d] Percentage of the total number of respondents in that column with less than four years of general education.
[e] Total N (number of people who responded to questions about reading scientific literature).
[f] The column total (497) is 54.7 percent of total N (908).

comparison cannot be made.[15] Again, the respondent's educational specialty was just as important as the general level of education. Those who had studied the natural sciences claimed to have been more attentive to Soviet scientific achievements than did those who had studied other subjects.[16]

> *Hypothesis 2*
> The more closely related the respondent's occupation was to the science sector, the more attention the respondent gave to science and technology in the USSR.

I expected to find that the people who worked in scientific-technical occupations (that is, those who worked in the science sector of the economy and those who had scientific or engineering technical occupations) would be the ones most likely to follow scientific events closely. The difficulty in testing this hypothesis is that most branches of the economy, broadly defined, are related in one way or another to science and technology. Also, initial occupational categories for the SIP general sample were defined so broadly that scientists were coded into the same professional category as artists and government planners. To get a finer distinction, I decided to focus on people with occupations in the science sector by identifying a group of respondents who met at least one of two criteria: (1) employment in establishments conducting scientific research work, and (2) employment as scientific workers, including science teachers and administrators in institutions of higher education (*vysshie uchebnye zavedeniia*, or VUZy). The number of

[15] Among those who had less than a secondary school education in the USSR or less than a high school education in the United States, 16.4 percent or 4 percent, respectively, are attentive to organized science. Among those who completed Soviet secondary school or American high school, the difference is 25.5 percent to 12.0 percent, respectively. Among those with some higher education in the USSR or some college in the United States, the difference is 34.7 percent to 28 percent, respectively. But among those who completed higher education or had advanced graduate training in each country, the proportion of attentives is 46.6 percent for the Soviet Union and 47.9 percent for the United States. (American figures are adapted from Miller, Prewitt, and Pearson 1980: 46.)

[16] The distribution of responses for respondents who had studied the natural sciences was: very closely, 32.3 percent; fairly closely, 32.3 percent; not too closely, 22.6 percent; not at all, 12.9 percent ($N = 31$, with the chi-square statistically significant at the 0.00005 level).

Table 5.2. *Respondents' education and following scientific achievements*

	Followed very closely	Followed fairly closely	Followed not too closely	Followed not at all	Row total
Less than 4 yrs. gen. educ.			1[a] 12.5[b] 0.2[d]	7 87.5 3.3	8 0.9[c]
4–6 yrs. gen. educ.	1 2.6 1.5	3 7.7 1.3	11 28.2 2.7	24 61.5 11.3	39 4.3
Either 7–8 yrs. gen. educ. or 1 yr. trade sch.	5 10.0 7.5	4 8.0 1.7	16 32.0 4.0	25 50.0 11.8	50 5.5
More than 8 yrs. gen. educ. or 1 yr. spec. sec.	1 5.3 1.5	4 21.1 1.7	5 26.3 1.2	9 47.4 4.2	19 2.1
Either 2 yrs. trade sch. (diploma) or 3 yrs. (no diploma)	1 16.7 1.5	1 16.7 0.4	1 16.7 0.2	3 50.0 1.4	6 0.7
Sec. sch. diploma w/ wo 2 yrs. trade/ 1 yr. spec. sec.	12 7.3 17.9	31 18.8 13.3	67 40.6 16.7	55 33.3 25.9	165 18.1
Comp. spec. sec. sch.	7 3.3 10.4	47 21.9 20.2	118 54.9 29.4	43 20.0 20.3	215 23.5
Higher educ. w/o degree	5 6.9 7.5	20 27.8 8.6	36 50.0 9.0	11 15.3 5.2	72 7.9
Comp. higher educ. or grad. study	35 10.3 52.2	123 36.3 52.8	146 43.1 36.4	35 10.3 16.5	339 37.1
Column total	67 7.3[f]	233 25.5	401 43.9	212 23.2	913[e] 100.0

Note: Chi. square = 155. 30746; D. F. = 24; 519. = 0.00.

[a] N (number of respondents with less than four years of general education who did not follow scientific achievements too closely).

[b] Percentage of the total number of respondents in that row who did not follow scientific achievements too closely.

[c] The row total (8) is 0.9 percent of total N (915).

[d] Percentage of the total number of respondents in that column with less than four years of general education.

[e] Total N (number of people who responded to questions about following scientific achievements).

[f] The column total (67) is 7.3 percent of total N (915).

Table 5.3. *Scientists and reading scientific literature*

	Read neither scifi/ST	Read only scifi	Read only scitech	Read both scifi/ST	Row total
Scientists	28[a]	14	33	23	98
	28.6[b]	14.3	33.7	23.5	10.8[c]
	5.6[d]	10.1	21.0	19.8	
Nonscientists	469	124	124	93	810
	57.9	15.3	15.3	11.5	89.2
	94.4	89.9	79.0	80.2	
Column total	497	138	157	116	908[e]
	54.7[f]	15.2	17.3	12.8	100.0

Note: Chi-square = 40.68636; D. F. = 3; sig. = 0.00.
[a] N (number of scientists who read neither science fiction nor scientific-technical nonfiction).
[b] Percentage of the total number of respondents in that row who read neither science fiction nor scientific-technical nonfiction.
[c] The row total (98) is 10.8 percent of total N (908).
[d] Percentage of the total number of respondents in that column who were scientists.
[e] Total N (number of people who responded to questions about reading scientific literature).
[f] The column total (497) is 54.7 percent of total N (908).

respondents who met these criteria was 299, or 10.7 percent of the SIP general sample. One hundred of these were also in the sample that answered the green supplement.

Characteristics of Soviet emigrant scientists resembled those of the attentive general public in several ways. Most of the scientists came from families where the fathers were highly educated and in professional occupations. Their parents were usually not religious, and neither were they. Scientists were significantly more likely to live or work in an urban area than were nonscientists. A majority of the scientists were male, and most of them (72.9 percent) were between the ages of 33 and 52. When the reading habits of scientists were compared to those of nonscientists, I found, as expected, that the former were significantly more likely to read scientific-technical nonfiction. They were less likely, however, to read science fiction (see Table 5.3). Turning to the question of how closely the respondents claimed to follow Soviet scientific achievements, I found that scientists (especially those who were employed as scientific workers in VUZy) were significantly more attentive than were nonscientists, thus confirming hypothesis 2 (see Table 5.4).

The interpretation of these data varies depending on whether one focuses on the positive or the negative responses. On the positive side, the SIP

Table 5.4. *Scientists and following scientific achievements*

	Followed very closely	Followed fairly closely	Followed not too closely	Followed not at all	Row total
Scientists	20[a]	37	30	13	100
	20.0[b]	37.0	30.0	13.0	11.0[c]
	29.9[d]	15.9	7.5	6.1	
Nonscientists	47	196	371	199	813
	5.8	24.1	45.6	24.5	89.0
	70.1	84.1	92.5	93.9	
Column total	67	233	401	212	913[e]
	7.3[f]	25.5	43.9	23.2	100.0

Note: Chi-square = 40.33880; D.F. = 3; sig. = 0.00.
[a] N (number of scientists who followed scientific achievements very closely).
[b] Percentage of the total number of respondents in that row who followed scientific achievements very closely.
[c] The row total (100) is 11.0 percent of total N (913).
[d] Percentage of the total number of respondents in that column who were scientists.
[e] Total N (number of people who responded to questions about following scientific achievements).
[f] The column total (67) is 7.3 percent of total N (913).

sample is more attentive to organized science than are American citizens. Focusing on the negative, one could ask why more than two-thirds of the respondents reportedly devoted so little attention to Soviet scientific achievements. Even among scientists, 43 percent said that they did not follow scientific achievements very closely or did not follow them at all. Do the negative responses to this question mean that there was little interest in science, or little interest in Soviet achievements and programs? Were Soviet scientific achievements seen as indications of scientific progress per se or as measures of Soviet prestige and power? The real import of this question can be understood only in comparison with questions on how closely the respondents followed other types of Soviet achievements and programs. Unfortunately, comparable questions were not included in the SIP survey.

As an alternative check on the validity of the subjective measure of attentiveness to organized science, I correlated emigrant responses to this question with the reading of scientific literature, where the questions were more straightforward. More than 52 percent of those who followed Soviet scientific achievements very closely read science fiction, and almost 54 percent read scientific-technical nonfiction. By contrast, only 20 percent of those who did not follow Soviet scientific achievements at all read science fiction, and only 11 percent read scientific-technical nonfiction.[17] Moreover, the two variables (reading scientific literature and being attentive to scientific achievements) behaved the same way in relation to other variables. This reinforced my confidence in using the subjective measure of attentiveness to report the results for hypotheses 4 through 9.

> *Hypothesis 3*
> The respondents who are male, younger, and/or less religious were more likely to have been attentive to science and technology in the USSR than were the respondents who are female, older, and/or more religious.

Studies of the American public have shown that men are more attentive than women to science, technology, and other areas of public policy. One might argue that this is the result of the lower educational achievements of women and the low proportion of women in scientific and technical occupations. Indeed, my examination of the SIP data shows that women in the general sample were less likely than men to have completed higher education and to have worked in engineering/technical occupations. To test the impact of gender and age on attentiveness to science and technology, I used them as control variables in other hypotheses, and I also correlated them directly with each of the variables discussed above. Women and older emigrants (especially those over 53 years old) were indeed less likely than men and younger emigrants to read science fiction or scientific-technical nonfiction or to follow Soviet scientific achievements closely, thereby partly confirming hypothesis 3.[18] The gender variable had no significant impact on the direct correlations between the education or occupation variables and the variables of attentiveness to organized science. Those correlations did not remain consistent for all age groups, however. Relationships between the education and occupation variables, on the one hand, and attentiveness to science and technology, on the other, were significant only for the middle and older age groups (especially those 43–57 and 63–72 years old). This suggests that age may be more important than gender as a factor affecting respondents' attentiveness to organized science.

The SIP data reveal, not surprisingly, that religiosity is associated with some of the other variables that result in low attention to science and technology. Indeed, among the emigrants interviewed, there was a greater probability that respondents would be religious if they were older, less educated, in low-status occupations, and/or living in rural areas. By

---

[17] In the correlation between reading scientific literature and following scientific achievements, the chi-square is statistically significant at the 0.00005 level.

[18] For the correlations of gender and age with reading scientific literature and following scientific achievements, the chi-squares are statistically significant from level 0.0024 to level 0.0005.

Table 5.5. *Respondents' religiosity and following scientific achievements*

	Followed very closely or fairly closely	Followed not too closely or not at all	Row total
Religious	69^a	184	253
	27.3^b	72.7	27.9^c
	23.1^d	30.3	
Not religious	230	423	653
	35.2	64.8	72.1
	76.9	69.7	
Column total	299	607	906^e
	33.0^f	67.0	100.0

Note: Chi-square = 5.21148; D.F. = 1; sig. = 0.0224.

[a] N (number of respondents who were religious and who followed scientific achievements very closely or fairly closely).

[b] Percentage of the total number of respondents in that row who followed scientific achievements very closely or fairly closely.

[c] The row total (253) is 27.9 percent of total N (906).

[d] Percentage of the total number of respondents in that column who were religious.

[e] Total N (number of people who responded to questions about religiosity and following scientific achievements).

[f] The column total (299) is 33.0 percent of total N (906).

contrast, students of the natural sciences and respondents who had worked in the science sector (especially engineering/technical personnel) were among the least religious. Proportionately more women believed in God, and more men believed in science. But the nonreligious (including scientists) were more apt to say they believed in humanity rather than in science, as an alternative to a belief in God.[19] As in the United States, religious people were less attentive to science and technology than were the nonreligious, thus confirming the rest of hypothesis 3 (see Table 5.5). When controlled for other variables, however, religion appeared to be less significant than gender in affecting the respondent's attentiveness to organized science.

Thus far, the study demonstrates that variables that are salient for the development of attentiveness among American citizens are important also for the SIP sample. I have not done a multivariate analysis of the SIP data to

[19] Thirty percent of the scientists said they believed in a suprahuman power, 30.7 percent said they believed in humanity, 13.1 percent said they believed in science, and 9 percent said they believed in God.

compare the relative importance of each variable in the formation of attentiveness. At this stage of analysis, however, it is clear that education, family background, urban living, occupation, age, gender, and religiosity each play a role in the identification of an attentive public for science and technology in both countries. Moreover, the relationship of each variable to attentiveness is similar in the American studies and the Soviet Interview Project. The more attentive are those who had higher education, those who worked in professional and technical occupations, and those who are male, younger, and less religious. Having identified the characteristics of those who were most attentive to science and technology in the USSR, let us now examine the attentive public's attitudes toward science, scientists, and science policy.

Attitudes toward science and technology

American scholarship on public attitudes toward science and technology suggests that the people who are more informed about and more interested in science are generally those who strongly support scientific programs and the traditional values of scientific research. This is also the case for those who work close to the science sector of the economy. Scientists tend to be more sympathetic toward the funding of projects that contribute directly to their own work and to the protection of values such as the freedom of scientific inquiry. An informed assessment of science and technology often extends to a broad appreciation of the impact of science and technology on society as a whole. One might expect, therefore, that scientists and the attentive public would be highly confident in the capacity of science and technology to solve social problems. At the same time, however, we could argue that the closer one is to the scientific enterprise, the more one sees its shortcomings, its problems, and its pockets of corruption. The lofty image that scientists and scientific institutions project to the general public may seem tarnished to those who experience them directly.

In this section I test six hypotheses regarding the attitudes of SIP respondents toward science and technology, with attentiveness to organized science as the key independent variable. The maximum sample size for each hypothesis (based on responses to the green supplement) is 913.

> *Hypothesis 4*
> The more closely the respondent followed Soviet scientific achievements, the more likely the respondent was to support Soviet funding for exploration in outer space.

In 1957 the world acknowledged the launching of Sputnik as a major accomplishment for Soviet science and technology. By 1965 Soviet investment in science had increased dramatically, and the commitment to the space program continued into the 1970s, albeit at a slower pace. Estimated expenditures for space exploration were approximately 1 to 2 percent of Soviet gross national product (GNP) from 1967 to 1980.[20] Using support for the space program in the 1970s as an indication of support for Soviet science and technology, SIP interviewers asked the respondents whether they thought the Soviet Union was spending too much, too little, or about the right amount of money on space exploration, along with several other areas of public policy.[21]

General public support for Soviet space exploration was very low compared with support for other program areas.[22] More than 67 percent of the respondents thought that the government was spending too much money on space. The only two areas where a greater percentage of respondents thought that the Soviet Union was spending too much money were defense (79.3 percent) and aid to Eastern Europe (72.9 percent). Indeed, emigrants may have viewed the space program as a component of Soviet military research and foreign policy. The preference for a reduction of expenditures on the space program was evident among all respondents regardless of how closely they followed Soviet scientific achievements. The difference between the attentive public and the nonattentive public is not statistically significant on this issue. Hypothesis 4 is therefore false (see Table 5.6).

Hypothesis 5
The more closely the respondent followed Soviet scientific achievements, the more likely the respondent was to believe that scientific leaders were honest.

Was the low public support for space exploration indicative of public distrust of scientists and scientific institutions? To test whether the public viewed scientific leaders as basically honest or dishonest, respondents were asked about scientists in the USSR Academy of Sciences. For comparative purposes they were also asked about the leaders of other institutions in the USSR. The Academy remains a highly prestigious establishment, and this was clearly reflected in the emigrants' assessments. Almost 26 percent of all respondents in the general sample ($N = 2,793$) said that "most" or "almost all" Academy leaders were honest, a higher percentage than for the leaders of any institution other than the military, which was 27.3 percent. More

[20] From 1955 to 1965 the Soviet science budget grew more than fivefold. For an estimate of space expenditures, see U.S., Congress, Senate, *Soviet Space Programs: 1976–80*, pt. 1, 97th Cong., 2d sess., 1982, pp. 334–35, and earlier reports for 1966–70 and 1971–75.
[21] The other areas were health, defense, agriculture, foreign aid (to Eastern Europe), crime, and education.
[22] Public support for exploration in outer space has also been very low in the United States. See Miller, Prewitt, and Pearson 1980: 84–96.

Table 5.6. *Attentiveness and support for the space program*

	Amount spent on space program			
	Right	Too little	Too much	Row total
Followed sci. achievements				
Very closely	13[a]	3	47	63
	20.6[b]	4.8	74.6	7.7[c]
	7.6[d]	21.4	7.5	
Fairly closely	47	5	169	221
	21.3	2.3	76.5	27.2
	27.3	35.7	27.0	
Not too closely	84	5	279	368
	22.8	1.4	75.8	45.3
	48.8	35.7	44.5	
Not at all	28	1	132	161
	17.4	0.6	82.0	19.8
	16.3	7.1	21.1	
Column total	172	14	627	813[e]
	21.2[f]	1.7	77.1	100.0

Note: Chi-square = 7.38364; D.F. = 6; sig. = 0.2868.

[a] N (number of respondents who followed scientific achievements very closely and said that the right amount was being spent on the space program).

[b] Percentage of the total number of respondents in that row who said that the right amount was being spent on the space program.

[c] The row total (63) is 7.7 percent of total N (813).

[d] Percentage of the total number of respondents in that column who followed scientific achievements very closely.

[e] Total N (number of people who responded to questions about following scientific achievements and support for the space program).

[f] The column total (172) is 21.0 percent of total N (813).

than 33 percent said that "some" Academy leaders were honest, and only 13.6 percent said that "none" or "hardly any" were honest, a lower percentage than for the leaders of any other institution. Although a favorable view of the Academy was widespread, respondent perceptions of honesty in the Academy leadership were expressed more frequently by the attentive public than by the nonattentives, thus substantiating hypothesis 5 (see Table 5.7). As expected, scientists were more likely than nonscientists to view Academy leaders as honest. But they did not have as much confidence in the Academy's competency, as we shall see.

Table 5.7. *Attentiveness and the honesty of scientific leaders*

	Leaders considered honest					
	None	Hardly any	Some	Most	Almost all	Row total
Followed sci. achievements						
Very closely	5[a]	5	28	9	4	51
	9.8[b]	9.8	54.9	17.6	7.8	7.6[c]
	7.9[d]	8.9	8.3	5.9	6.1	
Fairly closely	9	17	99	49	15	189
	4.8	9.0	52.4	25.9	7.9	28.1
	14.3	30.4	29.5	32.2	22.7	
Not too closely	31	27	162	72	22	314
	9.9	8.6	51.6	22.9	7.0	46.7
	49.2	48.2	48.2	47.4	33.3	
Not at all	18	7	47	22	25	119
	15.1	5.9	39.5	18.5	21.0	17.7
	28.6	12.5	14.0	14.5	37.9	
Column total	63	56	336	152	66	673[e]
	9.4[f]	8.3	49.9	22.6	9.8	100.0

Note: Chi-square = 33.95751; D.F. = 12; sig. = 0.0007.

[a] N (number of respondents who followed scientific achievements very closely and said that none of the scientific leaders were honest).

[b] Percentage of the total number of respondents in that row who said that none of the scientific leaders were honest.

[c] The row total (51) is 7.6 percent of total N (673).

[d] Percentage of the total number of respondents in that column who followed scientific achievements very closely.

[e] Total N (number of people who responded to questions about following scientific achievements and the honesty of scientific leaders).

[f] The column total (63) is 9.4 percent of total N (673).

Hypothesis 6

The more closely the respondent followed Soviet scientific achievements, the more likely the respondent was to believe that scientific leaders were competent.

Soviet emigrants were asked about the competency of Academy leaders in comparison with leaders of other institutions. Again, the public's view of the Academy was a very positive one. The proportion of respondents in the general sample who said that Academy leaders were incompetent (2.4 percent) was smaller than for leaders of any other institution. "Most" or "almost all" military and Academy leaders were viewed as competent by the

Table 5.8. *Attentiveness and the competency of scientific leaders*

	Leaders considered competent					
	None	Hardly any	Some	Most	Almost all	Row total
Followed sci. achievements						
Very closely			16^a	25	11	52
			30.8^b	48.1	21.2	7.7^c
			8.0^d	8.0	7.5	
Fairly closely	2	1	59	90	41	193
	1.0	0.5	30.6	46.6	21.2	28.6
	18.2	16.7	29.4	28.9	27.9	
Not too closely	5	4	91	148	63	311
	1.6	1.3	29.3	47.6	20.3	46.0
	45.5	66.7	45.3	47.6	42.9	
Not at all	4	1	35	48	32	120
	3.3	0.8	29.2	40.0	26.7	17.8
	36.4	16.7	17.4	15.4	21.8	
Column total	11	6	201	311	147	676^e
	1.6^f	0.9	29.7	46.0	21.7	100.0

Note: Chi-square = 7.68627; D.F. = 12; sig. = 0.8091.

[a] N (number of respondents who followed scientific achievements very closely and said that some scientific leaders were competent).

[b] Percentage of the total number of respondents in that row who said that some scientific leaders were competent.

[c] The row total (52) is 7.7 percent of total N (676).

[d] Percentage of the total number of respondents in that column who followed scientific achievements very closely.

[e] Total N (number of people who responded to questions about following scientific achievements and the competency of scientific leaders).

[f] The column total (11) is 1.6 percent of total N (676).

largest proportion of respondents, that is, by 50.2 percent and by 49.2 percent, respectively. Generally, the public viewed the leaders of all Soviet institutions as more competent than honest. Public perception of Academy competence did not seem to vary with one's attentiveness to scientific achievements, however, and hypothesis 6 was found to be false. Between 40 and 48.1 percent of the respondents said that "most" Academy leaders were competent. The rest were divided fairly evenly between the views that "some" or "almost all" Academy leaders were competent (see Table 5.8). Although in general agreement with the rest of the respondents, scientists tended to be more skeptical about the Academy's competency. Only 15.1

percent of the scientists thought that "almost all" Academy leaders were competent, compared with 23.4 percent of the nonscientists who thought so.

Hypothesis 7

The more closely the respondent followed Soviet scientific achievements, the more likely the respondent was to support the relative importance of fundamental over applied research.

Respondents were asked if during their last normal period in the USSR they thought it was more important for scientists to create new ideas and theories or to solve practical problems. The people who were most attentive to organized science said that fundamental research was more important. Almost 37 percent of them preferred the creation of new ideas, compared with 30 percent who preferred the solution of practical problems. All other respondents said that applied research was more important, by an increasingly greater margin for the less attentive. Among those who followed scientific achievements fairly closely, there was only a small difference in the proportion who preferred applied over basic research (36.5 percent compared to 36.0 percent). Among those who did not follow scientific achievements very closely, there was a somewhat larger difference (40.7 percent compared to 37.7 percent); but for those who did not follow scientific achievements at all, the difference was almost 17 percent (51.5 percent compared to 34.6 percent) (see Table 5.9). Hypothesis 7 is obviously true.

A separate cross-tabulation reveals that scientists were the most likely to support both kinds of activities (36.1 percent of scientists, compared to 26.4 percent of the attentive public and 18.2 percent of the nonattentive public). A similar decline in the relative support for both basic and applied research can be seen in Table 5.9 (from 32.3 percent of the most attentive to 13.8 percent of the nonattentive). Attentiveness and employment in the science sector, therefore, are important factors in providing public support for balanced government programs in basic and applied research.

Hypothesis 8

The more closely the respondent followed Soviet scientific achievements, the more likely the respondent was to value the freedom of scientific inquiry.

To see whether respondents supported freedom of scientific inquiry, they were asked to comment on the placement of restrictions on scientific research. Should scientists be permitted to study whatever they want (even if they sometimes discover things that might be harmful), or should there be restrictions on their research? Support for the principle of scientific freedom was widespread regardless of whether the respondent was generally attentive or nonattentive to science (see Table 5.10). Support for freedom of scientific research was even higher among emigrant scientists (75 percent

Table 5.9. *Attentiveness and support for fundamental research*

	Research considered most important			Row total
	Fundamental	Applied	Both	
Followed sci. achievements				
Very closely	24[a]	20	21	65
	36.9[b]	30.8	32.3	8.4[c]
	8.4[d]	6.3	11.8	
Fairly closely	80	81	61	222
	36.0	36.5	27.5	28.5
	28.1	25.7	34.3	
Not too closely	136	147	78	361
	37.7	40.7	21.6	46.4
	47.7	46.7	43.8	
Not at all	45	67	18	130
	34.6	51.5	13.8	16.7
	15.8	21.3	10.1	
Column total	285	315	178	778[e]
	36.6[f]	40.5	22.9	100.0

Note: Chi-square = 16.06310; D.F. = 6; sig. = 0.0134.

[a] N (number of respondents who followed scientific achievements very closely and said that fundamental research was most important).

[b] Percentage of the total number of respondents in that row who said that fundamental research was most important.

[c] The row total (65) is 8.4 percent of total N (778).

[d] Percentage of the total number of respondents in that column who followed scientific achievements very closely.

[e] Total N (number of people who responded to questions about following scientific achievements and support for fundamental research).

[f] The column total (285) is 36.6 percent of total N (778).

of them were opposed to any restrictions on science, compared with 69.5 percent of the nonscientists who opposed restrictions), but this was not statistically significant. Hypothesis 8 appears to be false. However, the survey question may have elicited a response to two different issues – freedom of scientific research, on the one hand, and social risks from science, on the other. The full implications of this question will have to await further analysis.

Hypothesis 9

The more closely the respondent followed Soviet scientific achievements, the more likely the respondent was to believe that science and technology

Table 5.10. *Attentiveness and freedom of scientific research*

	Free research	Restricted research	Row total
Followed sci. achievements			
Very closely	47[a]	18	65
	72.3[b]	27.7	8.1[c]
	8.4[d]	7.5	
Fairly closely	150	67	217
	69.1	30.9	27.1
	26.7	28.0	
Not too closely	266	100	366
	72.7	27.3	45.8
	47.4	41.8	
Not at all	98	54	152
	64.5	35.5	19.0
	17.5	22.6	
Column total	561	239	800[e]
	70.1[f]	29.9	100.0

Note: Chi-square = 3.70703; D.F. = 3; sig. = 0.2949.
[a] N (number of respondents who followed scientific achievements very closely and said that scientific research should be free).
[b] Percentage of the total number of respondents in that row who said that scientific research should be free.
[c] The row total (65) is 8.1 percent of total N (800).
[d] Percentage of the total number of respondents in that column who followed scientific achievements very closely.
[e] Total N (number of people who responded to questions about following scientific achievements and freedom of scientific research).
[f] The column total (561) is 70.1 percent of total N (800).

could solve problems in the areas of agriculture, health, consumer goods, energy, pollution, and crime.

More than 40 percent of the respondents said that the solution of practical problems was more important than theory building. But did they have faith in science and technology to solve problems in areas of social and economic policy? To test hypothesis 9 the emigrants were asked whether they believed (during their last normal periods in the USSR) that Soviet science and technology could eventually solve most of the problems, some of the problems, or none of the problems in several policy areas. The results differed, of course, depending on the area of public policy. The interpretation of these differences is somewhat ambiguous. In some cases, differences may reflect the respondents' perceptions of the relative distances

Table 5.11. *Public confidence in the ability of science and technology to solve problems*

Area of public policy	Most problems	Some problems	No problems	N
Agriculture	9.1	37.9	53.1	795
Health	18.5	67.2	14.4	807
Consumer goods	8.4	37.6	53.9	805
Energy	32.8	60.6	6.7	720
Pollution	17.5	52.7	29.8	766
Crime	14.0	48.6	37.4	771

Note: Table shows percentage of all respondents (N) who answered in each policy area. Each row totals 100 percent.

between science and technology, on the one hand, and the substantive policy areas, on the other. Or, the differences may reflect the respondents' perceptions of how amenable each problem was to any kind of a solution. In other cases, respondents may have been expressing their confidence in the Soviet system, that is, in the ability of the Soviet political leadership to use science and technology in the solution of certain social problems. Therefore, we do not know whether the emigrants were focusing on the research potential of science and technology or on the Soviet system in general. With this in mind, let us review the results.

The people who followed Soviet scientific achievements closely were no more likely than the nonattentives to believe that science and technology could solve the problems in agriculture, health, energy, or crime. There was a statistically significant difference in the correlations for pollution and consumer goods,[23] but the distribution of responses did not clearly correspond to what was stated in the hypothesis. For most policy areas, therefore, hypothesis 9 appears to be false.

The policy areas where respondents expressed the most confidence were health, energy, and pollution. In each case, a majority said that science and technology could solve at least "some" of the problems. The most positive responses were in the area of energy, where 32.8 percent said that science and technology could solve "most" of the problems. At the other extreme, a majority of respondents said that science and technology could solve "none" of the problems in agriculture and consumer goods (53.1 and 53.9 percent, respectively) (see Table 5.11). The most plausible interpretation, at this stage of analysis, is that the emigrants' confidence in science and technology

[23] Chi-squares for the correlations between attentiveness and pollution/consumer goods are statistically significant at the 0.0018 and 0.0745 levels, respectively.

164   **Linda L. Lubrano**

Table 5.12. *Inability of science and technology to solve problems*

Area of public policy	Scientists[a]	Nonscientists[a]		Level of significance[b]
		Attentive	Nonattentive	
Agriculture	64.9	49.8	52.2	0.0637
Health	17.7	10.8	15.4	0.0044
Consumer goods	70.8	50.4	52.2	0.0028
Energy	8.8	5.1	7.0	0.2494
Pollution	40.6	27.3	28.7	0.0640
Crime	46.7	37.7	35.4	0.0922

[a] Percentage of each group who said that science and technology could solve "none" of the problems in that policy area.
[b] The levels at which the chi-squares are statistically significant in cross-tabulations of responses from scientists and nonscientists.

to solve problems depends not so much on their attentiveness to organized science as it does on the perceived distance of science and technology from the problem area. Health, energy, and pollution are closely related to science and technology, whereas crime, agriculture, and consumer goods are usually viewed by the public as areas that are primarily social and economic.

For a better delineation of responses, I created a new variable that separated scientists from other emigrants in their responses to the question on attention to Soviet scientific achievements. Since people who worked in the science sector of the economy or in science occupations were among the most attentive members of the sample, I put them in the top category of attentiveness and combined the four response categories to two for the nonscientists as follows:

Scientists/Attentive Public variable	N
1. Scientists (respondents who worked in the science sector or in science occupations)	100
2. Attentive Public (nonscientists who followed scientific achievements very closely or fairly closely)	243
3. Nonattentive Public (nonscientists who followed scientific achievements not too closely or not at all)	570
Total number of respondents who answered the question on attentiveness to science	913

I then correlated this variable with emigrant responses on the ability of science and technology to solve social and economic problems.

It is significant that scientists were consistently more negative than nonscientists in their responses. In all six areas of public policy, scientists were the most likely to say that "none" of the problems could be solved by science and technology. By contrast, attentive nonscientists were the most optimistic (see Table 5.12). One possible explanation is that attentive nonscientists were people who supported organized science, but they did not know as much about the country's scientific and technical capabilities as the scientists did.

Conclusion

What conclusions can be drawn about the attentive public for Soviet science and technology? Approximately 33 to 45 percent of the SIP respondents (who answered the green supplement) could be considered members of the attentive public, as measured by attention to Soviet scientific achievements or by reading habits, respectively. Many read science fiction and acquired information on organized science by reading scientific-technical nonfiction. Those who were attentive to science and technology, had a more positive image of the honesty of scientific leaders, and they were more likely to support the relative importance of fundamental research. The concept of attentiveness was significant in drawing these distinctions, but it was not very helpful in differentiating respondent attitudes in areas where there was a high degree of consensus.

On the whole, SIP respondents had a positive view of science and scientific leaders. There was widespread support for freedom of scientific inquiry and a prevailing consensus that scientists were competent in their work. Confidence in the enterprise of science and in the professional behavior of scientists apparently did not extend to the Soviet system in general. The different assessments of organized science in contributing to each area of social and economic policy reflected a discriminating but somewhat negative view of the system's ability to utilize its scientific and technical capabilities effectively.

Where there was confidence that Soviet organized science *could* solve some of the problems – for example, in the area of health – there was criticism that the Soviet government was not investing enough resources to do so. In other areas, such as agriculture, respondents were pessimistic about the application of scientific and technical achievements, possibly also because of inadequate government investments.[24] This would be all the more frustrating for those who considered the main task of science to be the solution of practical problems. The pragmatic orientation toward science and tech-

[24] Almost two-thirds of the emigrants said that the Soviet government was spending too little on health and agriculture.

nology, especially among nonscientists, might account for the low priority of the space program. Respondents may have seen the exploration of outer space as frivolous or as a military venture not directly relevant to the daily needs of the average citizen.

Perhaps the most revealing aspect of our study is the negative attitude of Soviet emigrant scientists toward Soviet scientific and technical capabilities. It is true that they were significantly more attentive to organized science than were nonscientists. Fifty-seven percent of the scientists followed scientific achievements closely and 71.5 percent read scientific literature. But there is another side to these statistics. Forty-three percent of the scientists admitted that they had *not* been reading scientific-technical nonfiction and that they had *not* followed scientific achievements closely. This might explain their view that scientists were not as competent as the public believed. Also, scientists may have had higher expectations for the scientific community than did the rest of the public. Their dissatisfaction with the quality of Soviet science and technology may have been tied very closely to their disaffection with the Soviet Union and the decision to emigrate.

The attentive public identified in this study was once part of a larger public attentive to science and technology in the USSR. Although we have no comparable statistics on the proportion of the Soviet population that follows scientific achievements closely, we would probably find that the characteristics of the Soviet attentive public would be similar to the characteristics discussed here. Both on a theoretical and on an empirical level, one could argue that education, occupation, age, gender, and religiosity are important factors in the development of attentiveness to organized science in the USSR. Clearly, it is problematic to speculate about whether the Soviet attentive public shares the attitudes of the emigrant attentives toward science, scientists, and science policy. Similarly, one could question whether Soviet scientists would agree with the scientists who emigrated in their assessments of Soviet scientific and technical capabilities. Nonetheless, the above data suggest issues that could be explored in further research on Soviet science and society.

First, it appears that regime messages about the importance and high quality of science and technology are being received favorably, at least among educated and urban elements of the Soviet population. The regime has been highly successful in promoting positive images of organized science, even among those who are generally not very attentive to science and technology. However, the government's advocacy of a strong system of science has also raised citizen awareness of scientists' needs and capabilities. In some ways public support for the principles of science appears to be stronger than public support for government policies. Negative perceptions of Soviet scientific and technical capabilities probably mean, therefore, that there is low confidence in the Soviet system rather than in science per se.

Second, the regime has fostered expectations that science and technology must be utilized in the solution of social and economic problems. The criterion of success in Soviet science, at least since the days of Stalin, has been *praktika*, namely, the practical implementation of the results of scientific research. The strong sense of utilitarianism, where performance is valued above rhetoric, contributes further to the erosion of public confidence in regime policies, among both attentives and nonattentives. In the area of science and technology, therefore, it appears that the Soviet regime may be a victim of its own campaign to promote the high prestige and practical consequences of organized science.

Finally, the above findings on the attentive public for Soviet science and technology will acquire greater theoretical significance it they are related to future analyses of attentiveness in other policy areas. In the present study, the concept of attentiveness did not provide a high degree of differentiation in responses to questions on Soviet science policy. Is this consensus of public views unique to science and technology, or is there consensus between attentives and nonattentives in other areas as well? At the same time, the above data reveal a differentiation in emigrant assessments of science and science policy, which may be extended to other policy areas. Do Soviet citizens generally make a distinction, for example, between their support for professional elites and their skepticism about the contribution of those elites to the solution of social problems? Does this reflect a serious discrepancy between the high prestige of institutions and low public confidence in system performance? Such questions remind us that the issue of attentiveness to science and technology is not an isolated one but is part of a broad range of issues that characterize the citizen's relationship to public policy.

References

Dobson, Richard. 1980. "Education and Opportunity." In *Contemporary Soviet Society*, ed. Jerry Pankhurst and Michael Paul Sacks. New York: Praeger.

La Porte, T.R. 1980. "Indicators of Public Attitudes toward Science and Technology," *Scientometrics*, 2: 439–48.

Miller, Jon, Kenneth Prewitt, and Robert Pearson. 1980. *The Attitudes of the U.S. Public toward Science and Technology*. Chicago: National Opinion Research Center/University of Chicago.

Miller, Jon, Robert Suchner, and Alan Voelker. 1980. *Citizenship in an Age of Science*. New York: Pergamon Press.

Pion, Georgine, and Mark Lipsey. 1981. "Public Attitudes toward Science and

Technology: What Have the Surveys Told Us?" *Public Opinion Quarterly*, 45: 303–16.

Yanowitch, Murray. 1977. *Social and Economic Inequality in the Soviet Union*. New York: Sharpe.

PART III

Work: economic/demographic trends

Inequality of earnings, household income, and wealth in the Soviet Union in the 1970s

AARON VINOKUR and GUR OFER

Introduction

At least in the popular mind, socialism is associated with economic equality. The issue of whether or not incomes on the Soviet Union and the other members of the "socialist" bloc are distributed in a more equal fashion than in the mixed economies of the West has, therefore, been addressed by students in both the East and the West.

The scarcity of relevant data published in the Soviet Union adds to the many natural and methodological problems that any attempt at international comparison of equality must face. Raw data are completely unavailable to Western scholars, and whatever is published in Soviet scientific work is usually restricted to a very few measures of dispersion, mostly the decile ratio, and both the methodology and information about the nature of the samples that have been studied are at best obscure. As it is quite clear that Soviet authorities possess that necessary information, withholding it from the public eye must be attributed to the embarrassment that publication would cause. The source of such embarrassment is not entirely clear. Peter Wiles suggests that the main problem is that income in the Soviet Union is distributed less equally than in other East European countries (1974: 1–2), but one cannot exclude internal considerations or embarrassment on the basis of international, East–West comparisons.

Given the problem of data and the ideological sensitivity of the issue, it is no wonder that views on Soviet income inequality are open to dispute. Soviet scholars almost in one voice claim that both wage and income distributions in the Soviet Union are much more equal than in the "capitalist" world and that historical wage and income gaps in the Soviet Union are diminishing as

Analysis based on the Soviet Interview Project data was done with the unrestricted help, attention, and excellent hard work of Pamela J. Hohn, Mary A. Cummings, and Chong-Ook Rhee. Matilda Frankel provided very useful editorial advice. We would like to acknowledge their assistance warmly. The present version of this paper benefited from many useful comments offered by Janet G. Chapman, Abram Bergson, Joseph Berliner, and Gertrude Schroeder.

Soviet society becomes more homogeneous in all aspects of social life. Soviet studies demonstrating a rather marked decline in the size distribution of wages since 1947 are better documented and more convincing than those related to household incomes. As wages constitute the lion's share of incomes in the Soviet Union, however, it is reasonable to assume that incomes followed the same trend. As regards inequality trends for the seventies, and even the sixties, there seems to be some dispute even among Soviet scholars. According to the well-informed Soviet economist V. F. Maier (writing in 1977), for example, "analysis of data that relate to the last 15–20 years shows that differentiation of incomes has not changed. And this conclusion is relevant not only for the total population, but also for the two main social groups, especially for kolkhozniks" (1977: 51). In 1979, however, the comparably well-informed Soviet scholars L. A. Migranova and N. E. Rabkina published a different conclusion. They claimed that income inequality measured by decile ratios and relating to per capita income for the entire Soviet population did decline over the "last 15–20 years, from 4.4 to 3.3" (1979: 106).

With respect to the more central question of comparison with the West, there are some Western scholars who support the Soviet claim of higher equality. J. Cromwell concluded in a recent paper that, in comparative perspective, "socialism as carried out in Eastern Europe has resulted in a true 'income revolution'" (1977: 305). If we accept the estimates presented by Alastair McAuley's very careful study (1979), which was based on Soviet data, we must reach a similar conclusion, though somewhat less enthusiastically phrased. An extreme formulation of just the opposite conclusion is Christian Morrison's: "Czechoslovakia excepted, Eastern European countries do not have a more egalitarian income distribution. Admittedly, Czechoslovakia is the most egalitarian of all the countries, but all the other East European countries belong in the same range of income distribution as the most advanced of the Western countries" (1984: 126–27). Abram Bergson came to the same conclusion regarding the size distribution of wages: "What emerges is a rather striking similarity in inequality between … the USSR and Western countries. Inequality in the USSR fluctuates in the course of time, but only rarely does any particular percentile ratio fall outside the range delineated by corresponding measures for Western countries" (1984: 1065). On the comparison of income distribution, however, Bergson is a little more cautious in asserting similarities (pp. 1072–73). The careful studies by Wiles and Morkowski (1971, 1972), Wiles (1974), Pryor (1973), and Chapman (1977b, 1979, 1983), all based on Soviet data, reach conclusions not far from Bergson's.

The opportunity to study questions of economic life in the Soviet Union independently was opened with the wave of emigration from the Soviet

Union beginning in the late sixties. The first full-fledged family budget survey (ISIP) was conducted in the West with a sample of 1,250 families who emigrated from the Soviet Union to Israel during the mid-1970s. In this survey, respondents reported retrospectively on their lives in the Soviet Union during the last "normal" year there; this is the last year before their lives started to be affected by the decision to emigrate. For most families this turned out to be 1972, 1973, or 1974 in about equal proportions. Therefore, 1973 was considered as the reference year for most comparisons with Soviet data.

The second independent source of information is the Soviet Interview Project (SIP). In this project, 2,793 individuals who emigrated from the Soviet Union to the United States during the late 1970s and the early 1980s were interviewed. In this survey respondents also reported retrospectively on their lives in the Soviet Union during the last normal period (LNP). In the framework of SIP, 1979 was considered as the last normal year and the reference year for most comparisons with Soviet data.

Many similarities and differences exist between ISIP and SIP. The Israeli project dealt only with the economics of Soviet urban households and was, therefore, properly termed a family budget survey. The U.S. research project, on the other hand, is interdisciplinary, and questions related to the family budget compose only a small part of the total questionnaire. From the outset of SIP, however, the intention has been to compare the results of the two surveys. Consequently, basic questions about personal wages and household income were included in the SIP questionnaire, and where possible, exactly in the form of the ISIP survey.

The surveys have similar problems. All respondents in the Israeli sample and the vast majority in the SIP sample are Jews who came to the West from various urban areas of the Soviet Union. The socioeconomic and demographic structures of both samples are, therefore, different from the comparable structures of the Soviet urban population. Both original samples have similar ethnic, emigrational, and structural biases. As is discussed elsewhere in this volume, it is impossible to eliminate the first two biases. They can only be minimized. Structural bias can, however, be overcome by reconstructing the original sample to match the referent population.

With all these considerations in mind, the main goals of this chapter are: first, to describe the empirical base of the SIP General Survey; second, to analyze the degree of inequality of personal wages, household income, and wealth in the Soviet Union in 1979, as revealed by the SIP data; third, to compare the principal results of the ISIP and SIP surveys. The comparison is badly needed for many reasons. One of them is to check the "credibility" of both designs as valid and important sources of information on Soviet inequality. The second reason is to trace changes in wage, income, and wealth inequality that have occurred in the Soviet Union during the last decade.

The fourth goal is to compare the results of the two surveys with patterns of wage, income, and wealth inequality that are typical for Western countries. With the help of this comparison, a third Soviet claim may be tested, namely, that wages, household income, and wealth in Soviet "socialist" society are more equally distributed than in Western "capitalist" countries and that the gap between the two socioeconomic systems is so wide that it is possible in comparative perspective to define what has happened in the Soviet Union as an "income revolution."

The methodology developed by ISIP has been used systematically in calculations and comparative analyses of the "raw" data of both surveys. Some changes were introduced specifically to deal with the SIP sample.

The results presented in this chapter are preliminary and cannot be taken as final. Subsequent analysis may change some of our conclusions.

Inequality of wages

Methodology

For the majority of adult Soviet citizens, work in the public sector is the main source of personal wages and family income. For this reason, the employment status of respondents and their spouses at the end of the last normal period of their lives in the Soviet Union must be determined, and labor-force participation by sex, age, and marital status must be calculated.

Of the 2,793 respondents in the SIP sample, 2,045 (1,027 men and 1,018 women) were employed and received wages in the public sector. This sample is not representative of the employed urban population of the Soviet Union in the late 1970s, for there are discrepancies between the original sample and the referent population (the "active population" of large and medium-sized cities of the Soviet Union). The main differences stem from the educational and occupational structures of the two populations. To match the referent population, the original sample was weighted or reconstructed. In weighting the original sample, only two dimensions were used: the sex and educational structures of the total active urban population of the Soviet Union in 1979 according to the last Soviet census. We assume that the educational structure of this population is very close to the relevant active population living in the Soviet Union in large and medium-sized cities. The final result is a reconstructed sample of 2,045 respondents that closely approximates the referent population along these two dimensions. All results presented in this paper concerning the size distribution of wages are based on the weighted sample (see the Appendix to this chapter for additional explanation).

Respondents who worked in the end of the LNP were asked to report their gross and net wages at their main place of work in the public sector and at any additional place of work in the public sector. In addition, respondents were asked to report their net income (or wage) from any private work. The responses to these three questions were used to define the following concepts of wages (including salaries):

1. Gross wage at the main place of work in the public sector
2. Gross wage at the second place of work in the public sector
3. Income from private jobs
4. Gross public wage (1 + 2 above)
5. Total wage (1 + 2 + 3 above)

Several measures of inequality of wages were used: coefficient of variation and the Gini coefficient, ratios between earnings at specific percentiles of the distribution (percentile ratios), and distributions of respondents by wage categories and wage deciles. Dispersion measures were chosen to facilitate comparisons with studies on the Soviet Union and on other countries.

Findings: inequality of wages in the Soviet Union

Table 6.1 presents findings on wage dispersion in the Soviet Union for three wage concepts: categories 1, 4, and 5 above. Only 5.3 percent of all employed respondents reported an additional job in the public sector, and, on the average, such jobs added less than four rubles to the average gross wage. For these reasons the impact of extra public work on the distribution of wages is marginal. The discussion will, therefore, concentrate on wages at main place of employment only.

The impact of private wages on both wage levels and distribution is more substantial, however. Of all workers, 263 (12.9 percent) reported private wages. When averaged for all workers, private wages are estimated at 21.2 rubles per month. Tables 6.2 and 6.3 present selected findings on the incidence of private work by sex and occupation and on hourly rates of pay. We shall return to these findings when the distributive impact of private wages is analyzed.

When only public wages are considered (Table 6.1), it is found that the wage gap between the top and bottom two percentiles (P_{98}/P_2) is 5.75 (6.0 for all public wages); it narrows to 4.29 between the corresponding five percentile points (P_{95}/P_5) and becomes 3.33 for the decile ratio (P_{90}/P_{10}). The overall level of inequality as measured by the Gini coefficient stands at 0.244 for wages at main place of work. Only 6.2 percent of all earners make

Table 6.1. *Distribution of gross wages per earner, 1979*

	Wages at main workplace (1)	All wages in public sector (2)	Total wages (public and private) (3)
Mean, rubles per month	150.7	154.5	175.7
Coefficient of variation	0.51	0.54	0.89
Gini coefficient	0.244	0.249	0.304
Ratios between wages at indicated percentiles of distribution			
P_{98}/P_2	5.75	6.00	7.74
P_{95}/P_5	4.29	4.29	5.29
P_{90}/P_{10}	3.33	3.33	3.75
P_{75}/P_{25}	1.80	1.80	1.90
P_{95}/P_{50}	1.87	1.87	2.47
Mean monthly wages in given decile, rubles			
I	67.7	68.0	69.0
II	83.8	84.4	86.2
III	101.1	102.1	104.9
IV	117.1	117.8	120.4
V	128.7	130.2	140.3
VI	147.2	147.9	150.7
VII	155.1	156.8	169.1
VIII	179.1	182.8	199.9
IX	210.1	217.8	261.7
X	312.7	324.0	442.8
X/I	4.62	4.76	6.42

less than 70 rubles per month, and a similar segment of the employed make more than 275 rubles.

Who, in the Soviet Union, belongs to the group of lowest-paid workers, and who belongs to the highest-paid group? According to the SIP results, women compose more than 80 percent of the lowest decile of wage earners, and men 80 percent of the highest decile. In the lowest decile, more than 30 percent are blue-collar workers in the service sectors, 25 percent are employees in positions that require special secondary education (technicians, nurses and midwives, accountants, etc.), and more than 10 percent are nonprofessional white-collar workers. This lowest decile includes a relatively small number of workers with higher education.

By contrast, more than 60 percent of the highest-paid decile occupy positions that require higher education. It is interesting and important to point out that in the highest-paid decile more than 20 percent are blue-collar workers in the production sectors.[1] This reflects the preferential treatment of certain highly skilled blue-collar workers in the Soviet Union, who may be called a "labor aristocracy."[2]

When we move to total wages (Table 6.1, column 3), we find much wider differentials. The Gini coefficient moves from 0.249 to 0.304, and the decile ratio from 3.33 to 3.75. In general, the impact of an additional element on the overall distribution of total wages depends on the relative importance of the segment, on the level of inequality of the distribution of the specific elements among all employed, and on the correlation between the two distributions (of the particular element and the rest). A full analysis of the impact of private wages will be forthcoming, but Tables 6.2 and 6.3 imply that private wages are distributed in an extremely unequal fashion. Only 13 percent engage in private work at all, and in some cases hourly private wages are very high (see Table 6.3). The evidence is mixed as to the correlation between wages from public and private sources. There are rather high rates of participation in private work by groups with relatively low public wages. It may well be that there is even a negative correlation between the two, and private wages may reduce inequality by compensating individuals or groups with low public wages or low participation rates.

Comparison with other studies

Thanks to the contribution of Soviet researchers N. E. Rabkina and N. M. Rimashevskaia (1972, 1978), the careful analysis and compilations by Chapman (1977b) and McAuley (1979), and the pioneering Western work on Soviet wages by Bergson (1944), we have a reasonably detailed picture of the trends in the distribution of wages in the Soviet Union from 1924 to 1970. For the years 1968, 1972, and 1976, Rabkina and Rimashevskaia compiled and published decile ratios only (1978: 20). Two other Soviet researchers, A. Aleksandrova and E. Federovskaia, published decile ratios for 1981 (1984: 21). As for Western studies, we have at our disposal only estimates based on ISIP for circa 1973 and SIP for around 1979.

Table 6.4 compares measures of dispersion of wages in 1968, based on Chapman (1977b), and in 1973 and 1979, based on ISIP and SIP. The SIP and ISIP numbers refer to wages received from main place of work in the public sector. We assume this is also so for Chapman's estimates for 1968, which are based on her interpretation of official Soviet data that were presented in the bizarre and obscure fashion of noncalibrated

[1] For more detailed results, see Vinokur and Ofer 1986.
[2] See Nove 1982.

Table 6.2. *Instances of private work, by occupational groups and sex*

	Public work			Private work			Rate of participation in private work (%)		
	Total (2,045)	Men (1,027)	Women (1,018)	Total (263)	Men (176)	Women (87)	Total (12.9)	Men (17.1)	Women (8.5)
Faculty members and researchers	128	72	56	27	19	8	21.1	26.4	14.3
Engineers	484	318	166	49	46	3	10.1	14.5	1.8
Medical doctors and dentists	93	28	65	19	10	9	20.4	35.7	13.8
Employees in administration and planning	77	19	58	3	1	2	3.9	5.3	3.4
Teachers at high school	152	35	117	30	8	22	19.7	22.9	18.8
Employees in culture	144	70	74	31	15	16	21.5	21.4	21.6
Employees with special secondary level of education	272	70	202	10	6	4	3.7	14.3	3.0
Nonprofessional white-collar employees	91	23	68	10	2	8	11.0	8.7	11.8
Blue-collar workers in production sectors									
Skilled	110	101	9	19	19		17.3	18.8	
Semiskilled	108	83	25	21	20	1	19.4	24.1	4.0
Unskilled	23	16	7	3	3		13.0	18.8	
Other[a]	87	66	21	14	12	2	16.1	3.0	9.5
Drivers	48	48		6	6		12.5	12.5	
Blue-collar workers in service sector	189	61	128	16	5	11	8.5	8.2	8.6
Other	39	17	22	5	4	1	25.8	23.5	4.5

Note: All results presented in this table are based on the original *nonweighted* sample of 2,045 respondents.
[a] Workers who did not report their "grade" skill.

Table 6.3. *Per hour gross wages at the main place of work in the public sector and in the private sector, by occupational groups*

	Per hour gross wages (rubles)		Ratio between private and public per hour wages
	Public sector	Private sector	
Mean	1.08	8.14	7.5
Faculty members and researchers	1.38	8.18	5.9
Engineers	1.07	5.62	5.3
Medical doctors and dentists	1.21	32.96	27.2
Employees in administration and planning	0.97	3.5	3.6
Teachers at high school	1.15	4.94	4.3
Employees in culture	1.60	6.95	4.3
Several kinds of employees with special secondary level of education	0.84	8.60	10.2
Non-professional white-collar workers	0.77	3.26	4.2
Blue-collar workers in production Sectors			
Skilled	1.23	7.93	6.45
Semiskilled	0.98	6.19	6.32
Unskilled	0.96	18.17	18.9
Other[a]	1.04	6.85	6.59
Drivers	1.24	6.24	5.03
Blue-collar workers in service sector	0.85	5.54	6.52

Note: All results presented in this table are based on the original nonweighted sample of 2,045 respondents.
[a] Workers who did not report their "grade" skill.

histograms. Given the span of 11 years, when average wages rose by more than half (see above), and the fact that the three estimates are entirely independent of each other, the similarity of results must be considered amazing. Although other possibilities exist, our inclination, which cannot be considered entirely unbiased, is to conclude: (1) that the individual SIP and ISIP estimates are quite reliable, and (2) that there were relatively

Table 6.4. *Size distribution of Soviet gross monthly wages, 1968, 1973, 1979*

	Wages at main work place (public sector)			Total wages (public and private)[a]	
	1968	1973	1979	1973	1979
Mean, rubles per month	105.2	139.6	150.7	152.5	175.7
Mode, rubles per month	77.6		150.0		150.0
Coefficient of variation		0.50	0.51	0.58	0.89
Gini coefficient		0.275	0.244	0.291	0.304
Ratios between earnings at indicated percentiles of distribution					
P_{98}/P_2		5.46	5.75	6.85	7.74
P_{95}/P_5		4.28	4.29	5.29	5.29
P_{90}/P_{10}	2.83–3.17	3.11	3.33	3.63	3.75
P_{75}/P_{25}	1.83	1.80	1.80	1.86	1.90
P_{95}/P_{50}	2.10	2.01	1.87	2.48	2.47
P_{90}/P_{50}	1.78	1.70	1.67	1.92	2.00
P_{25}/P_{50}	0.74	0.73	0.67	0.74	0.65
P_{10}/P_{50}	0.56	0.55	0.50	0.53	0.53
Ratio between averages of highest-paid and lowest-paid 10%	5.0	4.69	4.62	6.05	6.42

[a] Gross wages from public sector and net income from private work.

Sources: Decile ratio for 1968 (2.83) from Rabkina and Rimashevskaia 1978. All other figures for 1968 from Chapman 1977b: 261. Data related to 1973 based on weighted Israeli sample, and data related to 1979 based on weighted SIP sample.

small changes in the distribution of wages in the Soviet Union over the decade of the seventies. This conclusion seems to be borne out also by Soviet decile ratio estimates (see Table 6.5). According to these data, published by different scholars, the decile ratio rose from 2.83 in 1968 to 3.4 during the mid seventies and returned to 3.0 by 1981. Such a cycle seems to be consistent with the various wage reforms that took place during the period. With the raising of the minimum wage to 60 rubles in 1968, Soviet wage distribution attained the highest level of equality thus far. A natural widening of gaps following the reform, and the gradual introduction of the next reform, including another increase of the minimum wage to 70 rubles, could have created the cycle of the seventies (McAuley 1979).

The last two colums of Table 6.4 present information on the distribution of total wages as estimated by ISIP and SIP. Both show higher levels of inequality than that of public wages, but again the results are remarkably similar.

Table 6.5. *Selected percentile ratios, distribution of wage earners and salaried workers by gross earnings, USSR and Western countries, specified years*

Country and year	P_{10}/P_{50}	P_{90}/P_{50}	P_{95}/P_{50}	P_{90}/P_{10}
USSR, official release, "public" earnings				
1970	0.58	1.7	2.0	
1972				3.2
1976				3.4
1981				3.0
ISIP sample, 1973				
"Public" earnings	0.55	1.7	2.0	3.1
Total earnings	0.53	1.9	2.5	3.6
SIP				
"Public" earnings	0.50	1.7	2.0	3.3
Total earnings	0.53	2.0	2.5	3.8
U.S.				
1972	0.47	2.1	2.6	4.5
1975	0.45	1.8		4.0
Japan, 1968	0.52	1.9	2.3	3.7
U.K., 1976	0.60	1.7	2.0	2.8
France				
1972				3.8
1977				3.2
Netherlands,[a] 1977				2.8

[a] Data are for full-time employment in all *private* sectors of the economy (Netherlands) and also semipublic sectors, like education (France).
Sources: USSR: P_{90}/P_{10} for 1972 and 1976, Rabkina and Rimashevskaia 1978. For 1981, Aleksandrova and Federovskaia 1984. For 1976, calculations based on official Soviet release made by Chapman 1979.
U.S.: Chapman 1977, 1979.
Japan and U.K.: Bergson 1984.
France and The Netherlands: Saunders and Marsden 1981: 52, 55.

As was pointed out by Bergson, "measures of inequality of wages for different countries are apt to be less than fully comparable statistically" (1984: 1066). Nevertheless, many Western scholars still attempt to do this kind of comparison. The data in Table 6.5 present some measures of the inequality of wages for five Western countries and the Soviet Union.[3]

3   Table 6.5 is a short version of a table prepared originally by Bergson, but the part of the data related to the Soviet Union is new and based on the Israeli and SIP weighted samples. Also new in this table are data related to France and the Netherlands.

Inequality of *"public"* earnings in the Soviet Union, measured by decile ratio, is much lower than in Japan (in 1968), the United States (in 1975), or France (in 1972). These results indicate that perhaps the gap between the highest and lowest wage groups, measured by P_{95}/P_5 and P_{98}/P_2 ratios, is also wider in the United States, Japan, and France than in the Soviet Union. Currently, however, we have these ratios only for the USSR.

On the other hand, the Soviet ratios are similar or even higher than those for the United Kingdom and the observation for France in 1977. When the distributions of total Soviet wages, including private wages, are considered, Soviet decile ratios clearly fall well within those for the market economies presented. It may, however, be claimed that such a comparison is unfair because there may also be side earnings in market economies that are not captured by the data presented. Finally, it must be pointed out that the comparisons presented in the table are for pretax wages. Given the very low income tax rates in the Soviet Union and its relative proportionality, as compared with higher and more progressive rates in most other countries, it is reasonable to assume that a post–income tax comparison would turn out even less impressive for the Soviet Union.[4]

So much for the comparisons themselves, but a word must also be said about the countries upon which they were based. It is reasonable to assume that the degree of equality of wage distribution rises with the level of economic development. The main reason for this, it is hypothesized, is the spread of modern education into all parts of the society as it develops, resulting in a decline of quasi rents for scarce skills. If this hypothesis is reasonable, then the Soviet Union must be given credit for achieving a higher degree of wage equality at a lower level of development than the other countries in the comparison presented above. One major explanation for this achievement is no doubt the early and dynamic development of the Soviet education system at all levels and opening access to it to everybody, especially to women. The resulting rapid increase in the supply of skilled workers for the industrialization drive has allowed the Soviet Union to reduce wage differentials drastically ever since the late fifties.

The level, structure, and size distribution of household income

Methodology

Soviet statisticians refer to "family" (*sem'ia*) rather than to household. "Family is understood to be a group of individuals not necessarily related by

---

[4] The ISIP estimates for posttax decile ratio of wages is 2.8 as compared with 3.1 for pretax wages.

blood or marriage who share a common budget" (McAuley 1979: 15). This definition of household was used by both ISIP and SIP. In ISIP, the basic unit of analysis is the household. In the framework of this unit any member aged 17 or older was asked to report on any source of personal or family income. In SIP, however, the basic unit of analysis is the individual, not the family or household. The individual respondent could be any member of a household, not necessarily its head. SIP respondents were asked a more limited number of questions concerning income than were ISIP respondents. Defining total family income and its major components has, therefore, posed certain problems of comparability.

Total income may be estimated by the declared total or by summing up the separately reported component elements. As the latter include only the respondent's gross wages from all sources and the spouse's gross wage in the main place of work, the declared total family income should by definition be equal to or greater than the sum of reported components. Due to problems of recollection and some ambiguity as to the relevant period, this is not so in all cases. The decision was to assume that recollection of components, most related to the respondent himself, was more reliable. Thus, whenever the sum of components was higher than the declared family income, the former was used instead.[5]

The restricted number of questions on income in SIP restrict also the investigation on equality to fewer income concepts and components than in ISIP. At one end of the spectrum we can study household income derived only from public sector wages. Here we lack only spouse's wages from a second job in the public sector and any public wages received by a third earner in the household. As both are relatively rare, distortion is minimal. At the other end we can study the distribution of total money income, including in addition to all the above elements of private income, wages of others and all money contributions out of the Social Consumption Fund (SCF), mostly pensions, and also other allowances. Unfortunately, we cannot study separately the distributional effect of all private wages and income and that of the SCF payments, for we believe that the two elements have opposite distributional effects.

A second major methodological problem is to define and restructure a representative sample for the Soviet referent population. This involves two steps. The first is to exclude from the original SIP sample of 2,793 respondents two groups: a group of some 400 spouses who were also respondents in the sample. In this way each family appears only once.

5 The question on total income was: "On the average, what was the total gross income received per month by you (and all the members of your family) during the [last year of the LNP]?" The marginals for this question show that there are 2,749 valid cases, two cases with income equal to zero, and 44 missing cases.

Second, we must exclude all households represented by a respondent who was neither the head of the household nor the spouse. For such households there is no information on wages of head and spouse or on the employment status and occupation of the head, all of which are essential for the present analysis. These two exclusions leave a SIP subsample of 1,995 households that must be reweighted in order to resemble the referent Soviet urban population.

Reweighting was done according to two criteria, the demographic-economic character of households and the educational level of their heads. According to the first criterion, all households were first classified by their working status into active and nonactive. If any member of the family was employed in the public sector, the household was considered active. Second, households were classified according to type – complete families, incomplete families, and singles – and by sex of head. Complete, active families were classified also by work status of the husband and wife. Weighting according to this criterion was done according to data provided by the 1970 census (as for ISIP) with a few marginal changes to take account of whatever data are available from the 1979 census.

Each type of household was subsequently reconstructed according to the educational structure of the active urban population of the Soviet Union. The reconstruction was done on the basis of the last Soviet census. When the head of the household was male, the educational structure of the working male population as provided in the 1979 census was used. If the head of the household was female, the female educational structure was used. The resulting reconstructed, or weighted, original subsample is not ideal, but it is a very close approximation of the referent population (along the two dimensions noted above).

The final reweighted sample includes 1,995 households, of which 221, or 11 percent, are nonactive.

Findings: income inequality in the Soviet Union

According to the results based on the SIP reweighted subsample, the average money gross monthly income per household in 1979 was 338.6 rubles for the total population, and 357.7 rubles for the active population. Comparison of these figures with the equivalent Soviet values is problematic for many reasons. First of all, data on average household income of the total population or the total urban population have not been published in the Soviet Union. Data on the average family income of state workers and employees are published by the official Soviet Central Statistical Administration, but in the following form. The total average income per employed person, which includes only two sources – the average gross wage and the total income from the Social Consumption Fund – is multiplied by the suggested average number of employed persons in the family (or household). The Statistical Administration published four figures for 1979: (1) total average income per worker or employee, − 224 rubles per month; (2) average gross wage per employed person, − 163 rubles; (3) average value of total income from social services per employed person, − 61 rubles; and (4) total income per family, − 400 rubles per month (*NK SSSR* 1980: 393). By simple division of the first number into the last, it is possible to arrive at the average number of persons employed per family.

The concept of total household (or family) income used in the Soviet Union includes "free" social services but does not include private income from private work (except income from private garden plots). The concept of gross money income, by definition, does not include "free" social services but does include private income from private work. To compare the results of the SIP survey with Soviet data, the following procedure has been followed:

1. The value of "free" social services (58.4 rubles per month or 14.6 percent of total income) was excluded from the average total income calculated in the Soviet Union for families of workers or employees.[6]

2. Private income from private work was excluded from the average "actual" gross monthly income based on the reweighted SIP subsample. Because SIP respondents were asked to report only their income from private work and not their spouses' also, the average actual private income of complete active households was doubled. This assumes that the relevant characteristics of the group of respondents and their spouses are approximately the same.

The final results of all the considerations mentioned above are presented in Table 6.6. It was necessary to include in this table averages for two different populations – complete and incomplete families – because the definition of family (or household) used by the Soviets in their calculation is not clear. Complete families include families where both husband and wife are present. Incomplete families are one-parent families. Unrelated persons were excluded from the calculations presented in Table 6.6. The data presented in this table reveal similarities between the Soviet and SIP data for both types of families. This similarity has to be taken very cautiously due to the relatively "crude" character of the comparison.

Findings on the size distribution of income are presented for two populations, active households (Table 6.7) and the entire population

<hr/>

[6] According to the results of family budget surveys done in the Soviet Union, in 1980 the "free" social services were 14.6 percent of total income (Nk SSSR 1981: 383).

Table 6.6. *Level and structure of average gross monthly household income for active population in USSR and SIP weighted subsample, 1979*

| | USSR | SIP subsample | |
		Complete families	Complete and incomplete families
Total "actual" gross monthly income	—	390.3	375.7
Total income from private work	—	46.6	37.9
Total comparable gross monthly income	341.6	343.7	337.8
All gross wages from public sector			
Rubles	291.8	286.6	264.9
Percent[a]	85.4	83.4	78.4
Number of persons employed	1.79	1.73	1.62

[a] As a percentage of comparable gross monthly income.

Source: For the USSR, calculations were based on Nk SSSR 1982: 383, 393.

(Table 6.8). All the estimates are for the distribution of income per household member over *all households*. We consider this distribution to be more meaningful than that of the distribution of the same income over all people, mainly because the household as a unit earns all incomes. (See Ofer and Vinokur 1980a; Kuznets 1981.)

The main link between the distribution of incomes and the distribution of wages is through the distribution of earnings from the public sector to the active population. In both cases it is the same total wage fund that is distributed once among workers and, through them, among their families. Starting from inequality of wages, the level of inequality per household member depends on the distribution of workers among the families, on the correlation between wages of workers in the same family, and on the distribution of family size. The two distributions will come close to each other when these additional factors behave in a uniform way or cancel each other out. If, for example, each active household "gets" two workers with

Table 6.7. *Distribution of households by income per household member: active population, 1979*

	All earnings in public sector (1)	Total income (2)
Median, rubles per month	81.4	100.0
Gini coefficient	0.324	0.374
Ratios between per capita income at indicated percentiles of distribution		
P_{98}/P_2	13.9	12.0
P_{95}/P_5	7.9	5.7
P_{90}/P_{10}	5.2	3.5
P_{90}/P_{50}	2.1	1.9
P_{75}/P_{25}	2.2	2.0
P_{10}/P_{50}	0.41	0.55

Lorenz statistics	Income shares of given groups (%)	
Lowest 5%	2.0	1.3
Lowest 10%	2.5	3.1
Lowest 20%	6.8	7.6
Lowest 25%	9.6	10.3
Lowest 50%	32.1	26.4
Highest 5%	14.2	25.1
Highest 10%	23.7	33.0
Highest 20%	39.5	45.8
Highest 25%	46.0	51.5

Decile income groups	Average per capita income in given decile (rubles)	
I	23.5	43.9
II	40.3	65.7
III	53.4	78.0
IV	65.7	89.3
V	76.6	100.5
VI	87.8	112.1
VII	100.7	130.2
VIII	116.2	157.4
IX	151.6	183.4
X	220.0	472.5
X/I	9.4	10.8

Table 6.8. *Distribution of households by income per household member: total population, 1979*

	All earnings in public sector (1)	Total income (2)
Median, rubles per month	76.0	100.0
Gini coefficient	0.396	0.382
Ratios between per capita income at indicated percentiles of distribution		
P_{98}/P_2		12.0
P_{95}/P_5		5.8
P_{90}/P_{10}		3.8
P_{90}/P_{50}	2.1	2.0
P_{75}/P_{25}	2.8	1.97
P_{10}/P_{50}		0.53

Lorenz statistics	Income shares of given groups (%)	
Lowest 5%		1.2
Lowest 10%		3.0
Lowest 20%	2.6	7.4
Lowest 25%	4.9	10.0
Lowest 50%	22.6	25.3
Highest 5%	15.6	25.3
Highest 10%	25.9	33.4
Highest 20%	42.8	46.4
Highest 25%	49.8	52.1

Decile income groups	Mean per capita income in given decile (rubles)	
I		41.6
II	21.7	61.4
III	41.4	75.1
IV	55.5	86.3
V	69.3	98.0
VI	81.0	109.1
VII	95.1	125.0
VIII	110.7	152.1
IX	140.8	182.0
X	214.5	467.9
X/I	9.9	11.2

correlated wages and household size is also uniform, the inequality of income will not be much greater than that of wages.[7]

As it turns out, when inequality is measured by the Gini coefficient, dispersion of public sector wages increases from 0.249 to 0.324 when we move from workers to their households, which is a significant difference but not extreme. Corresponding estimates by ISIP are 0.275 and 0.293. Given the problems in estimating income in SIP mentioned above, there is reason to believe that the Gini coefficient of 0.324 is biased upward and that the effect of moving from workers to households is nearer the ISIP estimate of 0.293. The reason for this is that SIP household income received from the public sector does not include wages of a third or higher-order worker or second-job earnings of anyone other than the respondent. This omission is relevant mostly for large families located in many cases at the lower end of the income (per household member) scale. Further support that this is so is provided by the very high and unreasonable decile ratio for public earnings per household members: 5.2 as compared with the corresponding figure of just 3.33 for public earnings per worker.[8]

As we move from public earnings to total money income (still for the active population), we add, in addition to the omitted element of public earnings just mentioned, all private incomes and all money payments from SCF. We expect the first element to raise the level of inequality and the second to reduce it. As the latter is not very large for the active population, however, the combined impact is to raise the Gini coefficient from 0.324 to 0.374.

When we turn from the active population to the entire population (Table 6.8) we see first that the overall distribution of public earnings becomes less equal. The Gini coefficient rises from 0.324 to 0.396. This is the obvious result of adding 10 percent of nonearning households to the bottom of the sample. The interesting result is, however, that when private income and a very significant increment of pensions and other SCF payments are added the distribution of income per household member is almost as equal for the entire population as for the active population alone. The meaning of this finding is that pensions and other SCF payments, and possibly also private incomes, are concentrated in the group of nonearners to a sufficient degree to assure that their addition to the population does not widen income gaps. This is definitely an achievement of the support system and of private activity. A similar finding emerges also from the ISIP estimates (see Table 6.9 and Ofer and Vinokur 1980a). What is somewhat surprising is that the Gini coefficient does not decline for the entire population when

[7] In principle, it can be even more equal, depending on the above. See Kuznets 1981; Gronau 1984.
[8] The fact that the decile ratio declines sharply to 3.5 also supports the claim about the bias in the distribution of public earnings in SIP.

nonwage income is added. It may be an artifact of the less than full account of wages discussed above.

Comparison with other studies

Information on the distribution of household income is far more scarce in the Soviet Union than are data related to the size distribution of wages. In the rare instances when some statistics do appear, the types of population, concepts of income, and the structure of the sample are not clear. For these reasons, our comparative analysis is restricted to only three sources of data: Western computations based on Soviet literature as presented by McAuley and the results of ISIP and SIP surveys. They are shown in Table 6.9. As presented, most measures of dispersion, with the small exception of the decile ratios, demonstrate a clear rise in the level of income inequality over the period 1967–79. However, a careful analysis of differences in methodology and biases in the data put this conclusion in some doubt. First, McAuley himself and others pointed out that his estimates understate inequality in 1967–68. This is a conclusion reached by Bergson (1984: 1068–69), among others, on the basis of an alternative estimate by Wiles (1974) of a decile ratio of 3.5–3.7 for 1966, which is similar to those estimated by both SIP and ISIP for later dates. Considering McAuley's sources, mostly Soviet official sources, it is highly likely that he was not able to take full account of private sources of income that contribute in the other two samples to a higher level of inequality.

Second, the rising level of inequality between ISIP (1973) and SIP (1979) also raises some questions of comparability. There is a much stronger impact on inequality by the group of unrelated active individuals on SIP results than in the case of ISIP. This difference alone explains about half of Gini differences between the two estimates, and it is unlikely that it can be exclusively linked to time trends. More likely, the difference results from sampling and reporting differences, one of which may be the different nature of the two samples. A higher concentration in the SIP sample of individuals who made a lot of money in the Soviet Union, especially through private activities, may be explained by a greater entrepreneurial spirit of emigrants who chose to go to the United States rather than to Israel. A similar argument may be extended to the entire SIP sample, namely, that it includes a higher proportion of people with higher, sometimes very high, private incomes, another contribution to the higher level of inequality. If one adds to this the fact that the decile ratios of ISIP are somewhat larger than those of SIP, it becomes doubtful whether any residual is left for a trend toward increasing inequality over the seventies.

The last relevant piece of evidence on the issue is a pronouncement by

Table 6.9. *Distribution of households by per capita household income, different estimates*

	Income share (%) of:					Percentile ratios			
	Lowest 10%	Lowest 20%	Highest 20%	Highest 10%	Gini coefficient	P_{98}/P_2	P_{95}/P_5	P_{90}/P_{10}	P_{10}/P_{50}
Nonfarm active households, pretax 1967 (McAuley) (USSR)	4.4	10.4	33.8	19.9	.229			3.0	
Urban households, pretax									
Total, 1973 (ISIP)	3.7	8.7	39.5	24.5	.305	9.6	5.4	3.7	0.55
Active, 1973 (ISIP)	3.9	9.2	38.4	24.0	.293	9.3	4.9	3.7	0.58
Urban households, pretax									
Total, 1979 (SIP)	3.0	7.4	46.4	33.4	.382	12.0	5.8	3.4	0.53
Active, 1979 (SIP)	3.1	7.6	45.8	33.0	.374	12.0	5.7	3.5	0.55

Source: Income shares and Gini coefficient for 1967 calculated by Bergson from frequency distributions that were compiled by McAuley (Bergson 1984: 1070; McAuley 1979: 57). Decile ratio for 1967 from McAuley 1979: 57.

Soviet scholars that the decile ratio for per capita income in 1973 for the entire Soviet population (including farm population) was 3.7 (Aleksandrova and Federovskaia 1984: 21). Since the addition of the rural population may add about 0.2 to the ratio, the implied urban ratio comes to about 3.5, almost exactly that for SIP and ISIP. It is hard to believe that the Soviet estimate fully includes private incomes, which makes the estimate even more of a surprise. It is also much higher than McAuley's similar estimate for 1968 of 3.1 (1979: 65).

Our conclusion at this time is that there is no evidence in the data so far for a trend of declining inequality of incomes in the Soviet Union over the seventies, as sometimes claimed by Soviet scholars. In fact, our results point to a stable distribution of income and do not rule out the possibility of rising inequality.

Comparison with other countries

Are incomes in the Soviet Union distributed more equally than in Western developed countries? A priori reasoning has it that indeed this should be the case, at least for public incomes of the urban European Soviet population. It goes as follows: Start with a distribution of wages per worker that is as equal as or even slightly more equal than in the West. The exceptionally high level of participation of women in the labor force should make wage distribution per household member even more equal. The small size of the average family and the small variance in family size that goes with it should keep the distribution of wages per household member almost as equal as that of wages per worker. Finally, considering that nonwage sources of public earnings, such as property income and the like, are almost completely absent and that the impact of SCF payments is similar to that for other countries, it follows that a greater degree of equality ought to be found in the Soviet Union. These considerations exclude, however, a number of factors working in the opposite direction in the Soviet Union, namely, the existence of a substantial Moslem population with demographic characteristics that tend to raise inequality, the relatively large rural sector with a similar effect, and the phenomenon of private incomes.

The SIP and ISIP data in Table 6.10 for the USSR exclude the Moslem and rural populations, and some entries exclude private income. They are compared with data compiled by Sawyer (1976) and with further calculations by Bergson (1984) for Western countries. By and large, it can be stated that the 1973 ISIP estimates with or without private incomes are consistent with the above considerations and show a more equal distribution of income in the Soviet Union than in six of the seven countries presented. The differences are significant between the Soviet Union and France, Canada

Table 6.10. *Income shares of selected percentile groups and Gini coefficients: distribution of households by gross money income per household member (USSR and Western countries, specified years)*

Population, country, and year	Income share (%) of:				Gini coefficient	Ratio between income shares at highest and lowest deciles
	Lowest 10%	Lowest 20%	Highest 20%	Highest 10%		
Urban households (USSR, ISIP, 1973)						
Pre-tax total money income	3.7	8.7	39.5	24.5	0.305	6.6
Posttax total money income	3.8	9.0	39.5	24.6	0.302	6.5
Posttax money income from public sector	3.7	9.3	36.7	22.0	0.270	5.9
Urban households (USSR, SIP, 1979)						
Pre-tax total money income	3.0	7.4	46.4	33.4	0.382	11.1
All households, pretax						
Australia, 1966–67	3.5	8.3	41.0	25.6	0.317	7.3
Norway, 1970	3.5	8.2	39.0	23.5	0.306	6.7
France, 1970	2.0	5.8	47.2	31.8	0.398	16.3
Canada, 1972	2.2	6.2	43.6	27.8	0.363	12.6
U.S., 1972	1.8	5.5	44.4	28.6	0.376	15.9
All households, posttax						
Sweden, 1972	3.5	9.3	35.2	20.5	0.254	5.9

Sources: For all Western countries, income shares from Sawyer 1976: 17. All Gini coefficients for Western countries computed by Bergson from income shares of decile groups (1984: 1070).

and the United States, and marginal when compared with Australia, Norway, and the United Kingdom. The comparison with Sweden, on a posttax income basis, shows obvious greater Swedish equality. However, when the Soviet 1979 SIP estimates are considered, they show a higher Gini coefficient than that of all other countries with the sole exception of France. In both comparisons the Soviet distribution is "stronger" in terms of equality at the lower end: The lowest tenth and fifth of households are receiving relatively higher shares of total (per capita) income than in most countries. Even according to the 1979 estimates these shares are higher than those in France, Canada, and the United States. Although not shown in the table,

McAuley's estimates for 1967 put the Soviet Union at a much more equal point than all other countries on the equality scale.

It is our feeling that, due to the considerations given above, inequality as estimated by the SIP sample may be somewhat exaggerated. It must be considered highly unlikely that income in the Soviet Union would be distributed as unequally as in the United States. Even so, the SIP estimate certainly brings the Soviet Union nearer to the other countries for which data are available.

A number of additional considerations qualify the comparisons as presented in Table 6.10 in different directions. First, according to Sawyer, the data related to Western countries tend to underestimate the inequality of income due to possible underreporting or entire omission of capital gains, fringe benefits, and investment and entrepreneurial income (Sawyer 1976: 4). Most of these income elements are distributed rather unevenly. Their omission may justify comparisons with only public incomes in the Soviet Union. On the other hand, although there are good reasons to assume that in both SIP and ISIP there was fuller reporting of incomes, the Soviet samples exclude households that belong to the "elite" group in the Soviet Union, a group that enjoys many extra monetary and nonmonetary benefits. On the basis of data assembled by Matthews (1978), Bergson estimated those perks as adding about 1.5 percent of all incomes to the upper tenth or fifth of all households (1984: 1070–71). Such a correction may add a noninsignificant degree of inequality to the Soviet estimates.

Second, there is reason to believe that free services and subsidies provided to the Soviet household by the government have a higher impact on equality of total income than in most Western countries. Education and health services in the Soviet Union are almost entirely free, and there is a very substantial rent subsidy. Estimates based on ISIP for 1973 show that the overall impact of nonmoney SCF allowances on overall inequality, like the Gini, amounts to more than 10 percent (the Gini coefficient for the entire population declines from 0.305 to 0.260) (Ofer and Vinokur 1986).

Third, one has to consider the impact of taxes. Unlike those in the West, Soviet income taxes are very low and of limited progressivity. Most taxes are turnover taxes with different rates on different consumption goods. There is reason to believe that posttax data for Western distributions would move them nearer to the Soviet distribution. The comparison with Sweden in Table 6.10 may also point in this direction.

Finally, Bergson brings up the point that in such comparisons some normalization for different levels of economic development must be made. Distributions are typically much less equal for countries at earlier levels of development and tend to become more equal as development progresses. Among the groups of countries represented in Table 6.10, the Soviet Union has the lowest level of gross national product (GNP) per capita, a common approximation of the level of development (see Bergson 1984: 1070). Thus, normalization for this factor gives the Soviet distribution some more credit in the comparison. Part of this credit, however, is taken away because rural and Moslem populations are excluded. This exclusion is important as an offset because one of the reasons for a lower level of income equality in less-developed countries is the higher share of rural population and the larger variance of rural household size. A small additional measure of "credit" may also be allowed to the Soviet distribution on account of its very large size, which is bound to create higher variance of conditions of life and thus incomes, compared with smaller countries of more uniform character (see Wiles 1974).

In the end, the analysis must of necessity prove inconclusive to some extent. We conclude, however, that it is still reasonable to assume that, with normalization for level of development, income in the Soviet Union is distributed in a more equal fashion than in most Western countries. We also conclude that this holds, in all probability, even without normalization. The fact that those conclusions are not easy to demonstrate, however, testifies that the edge in equality for the USSR is not very significant.

A preliminary note on the concentration of wealth

Under Soviet socialism the ownership of "means of production," that is, productive capital, is almost completely excluded. Exceptions are mostly private agricultural plots. In addition, most residential capital is also publicly owned. Accumulation of wealth is therefore limited to some private houses and cooperative apartments, to private plots, to household appliances and cars, to valuables like jewelry, and to a limited list of financial assets – savings accounts and government bonds and cash. There is also the illegal production capital of the second economy. These limitations, plus the relatively short time span over which wealth could have accumulated and the rather low level of private income, must limit the extent of accumulation thus far and in the future as well. Nevertheless, both ISIP and SIP asked about wealth, and they provide one of the first opportunities to look into this aspect of equality in the Soviet Union. At this point our observations are very preliminary.

The conventional definition of wealth relates to the sum of several kinds of assets. In both our surveys, these assets include family possessions (such as houses, cooperative apartments, dachas, and cars) and family financial assets (such as savings in the bank, cash, and government bonds). The SIP survey also asked about furniture and other valuable items like jewelry. Another difference is that ISIP asked about the purchase price, whereas SIP asked

Table 6.11. *Concentration of wealth and financial assets in USSR, UK, and US (total population)*

Lorenz statistics	Gross wealth, USSR		Wealth		Financial assets, USSR	
	ISIP, 1973	SIP, 1979	UK, 1979	US, 1972	ISIP, 1973	SIP, 1979
Share of given group						
Lowest 25%	0.0	0.3	—	—	0.0	0.0
Lowest 50%	0.0	8.9	—	—	0.0	5.9
Highest 1%	4.8	7.0	24.0	26.0	8.3	11.5
Highest 5%	23.4	28.7	45.0	45.0	35.8	28.6
Highest 10%	41.2	42.9	59.0	—	54.9	43.1
Highest 25%	70.7	69.5	—	—	83.0	72.8
Gini coefficient	.77	.61	.74	.76	.83	.64
Percentage of households with no wealth or financial assets[a]	58.0	19.0	—	—	68.0	28.0

Note: "Wealth" and "financial assets" in ISIP and SIP contain the *same* elements.
[a] Differences in the percentage of households without financial assets, 68 and 28, may be explained by "anticipation of emigration."
Source: Atkinson 1983: 164, 173–74. For U.K., shares of adult population; for U.S., shares of families. Gini coefficient for U.S. is relevant for 1962.

about current, resale value. Questions about liabilities, such as mortgage and money owed, were included only in ISIP. On the basis of ISIP, therefore, it is possible to calculate gross and net wealth; on the basis of SIP, only the former.

The main results concerning the size distribution of total wealth and financial assets in 1973 and 1979 are presented in Table 6.11. The results show that inequality of wealth is much greater than inequality of personal wages or income of households. The top 1 percent of the households own approximately 5–7 percent of the total sum of wealth; the top 5 percent own 23–28 percent and the top 10 percent own more than 40 percent. On the other end, nearly half of all households under ISIP and a quarter under SIP reported no assets. The Gini coefficients for all households are 0.77 in ISIP and 0.61 for SIP.

The size distribution of financial assets is more unequal than the distribution of total wealth. The top 1 percent of all households own between 8 and 11 percent of the total sum of these assets, and the top 10 percent own approximately 45–55 percent. The lowest 50 percent of households have

0–6 percent of the total sum of financial assets. The Gini coefficients are 0.83 for ISIP and 0.64 for SIP.

Table 6.11 also presents information on the distribution of wealth in Western countries. Needless to say, comparability with the Soviet data is highly problematic. Even so, there is a much higher concentration of wealth in the West among very few rich families than in the Soviet Union. The differences between the Gini coefficients seem to be narrower, but the main reason for this is most likely that the proportion of households without wealth in the Soviet samples (at least those reporting no wealth) is much higher than in the West. In principle, current income derived from wealth should have been included as part of income and its offset on inequality already taken into account. We have seen that for both the Soviet Union and the West the inclusion of income from assets was not complete. But, even if it were, the distribution of wealth itself contributes to the degree of economic inequality, in the form of economic security, attending emergencies, and social and political status and influence. The impact of the distribution of wealth on overall economic equality depends (in addition to its own size distribution) also on its quantitative weight, relative to current incomes, and on the correlation between the distributions of income and wealth. It is very likely that, as in the West, the correlation between income and wealth in the Soviet Union is also rather high. The impact of wealth on economic equality in the Soviet case is also weaker by comparison, for the amount of privately owned wealth relative to income is less than in the West.

Conclusions

Without normalization for the level of development, and also for the large size and the heterogeneity of the Soviet Union, the findings in this chapter support the view that public income per household member is distributed among households more equally than in most advanced Western countries. Wages per worker are also somewhat more equally distributed, but the Soviet advantage here is narrower. The incorporation of privately earned incomes draws the Soviet distribution even closer to earned incomes in the West. Normalization, however, especially for the level of development, may put the Soviet Union one step above most Western countries on the equality chart. If indeed, after normalization, even wages are more equally distributed than in the West, then credit should be given to the historically intensive process by which the USSR has raised the educational level of the labor force. It is very likely that the resulting increased supply of highly trained academics, technicians, and skilled workers made possible the significant reduction of the earnings differentials that took place in the fifties and sixties. According to Soviet sources, the decile ratio of wages fell between 1946 and 1967 from 7.2 to 2.8 (Rabkina and Rimashevskaia 1978: 20). Further study is needed to substantiate this proposition.

A second probable explanation for the better showing of the Soviet Union is the high level of participation of workers in the labor force. The exact effect of this factor on the size distribution of income also deserves further study, but here too, as in the sphere of education, the Soviet Union started the process earlier than others. A third contributing factor is the high level of demographic uniformity in household size and structure achieved in the Soviet Union, at least as far as non-Moslem populations are concerned. Variation in household size, especially in the number of children, is an important explanation for differentiation in income per capita. The hardships and economic pressures imposed on the Soviet population by the regime helped to expedite the natural process of declining fertility and household size. It also probably contributed to raising the level of income equality at a relatively early developmental stage. To the extent that these policies in the spheres of education and female participation in the labor force, plus the demographic consequences of Soviet consumption policies, may all be included as integral components of "Soviet socialism," it deserves credit for the higher degree of equality that has been achieved. The fact is, however, that the elements that are considered the essence of socialism – that is, a higher degree of equality brought about by the elimination of property income, by better welfare programs, and by given demographic and human capital conditions – have yielded only a marginal difference and that a portion of even this contribution is offset by inequality in the distribution of income derived from the second economy on the one side and the special privileges to the elite on the other.

Socialism was established for a number of reasons, and this is not a place for its overall evaluation. When we consider its achievements in the sphere of income equality, however, our conclusion is that it is highly doubtful whether this small advantage in equality, assuming it is there, outweighs the heavy cost that the Soviet society has been paying in terms of denial of basic freedoms, not to mention the price in terms of the level of income. When socialism was advocated or even when it was established, its claim for greater equality was based on comparison with the more or less pure market economies. Since then, the market system has undergone rather drastic changes in the direction of mixed economies with a substantial degree of government intervention in the supply of public services and in income maintenance and distribution. This alternative has presented a constant challenge to Soviet socialism. It seems that in the sphere of income distribution the Soviet Union may be a slight winner but, even at that, a Pyrrhic winner.

Appendix

One way to check the improvement brought about by the reconstruction of the sample is to compare the average monthly wage after reweighting with Soviet official figures for average wages. The official Soviet figure is 163 rubles (for 1979), and ranges for SIP reweighted figures are between 150.7 (average wage in the main place of work) and 154.5 (in the entire public sector). The relatively small remaining difference may be due to a host of reasons, including the fact that at present the weighting does not consider all possible criteria, such as age or size of city. Even so, the estimates are close enough to raise our confidence that wage differentials in the weighted sample also approximate the true differentials in the Soviet Union.

To compare the results based on the SIP sample with results published in the Soviet Union, it is necessary to choose not only a referent population but also a specific year or years. Following is the distribution of respondents by the last normal year of their work in the public sector:

Year	Percentage
1972–76	1.6
1977	2.3
1978	26.1
1979	47.0
1980	16.2
1981–82	6.7

On the basis of this distribution, 1979 was accepted as the reference year for comparison of SIP data with that published in the Soviet Union. Clearly, some variance among wages is due to the rise of wages over time, from 1972 to 1982. Ideally, this part of the variance should be eliminated, and only wage differentials at a given year should be measured. A number of attempts were made to adjust non-1979 wages to those of 1979, using Soviet official data on wages. The differences found were too small to justify the arbitrary adjustment of individual wages on the basis of group averages.

References

Aleksandrova, A., and E. Federovskaia. 1984. "Mechanism formirovaniia i vozvysh-
eniia potrebnostei," *Voprosy economiki*, 1: 15–25.
Atkinson, Anthony B. 1983. *The Economics of Inequality*. Oxford: Clarendon Press.
Bergson, Abram. 1944. *The Structure of Soviet Wages*. Cambridge, Mass.: Harvard
University Press.

200   **Aaron Vinokur and Gur Ofer**

1984. "Income Inequality under Soviet Socialism," *Journal of Economic Literature*, 22: 1052–99.

Chapman, Janet G. 1977a. "The Distribution of Earnings in Selected Countries, East and West." Paper presented at Symposium on Technology, Labor Productivity, and Labor Supply, Racine, Wisc., November.

1977b. "Soviet Wages under Socialism." In Alan Abouchar (ed.), *The Socialist Price Mechanism*. Durham, N.C.: Duke University Press.

1979. "Are Earnings More Equal under Socialism?" In John R. Moroney (ed.), *Income Inequality*. Lexington, Mass.: Lexington Books.

1983. "Earnings Distribution in the USSR, 1968–1976," *Soviet Studies*, 35(3): 410–13.

Cromwell, J. 1977. "The Size Distribution of Income: An International Comparison," *Review of Income and Wealth*, 23: 291–309.

Gronau, Ruben. 1984. *Effect of Women's Earnings on the Inequality of Income Distribution: Israel, 1968–1980*. Maurice Falk Institute for Economic Research in Israel.

Karpukhin, D. N., and N. P. Kuznetsova. 1968. "Dokhody i potrebleni trudiashchikhsia." In *Trud i zarabotnaa plate v SSSR*. Moscow: "Economika."

Kuznets, Simon. 1981. "Size of Households and Income Disparities." In Julian Simon and Peter A. Lindert (eds.), *Research in Population Economics*, 3: 1–40. Greenwich, Conn.: JAI Press.

McAuley, Alastair. 1977. *Soviet Anti-poverty Policy, 1955–1975*. Discussion papers, Institute for Research on Poverty. Madison: University of Wisconsin.

1979. *Economic Welfare in the Soviet Union*. Madison: University of Wisconsin Press.

1982. "Sources of Earnings Inequality: A Comment on A. Nove's 'Income Distribution in the USSR," *Soviet Studies*, 34(3): 443–47.

Maier, V. F. 1977. "Aktual'nye problemy povyshenii narodnogo blagosostoianiia," *Voprosy economiki*, 11: 47–56.

Matthews, M. 1978. *Privilege in the Soviet Union: A Study of Elite-Styles under Communism*. London: Allen and Unwin.

Migranova, L. A., and N. E. Rabkina. 1976. "Izmenenie differentsiatsii pri prevrashchenii zarabotnoi platy v dokhod sem'i." In N. M. Rimashevskaia (ed.), *Sotsial'no economicheskie problemy blagosostoianiia*. Moscow: Tsentral'nyi economico-matematicheskii institut.

1979. "Izmenenie differentsiatsii pri prevrashchenii zarabotnoi platy v dokhod sem'i." In *Potrebnosti dokhody potreblenie*. Moscow: Akademia Nauk SSSR.

Morrison, Christian. 1984. "Income Distribution in East European and Western Countries," *Journal of Comparative Economics*, 8: 121–38.

Narodnoe khoziaistvo v 1979 g. [*Nk SSSR*]. 1980. Moscow: Tsentral'noe statisticheskoe upravlenie.

Nove, Alec. 1982. "Income Distribution in the USSR: A Possible Explanation of Some Recent Data," *Soviet Studies*, 34(2).

Ofer, Gur, and Aaron Vinokur. 1979a. "Family Income Levels for Soviet Industrial Workers, 1965–1975." In A. Kahan and B. A. Ruble (eds.), *Industrial Labor in the USSR*. New York: Pergamon Press.

1979b. "Family Budget Survey of Soviet Emigrants in the Soviet Union" (with Yechiel Bar-Chaim). Research Paper no. 32, Soviet and East European

Research Center, Hebrew University, Jerusalem. Updated version, RAND Corporation, 1979.

1980a. "The Distribution of Income of the Soviet Urban Population." Paper presented at the Second World Congress of the Association of Soviet and East European Studies, Garmisch, West Germany.

1980b. "The Distributive Effects of the Social Consumption Fund in the Soviet Union." Paper presented at a Conference on Social Welfare and the Delivery of Social Services USA/USSR, Berkeley, Calif.

1980c. "Private Sources of Income of the Soviet Urban Household." R-2359 NA. RAND Corporation. Forthcoming in Gregory Grossman (ed.), *The Second Economy in the Soviet Union*. Berkeley: University of California Press.

1982. "Earnings Differentials between Men and Women in the Soviet Union: A First Look." In S. Rosenfield (ed.), *Economic Welfare and the Economics of Soviet Socialism: Essays in Honor of Abram Bergson*. Cambridge: Cambridge University Press.

1983a. "The Labor Force Participation of Married Women in the Soviet Union: A Household Cross-Section Analysis," *Journal of Comparative Economics*, July.

1983b. "Work and Family of Soviet Women: Historical Trends and Cross Section Analysis." Paper presented at a Conference on Trends in Education, Chelwood-Gate, England.

1986. "The Distributive Effects of the Social Consumption fund in the Soviet Union." Forthcoming in Gail Lapidus and Guy E. Swanson (eds.), *Social Welfare and Social Services in the U.S.S.R.* Berkeley, Calif.: Institute of International Studies.

Pryor, Frederic L. 1973. *Property and Industrial Organization in Communist and Capitalist Nations*. Bloomington: Indiana University Press.

Rabkina, N. E., and N. M. Rimashevskaia. 1972. *Osnovy differentsiatsii zarabotnoi platy i dokhodov naseleniia*. Moscow.

1978. "Raspredelitel'nye otnosheniia i sotsial'noe razvitie." *Economica i organizatsiia promyshlennogo proizvodstva*, no. 5.

Rimashevskaia, N. M. 1965. *Ekonomicheskii analiz dokhodov rabochikh i sluzhashchikh*. Moscow.

Sarkisyan, G. S., and N. P. Kuznetsova. *Potrebnosti i dokhod sem'i*. Moscow: Publishing House "Economika."

Saunders, C., and D. Marsden. 1981. *Pay Inequality in the European Community*. Redmond, Wash.: Butterworths.

Sawyer, Malcolm. 1976. "Income Distribution in OECD Countries." *OECD Economic Outlook: Occasional Studies*, July: 3–36.

Schroeder, Gertrude E., and Barbara S. Severin. 1976. "Soviet Consumption and Income Policies in Perspective." In U.S. Congress, Joint Economic Committee, *Soviet Economy in a New Perspective*. Washington, D.C.: Government Printing Office.

Vestnik statistiki. 1983. 9: 38.

Vinokur, A. 1975. "Surveys of Family Budgets in the USSR: A Review." Mimeographed. Hebrew University of Jerusalem.

Vinokur, A., and G. Ofer. 1986. "Inequality of Earnings, Household Income, and

Wealth in the Soviet Union in the 70s." University of Illinois SIP working Paper Series, no. 25.

1976. "Average Net Monetary Income of Worker and Employee Families in the USSR from 1964 to 1973." Mimeographed. Hebrew University of Jerusalem.

Wiles, P. J. D. 1974. *The Distribution of Income East and West.* Amsterdam.

Wiles, P., and S. Markowski. 1971. "Income Distribution under Communism and Capitalism" (Part 1). *Soviet Studies,* 22(4): 344–69.

1972. "Income Distribution under Communism and Capitalism" (Part 2). *Soviet Studies,* 22(5): 487–511.

CHAPTER 7

The life course of Soviet women born 1905–1960

BARBARA A. ANDERSON

The Soviet European urban population has low fertility, high female labor-force participation, and a high level of educational attainment. Low fertility in the urban part of the Soviet Union in combination with large Soviet losses in World War II led the Soviet government to encourage all able-bodied citizens to work for pay. The shortage of adult males after World War II helps to explain why the Soviet Union has the highest female labor-force participation rate of any country in the world. Partly to increase the productivity of labor, the building of a high-quality educational system has been a priority, and educational attainment has increased rapidly since the 1917 Revolution for both sexes.

The women interviewed in the Soviet Interview Project (SIP) General Survey are characterized by low fertility, high educational attainment, and high rates of labor-force participation to an even greater extent than Soviet urban women as a whole. The bulk of the SIP respondents are from very large cities. Most are Jews, and Jews have the highest average educational level of any nationality[1] in the Soviet Union.

The lives of these well-educated Soviet urban women are relevant both to Soviet manpower policy and to understanding the implications of recent changes in female labor-force participation and fertility in the West. Figure 7.1 shows female labor-force participation rates by age in the United States for 1950 through 1983.[2] Labor-force participation rates of women over 40 rose throughout the postwar era, as more and more women returned to the labor force as their children grew older. Since the early 1960s, however, labor-force participation rates of American women in their twenties and thirties also have risen sharply. This has been partly due to

I would like to thank Brian Silver, Cynthia Buckley, Reynolds Farley, William Frey, and Victoria Velkoff for helpful comments. I also would like to thank Cynthia Buckley and Victoria Velkoff for research assistance; Mike Coble, Amy Hsu, and Kathleen Duke for assistance with graphics; and Judy Mullin for help with preparation of tables.

[1] In Soviet usage, "nationality" has the meaning of "ethnic group" in Western usage. Jews are considered a separate nationality in this sense.
[2] The values plotted at age 65 in Figure 7.1 refer to women 65 or older.

declining fertility after the baby boom, but it also has been marked by increases in the tendency of women with young children to work for pay (Waite 1981). As shown in Figure 7.1, the dip in labor-force participation traditionally associated with childbearing and the care of young children disappeared by 1983.

The women in the SIP General Survey have even higher labor-force participation rates than American women. Figure 7.2 shows the labor-force participation rates by age of the women in the SIP General Survey from about 1950 to about 1975.[3] The dip associated with childbearing disappeared in the SIP data by 1965.[4] Also, labor-force participation rates of the women in the SIP General Survey were higher even in *1960* than the rates for American women in *1983*.

The Soviet government has been concerned with how to bring "labor reserves" into work for pay, since the Soviet economy faces an increasing labor shortage as the small post–baby boom cohorts move into the prime working ages (Feshbach and Rapawy 1973, 1976; Anderson and Silver 1985; Anderson 1986b). Especially in cities, efforts have been made to increase the labor-force participation rates of all residents, including those past normal retirement age. However, the labor-force participation rates of well-educated urban women, such as those in the SIP survey, are not a likely source of any *greater* contribution to the labor force. Other solutions, such as greater investment of capital or the recruitment of untapped labor from rural areas, must be sought in order to increase production in the future.

The recent increases in female labor-force participation rates for American women have led to speculation about how high female labor-force participation rates might rise and about what combinations of work and family life are possible when almost all women hold paid jobs (cf. Bumpass 1973; Westoff 1978; Butz and Ward 1979). Does a very high female labor-force participation rate eventually force women to choose among childlessness combined with a career, having children and forgoing market work, or settling for a substantially less successful career than would have been possible otherwise? What are the inevitable trade-offs for women between

3   The data in Figure 7.2 are from retrospective reports of women in the SIP General Survey. They refer to a five-year period centered on the year for which the data are plotted. For example, the data for 1950 refer to 1948–52, and the data for 1975 refer to 1973–77. The data in Figure 7.2 refer to employment in *public sector* jobs. The vast majority of working people in the Soviet Union hold public sector jobs. Public sector employment does not include legal private work, such as marketing home-produced vegetables, or illegal private work, such as black market transactions. It also does not include unpaid home production. In this chapter, when referring to the behavior of people in the SIP General Survey, the term "work for pay" or "paid work" will be used interchangeably with "employment in a public sector job."

4   The dip in Figure 7.2 for women in their early twenties is primarily related to school attendance rather than to childbearing.

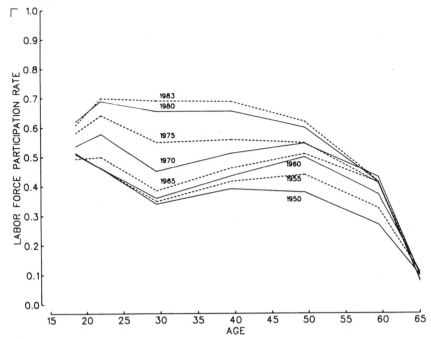

Figure 7.1. Labor-force participation rates of American women. *Source*: U.S. Bureau of Labor Statistics

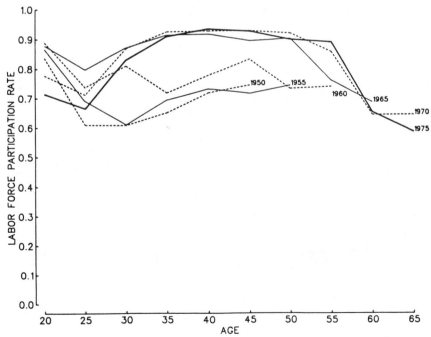

Figure 7.2. Labor-force participation rates of women in SIP General Survey

childbearing and work for pay? The experience of women from the Soviet Interview Project points to one possible pattern of labor-force participation and childbearing.

The life course approach

I use a life course approach to examine the order in which women complete their education, begin to work for pay, and begin childbearing. How does the sequence in which these events occur affect a woman's work career and the income she receives?

There has been growing interest among Western sociologists in the life cycle or the life course (cf. Elder 1985). The life course approach focuses on sequences and timing. This orientation grew out of the study of "career contingencies" in models of achievement. As Duncan, Featherman, and Duncan (1972: 205) write,

The notion of career contingencies used in this research is that of events occurring subsequent to the determination of family background, that may have a bearing upon the level of ultimate occupational achievement.... A man who undergoes a period of poor health, for example, may thereby be handicapped in his subsequent career.[5]

I am able to use a life course approach because the SIP General Survey collected a large amount of data pertaining to household and family demography. The amount of detail about life experiences collected in the SIP General Survey is unusual even by Western standards. For the respondent and for the respondent's spouse, we know in what years that individual did not hold a public sector job for six months or more, when the household migrated from one city or town to another city or town, when children were born, and when children died.

We have even more detailed information for a random one-third of the sample. For this subsample, we know about the use of and attitudes toward contraception, the number of abortions, views of the ideal number of children, and the number of children that the mother of the respondent bore.

Table 7.1 shows when various important life events occurred on average for each cohort of respondents.[6] The women in the SIP General Survey

---

[5] For a more detailed discussion see Sweet 1977.

[6] We know the actual year that schooling ended for respondents who had some specialized schooling. We do not know the actual year that schooling ended for respondents who had no specialized schooling. Specialized schools include all institutions of higher education, including *tekhnikums* and VUZs (higher educational institutions). They also include specialized secondary schools and vocational-technical schools. Michael Swafford assigned years of schooling equivalent to 11 education levels. For respondents who had no specialized

tended to begin working at about age 21 and to marry at about age 22. Earlier cohorts tended to have their first child at about age 25, whereas more recent cohorts have tended to begin childbearing at a younger age.[7]

Table 7.1 also shows the proportion of women by cohort who were ever married, the proportion who had no children, the proportion who never held a public sector job, and the proportion who held a public sector job every year from the time they first worked through the end of the last normal period (LNP) of life in the Soviet Union (or retirement age if that came earlier).[8]

Table 7.1. *Occurrence of major life events for women born 1905–1960*

| | | Average age at | | | Percentage who | | | |
| | Completion | | | | | | | |
Year of birth	of education	First job	First marriage	First birth	Ever married	Had no children	Never worked	Always worked
1905–10	17.9	22.1	25.3	24.7	100.0	0.0	15.9	25.0
1911–15	18.5	20.6	23.5	25.5	100.0	0.6	2.9	21.2
1916–20	19.6	21.9	22.5	24.6	98.1	1.9	3.8	17.0
1921–25	21.7	22.4	23.1	25.0	100.0	2.6	1.9	22.1
1926–30	21.3	21.3	22.2	23.9	100.0	1.7	0.9	21.7
1931–35	23.7	21.9	23.6	26.0	98.2	5.3	1.8	32.5
1936–40	23.8	21.3	23.0	25.0	98.7	7.5	0.9	37.3
1941–45	23.8	21.0	22.8	24.8	96.2	9.1	0.0	35.6
1946–50	22.9	21.2	22.1	23.3	96.2	13.0	0.8	28.0
1951–55	21.6	20.7	21.1	22.2	86.9	31.4	3.3	29.4
1956–60	20.3	19.5	19.8	20.9	70.7	56.0	13.0	35.5
Overall	21.8	21.3	22.5	24.4	95.5	11.5	2.8	28.3

schooling, age at completion of schooling was estimated by adding the years of schooling equivalent for the reported educational attainment to seven, the age at which schooling normally begins. The age at which the respondent's most recent marriage occurred and age at which the respondent's first marriage occurred were asked only of people who were married at the end of the LNP. The discussion of age at marriage, thus, is based on those people who were married at the end of the LNP. The data on age at first job refer only to women who ever held a public sector job.

[7] A retrospective survey done in Moskvoretskii raion of Moscow in 1965 estimated age at first birth to have remained close to 25 from 1945 through 1965 (Sisenko 1974: 31).

[8] The last normal period of life in the Soviet Union (LNP) is defined as the five-year period before the respondent's life changed substantially due to the decision to emigrate. Although the end of the LNP was defined however the respondent chose, for the majority of respondents the LNP ended the month before they applied for an exit visa. The LNP of most respondents ended in 1978 or 1979.

Although a mere 3 percent of the women in the SIP General Survey never held a public sector job, only 28 percent worked continuously from the time they first held a public sector job through the end of their last normal period of life in the Soviet Union or through reaching retirement age. Thus, the high female labor-force participation rates shown in Figure 7.2 occur because almost all women worked for most of their adult lives, but the majority spent some time without a public service job in the course of their careers. Although the women in the SIP General Survey worked 80 percent of the time between their first job and retirement, their high labor-force participation rate was not the result of 80 percent of the women having an uninterrupted career and 20 percent of the women never holding a public sector job.

The low fertility of this population does not result from a large proportion remaining childless while other women had many children. Only 12 percent of all women were childless, but the average number of children ever born, even for women who had completed childbearing, is only about two.

The focus of this chapter is on the experiences of these women while in the Soviet Union. However, in order to gain a perspective on what was typical of the *women* in the SIP General Survey and what was typical of *all* SIP respondents, some of the characteristics and experiences of the *men* in the SIP General Survey will be examined.

Educational attainment

Figure 7.3 shows the distribution of educational attainment by birth cohort and sex. For each sex, educational attainment increased substantially among recent cohorts, as indicated by the drop in the percentage who had less than seven years of education and the increase in the percentage with some higher education or completed higher education.

The educational attainment of the youngest cohorts was truncated. A larger proportion of those born since 1956 than of those who were born somewhat earlier had some higher education but had not completed higher education; many members of the youngest cohort were not old enough to have completed higher education before they left the Soviet Union. Even so, this is a highly educated population. Thirty percent of women born 1926–30 report that they completed higher education.

Education and cohort of birth are extremely intermingled, especially for women. The differences in educational attainment by cohort are so striking that, when one talks about people whose educational attainment was less than completion of secondary school, one is actually talking about people who were born before 1931; 77 percent of those with less than completed secondary education were born before 1931. A substantial proportion of men

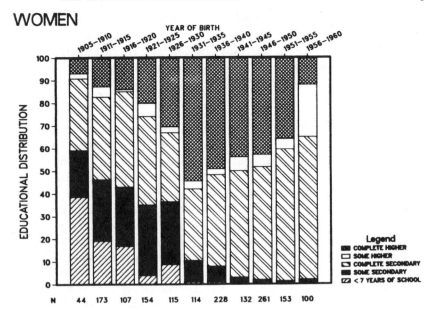

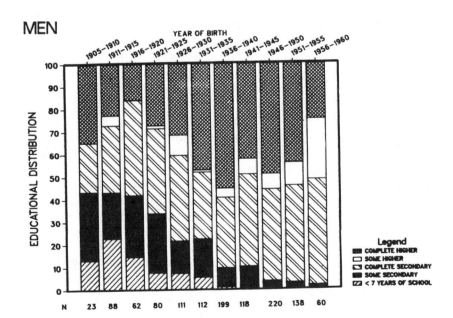

Figure 7.3. Educational distribution, by year of birth

in all cohorts had at least some higher education. However, 79 percent of all women with at least some higher education were born after 1930. The strong relation between cohort of birth and education means that analyses of the relation between education and other variables that do not take cohort of birth into account may misinterpret age effects as education effects.

Marital status

The marital status distribution at the end of the LNP by birth cohort by sex is shown in Figure 7.4. Most women married in their early twenties; 66 percent married between ages 20 and 25. Only 16 percent of the women first married at 26 or older. Only among those born after 1950 were over 5 percent never married while living in the USSR. These recent cohorts were still in the process of forming first marriages and probably would have ended up with proportions ever-married similar to those of earlier cohorts. For women born before 1921, the widowed outnumber the currently married.

Figure 7.4 shows a much higher proportion of young men never-married than of young women. For men, marriage occurred later than for women. Although 53 percent of the men married between age 20 and age 25, 43 percent of the men first married at 26 or older.

Figure 7.4 also shows a smaller proportion of older men widowed at the end of the LNP than of older women. This is because wives tend to be younger than their husbands and also because widowers are more likely to remarry than widows in most societies. The tendency of widowed or divorced men to remarry is even greater among those cohorts in which men were in short supply due to losses in World War II.

Childbearing

Figure 7.5 shows the distribution of the number of children ever born for each birth cohort of women. The average number of children ever born to each cohort also is shown.

It was unusual for a woman to have more than two children. Only 30 percent of the oldest cohort had three or more children. It also was unusual for a woman to have had *no* children. Only for women born since 1946, and still in the process of childbearing, are over 10 percent childless.[9]

---

[9] In a survey conducted in Moscow in 1970, women were asked whether they wanted to have more children. Only 16 percent of the childless women stated that they did not want to have any children. Among childless women under age 20, 91 percent planned to have children; 90 percent of childless women age 20–24 planned to have children; and 56 percent of childless women age 35–39 planned to have children (Kiseleva and Rilkova 1974: 59–61).

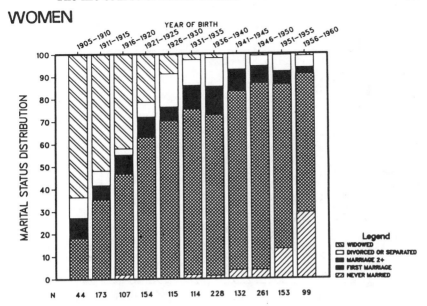

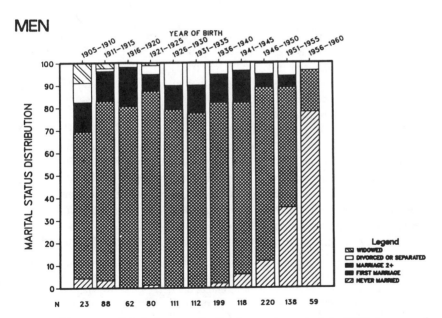

Figure 7.4. Marital status distribution at the end of the LNP, by year of birth

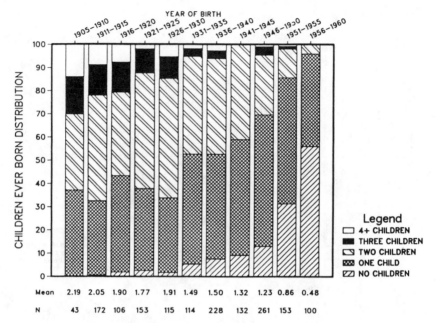

Figure 7.5. Distribution of children ever born, by birth year of women

Almost all children were born to married women. Only six women who never had been married reported having born any children. Of the women who were married at the end of the LNP, less than 2 percent report that their first child was born before the calendar year in which they first married, and 9 percent report that their first child was born in the same calendar year in which they first married.[10]

For those who started childbearing after marriage, children tended to follow the marriage quickly. For 47 percent of women, a child was born in the first calendar year after the marriage. For only 24 percent of the women was the first child born three or more calendar years after the marriage. Thus, unlike the United States in which there has been a trend toward postponement of childbearing (Baldwin and Nord 1984), for these women childbearing followed soon after marriage.[11]

Coale (1973) has suggested that three things must be true in order for

[10] We know the year and month that each child was born. We know the year that a woman first married, for women who were married at the end of the LNP. Thus, for a woman who was married at the end of the LNP, we know whether she bore a child in the same calendar year as the marriage, but we cannot be certain whether the date of the first marriage was before the date of the first birth.

[11] Volkov (1977) notes that the interval between the date of first marriage and the birth of the first child has grown shorter for Soviet women over time. For women

couples to limit their fertility. They must think it is morally acceptable to control fertility, they must have some effective means to control their fertility, and they must perceive that it is in their interest to limit their fertility.

Moral acceptability of fertility limitation and access to an effective means of limiting fertility were not a problem for most of the women in the SIP General Survey. Seventy-six percent of the women approved of contraception, 72 percent had used contraception, and 69 percent had had at least one abortion.

Abortion was extremely important in the control of childbearing. Figure 7.6 shows the distribution of the number of abortions by birth cohort. About one-third of the women had never had an abortion, one-third had had one or two abortions, and one-third had had three or more abortions.[12]

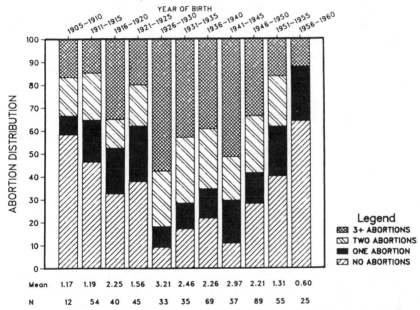

Figure 7.6. Distribution of number of abortions, by birth year of women

married in 1920–24, he reported that the average interval from marriage to birth of first child was 2.3 years, whereas for women first married in 1945–49, the average interval was 1.7 years. He comments that this decrease in the interval from marriage to first birth may be due to an increase in couples living together without formal marriage until they expect to have children. A study of Taganrog found that about 45 percent of women bore their first child within the first year after marriage (Rimashevskaia and Karapetian 1985: 43).

[12] The questions about abortions were not considered sensitive by most respondents. Less than 5 percent of the women refused to answer the question about whether they had ever had an abortion.

There has been some trend toward abortions becoming more common among the more recent cohorts, but the birth cohort of 1926–30 had the most abortions. These women were adolescents or young adults during and shortly after World War II.

Eleven percent of the women had more children than the number they considered ideal. The Soviet literature reports that women in Soviet European cities typically have fewer children than they consider ideal.[13] When asked why they do not have more children, practical considerations, such as a shortage of housing space, often are cited (cf. Belova 1971, 1973). The women in the SIP General Survey who had more children than they considered ideal had significantly more abortions than women whose number of children did not exceed their ideal number.

Some women, such as those just mentioned, had more children than they wanted. However, the use of contraception and abortion are so common in this population that the primary determinant of how many children a woman had is whether the woman or the couple thought it was in their interest to limit their fertility. Whether a couple perceives that it is in their interest to control their fertility depends on psychological, social, and economic factors.

Many studies have found that how many children a woman's mother had influences how many children the woman has, perhaps through its effect on the number of children that the woman views as desirable (cf. Gustavus and Nam 1970). One way that a woman's educational level is thought to influence her fertility is through making her relatively more interested in activities other than childbearing and childrearing.

Several studies have found that cultural factors, such as ethnicity, religion, or religiosity, affect childbearing independently of socioeconomic characteristics (cf. Westoff and Potvin 1967; Knodel and van de Walle 1979; Anderson 1986a). Most explanations of these effects relate to differences in subgroup norms about the value of children.

In the study of Soviet fertility, attention has most often been drawn to differences between traditionally Moslem and non-Moslem groups, but fertility differences also have been found between Finnic groups in the European part of the Soviet Union and Slavs who lived in the same region (Coale, Anderson, and Härm 1979). Soviet research has supported the point of view that members of traditionally Moslem groups in the Soviet Union tend to have more children than members of non-Moslem groups

---

[13] For example, in Minsk in 1969, women reported an average of 2.6 for the ideal number of children but reported an average of 2.0 as the number of children they expected to have (Shakhot'ko 1975: 136). A similar pattern occurs in Armenian cities (Rimashevskaia and Karapetian 1985: 32).

because they *want* more children rather than because of reluctance to use birth control (Belova 1973, 1975).

Studies of fertility differences among adherents of a single religion also have found that those who are more religious tend to have more children than those who are less religious. This has been found for Catholics in Portugal (Livi-Bacci 1971) and in Belgium (Lesthaeghe 1977). In this analysis, I examine whether being a religious Jew affected a woman's fertility.

Economic factors proposed to influence fertility are almost always viewed in terms of their effect on how many children the couple wants to have, that is, whether the couple perceives that limiting their fertility is in their interest (cf. Becker 1960; Willis 1973; Turchi 1975). Along this line, economists argue that a woman's education will be negatively related to the number of children she has, because the higher her education, the higher the wage she could command if she worked for pay.

This argument assumes that there is a trade-off for women between childbearing and labor-force participation and/or the wage rate that a woman will receive. The main cost of children typically is seen as the opportunity cost of the wife's forgone earnings because of the time she devotes to childcare (cf. Gronau 1973; Michael 1973).[14]

Economists also predict that the higher the income of the husband, the more children the wife will have.[15] This is because the higher the husband's income, the more children the couple can afford to support. These economists assume that children do not demand much of the father's time, or at least that they do not interfere with his labor-force activity or have a depressing effect on his income.

Analysis of the determinants of the number of children ever born

The effects of various factors on fertility were examined through multiple regression analysis, using a combination of dummy variables and interval-

---

[14] Typically, female education is used as an indicator of the wage that a woman could command rather than actual wages of women who work, since the entire structure of female labor-force participation and female earnings is assumed to be affected by childbearing.

[15] The economic argument actually is that the higher the family income, the more children the wife will have. However, economists also argue that a woman will have fewer children, the higher the wage she would have received if she worked for pay. Since the main source of family income aside from the wife's income is the husband's income, the economic argument reduces to the expectation that the higher the husband's income, the more children the wife will bear.

level variables.[16] All the variables used in the analyses are described in the Soviet Interview Project General Survey Codebook, cited in Chapter 1 and in the Glossary of this book.

In all the multiple regression analyses, cohort of birth is taken into account regardless of the statistical significance of coefficients for individual birth cohorts or for the set of birth cohorts as a whole. This is because I seek to analyze patterns of the life course after cohort of birth has been taken into account, or controlled. It is important to take cohort of birth into account in the analysis of the number of children ever born because many women had not reached the end of childbearing by the end of the LNP.[17]

The results of the multiple regression analysis of the number of children ever born, for women, appear in Table 7.2.[18] The results when only birth cohort and educational attainment are included in the analysis are shown in Panel A, and the results when additional variables are included are shown in Panel B. A schematic representation of the factors that were found to be important appears in Diagram 7.1.[19]

Birth cohort and educational attainment are important for the number of children that a woman has borne. When only birth cohort and education are considered, women with completed secondary education have on average 0.14 fewer children than women with less than completed secondary education, and women with some higher education or more have on average 0.40 fewer children than women with completed secondary education.

Factors other than birth cohort and education also are important for the number of children ever born. The results in Panel B show that religious Jewish women have 0.29 more children than women who are not religious Jews but who are the same age and have the same educational attainment.[20]

[16] Dummy variables are assigned a value of 0 or 1 for each respondent, according to whether or not the respondent had the given characteristic, such as having or not having completed higher education, or having or not having completed secondary education.

[17] The youngest cohort, those born 1956–60, were on average aged 20 at the end of the LNP. Many had not completed their education, and few were launched on a career. Because this youngest group had experienced few of the events analyzed in this chapter, they will be excluded from the regression analyses, although information about them will appear in the figures.

[18] The questions about the ideal number of children and how many children the woman's mother had borne were asked of only a random third of the respondents. The analysis without these two items was very similar for the entire sample and for the random third. Both the results presented that include only birth cohort and education as independent variables and the results presented that include all variables refer to the random one-third of the sample for which all items were available.

[19] Birth cohort is not explicitly represented in Diagram 7.1 and successive diagrams.

[20] Twenty percent of the women in the SIP General Survey were religious Jews, 58 percent were nonreligious Jews, and 22 percent were non-Jews. The non-Jews did not differ substantially from the nonreligious Jews in their fertility behavior.

Table 7.2. *Multiple regression results for the number of children ever born*

Variable	B	t	Significance of t
Panel A: Results when only birth and educational variables are included[a]			
Birth cohort			
BN1620	−.054923	−.383	.7021
BN2125	−.093698	−.696	.4870
BN2630	.232570	1.555	.1205
BN3135	.026185	.171	.8641
BN3640	−.190513	−1.474	.1413
BN4145	−.281393	−1.894	.0588
BN4650	−.395967	−3.236	.0013
BN5155	−.896302	−6.585	.0000
Educational attainment			
COMPSEC	−.136161	−1.316	.1889
SOMEH	−.400707	−3.705	.0002
Constant	2.912193	28.942	.0000
Panel B: Results when additional variables are included[b]			
Birth cohort			
BN1620	−.033255	−.238	.8119
BN2125	.019290	.145	.8844
BN2630	.367085	2.493	.0130
BN3135	.161136	1.075	.2832
BN3640	−.013502	−.105	.9167
BN4145	−.058243	−.391	.6962
BN4650	−.189242	−1.522	.1286
BN5155	−.648777	−4.657	.0000
Educational attainment			
COMPSEC	−.015325	−.149	.8814
SOMEH	−.221186	−2.017	.0442
Ideal number of children			
KIDSNO	.076587	2.659	.0081
Number of children woman's mother had			
MOMKIDS	.057906	3.127	.0019
Being a religious Jew			
RELJEW	.287442	3.329	.0009
Constant	2.248823	14.164	.0000

[a] $R^2 = .20854$; adjusted $R^2 = .19103$; overall $F = 11.90958$; sig. of overall $F = .0000$; $N = 463$.
[b] $R^2 = .26370$; adjusted $R^2 = .24238$; overall $F = 12.36979$; sig. of overall $F = .0000$; $N = 463$.

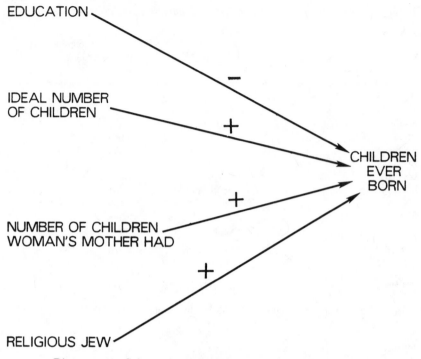

Diagram 7.1. Schematic model of determinants of the number of children ever born, for women

Also, the larger the number of children that a woman considers ideal,[21] and the more children that the woman's mother had, the more children the woman bore, even after birth cohort and education have been taken into account.[22]

Even after whether the woman was a religious Jew, the ideal number of children, and the number of children the woman's mother had are taken into account, educational attainment is still important, but its effect on the number of children ever born is much weaker. After these three additional

[21] In the SIP General Survey, the mean of the ideal number of children was 2.1. This accords well with the results of a survey in 1969, which reported the average ideal number of children among women living in Moscow to be 1.9 (Belova 1971:41).
[22] In regression analyses, some categories must be excluded for each independent variable that is converted into dummy variables. For education, the excluded category comprises those with less than completed secondary education. For cohort of birth, those born before 1916 are the excluded group. Thus, the coefficients can be interpreted as the net effect of a woman's having a given characteristic in comparison with women who were born before 1916, who were not religious Jews, and who had less than completed secondary schooling.

variables are taken into account, women with completed secondary education have, on average, 0.02 fewer children than women with less than completed secondary education, and women with at least some higher education have 0.22 fewer children than women with less than completed secondary education. The effects of education are weaker after these other variables are taken into account, because more-educated women were less likely to be religious Jews, less likely to perceive a large number of children as ideal, and less likely to have had many siblings themselves than women with less education.

The timing of the completion of education, first employment, and the beginning of childbearing

As suggested by the data in Table 7.1, the normal course of events for women in the SIP General Survey was to complete their education, begin working, and then bear their first child. For individuals, however, any sequence of completion of education, first employment, and birth of the first child is possible.

Table 7.3 shows for each sex the distribution of respondents among the various possible sequences of completion of education, first employment, and beginning of childbearing. For 64 percent of the women and for 50 percent of

Table 7.3. *Distribution of sequences of completion of education, first employment, and birth of first child*

	Women (%)	Men (%)
Completed education before first employment		
Completed education, first employment, first birth	45.1	35.4
Completed education, first birth, first employment	4.2	1.7
First birth, completed education, first employment	8.3	3.4
Completed education, first employment, no child	6.4	9.8
First employed before completion of education		
First employment, completed education, first birth	17.9	19.8
First employment, first birth, completed education	10.6	19.6
First birth, first employment, completed education	3.3	3.3
First employment, completed education, no child	4.3	6.8
Total	100.1	99.8
N	1,509	1,169

Note: People are excluded from this table who never worked or who could not recall the year they first worked or the year their first child was born.

the men, education was completed before the first full-time public sector job was begun. Thus, contrary to what is commonly perceived to be the conventional path of career development, only slightly more than half of the members of each sex completed their education before they began to work. The lower proportion for men than women is due partially to the greater tendency of men than women to accumulate additional education in midcareer.[23]

Forty-five percent of the women conformed to the conventional path: education, followed by the beginning of work, followed by the beginning of childbearing. However, a substantial proportion of women (22 percent) bore a child before they completed their highest education. Shortly, I shall investigate whether the sequence of the beginning of childbearing and completion of education affects a woman's working life.

The nexus of educational attainment and the early career

The SIP General Survey interview schedule asked when the respondent began the first job he or she held after completion of highest education. The SIP General Survey interview schedule also asked when the respondent entered the last specialized school he or she attended for at least one year and when the respondent left that school.[24] Over 70 percent of the respondents attended some kind of specialized school for at least one year. For these respondents, we know the year they began studying at that school and the year they left that school.

The expectation was that even if a person had worked before completing school, he or she would begin a *new* job after the completion of highest education. However, a surprisingly large proportion of respondents did not complete their education and then commence a new job.

The respondent could have *started* working at the job held after completing schooling before he or she stopped attending that last school. For example, a graduate student might begin teaching before she had completed all course work at the university. If the former student continued in the same teaching job after graduation, then she would have begun the first job she held after

---

[23] We know the year that work began for almost all respondents. For respondents with no specialized schooling, the age at completion of education was estimated as explained earlier. Often the year of completion of schooling, the year work began, and the year the first child was born did not all occur in different calendar years. We do not know for certain what the ordering was of events that occurred in the same calendar year. I have assumed, if the year that two events occurred is the same, that completion of education precedes beginning of work and that completion of education and beginning of work precede the birth of the first child.
[24] Recall the specialized schools include all higher educational institutions, specialized secondary schools, and vocational-technical schools.

completing schooling while she was still *attending* that last school. A white-collar worker might enroll in an evening higher educational institution (VUZ) but continue to work at the same job while attending the evening VUZ. If he continued at the same job after completing the work at the evening VUZ, then he would have begun the first job he held after completing his education *before* he entered that last school. Thus, knowing that a person *held* a certain job after he or she stopped attending a certain school does not tell us when he or she *started* that job.

Table 7.4 shows the distribution by sex of the number of respondents who began the first job they held after completing highest education: (1) *after leaving* the last school, (2) *while attending* the last school, or (3) *before entering* the last school. The distribution is shown with and without those who never attended a specialized school and with and without those who reported no job after completing highest education.

Only 61 percent of the men with some specialized schooling and 72 percent of the women with some specialized schooling completed their highest education and then began a new job. Thus, for many respondents, choice of occupational specialty may have led to choice of educational specialty, rather than vice versa.

Table 7.4. *Percentage distribution of timing of leaving last school and beginning first job after completion of highest education*

	All people		People who attended a specialized school	
	Men	Women	Men	Women
Job started *after* leaving last school	46.2	51.0	60.8	72.1
Job started *while* attending last school	13.2	10.4	17.3	14.8
Job started *before* entering last school	16.7	9.3	22.0	13.1
No job after last schooling	2.8	5.4		
No specialized schooling	21.1	23.8		
Total	100.0	99.9	100.1	100.0
N	1,211	1,582	920	1,118

Age at first employment

The age at which full-time employment starts marks the beginning of the career. In this section, I investigate what factors influence the age at which full-time employment first occurs.

The topic also is interesting because of recent changes in the average age at entry into the labor force in the Soviet Union. By conventional Soviet definition, the "able-bodied ages" begin at age 16 for both men and women. But the average age at actual entry into the labor force has increased over time. In 1959, 60 percent of the Soviet population aged 16–19 were employed, whereas in 1970 only 40 percent of those aged 16–19 were employed (Breeva 1984: 33).

Educational attainment is certainly likely to influence the age at which a person first worked. Whether a person became a parent before completion of highest education also might affect when that person first worked. For women, birth of a child before completion of highest education might postpone entry into the labor force. For men, birth of a child before completion of education might speed entry into the labor force. As being a religious Jew influenced a woman's childbearing, it also is possible that being a religious Jew affected the age that she first worked.

Analysis of the determinants of the age at first employment

Multiple regression analysis is again used to analyze the determinants of the age at which the respondent first worked. Both males and females are considered in the same analysis.[25] Dummy variables for educational attainment are again used.[26] These educational variables were considered in combination with whether the respondent was female, since the relationship between educational attainment and age that work began might be substantially different for males and females. As earlier, the cohort of birth also is taken into account. Multiple regression results appear in Table 7.5. A schematic representation of the factors that were found to be important appears in Diagram 7.2.

Educational attainment is the primary determinant of the age at which respondents first worked. Once educational attainment is taken into account, the sex of the respondent does not matter. Those who completed secondary education entered the labor force three-quarters of a year later than those with less than completed secondary education, and those with at

[25] Preliminary analysis showed that the pattern of relations of variables with age at first work was not distorted by including both sexes in one equation.

[26] A more detailed breakdown of educational attainment mattered for age at first work and for the multiple regression analyses in the remainder of the chapter than mattered for the number of children ever born to women.

Table 7.5. *Multiple regression results for age at first employment*

Variable	B	t	Significance of t
Birth cohort			
BN1620	1.113609	3.410	.0007
BN2125	1.208444	4.132	.0000
BN2630	−.181214	−.614	.5394
BN3135	−.286667	−.956	.3390
BN3640	−.915518	−3.505	.0005
BN4145	−1.044411	−3.551	.0004
BN4650	−1.000210	−3.874	.0001
BN5155	−1.236149	−4.274	.0000
Educational attainment			
COMPSEC2	.490599	2.051	.0404
SPECSEC2	1.626378	7.381	.0000
SOMEH2	2.566403	6.935	.0000
COMPH2	3.381919	15.811	.0000
GRADST2	3.717436	9.391	.0000
Female and first birth before end of education			
FEDBIR1	.933928	4.595	.0000
Constant	19.829877	91.387	.0000

Note: $R^2 = .15773$; adjusted $R^2 = .15308$; overall $F = 33.89519$; sig. of overall $F = .0000$; $N = 2,549$.

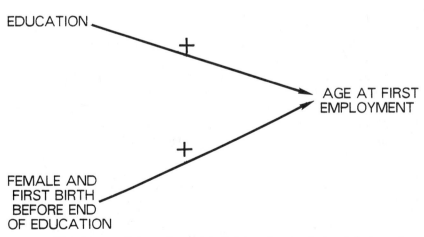

Diagram 7.2. Schematic model of determinants of age at first employment, both sexes combined

least some higher education entered the labor force almost three and a half years later than those with less than completed secondary education. Those who had at least some graduate study began work almost four years later than those who had less than completed secondary education.

Surprisingly, however, delays in the beginning of work for those with higher education are not due mainly to postponement of the beginning of work until *all* schooling had been completed. Rather, they are due to postponement of the beginning of work because of *earlier* schooling. Over 50 percent of those with some higher education first worked before they completed their education, and over 80 percent of those with at least some graduate study first worked before they completed their education.

For women, birth of a child before completion of highest education led to postponement of entry into the labor force by almost one year. Once cohort of birth and educational attainment have been taken into account, whether a person was a religious Jew did not affect age of entry into the labor force for either men or women. There is no statistical evidence that birth of a child before completion of highest education affected the age at which men began to work.

Work after reaching retirement age

Many respondents worked after they reached normal retirement age. Of the 144 men and 411 women interviewed who were past normal retirement age at the end of the LNP, 68 percent of the men and 53 percent of the women worked after they had reached retirement age.[27]

Table 7.6 shows the average earnings in their last job of people who were past retirement age at the end of the LNP. Some of these people ended their last job before reaching normal retirement age, and others ended their last job after reaching retirement age. For those who worked after reaching normal retirement age, some people continued in a job that they had held before reaching retirement age, and others began a new job after reaching retirement age. Thus, in Table 7.6, the average earnings in last job are shown, for men and women, by whether the last job *ended* after the respondent had reached retirement age and, for those who worked after reaching normal retirement age, by whether the last job *began* before the respondent reached retirement age.

[27] In the Soviet Union, the normal retirement age for women is 55 and for men is 60 years. A woman was classified as having worked after reaching retirement age if she was 56 or older when she last worked. A man was classified as having worked after retirement age if he was 61 or older when he last worked. Although some of the elderly took "retirement-type jobs" that they started after reaching retirement age, most continued in their preretirement jobs. Of those who worked after retirement, 90 percent of the men and 82 percent of the women began their last job before they had reached retirement age.

Table 7.6. *Average earnings in rubles per month in last job for people who were past retirement age at end of the LNP, by when job began*

	All	Less than complete secondary education	Complete secondary education	At least some higher education
Women				
No retirement job ($N = 148$)	118	105	—	125
Retirement job begun *before* retirement age ($N = 177$)	136	111	136	146
Retirement job begun *after* retirement age ($N = 38$)	88	81	—	93
Men				
No retirement job ($N = 42$)	187	160	—	193
Retirement job begun *before* retirement age ($N = 87$)	196	156	210	220
Retirement job begun *after* retirement age ($N = 10$)	131	143	—	123

Note: Dashes indicate cells with no cases.

In general, the lowest earnings in last job were received by people who started a new job after reaching retirement age. Women who began their last job after reaching normal retirement age tended to hold the manual and lower-level service jobs, such as museum guard or coat-check clerk, that often come to mind when one thinks of Soviet retirees working. However, at least among the SIP respondents, most retirement work was *not* of this type.

The age profile of men and women who work after retirement age differs. Men who worked after retirement age tended to work for only two or three years. The age gradient of leaving work after reaching retirement age is much more gradual for women. For those who worked after reaching retirement age, work was much more discontinuous than work before retirement age.

Twenty percent of the respondents in the SIP General Survey were past retirement age at the end of the LNP. Since the pattern of work and of earnings of those past retirement age is different from that of people before reaching retirement age, it is important that analyses of the career not be misled by assuming that the last job of people who were past normal retirement age is comparable to a preretirement job of a person at the height of his or her career.[28]

[28] See Mincer 1974 for a discussion of the typical pattern of earnings with age in the United States.

The course of the career

I now examine the continuity of women's work careers. The more years a woman is away from the labor force, either for childbearing or for some other reason, the less experience she gains. In addition, the more discontinuous her career, the less chance she has to build on earlier experience. In the Western literature, lesser job experience and more discontinuous careers, which inhibit obtaining promotions, have been suggested as reasons why women's earnings tend to be lower than those of men of the same age and educational attainment.[29]

I shall measure the discontinuity of men's and women's work careers by the number of years he or she did not hold a public sector job between the year the person *first* held a public sector job and the end of the LNP. If a respondent was past retirement age at the end of the LNP, I shall examine the number of years he or she did not hold a public sector job between the time the respondent first held a public sector job and the year the respondent reached retirement age.[30]

I expect that men will have taken few years away from public sector employment. Some men will take time off for activities such as additional schooling.[31] Women are likely to take much more time away from public sector employment than men. Most theories predict that the higher a woman's education, the greater her labor-force participation, both because she will have more "taste for work" and because her earnings will be greater. Also, the higher her actual earnings, the less time she is likely to spend without a paid job. In addition, the more children she bears, the less she is likely to work for pay, under the assumption that there is some incompatibility between raising children and working. Theories also predict that the higher the husband's income, the less his wife will work, since the higher his income, the more easily they can afford for her not to earn money.

Figure 7.7 presents information about women's and men's participation in public sector jobs between the time they first held such a job and the end of the LNP (or when they reached normal retirement age, if that occurred before the end of the LNP). It shows the percentage in each cohort that never

[29] Corcoran (1978) shows for the United States that, although lesser job experience and career interruptions play a role in the lower earnings of women, these factors do not account for all of the gap between men's and women's earnings. American women tend to earn substantially less than American men even after education, job experience, and work interruptions have been taken into account.

[30] I estimate the number of years a person did not work by counting the number of years that he or she indicated on the life history chart that he or she did not hold a public sector job for six months or more. To avoid major errors, it is necessary to make some adjustments to the reported data. See the Appendix to this chapter for more discussion of the life history chart and adjustments to the data.

[31] Military service was considered working for pay.

WOMEN

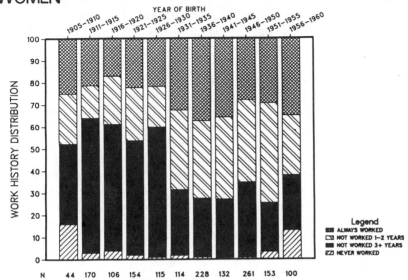

N   44   170   106   154   115   114   228   132   261   153   100

MEN

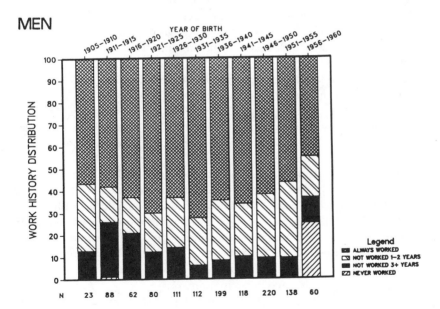

N   23   88   62   80   111   112   199   118   220   138   60

Figure 7.7. Distribution of years not working from first job through end of LNP or retirement age.

held a public sector job, the percentage that held a public sector job at some time but were without a public sector job for three years or more between the time they first worked and the end of the LNP, the percentage that was without a public sector job for one or two years between their first job and the end of the LNP, and the percentage that had a public sector job every year from first job through the end of the LNP.

The majority of men had uninterrupted careers. Those who did not have uninterrupted careers tended to take off only one or two years. A substantial proportion of the youngest cohort had never held a public sector job because they were still in school at the end of the LNP.

In contrast, only a minority of women had uninterrupted careers, and a large proportion of those who did not have an uninterrupted career took off three years or more. As with the men, a substantial proportion of the youngest cohort of women had not yet begun to work. Except for the oldest cohort, however, all cohorts of women had only a trivial proportion that had never held a public sector job.

Analysis of the determinants of the discontinuity of the work career

Next, I shall examine the factors related to how many years women did not hold a public sector job between the year they first worked and the end of the LNP or the year they reached normal retirement age, whichever came first. Naturally, cohort of birth must be taken into account. In addition to birth cohort, the most likely influences on the amount of time a woman did not have a public sector job are educational attainment, the number of children ever born, the woman's earnings, and her husband's income.

Although we do not know a woman's earnings at every point in her career, we do know her reported earnings in her first job. Those earnings will be used to indicate how much money she would lose by not holding a public sector job for some time, even though her education gives a general indication of her expected wage rate.

Based on the results of the earlier analysis, I also shall examine whether being a religious Jew or bearing a child before completion of schooling affects the number of years that a woman does not hold a public sector job. Do religious Jewish women have a different labor-force participation pattern than other women with the same educational attainment and number of children? Also, does bearing a child before completion of education indicate a disinclination to work, or is there some later "catching up" in increased labor-force participation?

Multiple regression analysis is again used. Dummy variables were introduced for having had one child, two children, and three or more children. Dummy variables for educational attainment also are included.

Earnings in first job and spouse's earnings from main job at the end of the LNP were entered in rubles per month.[32] The multiple regression results appear in Table 7.7, and a schematic representation of the important factors appears in Diagram 7.3.

Table 7.7. *Multiple regression results for number of years women did not work from first job through retirement age or end of LNP*

Variable	B	t	Significance of t
Birth cohort			
BN1620	− 2.407256	− 2.022	.0435
BN2125	− 5.669074	− 5.356	.0000
BN2630	− 5.517375	− 5.153	.0000
BN3135	− 7.327137	− 6.999	.0000
BN3640	− 8.634785	− 8.994	.0000
BN4145	− 8.662197	− 8.413	.0000
BN4650	− 8.425018	− 8.684	.0000
BN5155	− 8.754299	− 8.247	.0000
Educational attainment			
COMPSEC2	− .963015	− 1.276	.2023
SPECSEC2	− 2.163525	− 3.122	.0019
SOMEH2	− .731461	− .660	.5091
COMPH2	− 2.494798	− 3.572	.0004
GRADST2	− 2.896667	− 2.379	.0175
Children ever born			
CEB1	.252317	.330	.7412
CEB2	1.444870	1.788	.0740
CEB3	1.920616	1.802	.0719
First birth before end of education			
EDBIR1	− 1.019418	− 2.375	.0178
Monthly earnings in first job (rubles)			
GROSFTJ	− .007578	− 2.059	.0398
Spouse's monthly earnings in last job (rubles)			
SPGROSMO	.004937	3.568	.0004
Constant	12.019649	9.035	.0000

Note: $R^2 = .25171$; adjusted $R^2 = .23662$; overall $F = 16.67730$; sig. of overall $F = .0000$; $N = 962$.

[32] The only indicator of the spouse's income is the spouse's earnings from his main LNP job.

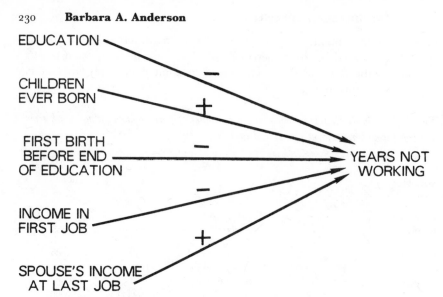

Diagram 7.3. Schematic model of determinants of the number of years women did not work from first job through retirement age or end of LNP

Educational attainment, whether a child was born before completion of highest education, the number of children ever born, earnings at first job, and husband's LNP earnings all influence the continuity of work. Women with completed general secondary education take one year less away from public sector employment than women with less than completed secondary education.

However, the relation between the number of years without a public sector job and education is not linear. Women with some higher education take more time out than women with completed general secondary education or women with completed specialized education. These women with incomplete higher education may have cut their education short because of childbearing and may be less inclined to work than otherwise similar women. However, women who have completed higher education spend two and a half years less without a public sector job than women with less than secondary education.

Women who bore a child before completion of highest education make up for this postponement of the beginning of their career by taking off one year less than otherwise similar women. Thus, bearing a child before completion of education does not indicate a disinclination to work. It only affects the *timing* of when a woman works.

Most childless women spent some time without a public sector job, but women with *one* child spent no more time without a public sector job than childless women. Women with two children, however, tended to spend one and a half more years without a public sector job than childless women, and women with three or more children took almost two more years away from public sector work than childless women.[33]

In recent years, Soviet women have been able to take maternity leave with pay for six months. In addition, if they want to take a longer leave, their jobs are supposed to be held for them for one year without change in job or any harm to their work record. Even so, the Soviet literature suggests that women are concerned about whether taking an entire year's leave due to childbirth will hurt their careers, especially if they have not held a given job for very long (Katkova 1978).[34] In the SIP General Survey results, we may be observing different labor-force behavior after the birth of the first child, when a woman would typically have had little accumulated experience in her job, than after a second or later child, by which time she would have accumulated more experience.

There are additional reasons why women with two or more children may have different labor-force participation patterns than women with no children or only one child. Whenever a family makes a change in its living arrangements, such as that related to geographical mobility, the situation is more complicated the more children there are in the family. Women with more children are likely to take more time away from public sector work in association with *any* change in living arrangements.

There also are income effects. The higher a woman's earnings in her first job, the more years she holds a public sector job. Also, the higher the earnings of the husband in his LNP job, the fewer years the wife holds a public sector job.

Even though women who were religious Jews tended to have more children than women who were not religious Jews, once the factors just discussed are taken into account women who were religious Jews did not spend significantly more time without a public sector job than women who were not religious Jews. Thus, although religiosity did affect childbearing, it did not increase the tendency of women to take time away from public

---

[33] The set of children-ever-born dummy variables are jointly significant at the .05 level, even though none of the individual dummy variables is significant at that level.

[34] Respondents in the SIP General Survey would reasonably have replied that they were not without a public sector job if they took six months' paid maternity leave, since they were paid during that time, as if they had taken sick leave. If they took less than the full six months of additional unpaid maternity leave, they still would have been less than six months without a public sector job and still would not have reported a work interruption. Thus, the *reported* work interruptions are fairly major work interruptions.

sector work, once their other characteristics, including the number of children they have borne, have been taken into account.[35]

Analysis of the determinants of earnings

In this section, I examine the life course factors that influence earnings in last job. This is done only for people who were not past retirement age at the end of the LNP. The focus is on the explanation of female earnings, but the role of life course factors in the determination of male earnings also will be examined for comparison.

Cohort of birth is again taken into account. It is reasonable to expect that the respondent's earnings in first job would be related to the respondent's earnings in last job before retirement. Educational attainment may have a persistent effect on later earnings, even after earnings in first job are taken into account. The number of years that a woman has actually worked also should affect her earnings in her last job, since the amount of work experience has typically been found to be very strongly related to earnings (Mincer 1974).

The results of the multiple regression analysis for women appear in Table 7.8.[36] A schematic representation of the factors that were found to be important appears in Diagram 7.4.

Birth cohort, educational attainment, and earnings in first job are all important. In addition, the number of years that a woman has actually held a public sector job is positively related to her earnings in her last job. Once these factors are taken into account, the number of children that a woman has borne does not significantly affect her earnings in her last job. It is particularly interesting that the effects of children on women's earnings all appear to be channeled through their effect on work experience.

[35] The inclusion of spouse's LNP earnings required that the analysis shown in Table 7.7 be restricted to women who had a living husband at the end of the LNP. This considerably reduced the sample size. The results when spouse's LNP earnings were not included and, thus, when women who did not have a living husband at the end of the LNP were included in the analysis were similar. Only cohort of birth was significantly related to the number of years that a man did not work.

[36] Earnings in last public sector job held are used to calculate the dependent variable. Earnings includes all bonuses and premiums. Income from a second job or from a private job are not included. One thousand times the natural logarithm of the earnings at the last job in rubles is used as the dependent variable. The logarithm was taken because of the typical curve of earnings with experience, in which, with increasing experience, the additional returns in income decrease (Mincer 1974). The natural logarithm was multiplied by one thousand to make the coefficients clearer. Analyses in which the actual earnings in rubles were used as the dependent variable yielded very similar results.

Table 7.8. *Multiple regression results for natural logarithm of earnings in last job* (× *1,000*), *women who were not past retirement age at end of LNP*

Variable	B	t	Significance of t
Birth cohort			
BN3135	58.553655	1.270	.2045
BN3640	119.084663	2.842	.0046
BN4145	105.855276	2.083	.0375
BN4650	52.516241	.981	.3271
BN5155	− 17.549731	− .278	.7814
Educational attainment			
COMPSEC2	186.474121	3.657	.0003
SPECSEC2	186.408636	4.064	.0001
SOMEH2	262.200065	3.780	.0002
COMPH2	391.329466	8.732	.0000
GRADST2	676.977092	8.804	.0000
Monthly earnings in first job (rubles)			
GROSFTJ	2.059740	8.746	.0000
Years worked			
YRSWK	11.594928	5.080	.0000
Constant	4158.467893	54.793	.0000

Note: $R^2 = .24939$; adjusted $R^2 = .24036$; overall $F = 27.60509$; sig. of overall $F = .0000$; $N = 1,010$.

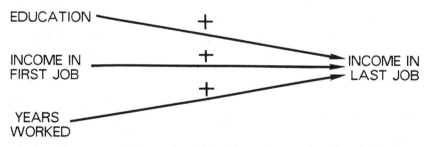

Diagram 7.4. Schematic model of determinants of earnings in last job

Table 7.9 shows the results of a multiple regression analysis for men, in which the variables appearing in Table 7.8 (for women) are entered. This set of variables explains less of the variance in men's earnings than it did in women's earnings. This is probably because specific characteristics of the job, such as industry and level of authority, are more important in

Table 7.9. *Multiple regression results for natural logarithm of earnings in last job (× 1,000) men who were not past retirement age at the end of LNP*

Variable	B	t	Significance of t
Birth cohort			
BN3135	60.834738	1.176	.2397
BN3640	89.159660	1.752	.0802
BN4145	67.604818	1.028	.3040
BN4650	65.144986	.917	.3592
BN5155	− 81.072631	− .951	.3419
Educational attainment			
COMPSEC2	142.879264	2.854	.0044
SPECSEC2	99.878370	2.060	.0397
SOMEH2	93.228691	1.386	.1661
COMPH2	237.795878	5.163	.0000
GRADST2	390.508384	5.797	.0000
Monthly earnings in first job (rubles)			
GROSFTJ	.696727	3.537	.0004
Years worked			
YRSWK	8.335643	2.822	.0049
Constant	4749.065326	43.282	.0000

Note: R^2 = .11118; adjusted R^2 = .09987; overall F = 9.82963; sig. of overall F = .0000; N = 956.

explaining the variability of men's than of women's earnings. Since men tended to have few years in which they did not have a public sector job, the number of years worked for men is almost totally determined by when they were born and their educational level.

Although the life course variables considered explain less of the variance in men's earnings than in women's earnings, it is surprising how *similar* the results are for the two sexes. For example, all of the coefficients for individual variables in the multiple regression equations for each sex are of the same sign. Even though the differences in the patterns of relations among variables for men and women required the estimation of a separate equation for each sex, these results suggest that the roles of education, job experience, and earnings in first job are similar in the determination of earnings for both men and women, even though on average women received lower earnings than men.

Concluding remarks

I have shown that life course factors are very important in the determination of the labor-force participation and earnings of women. Diagram 7.5 is a schematic representation of the relation of various life events to the number of years women held public sector jobs and to their earnings in their last job.[37]

I have shown that education is tremendously important for female labor-force participation and earnings. The higher a woman's educational attainment, the less time she takes out of the labor force and the higher her earnings, even after work experience and earnings in first job have been taken into account. Education is even more important for female labor-force participation when one considers its indirect effects through the number of children ever born.

The more children a woman has, the more years she does not hold a public sector job. But once job experience has been taken into account, having children has no further effect on women's earnings. In addition, although women who were religious Jews tended to have more children than women who were not religious Jews, once the number of children is taken into account, religious Jews are no more likely to take time away from public sector employment than other women.

Also, although women who bore a child before completing their education tended to begin to work in a public sector job about one year later than other women, they made up this delay later. These women, on average, took one year less away from public sector employment than otherwise similar women. Thus, childbearing before completion of education affected only the timing of work and did not indicate a distaste for paid work.

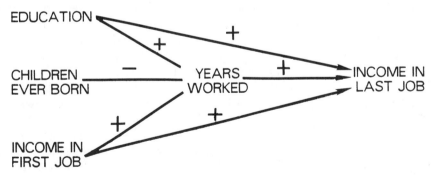

Diagram 7.5. Schematic model of interrelations of life course events for women

[37] Diagram 7.5 is not a statistical path model and should not be considered as such.

What do these results say about the status of Soviet women? That can be answered partially by examining the earnings of women in the SIP General Survey in comparison with the earnings of men in the SIP General Survey. The relation of women's and men's earnings in the SIP General Survey can be compared to the relation of men's and women's earnings in American data, in order to gain some insight into the status of the SIP women in comparison to that of American women.

A major part of the argument about the low status of American women has involved not just the lower average wages of American women but also that, for any given set of qualifications, such as education and work experience, American women are paid less than American men. In the United States, one source of the difference in women's and men's earnings is that women hold part-time jobs more often than men. One way to control for the difference in full- versus part-time work is to compare earnings of full-time female workers with earnings of full-time male workers.

Table 7.10 shows women's earnings as a percentage of men's earnings only for men and women who worked full-time (35 hours or more) for both the SIP General Survey respondents and for Americans in 1979 (U.S. Bureau of the Census 1981: 224–28). The table begins at age 25, since education often interferes with full-time work before that age. The table ends at age 55, since that is the normal retirement age for Soviet women. For those categories in which the female/male ratio in earnings is higher in the SIP General Survey than for the United States in 1979, the values in Table 7.10 are italicized.

Overall, women in the SIP General Survey aged 25–54 who worked full-time made 70.1 percent as much as men, whereas for American women in 1979 the comparable percentage was 56.8. The overall breakdown by education shows that within every education category the women in the SIP General Survey had earnings that were a larger proportion of the earnings of men in the SIP General Survey than American women's earnings were of earnings by American men in 1979. In the breakdown by age, the SIP women fared better than the American women for all age groups except the youngest, those 25–29. In the cross-tabulation of age by education, the SIP women fared better in every classification except for young women with fairly low education.[38]

The SIP data suggest that Soviet women, like American women, earn less than men and that the earnings differential by sex is not totally eliminated by controlling for characteristics such as age, education, and hours worked.

[38] In both the SIP and the American data, there were few people under age 35 who had less than completed high school education. Thus, the values for those aged 25–29 and 30–34 with less than completed secondary education are not presented, although their earnings are included in calculation of the marginal values by age and by education.

Table 7.10. *Women's earnings as a percentage of men's earnings by age and education for full-time workers, SIP General Survey and United States, 1979*

Age	Education			
	Less than completed secondary	Completed secondary	Some higher or more	Overall
SIP General Survey				
25–29	—[a]	54.8	*78.5*	66.1
30–34	—[a]	68.9	*72.8*	*69.3*
35–39	49.0	*81.9*	*75.9*	*76.3*
40–44	*63.2*	71.0	*82.3*	*76.1*
45–49	*69.0*	*59.1*	*67.3*	*66.5*
50–54	*67.3*	*59.1*	*74.0*	*62.3*
Overall	*63.7*	*66.1*	*75.6*	*70.1*
United States, 1979				
25–29	—	65.8	73.4	70.4
30–34	—	59.5	64.7	61.4
35–39	60.5	54.2	54.0	53.2
40–44	58.0	54.4	50.9	51.9
45–49	56.6	54.4	49.0	51.5
50–54	52.1	54.7	50.8	52.1
Overall	57.6	57.4	57.3	56.8

Note: The values for the SIP data are italicized when the percentage is higher than the corresponding percentages for the United States, 1979.
[a] Results not presented because of small number of cases.

However, in general, the differential between female and male earnings is not as great for the SIP respondents, and therefore possibly also for the Soviet European population in cities, as it is in the United States.

Appendix: Determination of first and last work

The data for studying the timing of labor-force participation come from a life history chart. On this chart one space appears for every year since the early twentieth century. The respondent was to place an X in the box pertaining to each year since reaching age 18 in which he or she did not have a public sector job for at least six months.

Examination of the results indicated that respondents recorded gaps in their employment accurately, but they sometimes did not place an X in boxes for years before they ever started to work, such as before finishing school, or for years after they stopped working, especially if they had been retired for many years.

All years before the first job and all years after the end of the last job were coded as indicating that the respondent was not working. In addition, those respondents who indicated that they had never held a public sector job were coded as having not worked in every year. Four respondents clearly had worked but could not recall when they had begun their last job or when they had ended it. Hence, the life history data for these four respondents were coded as missing.

All respondents were asked when they began their first job after completion of highest education. Respondents who completed their education at age 26 or older also were asked when they had their first full-time job, if they had one before completion of education. The first reported job was coded as first job – after completion of education for those who completed their education before age 25 and whatever was reported as first job for those who completed their education after age 25.

References

Anderson, Barbara A. 1986a. "Cultural Factors in the Decline of Fertility in Europe." In Susan Cott Watkins and Ansley J. Coale, eds., *The Decline of European Fertility*. Princeton, N.J.: Princeton University Press, pp. 293–313.

 1986b. "Family, Marriage, and Fertility in Russian and Soviet Censuses." In Ralph S. Clem (ed.), *Research Guide to the Russian and Soviet Censuses*. Ithaca: Cornell University Press, pp. 131–54.

Anderson, Barbara A., and Brian D. Silver. 1985. "Estimating Census Undercount from School Enrollment Data: An Application to the Soviet Censuses of 1959 and 1970," *Demography*, 22: 289–308.

Baldwin, Wendy H., and Christine Winquist Nord. 1984. "Delayed Childbearing in the U.S.: Facts and Fictions," *Population Bulletin*, 39, no. 4, Population Reference Bureau.

Becker, Gary S. 1960. "An Economic Analysis of Fertility." *Demographic and Economic Change in Developed Countries*. Universities-National Bureau of Economic Research Series 11. Princeton, N.J.: Princeton University Press.

Belova, V. A. 1971. "Velichina sem'i i obshchestvennoe mnenie" [The number of children and social attitudes]. In A. G. Volkov, ed., *Faktory rozhdaemosti*. Moscow: Statistika. pp. 35–51.

 1973. "Differentsiatsiia mneniia na zhlutshem i ozhidaemom chisle detei v sem'e" [Differences in attitudes toward the ideal and the intended number of children in the family], *Vestnik statistiki*, no. 7: 27–36.

 1975. *Chislo detei v sem'e* [The number of children in the family]. Moscow: Statistika.

Breeva, Ie. B. 1984. *Naselenie i zaniatost* '[Population and employment]. Moscow: Finansy i statistika.

Bumpass, Larry. 1973. "Is Low Fertility Here to Stay?" *Family Planning Perspectives*, 5: 67–69.

Butz, William P., and Michael P. Ward. 1979. "The Emergence of Countercyclical U.S. Fertility," *American Economic Review*, 69 (3): 318–28.

Coale, Ansley J. 1973. "The Demographic Transition Reconsidered." *International Population Conference, Liege, 1973*. Liege: International Union for the Scientific Study of Population, pp. 53–72.

Coale, Ansley J., Barbara A. Anderson, and Erna Härm. 1979. *Human Fertility in Russia since the Nineteenth Century*. Princeton, N.J.: Princeton University Press.

Corcoran, Mary. 1978. "The Structure of Female Wages," *American Economic Review*, 68: 165–85.

Duncan, Otis Dudley, David L. Featherman, and Beverly Duncan. 1972. *Socioeconomic Background and Achievement*. New York: Seminar Press.

Elder, Glenn H., Jr., ed. 1985. *Life Course Dynamics*. Ithaca, N.Y.: Cornell University Press.

Feshback, Murray, and Stephen Rapawy. 1973. "Labor Constraints in the Five-year Plan." *Soviet Economic Prospects for the 1970s*. U.S. Congress, Joint Economic Committee. Washington, D.C.: Government Printing Office, pp. 485–563.

   1976. "Soviet Population and Manpower Trends and Policies." *Soviet Economy in a New Perspective*. U.S. Congress, Joint Economic Committee. Washington, D.C.: Government Printing Office, pp. 113–54.

Gronau, Reuben. 1973. "The Effects of Children on the Housewife's Value of Time," *Journal of Political Economy*, 81: 200–33.

Gustavus, Susan O., and Charles B. Nam. 1970. "The Formation and Stability of Ideal Family Size among Young People," *Demography*, 7 (1): 43–51.

Iankova, Z. A., E. F. Achil'dieva, and O. K. Loseva. 1983. *Muzhchina i zhenshchina v sem'e* [Men and women in the family]. Moscow: Finansy i statistika.

Katkova, I. 1978. "Materinskii ukhod za novorozhdennym" [Maternal care of a newborn child]. In D. I. Valentei, ed., *Zhenshchiny na rabote i doma*. Moscow: Statistika, pp. 38–46.

Kiseleva, G., and I. Rilkova, 1974. "O motivakh ogranicheniia rozhdaemosti" [About motives for the limitation of fertility]. In O. I. Valentei, ed., *Demograficheskii analiz rozhdaemosti*, Moscow: Statistika, pp. 55–71.

Knodel, John, and Etienne van de Walle. 1979. "Lessons from the Past: Policy Implications of Historical Fertility Studies," *Population and Development Review*, 5 (2): 217–45.

Lesthaeghe, Ron J. 1977. *The Decline of Belgian Fertility, 1800–1970*. Princeton, N.J.: Princeton University Press.

Livi-Bacci, Massimo. 1971. *A Century of Portuguese Fertility*. Princeton; N.J.: Princeton University Press.

Michael Robert T. 1973. "Education and the Derived Demand for Children," *Journal of Political Economy*, 81: 128–64.

Mincer, Jacob. 1974. *Schooling, Experience, and Earnings*, New York: National Bureau of Economic Research.

Rimashevskaia, N. M., and S. A. Karapetian, eds. 1985. *Sem'ia i narodnoe blagosostoianie v razvitom sotsialisticheskom obschestve* [Family and popular well-being in a developed socialist society]. Moscow: Mysl.

Shakhot'ko, L. P. 1975. *Rozhdaemost'v Belorussii* [Fertility in Belorussia]. Minsk: Nauka i tekhnika.

Sisenko, V. 1974. "Differentsiatsiia rozhdaemosti v krupnom gorode" [Differential fertility in very large cities]. In O. I. Valentei, ed., *Demograficheskii analiz rozhdaemosti*. Moscow: Statistika, pp. 30–44.

Sweet, James A. 1977. "Demography and the Family." In *Annual Review of Sociology*, vol. 3. Palo Alto, Calif.: Annual Review.

Turchi, Boone A. 1975. *The Demand for Children: The Economics of Fertility in the United States*. Cambridge, Mass.: Ballinger.

U.S. Bureau of the Census. 1981. *Money Income of Families and Persons in the United States: 1979*. Current Population Reports, series P-60, no. 129. Washington, D.C.: U.S. Government Printing Office.

U.S. Bureau of Labor Statistics. 1985. *Handbook of Labor Statistics*. Washington, D.C.: U.S. Government Printing Office.

Valentei, D. I., ed. 1974. *Demograficheskii analiz rozhdaemosti* [Demographic analysis of fertility]. Moscow: Statistika.

Valentei, D. I., ed. 1978. *Zhenshchiny na rabote i doma* [Women at work and at home]. Moscow: Statistika.

Volkov, A. G., ed. 1971. *Faktory rozhdaemosti* [Factors in fertility]. Moscow: Statistika.

——— 1971. "Izmenenie polozheniia zhenshchiny i demograficheskoe razvitie sem'i" [Changes in the status of women and the demographic development of the family]. In Volkov, ed., *Faktory rozhdaemosti*, Moscow: Statistika, pp. 43–52.

Waite, Linda J. 1981. "U.S. Women at Work," *Population Bulletin*, 36, no. 2, Population Reference Bureau.

Westoff, Charles F. 1978. "Some Speculations on the Future of Marriage and the Family," *Family Planning Perspectives*, 10: 79–83.

Westoff, Charles F., and Raymond H. Potvin. 1967. *College Women and Fertility Values*. Princeton, N.J.: Princeton University Press.

Willis, Robert. 1973. "A New Approach to the Economic Theory of Fertility Behavior," *Journal of Political Economy*, 81: S14–64.

CHAPTER 8

Productivity, slack, and time theft in the Soviet economy

PAUL R. GREGORY

Introduction

This study uses eyewitness accounts of former Soviet workers and employees as an unconventional source of information on Soviet enterprise operations. The Soviet Interview Project (SIP) collected information in 1983 and 1984 from approximately 2,900 former Soviet citizens who reported on the jobs they held at the end of their last "normal" period (LNP) of life in the Soviet Union. For the vast majority of respondents, the end of this last normal period was 1978 or 1979. Soviet Interview Project respondents were asked a number of factual and perception questions concerning the Soviet workplace. They were asked for their assessment of productivity (whether it was rising or falling and the reasons why), their perception of the amount of labor slack and the seriousness of supply shortages, and their views on specific enterprise problems such as alcoholism, absenteeism, information flows, and worker apathy. They also responded to questions on dismissals and career advancement within the firm. Respondents were asked a wide range of factual questions concerning their primary job, second job, private economic activity, and time spent on personal business during work hours.

This chapter focuses attention on several issues. The first is how Soviet workers, as eyewitnesses at the firm level, assessed Soviet enterprise operations in the late 1970s. How do Soviet workers evaluate labor productivity, labor redundancy, alcoholism, apathy, and supply disruptions in their enterprises? The second issue is: What types of Soviet enterprises are systematically described as poor performers? What are the enterprise characteristics by branch, operating rules, and other features that eyewitnesses associate with poor performance? The third issue is the effect of specific operating characteristics of Soviet enterprises on the behavior of workers and employees. Do respondents who work in enterprises with one set of operating arrangements (such as merit advancement and few dismissals)

The author would like to thank Joseph Berliner, Janet Chapman, and Gregory Grossman for their comments and suggestions. I would also like to thank my colleagues Irwin Collier and Janet Kohlhase for their assistance. The weaknesses and errors that remain are the sole responsibility of the author.

behave differently from those who work in enterprises with different operating arrangements?

The picture of the Soviet enterprise that emerges from respondent descriptions is of interest in its own right. The official Soviet literature, which focuses on formal organization and operating procedures, provides few glimpses into the routine functioning of Soviet enterprises. The Western literature on the Soviet enterprise, on the other hand, is based upon accounts of a limited number of expert informants (describing an earlier period) and on anecdotal accounts from the Soviet press.[1] A relatively large sample of microrespondents could either confirm or refute the stereotypic view of Soviet enterprise operations found in the literature. Anecdotal accounts can establish only the existence of supply disruptions, overstaffing, alcoholism, time theft, second-economy job, worker absenteeism, and so forth. Unlike a large sample of microrespondents, anecdotal information cannot reveal the relative frequencies of such phenomena in routine enterprise operations.

Eyewitness reports represent a potential new source of information on the Soviet enterprise. The challenge is to use the material in a systematic, analytical fashion to understand Soviet resource allocation practices. Traditionally, Western economists have evaluated Soviet working arrangements either by examining aggregate outcomes (such as relative growth of gross national product or productivity growth) or by studying specific operating arrangements (such as the wage system, managerial bonuses, or procedures for allocating capital). Abram Bergson, for example, has attempted to isolate those Soviet operating arrangements for materials planning, capital allocation, and labor markets that contribute to economic inefficiency.[2] Joseph Berliner and David Granick have investigated Soviet managerial practices in the same light.[3] Padma Desai and Ricardo Martin and Judith Thornton have even attempted to place inefficiency price tags on Soviet working arrangements.[4] A number of problematic Soviet working arrangements – storming, inefficient investment allocation rules, ratchet

---

[1] The standard model of the Soviet enterprise is based primarily upon the writings of Joseph Berliner and David Granick. See Joseph Berliner, *Factory and Manager in the USSR* (Cambridge, Mass.: Harvard University Press, 1957), and David Granick, *Management of the Industrial Firm in the USSR* (New York: Columbia University Press, 1954). The Berliner study is based principally on interviews with a relatively small number of refugees who had worked in Soviet management. Granick's study is based primarily on published Soviet sources.

[2] Abram Bergson, *The Economics of Soviet Planning* (New Haven: Yale University Press, 1964).

[3] Berliner, *Factory and Manager*; Granick, *Management of the Industrial Firm*.

[4] Judith Thornton, "Differential Capital Charges and Resource Allocation in Soviet Industry," *Journal of Political Economy*, 79 (1971): 545–61; Padma Desai and Ricardo Martin, "Efficiency Loss from Resource Misallocation in Soviet Industry," *Quarterly Journal of Economics*, 98, no. 3 (1983): 441–56.

effects, overcommitment of construction funds, labor hoarding – have been identified, and they are typically offered as the causes of lagging Soviet growth and deteriorating productivity performance.[5]

The use of microeconomic eyewitness accounts to study Soviet enterprise working arrangements is novel. The average respondent is not an expert on the Soviet enterprise. Rather, the respondent is simply an observer of the very limited range of Soviet reality reflected in his or her former enterprise or working group. In fact, the average respondent's description of the Soviet enterprise may conflict with that of an expert from the same enterprise, such as a manager or chief accountant. The worker, operating from the restricted vantage point of limited personal observation, may have a different view of supply disruptions, alcoholism, or absenteeism than the manager, who has a better overview of enterprise operations.

Generally speaking, experts (managers, chief accountants, chief engineers, etc.) are a richer source of information on enterprise operations. Nonexperts, nevertheless, can provide valuable insights for a number of reasons. First, the number of expert informants on Soviet enterprises among an emigrant population is limited.[6] Researchers who deal with experts must generalize from a small number of reports and are unable to sort out the effects of different enterprise characteristics. Statistical inference can be applied to large samples of nonexperts to study the effects of enterprise characteristics (such as dismissals for poor work or merit advancement) on enterprise performance. Second, nonexperts should be able to identify obvious enterprise problems. If a high proportion of workers either failed to report to work every Monday or reported intoxicated, the nonexpert eyewitness could scarcely fail to notice. The average respondent would have observed if a high proportion of workdays were spent idle because supplies were not available.

A third reason for using nonexpert testimony is that nonexpert eyewitnesses can provide, in a number of instances, highly accurate information about enterprise operations. In a world of costly information, Soviet workers (like their Western counterparts) would specialize in the information of immediate relevance to them. They would be familiar with the wage and bonus system, criteria for advancement, and sanctions for poor work.

[5] It is difficult to establish empirically that Soviet productivity is low, holding the Soviet level of development constant. For a discussion of this issue, see Frederic Pryor, *A Guidebook to the Comparative Study of Economic Systems* (Englewood Cliffs, N. J.: Prentice-Hall, 1985), ch. 6. Also see Abram Bergson, "Comparative Productivity and Efficiency in the USA and USSR," in Alexander Eckstein (ed.), *Comparison of Economic Systems* (Berkeley: University of California Press, 1971), pp. 161–219.

[6] See Susan Linz, "Managerial Autonomy in Soviet Firms," Soviet Interview Project Working Paper, December 1985, for a description of the sample of former managerial personnel among the Third Soviet Emigration.

Although one could question the reliability of nonexpert responses on some enterprisewide questions (like overall productivity performance), non-experts should be able to provide accurate testimony on phenomena close to their own jobs.

Ideally, information from both nonexpert observers and expert informants should be combined to study Soviet enterprise operations. Ongoing special studies, supported by the Soviet Interview Project, have already provided some expert studies of enterprise operations that ask similar questions of expert informants.[7] At this juncture, it is too early to compare the results that emerge from small-scale expert and large-scale nonexpert studies of the Soviet enterprise.

The Soviet Interview Project Questionnaire

Introduction

SIP respondents were asked questions that cast them in the role of observers of enterprise working arrangements. They were also asked questions concerning their own personal experiences and backgrounds, questions that allow us to study the effects of respondent characteristics on descriptions of enterprise working arrangements. Background can affect responses because people with different backgrounds have different work experiences and because background characteristics may determine whether the respondent is an expert or nonexpert informant.

Labor productivity

Respondents who reported working during their last period of normal life in the Soviet were asked directly about their perceptions of labor productivity in the Soviet Union. Specifically, respondents were asked: "It has been said that the productivity of labor in the Soviet Union has been declining over the years. From your own experience during your last normal period, would you say that was true or not?" For those respondents answering affirmatively, an open-ended question was asked: "In your opinion, why was the productivity of labor declining?" Interviewers automatically probed to determine if respondents wished to give more than one reason. Respondents who volunteered more than one reason were asked to identify the main reason for the productivity decline.

These questions must be interpreted carefully for several reasons. First, the

7 Interview projects with expert informants from the Third Soviet Emigration are being conducted by Linz (see n. 6), Kenneth Gray ("The Soviet Food Complex"), Paul Gregory ("Planners"), and Helen Otto ("Construction").

extent to which responses are based upon the respondent's own work experiences is uncertain. Although respondents were asked to base their answers on their "own experience," they could have generalized from conversations, press reports, or other secondhand sources. Fortunately, this is an empirical issue: Systematically different responses, by type of enterprise, for example, would indicate that respondents had indeed answered on the basis of their own work experience. Second, it is not clear what an affirmative response to the "declining productivity" question actually means. The concept of productivity is inherently complex. The question asks specifically about declining labor productivity, a rare economic phenomenon, not about a declining rate of growth of labor productivity. It was feared that respondents would be confused by a question about declining rates of growth, and simpler but technically inexact language was chosen. The conservative interpretation is that affirmative responses are meant to signify subpar labor productivity performance as judged by some subjective productivity standard. The exact magnitude of the perceived productivity problem cannot and should not be read from affirmative responses, although Soviet respondents appear to understand the meaning of labor productivity.[8]

The respondent's volunteered explanation of the causes of "declining productivity" offers an unusual source of information on the unexplained productivity residual. Although growth accounting specialists have tried to penetrate the residual, their attempts have been based on guesswork and intuition.[9] In the absence of reliable conventional methods, unconventional information, such as eyewitness assessments, offers a new opportunity to study the residual.

Labor redundancy

SIP respondents were asked to report on the amount of labor slack they observed at their place of work: "On your last job, do you think it would have been possible to fulfill the plan with fewer workers and employees, or would it have not been possible?"

For those (with a plan) who answered affirmatively, a follow-up question was asked: "How many workers and employees do you think were

---

[8] Postinterview follow-ups with six emigrants appear to suggest that most former Soviet citizens can provide an accurate definition of labor productivity.

[9] See, for example, Denison's *Why Growth Rates Differ* (Washington, D.C.: Brookings Institution, 1967), and John W. Kendrick, "Survey of the Factors Contributing to the Decline in U.S. Productivity Growth," in Federal Reserve Bank of Boston, *The Decline in Productivity Growth*, Conference Series no. 22, June 1980.

really needed to fulfill the plan? On your job, could you have met the targets with X percent fewer workers?''

Respondents were started with the plan that could be fulfilled with 5 percent fewer workers and were allowed to build up to plan targets that could be fulfilled with 50 percent fewer workers.

These questions on labor redundancy force the respondent to speak directly about personal workplace experiences, so there is less danger of secondhand generalizations. The labor-slack questions address productivity only indirectly because respondents are asked to assess labor redundancy in terms of assigned plan targets. If an unrealistic target is set for the firm, and the respondent answers that there was no slack, this does not mean that the enterprise was operating more efficiently (in the economist's sense of the term) than one that was assigned easy targets and operating with slack. The question does, however, get at the issue of labor utilization, an important component of labor productivity.

The labor-redundancy question addresses the issue of "hidden labor reserves" in the Soviet economy. The literature has argued that Soviet managers tend to accumulate excess labor (to insure against future plan increases) and that there is little incentive for managers to fire redundant workers. In fact, Soviet authorities have sanctioned a series of economic experiments that encourage managers to dismiss redundant workers.[10] From these writings, one would expect widespread reportings of redundant labor staffing. The relatively large SIP sample provides an important opportunity to transcend anecdotal information on labor redundancy and to calculate relative frequencies.

Enterprise working arrangements

The SIP questionnaire asks a series of questions on enterprise operations. Respondents were asked to describe observed job-related problems (whether they typically had enough information to do their job well, whether they had sufficient equipment and supplies, whether they were given an opportunity to use their specialty, whether they could influence supervisor decisions that affected them, and the extent to which alcoholism and absenteeism were a problem),[11] the factors that were most important for career advancement at

[10] For a discussion of Soviet experiments to reduce redundant labor, see Paul Gregory and Robert Stuart, *Soviet Economic Structure and Performance*, 3d ed. (New York: Harper and Row, 1986), ch. 12.

[11] The question reads: "I'm going to read you some things that might have described your job. For each thing that I mention, tell me whether it was true of your job nearly all the time, often, sometimes, rarely, or never." The interviewer then read the following statements concerning the respondent's job: (a) "You had enough

their place of work,[12] whether "workers who performed poorly" were fired and how regularly, and whether the party committee and the trade union made things better or worse at their place of work.[13]

These questions allow respondents to make observations about routine enterprise operations. By asking respondents to assess problems such as alcoholism, lack of supplies, failure to use worker specialties, and so on, we can learn something about the relative frequencies of problems that have been identified as widespread by the anecdotal evidence. The question on merit advancement sheds light on an important aspect of enterprise operations. Presumably a merit-based advancement system is more conducive to efficient enterprise operations than other arrangements. The questions on trade union and party intervention give respondents the opportunity to rate the work of key organizations that supplement enterprise decision making. The available literature does not allow us to judge whether the interventions of the party organization or the trade union help or hurt enterprise operations.[14] With the exception of the party and trade union questions, these are issues on which the average respondent should be reasonably well informed.

information to do your job well." (*b*) "You had to do things against your better judgment." (*c*) "You were given an opportunity to make use of your specialty." (*d*) "You were able to infuence your supervisor's decisions that affected you." (*e*) "You had sufficient equipment and supplies to do your job." (*f*) "There was a problem with alcoholism and absenteeism among the workers."

[12] The question reads: "Many different things can help a person to advance his or her career. In your opinion, which item was the most important for career advancement at your job?" The card respondents were handed lists eight factors. The eight factors were higher education and a diploma, knowledge and experience, being a man and not a woman, being a member of the party, having *protektsiia* and connections, having talent and ability to organize the work of others, having ability and desire to get along with superiors, and being a member of a specific nationality.

[13] The party question reads: "At that place where you worked, what effect did the party committee have on production problems – did they make things better, did they make things worse, or did they have no effect?" The trade union question reads: "At that place where you worked, what effect did the trade union have on wage and premium problems? What effect did it have on working conditions and workers' welfare?"

[14] The writings of Berliner and Granick on Soviet management from the 1930s through the 1950s suggested that managers were sometimes hampered by the interference of the primary party organization and trade union. On the other hand, it is recognized that the party can assist managers in bargaining for plans and obtaining materials.

Descriptive statistics

Table 8.1 presents the frequency distributions of responses. It reveals that the overwhelming majority of respondents (74.5 percent) felt that productivity was declining. Over 60 percent cited problems related to material incentives (lack of incentives, unavailability of consumer goods, bad living conditions) as the main cause of declining productivity. Ten percent felt that alcoholism was the main cause of declining productivity, and another 10 percent cited worker apathy or laziness. Slightly over 8 percent felt that poor management was responsible for declining productivity.

Roughly one-half (47 percent) of those who had a plan reported that the plan could not have been fulfilled with fewer workers. Almost one-half (49 percent) felt the plan could have been fulfilled with 5 percent fewer workers. Twenty-two percent of respondents reported the plan could have been fulfilled with 20 percent fewer workers, and 11 percent felt that the plan could have been fulfilled with 50 percent fewer workers.

Slightly more than 15 percent (16.2 percent) reported that they rarely or never had sufficient supplies or equipment to do their jobs. One-third felt that alcoholism and absenteeism were problems nearly all the time or often. The vast majority felt that they had enough information to do their jobs well and that they were allowed to work in their specialty.

Forty percent of respondents cited merit factors (higher education, knowledge and experience, organizational ability) as the most important criteria for job advancement. Forty-five percent cited party membership, protection, and connections as the most important job advancement criterion, and 11 percent cited getting along with superiors.

The majority of respondents (52 percent) felt that the party committee had no effect on output, although a significant minority (33 percent) felt that the party committee made things better. An even larger majority felt that the trade union had no effect on wages (72 percent), although one-quarter felt that the trade union made things better. Similarly, 62 percent felt that the trade union had no effect on worker welfare, but more than one-third (37 percent) reported that the trade union had a positive effect on worker welfare.

These frequency distributions show the raw material upon which this study is based. Several of the results reported in Table 8.1 are interesting in their own right: First, SIP respondents do not report alarming problems with insufficient supplies and equipment. Almost 70 percent felt that they "often or nearly all the time" had sufficient supplies and equipment to do their jobs. Only 16 percent reported insufficient supplies and equipment to be a chronic problem. This result does not jibe well with the stereotypic picture of the Soviet enterprise as being plagued by constant supply problems. Second, SIP respondents confirm that alcoholism and absentee-

Table 8.1. *Descriptive statistics, SIP sample (in percentages)*

A. Was labor productivity declining?	
Yes	74.5
No	25.5
B. What was the main reason labor productivity was declining?	
Material incentives	
Lack of incentives	58.1
Unavailability of consumer goods	2.4
Bad living conditions	1.4
Bad working conditions	0.8
Poor workers	
Alcoholism	10.8
Apathy, laziness	10.0
Poor management	8.3
Insufficient resources, poor technology	2.6
The economic system	2.3
Other	0.6
C. Plan could have been fulfilled with:	
0 percent fewer workers (no redundancy)	47.0
5 percent fewer workers	49.0
10 percent fewer workers	35.0
20 percent fewer workers	22.0
50 percent fewer workers	11.0
D. Assessment of job-related problems	
How often had sufficient equipment and supplies?	
Nearly all the time	55.5
Often	11.7
Sometimes	14.5
Rarely, never	16.2
N.a.	2.1
How often were alcoholism/absenteeism a problem?	
Nearly all the time	9.0
Often	23.1
Sometimes	26.4
Rarely, never	40.4
N.a.	1.2
How frequently able to use specialty?	
Nearly all the time	70.5
Often	8.8
Sometimes	5.7

Table 8.1. (*contd.*)

Rarely, never	9.7
N.a.	5.3
How frequently had enough information to do job well?	
Nearly all the time	62.9
Often	15.0
Sometimes	11.9
Rarely, never	4.6
N.a.	5.6
E. Most important factors in career advancement?	
Higher education	6.3
Experience and knowledge	29.4
Talent and ability to organize work of others	4.4
Party membership	21.6
Protection and connections	23.5
Getting along with superiors and loyalty	11.3
F. Role of party organization and trade union	
Effect of party on production	
Made things better	32.9
Made things worse	15.2
Had no effect	51.9
Effect of trade union on wage matters	
Made things better	25.4
Made things worse	2.7
Had no effect	72.0
Effect of trade union on worker welfare	
Made things better	37.3
Made things worse	0.9
Had no effect	61.7

ism are serious but not overwhelming enterprise problems. One-third report alcoholism and absenteeism to be a problem "often or nearly all the time," but a higher proportion (40 percent) say that alcoholism and absenteeism were rarely or never problems. Third, SIP respondents do not report significant amounts of redundant labor. Sixty-five percent felt that the plan could not have been fulfilled with a 10 percent reduction in work force, and one-half (47 percent) felt that there were no redundant workers at their place of work. Fourth, there is a roughly even split on the importance of merit and nonmerit factors in job advancement. Fifth, although the majority of respondents felt that the party committee and the trade union made no difference, a significant minority felt they played positive roles in the Soviet enterprise.

Analysis of results

The frequency distributions of Table 8.1 are only the first step in analyzing the working arrangements of Soviet enterprises. The enterprise characteristics that are significantly related to enterprise outcomes can be isolated analytically using multiple regression. Ordinary least squares is used in this paper when the dependent variable is not dichotomous, and logit regression is applied to dichotomous dependent variables. Logit regression is suitable for capturing the factors that affect the probability of a respondent belonging to a specific dichotomous category. The logit functional form has convenient properties for dealing with dichotomous categories: The predicted value of the dependent variable must be between zero and unity (negative probabilities or probabilities greater than one are ruled out), the functional form is nonlinear (S-shaped) at the boundaries, and the probability coefficients depend upon the values of the exogenous variables. The logit regressions reported in this paper are estimated using a maximum likelihood convergence procedure.[15]

Productivity assessments

Figure 8.1 classifies respondents who felt that "productivity has been declining over the years" by the number of subordinates they supervised.

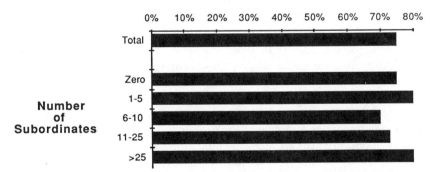

Figure 8.1. Positive responses to the question "It has been said that productivity of labor in the Soviet Union has been declining over the years; from your own experience during your LNP, would you have said that was true, or not?"

---

[15] For a discussion of the logit model, see Eric Hanushek and John Jackson, *Statistical Methods for Social Scientists* (New York: Academic Press, 1977), ch.7.

The number of people supervised at the workplace is not a perfectly reliable measure of the level of supervisory responsibility and hence of the "expertness" of the eyewitness. Some high-level respondents could have reported only the number of immediate supervisees, whereas foremen reported the total number of workers in their production unit. Postinterview analysis suggests, however, that the number of people supervised is a reasonable (but rough) approximation of level of supervisory responsibility.[16]

The classification of respondents by level of supervisory responsibility provides a rough reliability check on responses. More highly placed respondents could provide more reliable assessments of enterprise productivity. If the responses of low-level and high-level respondents are not systematically different, credence is added to the testimony of low-level respondents. The net gains are that the sample size is expanded considerably and that productivity assessments are the same at different vantage points within the enterprise. Figure 8.1 shows that 74 percent of the respondents answered that Soviet productivity was declining, and the percentages do not appear to vary systematically with the level of supervisory responsibility. Respondents at different levels in the firm's hierarchy are in basic agreement on the matter of poor productivity performance.

We interpret a report of declining productivity as a perception of productivity "problems" or of poorly managed resources. Respondents could have based their answers on personal observations from their place of work, or they could have generalized from experiences outside their immediate work experience. Respondents who used immediate work experience would be more valuable because, knowing the characteristics of their enterprise, we could isolate those enterprise characteristics that contribute systematically to productivity problems. In a sense, responses based upon personal work experiences allow us to learn something about the characteristics of poorly run enterprises in the Soviet Union.

Whether respondents answered the productivity question on the basis of actual work experience can be tested empirically. Responses based on actual work experience should be systematically related to enterprise characteristics. Responses based on other experiences would be either randomly distributed or associated with personal characteristics such as age, sex, marital status, and so on.

A logit regression of enterprise and respondent characteristics on reportings of "falling productivity" is presented in Table 8.2. The dependent variable is 1 if the respondent reports "declining productivity" and 0

---

[16] Postinterview surveys of six emigrants suggested that respondents tend to give the total number of people falling below them in the organization's hierarchy.

otherwise. A positive significant coefficient means that the exogenous variable raises the probability of reporting declining productivity.

A number of enterprise characteristics – branch (BRANCH), whether poor workers were fired (PINKSLIP), whether supply shortages (SUPPLYPROB) or alcoholism/absenteeism (ALCOHOL) were frequent problems, whether job advancement was based on merit (MERIT) – are included as exogenous variables to capture the impact of the enterprise work experience on the productivity assessment. Respondent characteristics – sex (FEMALE), age (AGE), supervisory responsibilities (SUBORD), and educational attainment (HIGHED) – are included for two reasons: First, if respondents answer on the basis of nonwork experiences, these responses may be systematically related to personal characteristics. Personal characteristics determine the after-work information environment in which the respondent lived. Second, even if respondents answer on the basis of work experience, respondents with different personal characteristics (such as more education) occupy different positions within the same enterprise and thus may assess productivity differently. Although our prime interest is the enterprise characteristics that contribute to poor productivity performance, other factors must be held constant if we are to have a complete model specification.

Table 8.2 shows that respondents who worked in enterprises where job advancement was based on merit were less likely to report falling productivity. Respondents who worked in enterprises in which poor workers were fired were more likely to report falling productivity. Enterprises with serious supply problems ("rarely or never had sufficient supplies/equipment") were more likely to be reported as experiencing productivity problems, although the statistical significance of this result is ambiguous. Surprisingly, enterprises with serious alcoholism/absenteeism problems did not have significantly higher reportings of productivity problems. The branches of the economy in which respondents were more likely to report falling productivity (with manufacturing productivity as the reference point) are construction, municipal economy and housing, science, and education.

Respondent characteristics also systematically affect productivity assessments. In particular, women and older respondents were more likely to report falling productivity than male respondents and young respondents. More highly educated respondents, however, did not differ systematically in their productivity assessments. It should be emphasized that personal characteristics are included principally to avoid specification error; these results are not of immediate interest in their own right. It is surprising, however, that older respondents systematically give more negative productivity assessments than their younger cohorts. This finding goes against

Table 8.2. *Logit regression: "productivity declining"*

	Regression coefficient	Standard error	*t*-statistic
Enterprise characteristics			
SUPPLYPROB	.24028	.15485	1.55170
ALCOHOL	−.12914	.11940	−1.08154
MERIT	−.35594	.10852	−3.28000
PINKSLIP	.11384	.04905	2.32065
BRANCH2[a]	−.75759	.60800	−1.24602
BRANCH3	.04338	.23050	.18820
BRANCH4	.65938	.22557	2.92314
BRANCH5	.21180	.17495	1.21061
BRANCH6	.55425	.39641	1.39817
BRANCH7	.40791	.23759	1.71687
BRANCH8	.13995	.18630	.75119
BRANCH9	.63855	.20798	3.07023
BRANCH10	.40047	.40937	.97824
BRANCH11	.35981	.21165	1.69999
BRANCH12	.96139	.38932	2.46941
Respondent characteristics			
FEMALE	.35726	.11538	3.09646
AGE	.00839	.00413	2.03175
SKILLED	−.02980	.12411	−.24009
SUBORD	.00120	.00136	.88682
Constant	4.77298	.23065	20.69342

Note: Number of observations = 571. Dependent variable: "It has been said that the productivity of labor in the Soviet Union has been declining over the years. From your own experience during your last normal period, would you have said that was true, or not?" If yes/true, coded 1. If no/not true/don't know, coded 0. Logit model: $(\text{LOG}(p/(1-p))/2+5)$ = Intercept + BX.
[a] See Appendix to this chapter for branches and other variables.

the general pattern encountered by SIP researchers, who find that older respondents generally tend to give a more optimistic assessment of Soviet economic life than their younger cohorts.[17]

Most of the above results confirm a priori expectations. Enterprises in which advancement is based upon merit would be expected to receive better productivity ratings, and they indeed do. That enterprises with frequent supply problems are associated with productivity problems comes as no surprise. It is also not surprising that construction and housing, branches

[17] See the contributions by Donna Bahry (Chapter 3), James Millar and Elizabeth Clayton (Chapter 2), and Brian Silver (Chapter 4), herein.

often singled out for criticism in the Soviet press, are identified as experiencing productivity problems. The high frequency of "falling productivity" reports from respondents in science and education – service branches in which it is conceptually difficult to estimate productivity – shows that Soviet science and education are perceived as functioning inefficiently relative to other branches. Notably, respondents fail to single out health care as a troubled-productivity sector, contrary to Western criticism of the "failing" Soviet health care sector.[18]

These results do not lend support to the proposition that Soviet productivity problems are due in a significant manner to human factors such as alcoholism and worker absenteeism.[19] Enterprises designated as having frequent alcoholism/absenteeism problems do not have a significantly higher incidence of poor productivity ratings.

The positive coefficient on the PINKSLIP (poor workers usually fired) variable seems to suggest that the discipline imposed by the threat of firing does not raise productivity. Instead, enterprises in which poor workers were "usually fired" have a higher frequency of reports of declining productivity. These findings seem to suggest that, although the "carrot" of merit advancement does have a positive effect on enterprise productivity, the "stick" effect of threatened firings has a perverse effect. We would not rule out that the positive coefficient is due to reverse causality (enterprises with more bad workers are forced to do more firing). However, the frequency of alcoholism/absenteeism is being held constant (a proxy for bad workers), so it is likely that this is truly a perverse result.

Reasons for productivity decline

Respondents who reported that productivity was declining were asked the main reason for this decline. As Table 8.1 showed, the reasons advanced fall into five general categories (in descending order of importance): incentive and pay problems (low pay, poor housing, bad working conditions, worker disappointment), bad workers (alcoholism, absenteeism, apathy, laziness), poor management, resource deficiencies (lack of sufficient workers, poor technology), and the economic system. To some degree, these categories can overlap. Absenteeism and apathy may be the consequence of lack of

---

[18] The most prominent studies of the crisis in Soviet health care have been conducted by Murray Feshbach. See, for example, Murray Feshbach, "Issues in Soviet Health Problems," in U.S. Congress, Joint Economic Committee, *Soviet Economy in the 1980's: Problems and Prospects*, pt. 2 (Washington, D.C.: U.S. Government Printing Office, 1983), pp. 203–27.

[19] For discussion of human factors and the Soviet productivity slowdown, see Gertrude Schroeder, "The Slowdown in Soviet Industry, 1976–1982," *Soviet Economy*, 1 no. 1 (1985): 42–74.

incentives. Poor management may ultimately be the consequence of the economic system. Thus, the dividing lines could be questioned.

Because the reasons for declining productivity do not fall into ready dichotomous categories, multiple regression is not a convenient tool for determining the enterprise characteristics that yield particular response categories.[20] Simple cross-classifications of the reasons for declining productivity by specific respondent and enterprise characteristics do, however, point to some explanatory factors.

Figure 8.2 gives the reasons for declining productivity by the number of persons supervised (none, 1–10, more than 10).[21] As noted above, higher-level respondents are more likely to give informed answers. In this particular case, the contrast between low-level and high-level respondents is particularly interesting because it reveals appraisals from different levels of the enterprise hierarchy.

Figure 8.2 shows a strong consensus across supervisory levels that incentive problems are the prime cause of "declining productivity." Over 55 percent of the respondents in each of the three supervisory categories blamed incentive problems. Human factors (alcoholism, absenteeism, apathy) are the second-most cited cause, with higher-level supervisors more likely to cite human factors (some 25 percent) as the prime cause of productivity problems than those with limited (or zero) supervisory responsibilities. Poor management comes in a distant third, with slightly less than 10 percent of the respondents citing it as the prime cause of falling productivity. Figure 8.3 shows a clear monotonic relationship: The higher the level of education, the more likely is the respondent to cite incentive problems as the prime cause of falling productivity.

Figure 8.4 reveals that the highest proportions of respondents citing incentive problems worked in culture, health, construction, manufacturing, and education (in declining order). Respondents are most critical of bad management in municipal economy and housing, transportation and communications, and construction. Thus, respondents appear to single out some branches of the economy that are more poorly managed than others.

The most important conclusion of this section is the overwhelming agreement that incentives are the key to Soviet productivity problems. According to the majority of respondents, poor productivity performance is caused not by the economic system, bad management, or apathetic or drunk

---

[20] A logit regression seeking to explain the factors that systematically explained material-incentive responses (respondents who gave an answer citing incentives were assigned a 1; 0 for any other answer) failed to yield any significant enterprise characteristics.

[21] The number of supervisory categories has been limited to three because of the relatively small number of respondents to this part of the question.

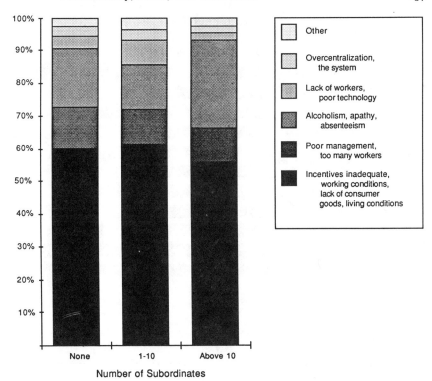

Figure 8.2. Main reason for productivity decline

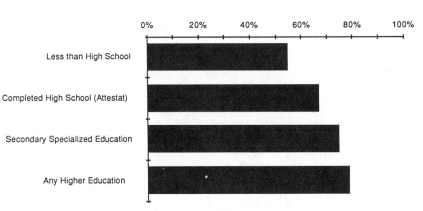

Figure 8.3. Reported incentive problems, by respondent's educational level

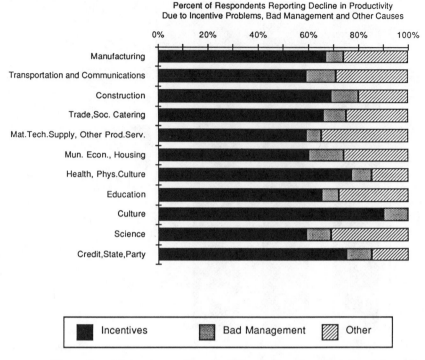

Percent of Respondents Reporting Decline in Productivity
Due to Incentive Problems, Bad Management and Other Causes

Figure 8.4. Main causes of productivity decline, by respondent's branch

workers but by the failure to provide personal incentives that motivate high levels of performance.

It is difficult to assess this result. Western analysts have typically argued that the Soviet wage and bonus system is the most rational element of Soviet resource allocation.[22] The degree of Soviet inequality may not be much different from that in the industrialized West.[23] Why, then, should Soviet workers single out the material incentive system as the prime cause of faltering productivity? The responses by branch and personal characteristics provide some clues: The strongest complaints of inadequate incentives appear to be voiced by those who work in poorly paid branches (culture, health, education), by the highly educated, and by those who work in highly paid branches that normally require compensating wage differentials (construction). From this, we conclude that the people who are most critical

[22] On this, see Gregory and Stuart, *Soviet Economic Structure*, ch. 10, and Abram Bergson, *Economics of Soviet Planning*, ch. 6.
[23] Abram Bergson, "Income Inequality under Soviet Socialism," *Journal of Economic Literature*, 22, no. 3 (1984): 1052–99. Also see Chapter 6, herein.

of the Soviet incentive system are those who receive low wages relative to the average, who receive low wages for their level of education, or who receive wages that do not compensate them for the negative features of the job.

These factors may explain the variation of responses within the sample; they do not explain the strong consensus that inadequate incentives are the prime cause of Soviet productivity problems. The most compelling explanation is that respondents are reacting to perceived "inadequate" absolute (as opposed to relative) material incentives. If the economy fails to provide what is generally perceived to be a "fair" average return for effort (at least relative to the return anticipated in light of the system's resources), participants may diminish effort, and labor productivity suffers. This reaction would occur even if the relative incentive system (what I receive relative to what you receive) is correctly calibrated for economic efficiency.

Respondent reports of personal real wage trends and of perceived poverty incidence support this interpretation. Table 8.3 shows that over 61 percent of the respondents felt that their real wages had fallen over the previous five years. Workers in the branches of construction, trade, supply, communal economy, and heavy manufacturing were more likely to report declining living standards, whereas scientific researchers, low-skilled white-collar workers, and medical personnel were more likely to report declining living standards among the various occupations.

Modern macrotheory teaches that the *perception* of falling real wages (whether true or not) should reduce labor effort and, hence, could depress productivity. It is clear that respondents judged the material rewards offered by the Soviet economy to the community to be deficient. Respondents thought that about one-third of the residents of their community lived in conditions of poverty (Table 8.3). Moreover, the feature of Soviet life that evoked the strongest dissatisfaction among respondents was the general unavailability of goods in their community (Table 8.3).

Statistical series on real wages and on income distribution cannot capture the effect of consumer market disequilibrium on incentives and morale. This is more likely to be captured by subjective responses, which clearly measure the level of dissatisfaction with material rewards. SIP respondents tell an internally consistent story about the causes of faltering productivity in the Soviet economy. They tell us that, although human-factor problems such as alcoholism and absenteeism are important, poor productivity performance is due to the failure of the system to provide real material rewards to elicit the appropriate human effort. There is systematic variation around this central tendency, but the shared perceptions of declining real wages, consumer market disequilibriums, and high poverty incidence account for the consensual blame of the material incentive system.

Table 8.3. *Living standards, poverty perceptions, goods availability*
(*SIP sample*) (*in percentages*)

A. Proportion of respondents reporting declining living standards	
All respondents	61.4
By branch	
Heavy manufacturing	62.3
Light manufacturing	55.0
Transportation & communications	57.9
Construction	69.3
Trade, supply, communal economy	64.1
Health, education, culture, science	60.3
By occupation	
Researchers	72.5
Engineers	59.8
Medical doctors	68.6
Schoolteachers	61.8
Workers in culture and arts	56.6
Skilled white-collar workers	62.1
Unskilled white-collar workers	71.7
Blue-collar workers	57.5
B. Percentage of people in community living below the poverty income level	30.0
C. Perceptions of shortages	
Did state stores have enough meat and dairy products?	
Usually had enough	18.9
Usually were short	81.1
Were other goods in short supply?	
Yes	94.9
No	5.1

Redundant labor

The labor-redundancy question provides respondents with another opportunity to assess enterprise operations. Rather than asking about output per unit of labor input, respondents are asked to judge the incidence of redundant labor. Redundancy is measured relative to staffing required to meet plan targets. The frequency distribution of responses was given in Table 8.1.

Figure 8.5 identifies those occupations in which more redundant labor was reported. Researchers, planners and administrators, culture and arts

PERCENT OF RESPONDENTS WHO REPORTED HAVING PLANS

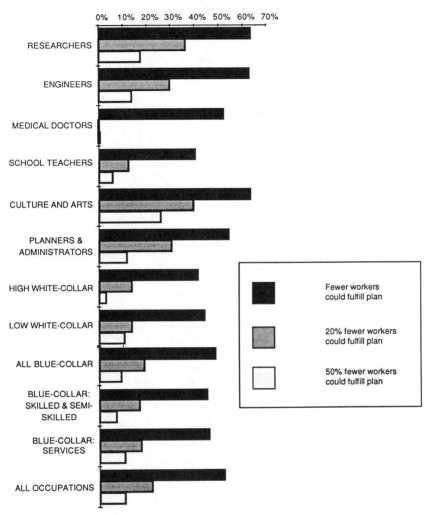

Figure 8.5. Perceived plan slack, by occupation

personnel, and engineers reported more redundant labor. Schoolteachers, skilled white-collar, low-skilled white-collar, and blue-collar workers reported relatively less slack. Judged in terms of proportions reporting that their "plan could be fulfilled with 50 percent fewer workers," the occupations with the least slack were medical doctors, skilled white-collar workers, teachers, and skilled and semiskilled blue-collar workers. Judged on the

Table 8.4. *Multiple regression: amount of redundant labor*

	Coefficient estimate	Standard error	t-statistic
Enterprise characteristics			
BRANCH2[a]	2.246920	6.770418	.332
BRANCH3	− 1.429125	2.967776	− .482
BRANCH4	2.254802	2.200402	1.025
BRANCH5	1.359631	1.984492	.685
BRANCH6	9.196858	4.195895	2.192
BRANCH7	9.000155	2.569370	3.503
BRANCH8	− .671275	2.666325	− .252
BRANCH9	− 2.373014	2.564582	− .925
BRANCH10	− 1.664234	4.881379	− .341
BRANCH11	10.110767	2.650443	3.815
BRANCH12	8.913987	3.479004	2.562
Respondent characteristics			
FEMALE	− 4.118873	1.315053	− 3.132
SUBORD	.012718	.006695	1.900
AGE	− .011890	.049047	− .242
HIGHED	.729914	.354148	2.061
Constant	5.641529	3.488273	1.617

Note: R-square, .10070; adjusted R-square, .07720; 589 observations. Dependent variable: "On your (last) job (in/before) [end of LNP] do you think it would have been possible to fulfill the plan with fewer workers and employees, or would it not have been possible?" Response = FEWERWRK. If FEWERWRK = 2, would not have been possible, then SLACK = 0%; if FEWERWRK = 1, would have been possible, then: "How many workers and employees do you think were really needed to fulfill the plan? On your job, could you have met the targets with . . . 2.5%, 5%, 10%, 20%, 50% fewer workers?" (Note: the 2.5% implicit in those who thought could fulfill with fewer workers but not with 5% fewer workers.)
SLACK = 2.5%, 5%, 10%, 20%, 50%.
[a] See Appendix to this chapter for branches and descriptions of other variables.

same basis, the occupations with the greatest incidence of redundant labor were workers in culture and arts, researchers, engineers, planners and administrators, and unskilled white-collar workers.

The multiple regression of reported labor slack on relevant enterprise and background characteristics is given in Table 8.4. The economic branches with relatively large amounts of redundant labor (with manufacturing as the reference point) are (in descending order) science, municipal economy and housing, material technical supply, credit, state and party apparatus, and construction (although the statistical significance of construction is unclear). The higher the level of supervisory responsibility, the more likely is the respondent to report redundant labor. Surprisingly, women report less redundant labor than men.

What conclusions should be drawn from this exercise? First, the amount of slack reported by respondents does not appear to be staggering. About one-half say that there were no redundant workers in their enterprises. Only about one in five felt that enterprise responsibilities could have been met with 20 percent fewer workers. Workers and employees performing the actual routine tasks of the economy felt that there was less slack than did their superiors.

We lack a frame of reference for these questions to judge what is a lot and a little. If the same questions were administered to American workers, we would not be surprised if the results were broadly similar. These results do indeed confirm the existence of redundant workers in the Soviet Union. There are too many scientists, engineers, and cultural workers and too few skilled white-collar workers and blue-collar workers. In fact, the patterns of redundancy are in accord with the stereotypic picture of the Soviet labor market as oversupplied with engineers and scientific workers and under-supplied with those who perform the routine tasks of the economy. The occupations with the lowest reported redundancy rates appear to be the skilled and semiskilled white- and blue-collar occupations.

There are no well-accepted procedures for measuring labor redundancy.[24] What we do know is that Soviet authorities are convinced that the Soviet economy suffers from a labor-redundancy problem. These findings intimate that official Soviet concerns may be misplaced, although, admittedly, we really do not know how to define the problem. David Granick in his interesting study of Soviet labor markets finds that Soviet officialdom can perceive problems (such as excessive labor turnover) that may not exist in a comparative sense.[25] The same could possibly be true of labor redundancy, but we can do no more than speculate at this point.

Supplies, alcoholism, and absenteeism

Table 8.1 presented the frequency distributions of reported supply problems and alcoholism/absenteeism problems at the respondent's place of work.

---

[24] The economic development literature has long attempted, without success, to develop measures of labor redundancy for less-developed countries. See Hla Myint, *The Economics of Developing Countries* (New York: Praeger, 1964), ch. 6, and John Fei and Gustav Ranis, *Development of the Labor Surplus Economy* (Homewood, Ill.: Irwin 1964).

[25] David Granick, "Job Rights in the USSR: Their Effect on the Total Organization of the Soviet Economy," Final Report to the National Council for Soviet and East European Research, August 15, 1985.

264   **Paul R. Gregory**

The branches and occupations in which these problems are relatively severe are shown in Figures 8.6 and 8.7.

Figure 8.6 shows that the three branches with the most frequent supply problems were (in descending order) transportation and communication, municipal economy and housing, and construction. In these branches, 20 to 30 percent complain that they "rarely" or "never" had sufficient supplies and equipment to do their jobs. The occupations that appear to be most plagued by supply and equipment problems are (in descending order) faculty and researchers, doctors and dentists, and semiskilled white-collar workers.

The principal conclusion is that, with the exception of certain branches (such as transportation, construction, and housing) and occupations (researchers, doctors, and some white-collar workers), typically two-thirds of the branches and occupations were reported as having sufficient equipment and supplies "nearly all the time" or "often." This picture diverges from the stereotype of the Soviet industrial enterprise as suffering

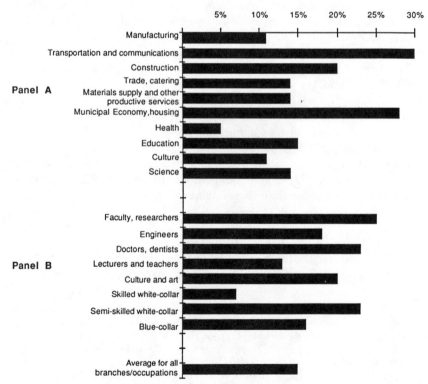

Figure 8.6. Proportion of respondents reporting rarely or never having sufficient supplies/equipment, by branch and occupation

from chronic supply and equipment problems. The supply situation of the Soviet industrial enterprise would be best seen in the reports of manufacturing workers, engineers, and blue-collar workers. Relatively small proportions of these workers (11 percent to 18 percent) reported chronic supply problems.

Figure 8.7 gives the branch and occupation breakdowns of reported alcoholism/absenteeism problems. Panel A shows a clear branch distribution: Alcoholism and absenteeism were reported with greatest frequency in transportation and communication, construction, and manufacturing and with least frequency in health and education. Panel B gives an even more sharply defined distribution: Alcoholism and absenteeism are most concentrated in the blue-collar professions and least concentrated among teachers, doctors, researchers, and white-collar workers. Alcoholism and absenteeism are also high among engineers and among workers in culture and arts.

The SIP questionnaire does not allow us to separate alcoholism from

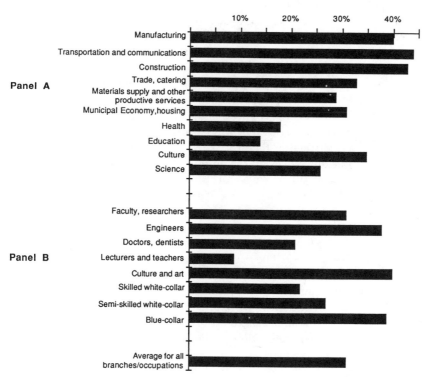

Figure 8.7. Proportion of respondents reporting alcoholism/absenteeism a problem often or nearly all the time, by branch and occupation

absenteeism, but both are indicative of human resource problems at the workplace. With certain exceptions (such as culture and arts and engineering), alcoholism and absenteeism appear to be more chronic problems among blue-collar workers. Almost 40 percent of the blue-collar respondents felt that alcoholism and absenteeism were a problem at their place of work "nearly all the time" or "often." The proportions of those reporting chronic alcoholism/absenteeism are much lower among white-collar workers, doctors, and teachers. The pervasiveness of the alcoholism/absenteeism problem is seen by the fact that teaching is the only profession in which less than one in five reported alcoholism/absenteeism to be a chronic workplace problem. Chronic alcoholism and/or absenteeism appear to be spread fairly evenly among branches, with health, education, and science reporting relatively less alcoholism/absenteeism than other branches.

Merit advancement

Presumably, job performance is affected by the perception that job advancement is due to merit. We have shown that respondents working in enterprises in which career advancement was based upon merit have a more favorable view of enterprise operations in the Soviet economy. Respondents were asked what factors determined who got ahead in the enterprise where they worked. Figure 8.8 gives respondent answers broken down into merit (higher education, expertise, talent, good work) and nonmerit advancement factors (party membership, connections, good relations with boss, being the right nationality). The pattern by supervisory levels is noteworthy. There is a general upward trend in the proportion of those citing merit reasons for advancement as one moves up the administrative ladder. However, at the highest level (those supervising more than 25 subordinates), a relatively small proportion (29 percent) cite merit at the most important reason for job advancement. Fifty-eight percent cite, instead, party membership and connections as most important. It should be noted that less than half the respondents (39 percent) believed that merit is the most important factor behind job advancement. The majority at all levels of supervisory authority cite nonmerit factors as dominating job advancement.

Given the important role attributed to merit factors in accounting for productivity and respondent complaints about the incentive system, it appears as if the widespread use of nonmerit advancement criteria has its economic costs. When enterprises choose to base career advancement on connections, party membership, good relations with the boss, and so on, productivity-enhancing factors like higher education and acquired knowledge come to be neglected insofar as there are personal costs to acquiring them. As a caveat, it should be mentioned that this is an area where sample

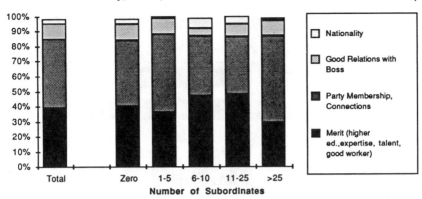

Figure 8.8. Most important reasons for job advancement

bias could distort the results. This sample was particularly exposed to job discrimination and would be more likely than the general Soviet population to emphasize nonmerit factors. The key question to interpreting these results is the extent to which respondents do indeed cast themselves in the role of *observers* of enterprise operations. The question on advancement criteria asks them to report on how things were generally done at their enterprise, not how they as individuals were treated.

Time theft and second jobs

Finally, we turn to the question of how enterprise working arrangements affect behavior. Specifically, we are interested in how enterprise working arrangements – such as firing patterns, use of merit criteria, and so on – affect actual behavior on the job. The two behavior variables that can be investigated using SIP data are "time theft" from the workplace and the propensity to take on second jobs and engage in second-economy activity.

Time theft

SIP respondents were asked whether they "sometimes used work time for personal business (like shopping or running errands)." If they answered affirmatively, they were asked to report how many times per week (on average) they took unauthorized time off from work and the average duration of the absence from work.

Fifty-nine percent of SIP respondents (with jobs) reported engaging in no time theft. The cross-tabulations in Figure 8.9 suggest that respondents were less likely to engage in time theft if they worked in enterprises where advancement was based upon merit (Panel A). They were less likely to steal

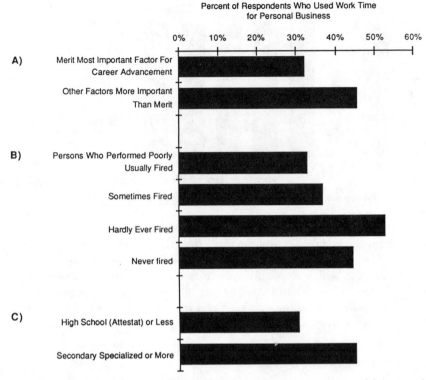

Figure 8.9. Time theft by importance of merit, frequency of firings and respondent's education

time from the workplace if they worked in enterprises where poor workers were fired (Panel B). More highly educated respondents reported more time theft than less highly educated respondents (Panel C).

The logit regression results are recorded in Table 8.5. The time-theft dependent variable is 1 if respondents stole time from the workplace and 0 if they did not. We hypothesize that time theft depends upon discipline conditions (PINKSLIP) and career advancement criteria within the enterprise (MERIT), upon the respondent's perception of whether he or she is working in a poorly run enterprise as proxied by whether productivity was falling (PRODOWN), upon the respondent's perception of whether his or her living standard was falling (LIVSTAND), and by background characteristics of the respondent (AGE, FEMALE, SKILLED). We are also interested to determine if time theft varies systematically by economic branch (BRANCH).

The logit regression confirms the cross-tabulations of Figure 8.9: Time

Table 8.5. *Logit regression: time theft*

	Regression coeff.	Standard error	*t*-statistic
Enterprise characteristics			
MERIT	− .23223	.09931	− 2.33833
PINKSLIP	− .09112	.04253	− 2.14231
PRODOWM	.24269	.11344	2.13929
BRANCH2	.90387	.59415	1.52129
BRANCH3	.19789	.21310	.92860
BRANCH4	.06721	.16936	.39683
BRANCH5	− .02297	.15735	− .14595
BRANCH6	.20836	.28359	.73473
BRANCH7	.07146	.18778	.38056
BRANCH8	− .22784	.17544	− 1.29871
BRANCH9	− .42842	.16783	− 2.55268
BRANCH10	− .30103	.35353	− .85151
BRANCH11	.26147	.18788	1.39169
BRANCH12	.09312	.24380	.38197
Respondent characteristics			
AGE	− .01383	.00367	− 3.76926
SKILLED	.28101	.10914	2.57477
STANDLIV	.07458	.09815	.75987
FEMALE	− .09618	.09598	− 1.00209
Constant	5.23676	.21253	24.64006

Note: Dependent variable (time theft): "While you were working at that job, did you sometimes use work time for personal business (like shopping or running errands)?" (Yes = 1). Number of observations = 582.

theft was systematically lower in enterprises that rewarded according to merit and in enterprises that fired poor workers. Workers who felt that they were working in poorly run enterprises were more likely to steal time. In general, branch effects appear to be weak. There is no strong evidence of systematic time-theft differences among branches.

More highly educated workers and younger workers were more likely to steal time. The positive relationship between time theft and education could be explained by the greater discretion of educated white-collar workers to come and go. Insofar as more educated workers tend to have higher income, it may also be indicative of a positive income elasticity of demand for leisure. Whether respondents felt that living standards were falling or rising did not systematically affect time theft. Women and men had the same incidence of time theft, other things equal.

An ordinary-least-squares regression was run on the sample of respondents reporting time theft to determine the factors that systematically affected the *amount* of time theft. These regressions (reported in Table 8.6) reveal that, of those who steal from the workplace, women and more highly educated respondents tend to steal more time. Although the perception of a declining standard of living does not affect the probability of time theft, it does increase the amount of time theft among those who engage in time theft. The factors that were shown in Table 8.5 to reduce significantly the probability of stealing work time – like working in enterprises that fire poor workers or that use merit criteria for career advancement – do not significantly affect the amount of time theft. Although there were no clear branch effects on the incidence of time theft, the amount of time theft (by those who steal time) is greater in material technical supply and other productive services and in municipal economy and housing.

Table 8.6. *Multiple regression: amount of time theft (of respondents who stole time)*

	Coefficient estimate	Standard error	*t*-statistic
Enterprise characteristics			
PINKSLIP	− 3.640750	16.160014	− .225
MERIT	− 11.511851	40.584287	− .284
BRANCH3	90.840790	74.804740	1.214
BRANCH4	− 16.735313	62.871817	− .266
BRANCH5	62.562898	62.246136	1.005
BRANCH6	183.506664	88.523359	2.073
BRANCH7	151.667627	68.202859	2.224
BRANCH8	− 52.214673	67.925311	− .769
BRANCH9	59.839575	65.191339	− .918
BRANCH10	− 125.758908	173.930483	− .723
BRANCH11	− 61.388081	65.291285	− .940
BRANCH12	− 76.519838	82.328070	− .929
Respondent characteristics			
STANDLIV	65.571989	36.873106	1.778
SUBORD	.054033	.110968	.487
FEMALE	− 61.064346	34.927739	− 1.748
SKILLED	72.956671	42.932003	1.699
AGE	− 1.908919	1.532172	− 1.246
PRODDOWN	− 33.587117	46.857800	− .717
Constant	183.539697	84.319952	2.177

Note: Multiple *R*, .36058; *R*-square, .13002; number of observations = 213. Dependent variable: "While you were working at that job, did you sometimes use work time for personal business (like shopping or running errands)?" If no, then observation dropped; if yes, "How many times a week did you do that?" If 0, then coded .333 times per week; otherwise, 1 to 7. Frequency times: "On average, when you used official work time to conduct personal business, how much time per day did you spend doing so?"

What conclusions can we draw from these results? The most important is that there are systematic determinants of time theft in Soviet enterprises. Enterprises in which discipline is tighter (in the form of firings of poor workers) are hit less hard by time theft. Enterprises that base career advancement on merit considerations suffer less time theft. Although the perception of a declining standard of living does not alter the probability of being a time thief, it does affect the amount of time theft. In a sense, workers who steal time retaliate against their enterprises for a perceived drop in real wages by stealing larger amounts of time.

Second jobs and the second economy

Respondents can react to enterprise working conditions by devoting their time and energies to activities outside their primary place of employment. The social consequences of this diversion of effort are not immediately clear because additional output is produced outside the primary enterprise, but perhaps at the cost of output from the primary enterprise.

SIP respondents were not particularly active in second jobs in the state sector or in second-economy activities. Only 6 percent held second state jobs at the end of the last normal period. SIP respondents participated more actively in private sector jobs. Some 13 percent reported having "private work or a private job other than a private plot."

We postulate that respondent perceptions of enterprise operating conditions, the enterprise reward system, and personal characteristics systematically affect the probability of having second jobs and private sector employment. A logit regression is given in Table 8.7 with the dependent variable a 1 if the respondent had a second job or a private job. The logit results show that women and older respondents were *less* likely to have second jobs or private activities. The two branches whose workers report higher incidences of second jobs and private activity appear to be health and education. These results (based upon a nonconverging logit regression, which is not reported in Table 8.7) appear reasonable insofar as private tutoring in education and private practice in medicine are well-known sources of private income in the Soviet Union.

The main finding·is that enterprise characteristics appear to have little impact on the incidence of private sector activity or second jobs. Economic activity outside of the regular job appears to be determined more by personal characteristics (like being young or being male) than by firm characteristics.

Conclusions

What have we learned from SIP interviews with former Soviet workers and employees that we did not know before? This exercise contributes to our

Table 8.7. *Logit regression: second state job or private job*

	Regression coeff.	Standard error	*t*-statistic
SUBORD	− .00201	.00214	− .93777
MERIT	− .21920	.13597	− 1.61216
PINKSLIP	.04992	.05537	.90165
FEMALE	− .36701	.12585	− 2.91621
AGE	− .01348	.00568	− 2.37292
SKILLED	.06749	.13882	.48616
PRODDOWN	.13693	.14784	.92621
Constant	4.86234	.29261	16.61706

Note: Number of observations = 458. Dependent variable: Respondent had either a second job (JOB2) in the state sector or a private job (PJOB). JOB2: "In [end of LNP], did you have any other job in a state or cooperative enterprise or organization at the same time as the job we just talked about?" PJOB: "In [end of LNP], did you do any kind of private work or have a private job other than a private plot?"

knowledge of Soviet enterprise operations in two ways: First, it provides information on the relative frequencies of phenomena such as alcoholism problems, supply disruptions, redundant labor, merit criteria, and so on. On a second and more analytical level, this study reveals the traits of enterprises that exhibit specific operating characteristics (such as poor performance), some of the reasons for these characteristics, and the impact of operating characteristics on worker behavior.

The information on relative frequencies supports some a priori expectations and yields surprises. According to respondent accounts, supply disruptions are less frequent in Soviet enterprises than one would expect from the literature. Less than one in five respondents reported regular supply and equipment problems, whereas two-thirds felt that they had sufficient supplies and equipment for their jobs. This result is puzzling because interviews with former managers stress supply problems as a constant source of irritation.[26] Microparticipants in the economy do not think that their job performance is particularly hampered by supply disruptions, whereas enterprise managers tend to feel differently.

SIP respondents felt that they had sufficient information to do their jobs well. The relative lack of complaints about information problems is a surprise. The literature depicts the command economy as plagued both by inadequate information and by confusing information. One would expect information problems to be perceived by microparticipants, but such does not appear to be the case.

[26] Linz, "Managerial Autonomy."

Respondents confirm the high incidence of alcoholism and absenteeism in Soviet enterprises (one-third report frequent alcoholism/absenteeism problems in their enterprises). Though depressing, the portrait of Soviet alcoholism/absenteeism is not drastic. The majority do not believe alcoholism/absenteeism to be a serious problem in their enterprises. It is difficult to say whether the incidence of alcoholism/absenteeism reported by respondents is greater than or less than one would expect from official Soviet complaints, but the notion of an economy paralyzed by alcoholism is not supported by this study.

SIP respondents report what this writer assesses to be relatively little redundant labor. One-half said that there was no redundant labor at all in their enterprises, and only a small proportion reported large amounts of redundant labor. The pattern of labor redundancy appears to fit well with a priori expectations. There appear to be too many engineers and scientists and too few skilled white and blue-collar workers. The scarce labor resource appears to be the worker with the industrial skills applied at the shop-floor level.

The strongest consensus among SIP respondents concerns poor productivity performance. Three-quarters believed that labor productivity was declining. There is a surprising consensus that inadequate material incentives, not bad management or the economic system, are the prime cause of Soviet productivity problems. Analysis indicates that respondents based their assessments on their own enterprise work experiences because of systematic patterns by enterprise characteristics. A profile of poorly functioning Soviet enterprises emerges from these patterns: In such enterprises, career advancement is not based on merit, poor workers are fired, and the patterns tend to concentrate in construction, housing, education, and science. Notably, supply problems and alcoholism/absenteeism are not associated systematically with poor enterprise performance.

It is clear why respondents appear so disenchanted with the material incentives offered by the economic system. There is a widespread perception that real wages are falling and that the incidence of poverty is high. The perception of falling real wages appears to be associated with consumer market disequilibriums (a point on which there is virtually no disagreement). Moreover, only a minority of respondents felt that career advancement where they work depended on merit factors. The majority felt instead that getting ahead depended on party membership, connections, and the ability to get along with superiors, and the more highly placed the job, the more important are nonmerit factors. The most disenchanted with the material reward system are those who work in poorly paid branches, those with higher education, and those who work in branches (such as construction) that typically require compensating wage differentials.

Enterprise working arrangements systematically affect the behavior of Soviet workers. Respondents working in enterprises in which poor workers were fired and advancement was based on merit were least likely to steal time from work. The more highly educated have a higher incidence of time theft, but time theft appears to be spread evenly among branches. Those most disenchanted with material rewards appear to steal more time.

This study confirms that certain Soviet working arrangements have predictable costs. The use of nonmerit advancement criteria promotes time theft; it also appears to cause disenchantment with the material reward system. Low rates of firing cause discipline to break down, again in the form of time theft. Most generally, workers feel that the low rate of return to effort is the prime cause of Soviet economic performance problems, eclipsing all other possible factors.

Appendix: independent variables

Branch:

BRANCH 1	Manufacturing (note that this branch has been used as the control branch in regressions; branch coefficients have the interpretation as the difference from the manufacturing branch effect)
BRANCH 2	Agriculture and forestry
BRANCH 3	Transportation and communications
BRANCH 4	Construction
BRANCH 5	Trade, soc. catering
BRANCH 6	Mat. tech. supply, other prod. serv.
BRANCH 7	Mun. econ. housing
BRANCH 8	Health phys. culture
BRANCH 9	Education
BRANCH 10	Culture
BRANCH 11	Science
BRANCH 12	Credit, state, party

Enterprise:

SUPPLYPROB	Rarely or never had sufficient equipment/supplies for job
ALCOHOL	Rarely or never had problem with alcoholism/absenteeism
MERIT	Most important for job advancement (high. ed., diploma, knowledge, experience, talent, ability)
PINKSLIP	Frequency of observed firings for poor performance (0 = never, ..., 3 = usually)

Respondent:

FEMALE	Female
AGE	Respondent's age
SKILLED	Completed secondary specialized school or higher
SUBORD	Number of subordinates in R's LNP job.
STANDLIV	Perceived decrease in living standard – those Rs reporting that prices had increased faster than own wages
PRODDOWN	Reported a decline in productivity during LNP
HIGHED	Highest educational attainment ($0 = < 14$ years of general education, ... , $8 =$ completed a program of higher education)

PART IV

Life: social status, ethnic relations, and mobilized participation

CHAPTER 9

Perceptions of social status in the USSR

MICHAEL SWAFFORD

The October Revolution produced a memorable spectacle. As one commentator later described it:

All classes were thrown like so much scrap into a melting pot beneath which burned the fires of the revolution dissolving all the old identities.... Court ladies cleaned the streets of snow, steel barons functioned as members of house committees and together with porters and shoemakers solved questions of keeping toilets clean and obtaining firewood.[1]

Of course, as Sovietologists well know, this venture into extreme egalitarianism was abandoned more than five decades ago, when Stalin himself denounced "the 'Leftist' practice of wage equalisation."[2] Yet, to this day, many Westerners remain curious about social stratification in the Soviet Union – the first country born of a Marxist revolution to overcome the injustices of capitalist class systems.

The question of Soviet stratification has much to recommend it, not just to Sovietologists but to social scientists in general. New findings on stratification could facilitate efforts to test or generalize Western findings. Consider, for example, the proposition that social perceptions help transmit social status[3] from parent to child. As Bowles and Gintis state, in a much acclaimed analysis of schools in capitalist American society: "Youth of different racial, sexual, ethnic, or economic characteristics directly perceive the economic positions and prerogatives of 'their kind of people.' By adjusting their aspiration accordingly, they...reproduce stratification on the level of personal consciousness."[4] Cannot the same claim be justifiably made about

I would like to thank Richard Dobson, Jack P. Gibbs, Deborah Narrigan, and Joseph Berliner for comments on a previous draft of this chapter.

[1] David J. Dallin, *The Real Soviet Russia*, trans. Joseph Shaplen (New Haven: Yale University Press, 1944), p. 95.

[2] J. V. Stalin, *Works*, vol. 13 (Moscow: Foreign Languages Publishing House, 1955), p. 58.

[3] In this chapter, "social status" means "relative standing in a prestige hierarchy." This usage should not be confused with the other sociological definition, in which the term means "social position" (e.g., father), with no connotation of rank.

[4] Samuel Bowles and Herbert Gintis, *Schooling in Capitalist America* (New York: Basic Books, 1976), p. 128.

the perceptions of people within a Soviet-style society – that they perceive a social hierarchy, peg themselves in that hierarchy, and adjust their aspirations accordingly, thereby maintaining the social order? Evidence from the USSR could help determine whether this process is generated by capitalism per se, as Bowles and Gintis suggest, or whether it is universal in industrial societies. More generally, such evidence could help social scientists determine the nature and extent of variation across human societies.

For Sovietologists, the question of social stratification takes on further significance. Given the importance of social status in explaining an enormous range of Western behavior – from child rearing to political participation, from language usage to artistic tastes – its parallel importance in explaining Soviet behavior is obviously worth exploring. But stratification offers more than a mere explanatory variable. The stuff of which any social system is made – values, norms, power, the distribution of goods, recruitment into adult roles, social solidarity, conflict, et cetera – inevitably manifests itself in the stratification system. Hence, any study of Soviet society in its totality should address the question of stratification.

Capitalizing on the exodus of Soviet citizens in recent years, the Soviet Interview Project (SIP) has provided an opportunity to examine an aspect of Soviet stratification rarely studied: ordinary citizens' perceptions of social status. This chapter presents the preliminary findings on the salience of four attributes that Soviets might take into account when judging others' social status: occupation, Communist party (CPSU) membership, education level, and ethnicity. The chapter also argues that the results accurately represent the perceptions of Soviet citizens, despite the fact that the study relies on interviews of emigrants.

Previous research on Soviet social stratification

It would be misleading to suggest that stratification in the USSR remains a great mystery. Even during the first three decades of Soviet rule, firsthand accounts provided a glimpse of the emerging social structure. Although many early journalistic reports saw promise in the "great experiment,"[5] by the late 1930s trenchant criticism of Soviet inequality was emanating from the ranks of Marxists,[6] and sympathetic Western socialists were becoming disillusioned.[7] And by 1944 the West had an informed introduction to Soviet

[5] Junius B. Wood, "Russia of the Hour: Giant Battle Ground for Theories of Economy, Society, and Politics, as Observed by an Unbiased Correspondent," *National Geographic Magazine*, 50 (1926): 519–98.

[6] Leon Trotsky, *The Revolution Betrayed: What is the Soviet Union and Where is it Going?*, 5th ed. (New York: Pathfinder Press, 1972).

[7] See, for example, the autobiography of Malcolm Muggeridge, who took a job as a correspondent in the USSR with the idea that he might settle there. *Chronicles of*

stratification in the work of David Dallin, a former member of the Moscow soviet, or city council.[8]

Only after World War II, however, did the first survey data on the subject materialize. The Harvard Project on the Soviet Social System, surveying some 2,700 Soviet citizens displaced by the war, established the utility of employing six categories in describing Soviet class structure: party and government elite, intelligentsia, low-level nonmanual employees, skilled manual workers, ordinary manual workers, and collective-farm peasants. In presenting these findings, Inkeles and Bauer concluded:

In a modern industrial society which lacks formal legal class divisions, any formula for dividing the population into classes will be somewhat arbitrary as to the number of classes it designates . . . . The crucial point is that by the late thirties the Soviet Union had a social class structure which, in its broad outlines, was very much like that in the other major industrial countries of Europe and America. True, there were no landowning or industrialist upper classes and no nobility, but there was an analogous class in the distinctive political elite which lived on a relatively lavish scale, and shared its material abundance with a managerial, scientific, artistic and literary elite.[9]

It is instructive to consider how Soviet authorities respond to conclusions such as these, and how they characterize social differentiation in their own country. Fortunately, since Soviet sociology was resuscitated in the early 1960s, we are no longer obliged to rely solely on official pronouncements of leaders and ideologists; we can also take advantage of some commendable analyses by Soviet scholars who have conducted relevant empirical research in the USSR.[10]

Wasted Time, vol. 1 (London: Collins, 1972). Other like-minded notables included Sidney and Beatrice Webb, and André Gide.

[8] Dallin, *The Real Soviet Russia*, pp. 87–185.

[9] Alex Inkeles and Raymond A. Bauer, *The Soviet Citizen: Daily Life in a Totalitarian Society* (Cambridge, Mass.: Harvard University Press, 1959), pp. 73–75. Using interviews with emigrants who left the USSR during the early 1970s, Zev Katz arrived at a very similar description of Soviet social structure in "Insights from Emigres and Sociological Studies on the Soviet Economy," in U.S. Congress, Joint Economic Committee, *Soviet Economic Prospects for the Seventies* (Washington, D.C.: Government Printing Office, 1973), pp. 94–120.

[10] Much Soviet work on stratification, especially that concerning social mobility, is beyond this chapter's scope. For a review covering both Western and Soviet research on stratification in the USSR through the mid-1970s, see Richard B. Dobson, "Mobility and Stratification in the Soviet Union," *Annual Review of Sociology* (1977), pp. 297–329. For English translations of Soviet research, see Murray Yanowitch and Wesley A. Fisher (eds. and trans.), *Social Stratification and Mobility in the USSR* (White Plains, N.Y.: International Arts and Sciences Press, 1973); and Murray Yanowitch (ed.), *The Social Structure of the USSR: Recent Soviet Studies* (Armonk, N.Y.: Sharpe, 1986).

282 **Michael Swafford**

Clearly, Soviet ideologists and sociologists alike reject any analysis like that set forth by Inkeles and Bauer.[11] They object not to Western claims that Soviet society has classes but rather to how those classes are defined. Not surprisingly, Soviet writers hew rigidly to the Marxist-Leninist sense of *klass*, in which the criterion of class membership is people's relationship to the means of production. Under Soviet law, the state owns the tools and factories used in production by manual workers (*rabochie*), whereas collective farms technically own the means of production used by collective farmers (*kolkhozniki*). Hence, these two groups are considered separate classes in Soviet society.

The 1977 Constitution of the USSR identifies yet a third social category, the "people's intelligentsia," which in its broadest sense comprises so-called "mental workers."[12] Statistical handbooks, as well as many Soviet sociologists, often instead refer to this third category as the *sluzhashchie* ("employees"), which again refers to all employed people who do not qualify for membership in the two official classes.[13] Whether labeled "intelligentsia" or "employees," this third category is never described as a class because its relationship to the means of material production is undefined in Soviet ideology. Instead, it is described as a stratum (*sloi*) in the service of the working class.

Soviet ideologists and sociologists, then, reject analyses such as those set forth by Inkeles and Bauer because such analyses employ a non-Marxist concept of class. For this reason, they also inveigh against common Western terms like "middle class," in which "class" denotes an arbitrary segment of a

---

[11] M. Kh. Titma, "Diskussii po problemam sotsial'noi struktury," *Sotsiologicheskie issledovaniia*, 1 (1979): 72–77; and M. N. Rutkevich, "Sovetskaia intelligentsiia kak obekt issledovaniia burzhuaznoi sotsiologii," *Sotsiologicheskie issledovaniia*, 3 (1980): 206–18.

[12] *Konstitutsiia obshchenarodnogo gosudarstva* (Moscow: Izdatel'stvo politicheskoi literatury, 1978), p. 111.

[13] Both "intelligentsia" and *sluzhashchie* are often used in a more narrow sense than here. When the entire third social category is labeled *sluzhashchie*, the term "intelligentsia" often refers only to the subset of mental workers having education and expertise in science and culture. On the other hand, when the entire third social category is labeled "intelligentsia," the term *sluzhashchie* often refers only to low-level mental workers such as salesclerks and bookkeepers, as contrasted to specialists with higher education. No English term properly translates *sluzhashchie*, since it comprises not only white-collar workers but some service workers as well; I shall follow the convention of translating it as "employee." It should be obvious, however, that "employee" does not mean "one who is employed," since manual workers and collective farmers are also employed, and many manual workers are salaried. I shall use quotation marks around the word "employees" whenever the word serves as a translation of *sluzhashchie*.

continuum based on, say, occupational prestige, education, and earnings.[14]
In keeping with Marxist philosophy, they instead identify two basic classes
in capitalist societies: the *bourgeoisie*, who own the means of production; and
the *proletariat*, who must sell their labor to the bourgeoisie. These two classes
are said to be antagonistic toward one another, in sharp contrast to the two
"friendly" (*druzheskie*) Soviet classes. It follows that Soviet ideology stren-
uously rejects claims that Soviet class structure is "much like that in the
other major industrial countries of Europe and America."

Although the Marxist concept of class is central to virtually every Soviet
publication on social structure in the USSR, it is by no means the only
recognized basis of social differentiation. The Constitution – which embodies the core of Soviet ideology – also discusses differences in earnings,
justifying them in terms of the "quantity and quality of work" (Articles 14
and 40). Several other social attributes are mentioned in Article 34, which
ostensibly guarantees equality before the law regardless of "social origin
[*proiskhozhdeniia*], social or property status [*polozheniia*], race or nationality,
sex, education, language, attitude toward religion, type or character of
employment, place of residence, and other circumstances."[15] Admittedly,
Article 34 speaks of equality, not of differentiation; however, the very fact
that the authors of the Constitution found it necessary to guarantee equality
irrespective of these attributes reveals their salience as potential bases of
differentiation.

Acknowledging social differentiation is not, however, the same as
acknowledging the existence of social stratification. Though hundreds of
Soviet authors have published on the relatively safe topic of social
differentiation, few have ventured into an empirical treatment of the
USSR's social hierarchy, an undertaking that might emphasize shortcomings in efforts to build a classless society.[16] Soviet sociologists' research
on this subject requires further consideration here, since it provides a natural
backdrop against which to view the Soviet public's perceptions of social
status.

The acknowledged bases of social differentiation can be separated into two
categories. First, there are attributes such as nationality and sex, for which
Soviet ideology offers no *official* rankings. Moldavians and Belorussians, for
example, belong to different nationalities, but Soviet ideology does not
officially confer higher rank to members of either ethnic group on the basis of

---

[14] O. I. Shkaratan, O. V. Filippova, and L. G. Demidova, "Sotsial'nyi sloi i
professiia," *Sotsiologicheskie issledovaniia*, 3 (1980): 26.

[15] *Konstitutsiia obshchenarodnogo gosudarstva*, p. 119.

[16] *Sotsial'naia struktura sotsialisticheskogo obshchestva, 1970–1977: Bibliograficheskii
ukazatel'*, vols. 1 and 2 (Tallin: Institute of History of the Academy of Science of
the Estonian SSR, 1980).

nationality per se. Likewise, neither sex is explicitly valued more than the other. It would be naive to suggest that authorities do in fact maintain entirely evenhanded policies toward these social groups; any favoritism, however, does not derive from ideological principles.

Much the same can also be said for class or stratum membership. Nowhere do authorities rank members of the intelligentsia higher than the collective-farm peasantry on the basis of class membership. Soviet ideology does admittedly bill the working class as the "leading revolutionary class," and this might be taken to bespeak a superior rank; but it would perhaps be more accurate to describe workers as "first among equals."

There are, however, several bases of differentiation about which Soviet ideology clearly expresses values. More education is considered better than less, and atheism is considered better than religious faith. Furthermore, recall that some work is considered to have more "quantity and quality" than other work; thus, some people are paid more than others. Ranking people on the basis of certain achieved characteristics, then, is sanctioned.

In describing the USSR's social hierarchy, most Soviet sociologists focus on these achieved characteristics. They are careful, however, to emphasize that their attention to these characteristics serves merely as an elaboration of, not an alternative to, a "proper" class analysis based on people's relationship to the means of production. This point is well illustrated in the work of M.N. Rutkevich, a prominent Soviet sociologist who has character-ized Soviet social structure as "hierarchical" and "multilevel." Rutkevich writes of the "skilled" versus the "unskilled" strata (*sloi*) *within* the working class, collective-farm peasantry, and intelligentsia. He explains further that such skill differences translate into social differences, which in turn "entail without fail differences in the sphere of distribution" (earnings and access to goods).[17] Notice particularly that he does not posit a single hierarchy of skill in which, say, unskilled laborers in the working class and collective-farm peasantry are assigned to the same low stratum. Such a hierarchy might well serve as an (objectionable) alternative way of looking at Soviet social structure. Rather, he maintains that a hierarchy exists within each class, attempting thereby to reaffirm the primacy of class as an analytical category.

Much the same strategy can be seen in the work of O. I. Shkaratan and associates, who have carried out some of the most outstanding sustained Soviet empirical research on social structure. Shkaratan and Rukavishnikov begin by acknowledging that social differences "are connected not only with the existing two forms of socialist property, but also with a certain

---

[17] M. N. Rutkevich, "Sotsial'no-klassovaia struktura sotsialisticheskogo obshchest-va i ee otrazhenie v sisteme poniatii," *Sotsiologicheskie issledovaniia*, I (1979): 24.

socioeconomic heterogeneity of work."[18] They attempt to capture this heterogeneity in the concept "character of work," which embodies two components: "the content of work" and "the socioeconomic conditions of work."[19]

What distinguishes the work of Shkaratan and associates is that they have actually applied their concepts in a large survey of adults in a major Soviet city (Kazan) in order to delineate the strata of an urban population. Following is the "typology of strata" they developed on the basis of their empirical work:

Manual Workers (i.e., working class)
1. manual workers with little or no skill;
2. skilled manual workers;
3. highly-skilled manual workers, combining mental and physical functions;

"Employees" and specialists
4. working people performing low-level mental labor not requiring higher or secondary specialized education;
5. working people performing skilled mental labor requiring a secondary specialized education;
6. working people performing skilled mental labor requiring a higher education;
7. working people performing skilled mental labor requiring a higher education and additional training (e.g., scientists and "the artistic intelligentsia");
8. working people performing highly-skilled managerial work.[20]

---

[18] O. I. Shkaratan and V. O. Rukavishnikov, "Sotsial'nye sloi v klassovoi strukture sotsialisticheskogo obshchestva," *Sotsiologicheskie issledovaniia*, 2 (1977): 62.

[19] To measure the content of work, they employ four indicators: (1) amount of routine activity entailed by the work; (2) administrative responsibility vested in the worker; (3) control over time at work and the sequence of work operations; and (4) education required by the work. To measure the socioeconomic conditions of work, on the other hand, they employ one indicator: the "mean socioeconomic value" of the work as reflected in earnings and housing provided by employers. Incidentally, their early work mentions yet another component of the socioeconomic conditions of work: "the social prestige [*obshchestvennyi prestizh*] of groups of people performing work of a given content." However, this component was dropped without explanation in later work. See O. I. Shkaratan and V. O. Rukavishnikov, "Sotsial'naia struktura naseleniia sovetskogo goroda i tendentsii ee rasvitiia," *Sotsiologicheskie issledovaniia*, 2 (1974): 39.

[20] Shkaratan and Rukavishnikov, "Sotsial'nye sloi," pp. 71–73. See also O. I. Shkaratan et al., "Kharakter vneproizvodstvennoi deiatel'nosti i sotsial'naia differentsiatsiia gorozhan," *Sotsiologicheskie issledovaniia*, 4 (1979): 104–10. For English translations, see sources given in no. 10. A discussion of Shkaratan's early work appears in Murray Yanowitch, *Social and Economic Inequality in the Soviet Union: Six Studies* (White Plains, N.Y.: Sharpe, 1977). For similar work on class structure in rural areas, see the work of Iu. V. Arutiunian, discussed in these same sources.

Shkaratan's description of urban social structure aptly represents Soviet research on this topic: Class membership remains the central category, and strata *within* each class or social group are defined on the basis of criteria considered legitimate for ranking – work and, indirectly, education and earnings. However, Shkaratan and his associates do wax bolder than most in positing a single hierarchy in which even the most skilled members of the working class fall below the lowest stratum of the intelligentsia, or "employees." Their work, then, brings us full circle to Inkeles and Bauer. Except for the omission of the collective-farm peasantry (due to their focus on urban populations), the hierarchy presented by Shkaratan and his associates bears a striking resemblance to the six levels proposed by Inkeles and Bauer: At the bottom fall the unskilled manual workers; at the top, high-level managers.

Perceptions of social status

Despite the substantial literature on Soviet social structure produced since World War II, a notable gap remains. Although we know what authorities say on the subject, we still know very little about ordinary citizens' perceptions of the social structure, because the subjective aspects of stratification have seldom been studied by the Soviets.[21] Marxist ideology downplays subjective factors, which might merely manifest the "false consciousness" of the populace; and the Soviet regime, perhaps fearful of embarrassing results, restricts the requisite survey research.

Readers familiar with Soviet sociology may question the assertion that the subjective aspects of stratification are given short shrift. After all, Soviet studies of occupational prestige exist, and these would seem to bear directly on citizens' perceptions of social status. These studies, however, fail to do justice to the question at hand. Consider, for example, the work of V.N. Shubkin and his students. Although the term "prestige" (*prestizh*) is used repeatedly in publications spanning two decades, their studies actually measure the "attractiveness" (*privlekatel'nost'*) of occupations – that is, occupational preferences. Shubkin's work is interesting and important, but it does not attempt to address the question of prestige directly.[22]

[21] Walter D. Connor, *Socialism, Politics, and Equality: Hierarchy and Change in Eastern Europe and the USSR* (New York: Columbia University Press, 1979), p. 92; and David Lane, *The End of Social Inequality?* (London: Allen and Unwin, 1982).

[22] Of course, the attractiveness of occupations correlates with their prestige, but the conceptual distinction is important. See V. N. Shubkin, *Sotsiologicheskie opyty* (Moscow: Mysl', 1970), and *Trudiashchaiasia molodezh'* (Moscow: Nauka, 1984), pp. 73–89. For an English account of Shubkin's early work, see Murray Yanowitch and Norton T. Dodge, "The Social Evaluation of Occupations in the Soviet Union," *Slavic Review*, 28 (1969): 619–41.

At least three other Soviet sociologists *have* made a clear distinction between the prestige and the attractiveness of occupations, and their studies constitute some of the most outstanding quantitative sociological research on any subject in the USSR.[23] However, by virtue of their focus on young people's vocational choices, they do not address directly the larger question of social stratification, including factors other than occupation that may contribute to social status. But other factors do contribute. Surprisingly, support for this claim can even be found in the *Great Soviet Encyclopedia*, in an article entitled "Social Status" (*Sotsial'nyi status*):

Marxist-Leninist class theory makes it possible to analyze the division of society into various classes, social groups, and strata, and to define the principles underlying people's status. In a socialist society, with its absence of class antagonism, the most important variables that determine the status of a group are occupation and educational qualifications (and consequently wages), as well as age, marital or family characteristics, and regional or local categories.[24]

This statement reads like a research-based conclusion, validated to such an extent that it has earned a place in one of the Soviet Union's most authoritative compendiums of knowledge. However, since the relative contribution of such factors as occupation and education to social status has apparently never been examined empirically in the USSR, this study treats it as a point of departure rather than a conclusion. In short, then, this study measures what Stanislaw Ossowski, in his seminal *Class in the Social Consciousness*, termed a "synthetic gradation": a social hierarchy based not on one attribute (say, occupation) but on information about several attributes, given weight and combined in a manner characteristic of members of a particular society.[25]

Measuring perceptions of social status

The best approach to measuring perceptions of social status derives from a method for studying occupational prestige developed over the past 60 years. In Western studies of occupational prestige, respondents are typically given tasks of the following sort: "For each job mentioned, please pick out the

[23] V. V. Vodzinskaia, "O sotsial'noi obuslovlennosti vybora professii," in G. V. Osipov and Ia. Shchepan'skii (eds.), *Sotsial'nye problemy truda i proizvodstva* (Moscow: Mysl', 1969), pp. 39–61; M. Kh. Titma, *Vybor professii kak sotsial'naia problema* (Moscow: Mysl', 1975); and V. F. Chernovolenko, V. L. Ossovskii, and V. I. Paniotto, *Prestizh professii i problemy sotsial'no-professional'noi orientatsii molodezhi* (Kiev: Naukova Dumka, 1979).

[24] *Great Soviet Encyclopedia* (New York: Macmillan, 1980), 24: 510.

[25] Stanislaw Ossowski, *Class in the Social Consciousness* (London: Routledge and Kegan Paul, 1963), p. 38.

statement that best gives *your own personal opinion* of the *general standing* that such a job has."[26] Notice that respondents are not asked to reveal their own occupational preferences; rather, they are asked to give their own impressions of how the general public views the social standing of each occupation. The mean rating given to each occupation, often transformed to a 100-point scale, constitutes the prestige score of that occupation.

Two findings of previous studies have added impetus to the research described below. First, the occupational prestige scores yielded by such studies are remarkably consistent with one another, despite methodological variations, time lapses, and cultural differences. The scores from the large-scale 1947 and 1963 National Opinion Research Center (NORC) studies, for example, correlate .99 (r) with one another.[27] More importantly, the prestige scores yielded by such procedures have proven quite useful in sociological inquiry during the past three decades.[28]

Second, people with disparate social attributes tend to agree with one another in rating occupations. For example, although men and women often experience different realms of the job market, they agree on average about the standing of occupations. Likewise, people with blue-collar jobs agree on average with managers and professionals, despite the fact that this requires them to acknowledge their own lesser status.[29] Since people with disparate social attributes render very similar ratings of occupations, we can assume that Soviet emigrants' perceptions of social status agree with those of the Soviet citizens who remain in the USSR, even though they differ from those citizens in ways that led them to emigrate. Evidence supporting this assumption is presented below.

In recent years, the techniques used to measure occupational prestige have been modified to show how factors other than occupation contribute to social status.[30] Consider the procedure employed in this study to examine the salience of education, ethnicity (*natsional'nost'*), CPSU membership, as well as occupation in emigrants' perceptions of social status. A randomly chosen subset consisting of 320 Soviet emigrants was handed a nine-page booklet in

[26] See Robert W. Hodge, Paul M. Siegel, and Peter Rossi, "Occupational Prestige in the United States, 1925–63," in Reinhard Bendix and Seymour Martin Lipset (eds.), *Class, Status, and Power*, 2nd ed. (New York: Free Press, 1966), p. 323. Statements were scored as follows: "excellent," – 100; "good," – 80; "average," – 60; "somewhat below average," – 40; and "poor," – 20.

[27] Ibid., p. 326.

[28] Donald J. Treiman, *Occupational Prestige in Comparative Perspective* (New York: Academic Press, 1977). See also Matti Alestalo and Hannu Uusitalo, *Prestige and Stratification: A Comparative Study on Occupational Prestige and Its Determinants* (Helsinki: Societas Scientiarum Fennica, 1980).

[29] Albert J. Reiss, Jr., *Occupations and Social Status* (Glencoe, Ill.: Free Press, 1961), pp. 162–238.

[30] See Peter Rossi and Steven L. Nock (eds.), *Measuring Social Judgments: A Factorial Survey Approach* (Beverly Hills, Calif.: Sage, 1982).

which the following two hypothetical Soviets were described (in Russian) on pages 1 and 2:

Page 1   Tatar
with incomplete secondary education
not a party [CPSU] member
works as a janitor.

Page 2   Russian
with a higher education
member of the party [CPSU]
works as a professor.

They then heard the following instructions in Russian:

Look at the description of the person on the first page and rate his social status (prestige) [*sotsial'nyi status* (*prestizh*)] in comparison to other Soviet people. On this scale, "1" means the person has the lowest social status (prestige), "9" means the person has the highest social status (prestige). Circle the number that represents this person's social status. Now turn the page. What is the social status of this person? Remember, 1 is the lowest, 9 is the highest.[31]

The ratings of these first two vignettes are presented in Table 9.1. Almost half the respondents agreed that the Tatar had the lowest possible social status (mean rating = 1.94), whereas more than half the respondents gave the Russian professor on page 2 a rating of 8 or 9 (mean rating = 7.91). As in all studies of this sort, there were a few anomalous answers, and approximately 10 percent of the respondents did not complete the task. On the whole, however, there was a substantial level of consensus.

The main purpose of the statistical analysis was to determine how much respondents weighed each piece of information when evaluating the status of each of the two hypothetical people. Since such an analysis would be mathematically impossible with only two vignettes, respondents were asked to complete seven more pages containing a total of 28 vignettes, each of which described a hypothetical Soviet person. The descriptions were based on a list of eight occupations, two states of CPSU membership (member and nonmember), six education levels, and five ethnic groups (all listed below). Thus, 480 (or 8 × 2 × 6 × 5) distinct vignettes were possible. However, only a subset was actually presented to respondents because (1) the statistical analysis (linear regression) did not require that all combinations be used, and (2) respondents could not be expected to rate a large number of vignettes carefully. The subset presented to respondents was as balanced as possible; however, as is customary in studies of this sort, combinations that

---

[31] This is a direct translation of the Russian version read to respondents. The published English version of the entire questionnaire does not record a last-minute change made in the Russian version.

Table 9.1. *Practice ratings of the social status of two hypothetical Soviet citizens*

	Tatar, incompl. secondary, not CPSU member, janitor		Russian, higher educ., CPSU member, professor	
	freq.	percent	freq.	percent
1 (low)	157	49.1	0	0.0
2	57	17.8	1	0.3
3	32	10.1	1	0.3
4	13	4.1	1	0.3
5	18	5.6	13	4.1
6	2	0.6	22	6.9
7	0	0.0	64	20.0
8	0	0.0	52	16.3
9 (high)	3	0.9	135	42.2
Refused	20	6.3	16	5.0
Don't know	12	3.8	13	4.1
Missing	6	1.9	2	0.6
Total	320	100.0	320	100.0
Mean rating		1.94		7.91

seemed highly unlikely (e.g., a scientist with an elementary education) were not presented.

Although the first two pages of the instrument were identical for all 320 respondents, the last seven pages differed considerably across respondents. First, the order of vignettes was varied to insure that ratings would not merely reflect positional differences. Second, to preclude uninteresting order effects, the order of attributes *within* vignettes varied (e.g., some respondents received vignettes in which occupational information appeared first, others rated vignettes in which CPSU membership appeared first, and so on). Finally, five independent designs, with different sets of occupations, were employed to test the replicability of the findings.

Before proceeding to the results, let us consider some possible outcomes. As regards the salience of occupational information, Soviet literature clearly identifies occupation as the most important objective determinant of the hierarchy within classes. Of course, this fact might merely reflect the ideological constraints under which Soviet sociologists work, not the perceptions of citizens; but if the experience of other industrialized countries is indicative, we would in fact expect occupational information to be quite salient to Soviet citizens.[32] Likewise, given the Soviet emphasis on education

[32] See, for example, Peter H. Rossi et al, "Measuring Household Social Standing," *Social Science Research*, 3(1974): 169–90.

and the intense competition for admission to institutions of higher education, educational achievement surely confers status.

The function of party membership in perceptions of status is more debatable. In Western countries, the salience of political affiliation in perceptions of status has rarely been studied, most likely because its contribution is captured by more fundamental correlates, such as education and earnings. In the Soviet Union, however, party membership directly affects people's daily lives and life chances far more than political affiliation does in the West. Its effect on perceived social status therefore seems well worth exploring.

Finally, consider the importance of ethnicity. Again, ethnic groups are not ranked officially, but this does not prove that the Soviet public refrains from ranking people according to ethnicity. Admittedly, indoctrination on the "friendship of nations" may have succeeded in training people to ignore ethnicity, and Soviet citizens' exposure to an uncommonly diverse range of ethnic groups may have reduced the salience of ethnicity. On the other hand, a disposition to maintain ethnic identity despite the daily onslaught of diverse ethnic stimuli might have instead heightened people's awareness of ethnicity.

Table 9.2 presents the results in the form of five regression equations, one for each of the separate designs. Respondents' 7,600 ratings of hypothetical Soviet citizens' status constitute the dependent variable. For each respondent, judgments were standardized to have a mean of 50 and a standard deviation of 15; they varied between approximately 10 and 90. Roughly speaking, then, the results are presented as though respondents gave ratings between 10 and 90 rather than between 1 and 9, as in the above example.[33]

Consider the regression equation for the first design, in column 1. One use of this equation is to predict the ratings earned by the vignettes in the study. For example, a vignette describing a salesclerk who served as a member of the CPSU, completed secondary education, and belonged to the Uzbek ethnic group would be predicted to receive a rating of 44.7

---

[33] Since numbers like, say, 18.8 are easier to comprehend than numbers with more decimal places, like 1.88, this transformation puts the results on a more human scale without affecting substantive conclusions in the least. Standardizing *each* respondent's ratings adjusts for the fact that some respondents utilized the full scale (from 1 to 9) in assigning social standing whereas others utilized only a restricted range (e.g., from 3 to 7). A methodological defense of standardizing each respondent's ratings lies beyond the scope of this chapter. Suffice it to say, standardizing in this manner increases the explained variance from 40 to 60 percent, which in this case constitutes prima facie evidence that the model does more justice to the process of making status judgments than models that do not standardize.

Table 9.2. *Regression of perceived social standing on four attributes*

	Replication number				
	1	2	3	4	5
Regression constant	27.4	23.0	27.9	27.5	29.5
Occupation					
State farmer (*sovkhoznik*)	0.0			0.0	
Collective farmer (*kolkhoznik*)					0.0
Tractor driver (*traktorist*)		0.0	0.0		
Driver (*voditel'*)	6.9				
Crane operator (*mashinist kranov*)				1.7	7.6
Telephone operator (*telephonist*)					4.0
Shipping clerk (*ekspeditor*)		7.6	4.5		
Decorator (*oformitel'*)					6.8
Jeweler (*iuvelir*)-		16.7	13.0		
Bookkeeper (*schetovod*)	8.7			−3.7	
Mail carrier (*pochtal'on*)		−1.5	−9.8	−7.4	
Salesclerk (*prodavets*)	10.1				
Journalist (*zhurnalist*)	32.5				
Writer (*pisatel'*)		31.1	28.1	21.9	
HS teacher (*prepodavatel'sr. shk.*)	17.9				
Auditor (*finansovyi inspektor*)					18.8
Chemical engineer (*inzh.-khimik*)				14.5	27.8
Physician (*vrach*)		30.1	25.0		
Lawyer (*advokat*)	32.5			21.9	
Economist (*ekonomist*)		22.1	21.2		
Professor (*professor*)					44.1
Army officer (*ofitser Sov. Armii*)					23.5
KGB officer (*ofitser KGB*)		34.3	33.8		
Mayor (*predsedatel' gorispolkoma*)	45.4			31.2	
Party					
Nonmember	0.0	0.0	0.0	0.0	0.0
Member	9.6	12.3	13.3	12.8	13.7
Education					
Low	0.0	0.0	0.0	0.0	0.0
Incomplete secondary	−.2	2.6	1.3	5.7	2.4
Vocational	2.7	10.4	6.1	9.0	5.5
Complete secondary	4.4	9.9	7.1	11.5	10.5
Specialized secondary	3.1	8.1	4.8	10.8	7.9
Higher	9.7	13.0	5.8	14.6	12.5
Ethnicity					
Russian	0.0	0.0	0.0	0.0	0.0
Ukrainian	−3.2	−2.9	−3.3	−1.0	−5.0
Estonian	−5.6	−4.6	−5.0	−2.3	−5.4
Uzbek	−6.8	−5.5	−4.3	−6.7	−8.5
Jewish	−12.1	−14.7	−10.5	−10.9	−11.0
Number of judgments	(981)	(687)	(1893)	(1574)	(2514)
Multiple-R	.78	.73	.72	.79	.75

Note: Eight occupational titles were included in each replication. Blanks for a given occupation indicate that the occupation was excluded from that replication. A "0.0" for an occupation indicates that the occupation serves as a point of reference, not that the occupation has no status (see text). Note that regression coefficients for occupations should not be compared across replications unless the replications have the same point of reference.

$(27.4 + 10.1 + 9.6 + 4.4 - 6.8 = 44.7)$ on a scale of approximately 100. Likewise, a vignette describing a state farmer who did not belong to the CPSU, who had a low education, and who was an ethnic Russian would be predicted to rate 27.4 $(27.4 + 0.0 + 0.0 + 0.0 + 0.0)$. The equation predicts unusually well: The predictions correlate .78 with the standardized answers given by respondents.[34] If respondents had assigned ratings randomly (in response to a meaningless task, for example), or if they had disagreed substantially with one another, the correlation would have approached zero.

For our purposes, however, the most important use of the equations lies not in their predictions but in the partial regression coefficients. Consider, for example, the "32.5" for journalist. This coefficient should be interpreted as follows: For vignettes *that were matched with respect to party membership, education, and ethnicity*, those with "journalist" on them were rated, on the average, 32.5 points higher than those with "state farmer" – a substantial difference on a scale from about 10 to 90. Similarly, those with "journalist" on them rated 23.8 points (i.e., $32.5 - 8.7$) above those with "bookkeeper" on them, again controlling on party membership, education, and ethnicity. The range of the regression coefficients is substantial: from 0 to 45.4.[35] The rank order of occupations implied by the coefficients is, in ascending order: state farmer, driver, bookkeeper, salesclerk, secondary school teacher, journalist and lawyer (tied), and head of the city executive committee (abbreviated "mayor" in the table). Perhaps the only surprise to most Westerners will be the low rating of bookkeepers, who scored below salesclerks in this study but 15 points *above* salesclerks in Treiman's Standard International Occupational Prestige Scale.[36] This can be largely explained by the fact that the Russian term (*schetovod*) presented to respondents denotes a low-level clerk who frequently works with an abacus, as opposed to a higher-level bookkeeper or accountant (*bukhgalter*).

Other occupations were rated in replications 2 through 5, with much the same results. The rankings implied by the coefficients seem reasonable. In

34 In technical terms, multiple-R = .78. It should be emphasized that the data were analyzed at the individual level. Had the *mean* rating given by all respondents to each vignette served as the dependent variable, as it does in many studies of this sort, multiple-R would have exceeded .90.

35 Bear in mind that, in regression equations with design or dummy variables, a coefficient of 0.0 represents the category that has been chosen arbitrarily as the point of comparison. If "journalist" had been chosen to serve as the occupation with which other occupations were compared, it would have received a coefficient of 0.0, and "state farmer" would have received a coefficient of -32.5. Hence, the substantive conclusion would have remained the same: Controlling on other variables, journalists were rated 32.5 points higher than state farmers.

36 Treiman, *Occupational Prestige*, pp. 235–60.

replication 5, for example, occupations are ordered as follows: collective farmer, telephone operator, decorator, crane operator, auditor, army officer, chemical engineer, and professor.

Though no surprises surfaced in replication 5, the ratings of two occupations included in other replications deserve special mention. Mail carriers received the lowest rating of all occupations in replications 2 through 4 – even lower than farm workers; this perhaps reflects their having to work in uncomfortable circumstances (lack of mechanization, large apartment complexes, and bad weather) for very low wages.

KGB officers, on the other hand, received the highest ratings in replications 2 and 3 – somewhat higher even than physicians. This high rating by no means indicates that emigrants *like* KGB officers, for they were not indicating their personal preferences. Rather, the rating seems to reflect the high influence and privilege enjoyed by officers of the KGB (not to be confused with rank-and-file agents). Evidence of their influence and privilege is provided by answers to a series of items in the core questionnaire, given to all 2,793 respondents. When asked to rank incumbents of nine occupations according to their influence (*vliianie*), respondents produced the following (ascending) order: collective farmer, worker in a truck plant, clerk in a department store, medical doctor, colonel in the army, professor at Moscow State University, manager of a large industrial enterprise, colonel in the KGB, and the first secretary of the oblast (provincial) committee (of the CPSU). The ranking of privilege (*privilegiia*) was identical, except that the rank orders of professor and army colonel were reversed.

Let us now turn from the effect of occupation to that of party membership. In replication 1 (Table 9.2), vignettes in which the hypothetical citizen was a CPSU member received ratings 9.6 points higher than those in which the hypothetical citizen was not a member, *holding occupation, education, and ethnicity constant*. Examining the coefficient for party membership in the other four replications (columns 2 to 5) reveals that they are all of similar magnitude. Again, this does not suggest that respondents necessarily *liked* party members more than others, only that they perceived members as enjoying higher social status than others in the USSR, controlling on three other characteristics.

The coefficients for education tell much the story one would expect, with higher education conferring higher status. The fact that incomplete secondary education (lasting eight years) supposedly confers less status than elementary education (lasting three or four years) should be overlooked because (1) the amount $(-.2)$ is minuscule and (2) the more sensible pattern is manifested in each of the other four replications (columns 2 to 5). Similarly, the anomalous low score for higher education in replication 3 should be overlooked in view of its consistently high score in the other four replications.

However, the fact that secondary specialized school (lasting 12 years) brings somewhat less status than complete secondary education (lasting 10 years) should not be entirely overlooked: The same pattern is observed in all five replications. General secondary schools may offer a slight advantage because they serve more frequently than secondary specialized schools as the avenue to higher education. In any case, the differences between the coefficients for the three kinds of secondary education are rather small in all replications. They speak more to the similarity in status conferred by various secondary schools than to the disparity. In other words, the social status of people *matched with respect to occupation, party membership, and ethnicity* does not differ appreciably as a result of the kind of secondary school they have attended. This, however, does not mean that secondary schools have no bearing on social status. Since vocational schools lead to low-status manual occupations, and other secondary schools normally lead to higher-status nonmanual occupations, differences in secondary schooling do exert an important indirect effect on social status.

Finally, consider the regression coefficients for ethnicity. The " − 6.8" for Uzbeks means that, on the average, vignettes of Uzbeks scored 6.8 points below vignettes of Russians when they were matched with respect to occupation, education, and party membership. The decrement for Jews (about 12 points) is even more striking. Discounting a minor anomaly in column 2, the coefficients from all five replications yield the following ranking of the nationalities (in descending order): Russians, Ukrainians, Estonians, Uzbeks, and Jews. Again, it must be emphasized that these rankings do not concern the ethnic preferences of the respondents; rather, they reflect perceptions of the social status enjoyed by the various groups. Furthermore, the rankings do not necessarily indicate that Jews have low status in the USSR. Although Jewishness per se causes a decrement in status according to these results, many Soviet Jews, despite widespread discrimination, manage to compensate with occupational and educational achievements.

Thus far, we have focused only on the magnitude of effects for each of the four attributes that were considered likely components of social status. Had this been the ultimate aim of the research, a much simpler research design could have been employed in which respondents simply rated occupations, party membership, education levels, or ethnic groups (nationalities) singly instead of in combination with one another. However, such ratings would have been potentially misleading. For example, in such an exercise a low rating for Uzbeks might merely manifest the fact that on the average they have lesser jobs than Russians and that lesser jobs, not ethnicity per se, bring lesser status.[37] The regression coefficients in Table 9.2 escape this potential criticism. The lower rating of Uzbeks obtained even when the vignettes were matched on the other attributes.

Another advantage of the regression equations is that they permit us to study the relative salience of the attributes. Notice that the coefficients for party membership, education, and ethnicity all have a range of 10 to 15 points at the extremes, suggesting that they are all roughly equivalent in salience. On the other hand, the coefficients for occupation vary about 40 points, depending on which replication one examines. In each of the replications, occupation appears three to four times as salient as any of the other attributes, but the other attributes still contribute appreciably to social status as judged by ordinary citizens.[38]

All four attributes, then, figure into the synthetic gradation of social status in the USSR. This, however, constitutes only a partial analysis. Other potentially important attributes readily come to mind: earnings, gender, and place of residence, to name a few.[39] A follow-up study will incorporate these attributes into the design. That study will also address three other questions. First, to what extent do respondents' personal attributes impinge on their judgments of social status? For example, do non-Jewish respondents rate ethnicity the same as Jewish respondents? Second, are there interaction effects among the attributes? Does earning a university degree, for example, confer the same status advantage to an Uzbek as it does to a Russian? Finally, to what extent are the results affected by the wording of the question put to respondents? The terms "social status" and "prestige" used in this study are more bookish in Russian than they are in English. The follow-up study will examine results based on the more common expression *pol'zovat'sia uvazheniem* ("to be held in respect").

---

[37] Darrell Slider, "A Note on the Class Structure of Soviet Nationalities," *Soviet Studies*, 37 (1985): 535–40.

[38] In attempting to measure the relative salience of the four attributes, many social scientists would instead examine the unique variance explained by each of the attributes. However, in experimental designs, such an approach is illegitimate because the unique variance to some extent merely reflects arbitrary features of the research design chosen by the experimenter. Unstandardized regression coefficients such as those presented in Table 9.2 escape this criticism.

[39] A pilot study based on 428 judgments from 16 respondents has suggested that earnings count heavily in perceived social status. However, earnings may well serve as a surrogate for occupation. These results will be explored in detail with the new data.

Some methodological considerations

Before turning to the substantive implications of these findings, let us deal with two likely methodological objections. First, some will doubtless object that this study, by relying on an experimental design using vignettes of hypothetical Soviet citizens, bears little relation to Soviet reality. Others may object that the task was too hypothetical for Soviet citizens who, after all, have rarely experienced the level of psychological testing that most Americans experience. Granted, the task (which lasted about six minutes) *was* different than anything most respondents had previously experienced. However, as the high multiple-Rs in Table 9.2 indicate, the responses embodied a great deal of order, not the randomness one would expect from people responding to a meaningless exercise.

An even stronger argument can be made for the "reality" of these findings by comparing them with the character-of-work index developed by Shkaratan and his associates (discussed above). The right-hand column of Table 9.3 reproduces their index for those occupations included in this study. The left-hand column presents comparable values from this study, based on partial regression coefficients for occupations (see the notes to Table 9.3). The correlation between the two is very substantial ($r = .88$). In other words, the occupational perceptions of the respondents corresponded greatly to the objective scale developed by an outstanding Soviet sociological team. This speaks well for the validity of these findings.

Much the same approach can be taken in addressing the second methodological objection – that results based on interviews with emigrants differ from those that would be obtained from normal Soviet citizens. Of course, the results in their entirety cannot be compared directly with Soviet studies, since no such studies have been conducted. However, it is possible to compare the results that pertain to occupations with the results of some uncommonly fine studies of occupational prestige conducted in the USSR. The relevant prestige scores from two such studies are reproduced in columns 2 and 3 of Table 9.3. Note that the prestige scores from the two Soviet studies correlate .89 with one another. The scores based on emigrants (column 1) correlate .92 with the scores from Kiev, and .77 with those from Leningrad. In other words, they are very comparable, especially if we take into account the fact that the Soviet results were obtained from secondary school students rather than from adults and were calculated in a manner that did not control for other factors contributing to social status. The available evidence, then, demonstrates that emigrants' perceptions of occupations correspond to those of Soviet citizens. There is little reason to doubt their perceptions of other attributes.

Table 9.3. *Comparison of occupational prestige scores from Soviet students and emigrants*

Adult emigrants,[a] SIP	Kiev students[b]	Leningrad students[c]	"Character of work" index[d]
11.2 mail carrier		4.6 pochtal' on	
21.9 tractor driver	−.02 traktorist	3.8 traktorist, kombainer	
22.4 state farmer	−.17 rabochii polevodcheskoi brigady	3.4 rabotnik polevodstva	2.7 ne- i malokvalifitsirovannye raboch. sel. khoz.
26.2 bookkeeper	−.28 schetovod	3.1 bukhgalter, schetovod	4.5 shetovod-kassir
29.4 driver	−.13 voditel' trolleibusa	5.1 shofer	5.0 shofer gruzovika voditel' tramvaia, taksi
35.2 salesclerk	−.21 prodavets	3.0 prodavets	4.2 prodavets
49.7 HS teacher	.51 uchitel'	6.2 prepodavatel' sred. shkoly	6.4 prepodavatel' v shkole (tekhnikume)
55.3 army officer	.34 kadrovyi ofitser	7.4 voennyi	7.3 ofitser armii
61.5 chemical engineer	.57 inzh.-geolog inzhener-radiotekhnik	7.3 nauchnyi rabotnik v oblasti khimii	7.0 inzhener-konstruktor, inzh.-tekhnolog
63.4 economist	.30 ekonomist	3.8 ekonomist-planovik	6.8 inzhener-ekonomist
74.7 doctor	.67 vrach	8.5 vrach	7.0 vrach
76.7 journalist			7.7 zhurnalist
85.2 professor	.75 uchenyi-fizik, kibernetik, medik, biolog	8.1 nauchnie rabotniki [10 subjects]	7.0 prepodavatel' v VUZe
100.2 mayor			8.0 otvetstvennyi partiinyi rabotnik

[a]This column lists the fourteen occupational titles in Table 9.2 that have also appeared in one of three important Soviet studies. In several cases, the occupational titles do not match exactly. Readers are free to judge the correspondence between job titles by examining the transliterations in Tables 9.2 and 9.3. Had the titles matched perfectly, the correlations discussed in the text might have turned out to be even greater. The numerical values in this column were calculated by (1) combining the regression coefficients for occupation in Table 9.2 (taking advantage of occupations that appeared in more than one replication) and (2) standardizing the results to yield a mean of approximately 50 and a standard deviation of 26. The procedure employed to combine the coefficients in Table 9.2 gives slightly different results depending on which replication is taken as the starting point. However, the correlations with the values in columns 2 through 4 are scarcely affected by such differences.

[b]*Source:* V.F. Chernovolenko, V.L. Ossovskii, and V.I. Paniotto, *Prestizh professii i problemy sotsial' no-professional' noi orientatsii molodezhi* (Kiev: Naukova Dumka, 1979), pp. 203–4. The values from their study "Va (b)" were used when possible. Otherwise, values from their study "IV" (1973)" were used. In the latter case, .03 was added to their reported values to compensate for a scaling difference between their two studies.

[c]*Source:* V.V. Vodzinskaia, "O sotial' noi obuslovlennosti vybora professii," in G.V. Osipov and Ia. Shchepan' skii (eds.), *Sotsial' nye problemy truda i proizvodstva* (Moscow: Mysl', 1969), pp. 39–61. Values were read from a foldout graph.

[d]*Source:* O.I. Shkaratan and V.O. Rukavishnikov, "Sotsial' nye sloi v klassovoi strukture sotsialisticheskogo obshchestva," *Sotsiologicheskie issledovaniia,* 2 (1977): 68–69. The values reported here are the natural logarithms of their index values. Logarithms were taken to adjust for the fact that their index was computed by using multiplication.

Some substantive implications

From the standpoint of social science, the Soviet Union is perhaps best viewed as a social experiment in which certain conditions have been changed, permitting us to determine whether such changes produce interesting social consequences. As Soviet authorities would themselves claim, Soviet rule has effected monumental changes in the USSR's political and economic orders, changes that were expected to transform the social stratification system. The question remains: To what extent has the Soviet stratification system actually been transformed? Numerous scholars since Inkeles and Bauer have addressed this question by studying social inequality and mobility as well as possible with the limited data made available by Soviet sources. Yet, virtually no attention has previously been devoted to Soviet citizens' perceptions of their stratification system.

Understanding these perceptions, however, is obviously very important for several reasons. In the first place, the objective conditions of stratification – for example, the distribution of income and of occupational opportunities – often take on social significance by virtue of people's perceptions and evaluations of those conditions. In other words, it is one thing to document the objective features of the occupational distribution; it is quite another to demonstrate that people perceive the distribution and weigh occupational differences heavily. Consider, for example, the changes in the Soviet occupational structure that now allow a greater proportion of the work force to perform so-called mental labor than was the case several decades ago. This study, by demonstrating that occupational information figures heavily in perceptions of Soviet social status, elaborates why the net upward mobility of the working population since the Revolution may have contributed to regime support. By the same token, it reveals the potential for disaffection should Soviet citizens' chances for upward mobility be blocked by a decrease in opportunities for professional advancement in a stagnant economy.

Understanding perceptions is also important because they obviously play a role in social recruitment. An informed Soviet view on this subject was well expressed by Vladimir Shliapentokh more than a decade ago, in an article entitled "Social Prestige" (*Sotsial'nyi prestizh*): "efforts to acquire or maintain a high level of social prestige play an important role in individual motivation and in the activity of organizations. Social prestige encourages activities beneficial to the functioning and development of society."[40] Status, like earnings, is a social reward that can attract people to functionally important

---

[40] Vladimir Shliapentokh, "Social Prestige," *Great Soviet Encyclopedia*, 24: 255. Since writing this article, Shliapentokh has immigrated to the United States, where he now spells his name Shlapentokh.

tasks in a complex, achievement-oriented society; or it can instead attach to ascribed characteristics such as sex or ethnicity. The results of this study demonstrate that, in the USSR, status is conferred on the basis of both achievements (such as occupation and education) and ascribed characteristics (such as ethnicity). In pragmatic terms, this represents a partial victory for the Soviet regime: Whatever other problems beset their efforts to build a highly productive work force, at least people see high status in occupational and educational achievement. In ideological terms, however, it represents something of a failure. People obviously do not revere the working class, and they do still make social distinctions based on ethnicity.

There is, however, a more important sense in which these results could be considered an ideological disappointment to Soviet authorities. Surveying Western studies of prestige, some accomplished Soviet sociologists have concluded: "The antagonistic character of that [capitalist] society is reflected in the prestige scale [of occupations]."[41] The results of this study do not set the USSR apart from the capitalist societies being criticized in conclusions such as these. Indeed, one is struck more by the similarities between Soviet and Western experience than by the differences. It would appear that industrialization and modernity exert a greater force than the unique features of Soviet state socialism.

Naturally, Marxists will object to the thrust of this argument because it seemingly ignores the paramount objective factor underlying their concept of stratification: people's relationship to the means of production. But the question of how best to describe a society, or to explain what goes on in it, ultimately requires that attention be given to empirical details. Surely, we may legitimately inquire whether the objective revolution in the Soviet Union's economic order has in fact affected its citizens' social consciousness. Indeed, given Soviet authorities' oft-stated concern about raising "conscious builders of communism," they themselves need to raise the same question.

[41] Titma, *Vybor professii kak sotsial'naia problema*, p. 143.

CHAPTER 10

Nationality policy and ethnic relations in the USSR

RASMA KARKLINS

Survey research with recent emigrants from the USSR is valuable not only because it provides new data but because it can be even more valuable as a means of determining the salience of one or another social science theory for the Soviet case. In assessing the applicability of comparative theories of ethnic relations and ethnopolitics it is necessary to look beyond statistical indexes and formal arrangements to examine the informal political dynamics of a system and the subjective inputs of various political actors. Analysts of Soviet politics have traditionally had great difficulty in gaining access to evidence about informal politics, and it is here that the knowledge derived from research with former citizens of the USSR fills a crucial gap.

The insights on nationality relations provided by the Soviet Interview Project (SIP) General Survey and by my previous in-depth interviews with Soviet German emigrants in 1979[1] indicate that one of the most volatile issues in unofficial Soviet politics is how various nationalities are treated in regard to political and socioeconomic advancement, and this points to the relevance of theories about the instrumental value of ethnicity. As pointed out by Crawford Young (1983), there are two basic strands in comparative theories of ethnicity: "primordialist" and "instrumentalist." Primordialists emphasize the assumed relevance of the givens of a shared culture. In contrast, instrumentalists view ethnicity essentially as a weapon in the pursuit of collective advantage. Thus, they stress the situational and circumstantial nature of ethnic solidarity and focus upon competition and interaction. In other words, ethnicity becomes politicized not only in the sense primordialists would suggest – namely, in the competition between alternative values and cultures – but also in the context of socioeconomic competition and the calculation of career threats and advantages. There have been a number of exponents of such theories (Shibutani and Kwan 1965; Hechter 1975), but the recent work of Joseph Rothschild (1981) stands out particularly.

These theorists argue that ethnic groups are concerned with the politics

---

[1] My earlier work is summarized in Karklins 1986. For other studies of ethnicity based on emigrant surveys, see Kazlas 1977; Kussmann and Schäfer 1982; Gitelman 1983; and Karklins 1987.

of manpower and tend to become interest groups in defense of particular advantages. Although ethnicity is used instrumentally in the pursuit of concrete goals, it also colors the perceptions of the protagonists about what is just and about how their particular group is treated. To the extent that injustices are perceived, they will press even harder to change the distributive balance. To the extent that they see themselves as falling short of their goals, however, they will develop political resentments against powerholders as well as ethnic resentments against competing groups.

It is contended here that these theories of ethnic socioeconomic and political competition are applicable to the Soviet Union and that they help explain numerous observed phenomena. Soviet policy has created a social context in which a person's official nationality is an important criterion for access to higher education, better jobs, and political positions. The policy has its origin in the twofold assumption that Russian cadres are most loyal to the central political system but that the loyalty of non-Russian nationalities can be enhanced by the pursuit of a modicum of proportional ethnic representation in selected areas. As noted by Bialer (1980: 213) "the crucial element in the Soviet political process which explains the leadership's ability to contain the nationality problem is the existence and development of indigenous elites in the basic ethnic regions." It has been the goal of Soviet nationality policy in the post-Stalinist era to have Russians dominate the politically most important positions in the USSR as a whole as well as in most non-Russian republics but also to draw non-Russians selectively into political and economic administration.[2] As first explicated by Zaslavsky (1980, 1982: ch. 5), the primary tool of ethnic cadre policy has been the inscription of all citizens' official *natsional'nost'* into their internal passports and other documents.

The differential treatment of various nationalities with regard to political and socioeconomic advancement is a sensitive issue that is rarely discussed in Soviet sources. Typically, official Soviet statements touch on just two points. First, as stipulated in the Soviet Constitution of 1977, "USSR citizens of different races and nationalities have equal rights," and "any direct or indirect advantages for citizens on a racial or national basis ... is punishable by law" (Article 36). Second, other statements refer to the policy of promoting proportional ethnic representation in state institutions and in the "building of scientific-technical cadre" (Ostapenko and Susokolov 1983: 10). As the history of other multiethnic societies shows, these two goals are frequently contradictory. Equal treatment for all implies that ethnicity is disregarded in the selection for certain positions or education; proportional representation requires specific attention to ethnic identity. There exists a

---

[2] For some recent statements on this, see Hodnett 1978: 38, 95, 392–93; Lubin 1984: esp. 83–89; Lapidus 1984: 569.

basic tension between the equal treatment of individuals and the equal treatment of groups. Emphasizing the latter implies the use of ethnic criteria for political and social upward mobility. This is in fact what we find in the USSR. The result is that – depending on regional and political context – Russians or union republic nationals are favored and members of other nationalities suffer.

Although it is difficult to find contemporary Soviet references to the preferential treatment of Russian nationals, the preferential treatment of indigenous, non-Russian nationalities has been mentioned occasionally.[3] Yet even these references are vague. This chapter will focus on the new insights provided by the SIP General Survey regarding regional differences in nationality treatment and links between cadre policy and the quality of ethnic relations.

The analysis faces a major difficulty created by the ethnic preselection of the potential sample population by the Soviet emigration authorities. With few exceptions, only people with close family ties abroad have been allowed to exit the USSR; for the Soviet Interview Project the result is that most respondents are Jewish, with a small Russian subgroup. Although the composition of this sample constitutes a liability by limiting the possibility of generalizing findings to the entire Soviet population, it can also be turned into an advantage if an appropriate research strategy is chosen.

Two strategies are applied in this chapter. The first focuses on the regional distinctions among union republics, hypothesizing that, as the sample is basically the same no matter where respondents resided, regional variance in responses reflects the environments in which they lived. It will be argued, for example, that variance in evaluations of the quality of ethnic relations between non-Jewish nationalities is less related to personal characteristics of the respondents than to actual differences between union republics. The second approach faces the possibility of ethnic bias directly and makes it the focus of an empirical test based on the partial ethnic diversity present in the sample.

Regional differentials in ethnic evaluations

Ethnic favoritism toward groups

Until recently, scholars have analyzed the question of differential treatment of nationalities within the entire USSR and within individual union

---

3 In recent years, such references have usually been made in the context of calls for ending such "nativization." See Litvinova and Urlanis 1982: 45, and sources cited in Lapidus 1984: 570. For an unusually open discussion of the role of ethnicity in access to higher education, see Ostapenko and Susokolov 1985: 47.

republics by focusing on official policy statements as well as on aggregate statistics about actual ethnic representation in various institutions (Hodnett 1978; Jones and Grupp 1984). Our data complement these studies by analyzing subjective evaluations of policy and its consequences as well as the correlates of differential evaluations made by subgroups of respondents.

Three survey questions asked about ethnic privilege in politics and in socioeconomic advancement in the union republic where each respondent last resided. The focus on the union republic level was deliberate because one can argue that the consequences of Soviet nationality policy are most pertinent in the republics and that the non-Russian union republics provide the context for politically the most relevant ethnic relations between groups, namely, between the titular nations and local Russians. The questions were: "In [R's republic] during your last normal period, which nationality did you think was treated best in:

a. access to government or party positions, or was everyone treated the same? What about...
b. getting good jobs?
c. access to higher education?"

The first substantive finding is that few respondents (less than 10 percent)[4] replied that everyone was treated the same. Although the low rate might be explained partly by the peculiarities of the sample as a whole, this could hardly explain differences within the sample about who was treated better. The pursuant analysis will focus on this internal variance in replies.

There is regional variance regarding the nationality viewed as receiving preferential treatment. As illustrated in Figures 10.1, 10.2, and 10.3 nearly all respondents perceived that Russians were treated best within the Russian Soviet Federated Socialist Republic (RSFSR),[5] but in non-Russian union republics significant privilege applied to the respective titular nationalities. There are additional regional differences in the intensity of ethnic privilege given to locals: It is perceived to be high in Central Asia, the Caucasus, Moldavia, Lithuania and Estonia (note the small N, which makes the last finding more questionable), middle-range in the Ukraine, and in Belorussia

---

[4] Of the one-third of the random sample responding to this question, 5.2 percent said "everybody was treated the same" in access to government and party positions, 8.5 percent in access to jobs, and 9.6 percent in access to higher education ($N = 924$).

[5] One could also have coded the Russians in the RSFSR as "local republic nationality," but this would be more confusing than the scheme used in Figures 10.1 to 10.3; logically, the "Russians are treated best" category means different things whether the reference is to the RSFSR or to the other republics.

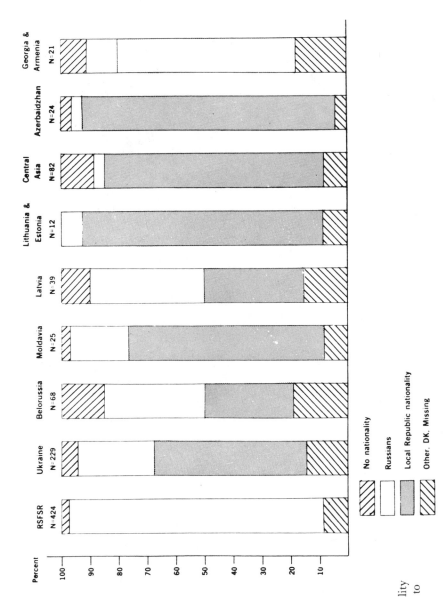

Figure 10.1. Nationality treated best in access to political positions

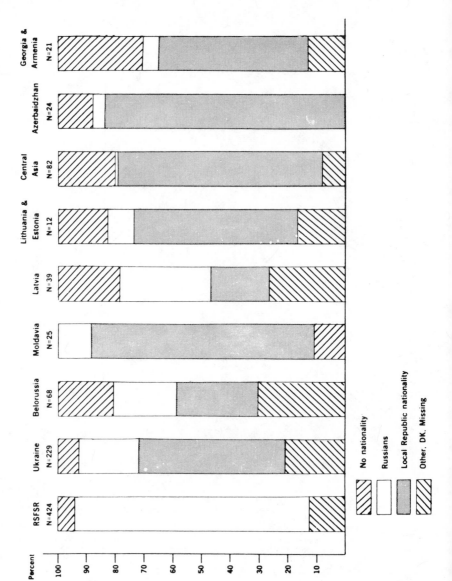

Figure 10.2. Nationality treated best in access to jobs

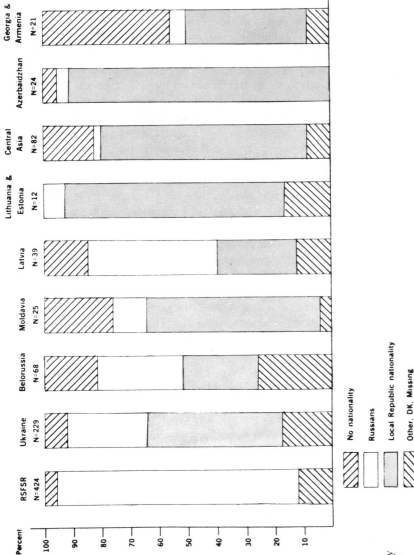

Figure 10.3. Nationality treated best in access to higher education

307

and Latvia the balance favors the Russians.[6] In other words, though in most non-Russian republics the titular nationality is perceived as treated best, in Belorussia and Latvia Russians are seen as holding an equal or even superior position.

The response pattern shows significant regional differences, but variance among the three fields of ethnic access is much less pronounced. A comparison of Figures 10.1, 10.2, and 10.3 shows that the strength of the respective ethnic privilege varies only slightly among political positions, jobs, and higher education. In non-Russian republics Russians are least likely to be mentioned as a preferred group if one asks about access to higher education and most likely to be mentioned if one asks about positions in government and the party. However, the "local republic nationality" is also dominantly cited as being preferred in government and the party and, except for Belorussia and Latvia, more so than Russians.

The role of nationality in political access and regional variation in the identity of the preferred group are seen also in replies given to a topically related question asked of a different subset of respondents. The first question asks directly whether any nationality was treated better in regard to access to government or party positions. The second question focuses only on the party and is formulated more generally: "In [end of LNP] did you feel that all people had about the same chance of being asked to join the party, or that some people were more likely to be asked than others?" In reply, 10 percent felt that "all have the same chance," 79 percent chose "some more likely than others," and 11 percent said they did not know.

Even though we are dealing with a different subsample, and even though the question is formulated differently and focuses only on membership in the CPSU, the overall thrust of these responses is similar to that of replies to the question about access to party and government positions. Roughly 10 percent of each group say that all people are treated equally or have no view to express, and about 80 percent feel that differentiations are made.

Respondents who mentioned differential treatment in recruitment to the party were asked to evaluate the importance of various factors; nationality was chosen most frequently by far, with class emerging as second in importance (see Table 10.1). Further replies show that, on a unionwide level, Russian nationals are most likely to be recruited into the CPSU. Republic nationalities are second most likely. On a regional level, however, differentials similar to those found in the question about access to

---

[6] Where there were few respondents from a certain republic and the distribution of replies was similar, republics were recoded into regions, namely, into Central Asia, Georgia and Armenia, and Lithuania and Estonia. Latvia and Azerbaidzhan appear separately in Figures 10.1 to 10.3 because the distributions of responses are unique.

Table 10.1. *Relative importance of characteristics of CPSU recruits (%)*

Perceived importance	Characteristic[a]				
	Nationality	Class	Leadership, influence, or hard work[b]	Education or experience	Sex
Very important	59	43	23	15	5
Somewhat important	32	33	35	29	22
Not important	7	18	38	53	68
Don't know, or missing	2	6	4	3	5

[a] All respondents saying that "some people are more likely to be recruited than others" ($N = 730$) were asked to evaluate each characteristic.
[b] Results for three separate questions are summarized due to similarity.

government and party positions appear: Within the RSFSR, Russians are overwhelmingly seen as the most likely party recruits; in Belorussia, Latvia, and this time the Ukraine, Russians emerge as holding a slight edge (33 percent), with the republic nationality a close second (30 percent). In all other non-Russian union republics, the titular republic nationalities are perceived to have the easiest access to the CPSU. Even in this case, however, Russians are mentioned more frequently than in replies about both government and party, which suggests that the locals are more likely to be recruited to government than to party positions.

Overall, the differentials found in these macrolevel evaluations of ethnic policies are plausible. Government positions are more visible and are therefore well suited to demonstrate the participation of indigenous nationals in politics. Government positions also tend to be more ceremonial and to wield less power than party positions. As concerns regional differentials, the dominant role of Russians in Latvia and especially in Belorussia is confirmed by other sources.[7] So is the quest for "affirmative action" by the Central Asian nationalities, who have in the past been significantly underrepresented in the higher ranks of administrators in their republics.

Although survey results seem to reflect political realities in the individual

[7] On the low representation of Belorussians in political positions, better jobs, and higher education, compare Hodnett 1978: 104 and Jones and Grupp 1984: 163, 165, 171. In the case of Latvia, the statistics are more contradictory – see Hodnett 1978, passim; Jones and Grupp 1984, passim; and Misiunas and Taagepera 1983: 198 – but *samizdat* protests support the view of Russian dominance. See the protest letter of 17 Latvian communists smuggled to the West in 1972, in George Saunders 1974: esp. 430–35.

union republics, it is also likely that assessments are affected by the characteristics and experiences of respondents, and we must test for this influence. The replies about access to both party and government positions are used as a test. Focus is on the non-Russian region as a whole and on a simplified response pattern that differentiates between respondents who perceived a preferential treatment of the republic nationality and those who did not.[8]

Respondent nationality is the first variable examined, but conclusive findings are unfortunately impeded by the ethnic composition of the sample. There were four types of responses to the question: (1) no nationality is treated better than any other; (2) Russians are treated better than everyone else; (3) titular republic nationalities are treated better; (4) everyone except smaller and/or dispersed groups is treated better. In order to test empirically for ethnic bias one should have data for all relevant groupings: Russians, non-Russian republic nationals, and individuals who belong to a smaller and dispersed group. The Soviet Jews are a good proxy for the latter, and there is a sizable group of Russian respondents from the RSFSR, but titular nationalities and Russians living outside of the RSFSR are underrepresented. Even though the marginals are small, Table 10.2 lists the latter two groups separately in order to show the thrust of replies. As may be seen, the clearest finding is that, compared to Russians and Jews, non-Russians in the "Other" category are least likely to say that republic nationalities are treated better. Since most of these respondents belong to republic nationalities, this suggests a tendency to deemphasize the advantages of one's own group. This same tendency is found among Russian respondents from the RSFSR, who were the least likely to say that Russians are treated better than others.[9] If the sample had been more diversified ethnically, results more likely than not would have shown even more divergent interpretations. The replies for Estonians seem, for example, highly problematic.

All respondent subgroups agree that the ethnic privilege of republic nationalities is most pronounced in regard to political positions, but the Russian subsample emphasizes this most clearly. Even though this is again suggestive of the influence of respondent nationality, the subsample of non-Jewish respondents is too small to draw definitive conclusions.

---

[8] The RSFSR is omitted here due to low variance (compare Figures 10.1 to 10.3). The responses are dichotomized in order to simplify analysis; alternative "cuts" in the data are substantively less interesting and are problematic numerically.

[9] Of those Russians who lived in the RSFSR ($N = 62$), just 77 percent stated that Russians were treated better in regard to government, compared to 93 percent of the rest of our respondents. The figures for access to jobs and higher education are similar.

Table 10.2. *Perception of titular nationality being treated best in non-Russian republics, by various factors* (%)

Factor	Areas where titular nationality is seen as treated best			
	Access to government or Party positions	Getting jobs	Access to higher education	N^a
Nationality				
Jewish only	59	54	56	(386)
Mixed Jewish	53	51	53	(49)
Russian	65	50	47	(20)
Other	42	31	35	(26)
Level of education				
Secondary or less	55	48[b]	52[b]	(322)
Some higher or more	64	61	59	(159)
Interest in politics				
Hardly interested	54	48	48	(211)
Interested	61	55	59	(270)
Job satisfaction				
Satisfied	56[b]	51	55[b]	(333)
Not satisfied	68	60	60	(95)
Not applicable	51	43	43	(53)

[a] Indicates total number of respondents on which percentage is based. The N listed refers to responses to first-column question; the Ns are very similar for the other two.
[b] Significant at 0.05 or less.

The data are more reliable when other respondent characteristics are examined. Thus, both a higher level of education and a self-declared "interest in politics" are associated with the belief that republic nationalities receive preferential treatment (see Table 10.2). This suggests that ethnic privilege is more evident to more educated and politically involved observers.

Job satisfaction also influences the pattern of responses significantly. People who did not work during their LNP were the least likely to say that republic nationalities were treated best (Table 10.2). Among those who were working, however, individuals who were satisfied with their jobs were the most likely to say that no nationality was treated better than another in access to government, jobs, or education. Also, in the non-Russian republics, decreasing levels of satisfaction with one's job are associated with an increasing emphasis on the statement that the republic nationality was treated best in all three areas, and especially so in government and party positions. This finding can be interpreted in several ways. The interpretation most closely in accord with the arguments of theorists of comparative ethnic relations and Soviet ethnosociologists is that job dissatisfaction is easily projected into general ethnic discontent or the perception of favoritism toward other groups.[10] But the causal chain could also be reversed, with favoritism toward the republic nationalities leading to higher levels of job dissatisfaction on the part of those who feel left out. Whatever the explanation, it appears that a politically interesting association between ethnic policy and economics exists in the USSR.

In summary, there is evidence that some characteristics of respondents affect their replies, but with differing intensity. As is suggested by Table 10.2, respondent nationality may be most influential, but our sample does not allow a clear conclusion about it. The data are more conclusive in pinpointing regional differentials of the extent to which Russians or union republic nationalities are perceived to receive preferred treatment in access to political and socioeconomic positions.

Trends in the quality of nationality relations

Relations between nationalities can be conceptualized as taking place on either an individual or a group level. Group-level relations are more affected by policy and are therefore more susceptible to fluctuations over time. In order to evaluate trends of the late 1970s – the primary period of reference for our respondents – the survey asked: "Would you say that relations among non-Jewish nationalities in [R's Republic] were improving, getting worse, or staying about the same during your last normal period?"

The quality of group ethnic relations in the Soviet Union as well as in other societies is influenced not only by long-standing characteristics of societies, such as their history and the closeness of cultural identity among the groups in contact, but also by changes in cultural and socioeconomic competition and in the perceptions of equity of politics (Glazer and Moynihan 1975; Azrael 1978; Rothschild 1981; Karklins 1986: ch. 2). As one thinks about individual regions of the USSR along these dimensions, and if one interprets "relations among non-Jewish nationalities" to refer to relations between the titular nations of the non-Russian republics and the local Russians, one would expect to find increasing strains in the Baltic and Central Asian areas, followed, with lesser severity, by the Caucasus, the Ukraine, Moldavia, and Belorussia.

As may be seen in Figure 10.4, this regional ranking is confirmed by our

[10] For Western theories, see Rothschild 1981, passim, and Blalock 1967: ch. 2. For Soviet findings, see Arutiunian and Kakhk 1979: 100; Drobizheva 1981: 96–99, 201; and Susokolov 1973.

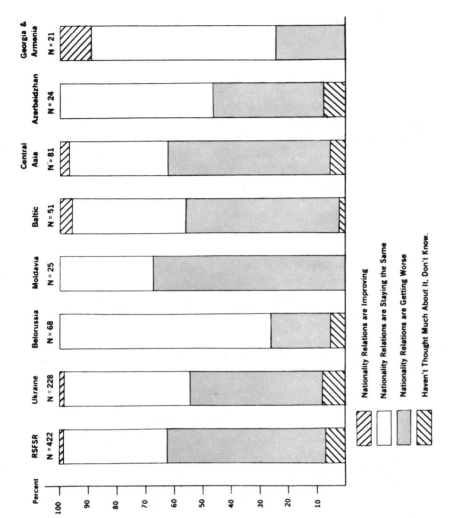

Figure 10.4. Quality of ethnic relations among non-Jewish nationalities

survey data, with two exceptions. The Caucasus emerges as decreasingly conflict-ridden, whereas Moldavia stands out as increasingly conflictual. Both these unexpected ratings are problematic because of the small numbers of respondents, but substantive explanations may also be found. There are comparatively few Russians in Armenia, Georgia, and Azerbaidzhan, and thus the statement, "relations are staying about the same," is plausible. As noted below, Moldavians appear for their part to react especially negatively to recent pressures on native culture.

Figure 10.4 shows that 56 percent of respondents who had lived in the RSFSR said that relations among nationalities were getting worse. This high rate is surprising and suggests that relations among the Russians and the other nationalities living within the RSFSR are more strained than the existing literature leads one to expect. Pressures on non-Russian cultures within the RSFSR appear to explain rising ethnic strains. Yet, it is also conceivable that respondents thought the question referred to the entire Soviet Union and not just the RSFSR.

As to explanations for worsening nationality relations in various regions, respondents had a chance to explain in a follow-up question. Most chose a reply about "growing pressures to forget traditional languages and cultures among non-Russians" (41 percent); others said "there was more competition for jobs and privileges" (28 percent); and a small group chose "material conditions among nationalities becoming more unequal" (10 percent). Looking again at regional distributions, one finds that the last reply category was most frequently given in regard to the RSFSR. The pressure to forget non-Russian cultures was most often cited for the Baltic republics and Moldavia (closely followed by the RSFSR), whereas job competition stands out in Central Asia and in the Ukraine.

This pattern of replies is plausible. Since the mid-1970s, pressures against minority languages have accelerated (Solchanyk 1982; Simon 1986: 382–95) and have weighed most heavily on those peoples such as the Balts whose identities revolve around distinct languages and cultures. Other sources confirm that the volatility of ethnic socioeconomic competition has increasingly emerged at the forefront of ethnic politics in Central Asia (Lubin 1981; Karklins 1986), and it was already highlighted for the Ukraine in the 1960s (Dzyuba 1968).

Again, one has to test how respondent characteristics may have affected their evaluations. The next section deals with this question systematically.

The role of respondent nationality in ethnic evaluations

Survey research by its nature focuses on the subjective experiences and evaluations of respondents. The extent and significance of ethnic subjectivity are assessed here in two ways. First, I shall measure the relative impact of ethnic variables on respondents' replies by comparing it to the impact of general demographic variables, political profiles, and job satisfaction. Second, I shall test the hypothesis that the impact of what I call "ethnic profile variables" differs depending on the question asked and is more intense in microlevel, respondent-related ethnic evaluations than in macrolevel evaluations of general ethnic trends in society. My supposition is that in the latter case respondents tend to take on the role of neutral observers, whereas in the former personal involvement is more influential.

Two survey questions are used to test these theses. The test question for microlevel evaluations is whether the respondent mentioned problems of nationality as a reason for emigration. Where this was the case (42 percent of the sample), respondents typically mentioned anti-Semitism and discrimination they themselves or family members had experienced or wanted to evade in the future.[11]

The core question about group-level ethnic relations in the USSR is whether relations among the major nationalities are improving or deteriorating over time. This is taken as the test question for macrolevel evaluations, as its wording deliberately underlined relations among non-Jewish nationalities, thus putting both Jewish and other respondents into observer roles. To recapitulate, the question asked was, "Would you say that relations among non-Jewish nationalities in [R's republic] were improving, getting worse, or staying about the same during your last normal period?" Responses for the entire USSR show that 2 percent thought that they were improving, 50 percent thought that they were getting worse, 42 percent said they were staying the same, and 6 percent did not know or had not thought much about it. Since the latter group of respondents is basically neutral in its evaluation, and since only 2 percent saw an improvement, these replies are merged with the "staying the same" category, transforming our test question into a dichotomous variable with a 50/50 frequency distribution.

Thus, we arrive at two replies treated as dichotomous dependent variables, and we want to compare how they are affected by several independent variables. The latter form three subgroups: demographic variables (sex, age, and level of education); ethnic profile variables (respondent's nationality, nationality of respondent's spouse and best friend, and interethnic attitude score); political profile variables (interest in politics, politics as a motive for emigration, and job satisfaction). These groups of variables are analyzed first separately and then collectively. My working hypothesis is that ethnic profile variables will have the strongest

---

[11] The survey recorded three emigration motives; I summarize responses into a dichotomous variable, whether discrimination was mentioned or not.

Table 10.3. *Comparison of the influence of demographic variables on evaluation of group ethnic relations and personal discrimination* (%)

	Percentage citing discrimination	Percentage seeing worsening of ethnic relations	N^a
Some higher education or more			
Male, 46 or younger[b]	46	57	(167)
Female, 46 or younger	37	55	(160)
Male, over 46	45	52	(31)
Female, over 46	37	54	(59)
Secondary education and less			
Male, 46 or younger	40	43	(129)
Female, 46 or younger	44	47	(152)
Male, over 46	49	56	(80)
Female, over 46	40	36	(146)

[a] Indicates total number of respondents on which percentage is based.

[b] The cutting point is between people born before and after 1931, with 1977 the median reference year for age during the LNP.

influence on the measure of discrimination because it is directly related to personal ethnic identity and that the political profile variables will have the most influence on answers about the status of group ethnic relations, as this relates more closely to general public affairs.

The two questions studied are dichotomous, which means that findings about correlates of one of the two responses are implicitly findings about the other response. For the sake of simplicity (note especially Tables 10.3 to 10.7), the pursuant analysis focuses on responses citing personal ethnic discrimination and on responses mentioning a worsening in ethnic relations among non-Jewish nationalities.

Demographic variables

Looking first at the demographic variables and the three-way cross-tabulations in Table 10.3, we find that the differentials are small and are inconsistent in sign. If one ignores the latter and calculates the relative effects[12] of the three variables on the perception of discrimination, it emerges that age is the least influential (with an average percentage difference of 3.5), followed by education (5), and sex (7.5). In other words, there is

[12] In calculating the relative effect of the variables I follow the logic and technique outlined in Rosenberg 1968: ch. 7.

very little difference in replies if one controls for age, and somewhat more if one controls for education (with the less educated tending to mention discrimination more, except for higher-educated males). Sex is the most influential in that males cite discrimination more often. In the case of evaluations of group ethnic relations, differentials are larger. Nevertheless, age again has the least pronounced influence, although younger individuals see a worsening of relations more often than any other group except older males. Males more frequently see a worsening of relations, and so do the more educated.

Being younger, male, and more educated are correlated with having more interest in public affairs; thus, it is conceivable that the latter is truly the "independent" variable determining evaluations of trends in nationality relations. Tests show, however, that higher levels of education remain associated with more negative evaluations of group ethnic relations, even when one controls for self-declared "interest in politics."

Ethnic profile variables

Three ethnic profile variables are used: nationality of respondents, and one score each for behavioral and attitudinal ethnic preferences. Each of these variables presents some complexities, but they are nevertheless useful measures of ethnic identity.

Three subcategories are used for respondents' nationality, namely, "Jewish only," "Mixed Jewish," and "Russian or other." It would of course theoretically be preferable to have more subcategories, especially for non-Russians/non-Jews, but, unfortunately, they are only minimally represented in the sample. I do, on the other hand, analyze separately those respondents who, according to self-identification and their official passport identification, were in part Jewish and in part belonged to another nationality (usually Russian).[13]

The "ethnic affiliation score" measures behavioral ethnic preferences in the choice of spouses and closest friends. The proposition to be tested with this score is that respondents' ethnic evaluations and perceptions are

---

[13] There were three questions about the respondent's own ethnic identity, two of which focused on self-identification: "what did you consider to be your nationality?" and "did you feel you belonged to another nationality besides. . .?"; a third asked about official identification in the internal passport. Most respondents with a mixed ethnic identity self-identified with two nationalities, one of which was inscribed in the passport. The large majority of the "mixed Jews" self-identified their nationality as both Jewish and Russian, with slightly more than half having "Jew" inscribed in the passport, the others having "Russian." For a detailed discussion of Soviet Jewish ethnic identification based on SIP data, see Karklins 1987.

influenced by the nationality of their closest personal affiliates. Persons affiliated only with members of their own nationality tend to focus more on their own group's concerns; those who have a spouse or best friend who is of another nationality than their own empathize more with the concerns of other nationalities. In other words, it is assumed that this score provides a behavioral measure of ethnocentricity.

The ethnic affiliation score is constructed to indicate the congruence of respondent nationality and affiliate nationality: a score of 2 indicates that both spouse and best friend are of the respondent's own nationality,[14] a 1 indicates that either the spouse or the best friend is of the respondent's nationality, and a 0 indicates that neither the spouse nor the friend is of the same nationality as the respondent.

It is typical that the affiliates are of the respondent's own nationality: A majority of the Jewish (59 percent) and mixed Jewish (52 percent) respondents have both a Jewish spouse and best friend. In contrast, only 31 percent of respondents who are "Russian or other" have both affiliates of their own nationality; the 0 and 1 scores are more heavily represented (24 percent and 44 percent). This nearly always means that one or both affiliates are Jewish. In the case of Jewish respondents, a non-Jewish spouse or friend usually refers to a Russian. It is rare that any respondent had affiliates who were other than Jewish or Russian.[15]

When one looks at relationships among the ethnic affiliation score, respondent nationality, and the two types of ethnic evaluations (Table 10.4) and examines those respondents who cited ethnic discrimination as a motive for emigration, one notes that the incidence of discrimination is highest among those who were "Jewish only." It is second highest among the mixed Jews and lowest among Russians and others. Russians and others mention discrimination most frequently if they have an ethnic affiliation score of 0 – for example, if both their spouse and friend were not of their own nationality. Since this is another way of saying that their closest affiliates were Jewish, the finding is logically in accord with that for the other respondent subgroups, which shows that individuals with more Jewish affiliates report discrimination more often. The percentage differentials are

---

[14] Affiliates of mixed Jewish respondents are considered to be of the same nationality if they are Jewish, since respondents rarely indicated a mixed ethnic identification for spouses or friends. If respondents were not married during LNP (22 percent), the second close friend was taken as a substitute in the score (157 cases, 17 percent); if there was no second friend, only the first friend was counted (18 cases, 2 percent). If there was a spouse but no friends, only the spouse was counted (78 cases, 8 percent). If there was neither a spouse nor a friend, the respondents were defined as missing cases ($N = 27$).

[15] Of the subsample, only 17 people (1.8 percent) had spouses who were neither Russian nor Jewish, and 74 (8 percent) had such as the closest friend.

Table 10.4. *Ethnic assessments, by ethnic affiliation score and by nationality*

Nationality and ethnic affiliation	Percentage citing discrimination	Percentage seeing worsening of ethnic relations	N^a
Jewish only, EF score[b]			
0	27	38	(45)
1	42	46	(229)
2	53	54	(394)
Mixed Jewish, EF score			
0	0	43	(7)
1	41	52	(42)
2	39	50	(54)
Russian and other, EF score			
0	28	34	(32)
1	21	46	(56)
2	5	50	(36)

[a] Indicates total number of respondents on which percentage is based.
[b] Indicates whether 0, 1, or 2 of respondent's closest affiliates (spouse and best friend) are of his nationality.

quite large both among the three nationality categories and among the subcategories of the ethnic affiliation score, thus supporting the proposition that respondent nationality and having a Jewish spouse and/or best friend are related to the experience and perception of ethnic discrimination against oneself or one's family.

By comparison, the percentage difference between subcategories of respondents is lower in their replies about trends in ethnic relations among non-Jewish nationalities, even though there again is a correlation, especially with the ethnic affiliation score. Respondents with a score of 0, indicating that neither their spouse nor their best friend was of their own nationality, have the lowest incidence of reporting ethnic strains, whereas those with a score of 2 have the highest rates. Those who are most ethnocentric in their behavior tend more often to perceive strains in ethnic relations, perhaps because of their subjective outlook on these matters. Alternatively, one could argue that individuals associating more with members of their own nationality may have lived in environments where a premium was put on affiliating with one's own ethnic group and that it is in this context that ethnic relations in the USSR are worsening.

Whereas the "ethnic affiliation score" measures personal behavioral preferences, the "ethnic attitude score" measures attitudinal ethnic preferences. It is a summary score derived from a series of questions about the desirability of intermarriage and ethnic interaction at work. We asked whether during the LNP it was "desirable," "undesirable," or "made no difference" for a close relative to marry a Russian, Armenian, Latvian, Uzbek, Ukrainian, Jew, or Buriat; similarly, we asked whether the respondent had had any preference among these nationalities for coworkers or immediate supervisor. Altogether, respondents gave 21 answers in this series.

The ethnic attitude score summarizing the responses can be constructed in several ways. Since the focus here is on the general role of ethnic preference or rejection, it is most appropriate to count the times that the "it made no difference" reply was chosen. Saying so consistently all 21 times indicates total indifference to the ethnoreligious identity of social partners, and a score of 0 is assigned to the respective respondents (23 percent). If the "no difference" category is chosen less often, people tend to express a single preference – usually for intermarriage with their own nationality – and a varying intensity of rejection of the alternative partners mentioned in the question series. If the rejection rate is low, this is indicated by a score of 1; if the rejection is high, the score is a 2.[16]

Although they do not emphasize the point, some Soviet sources have shown that nationalities differ in the extent to which ethnic preferences are expressed, especially regarding intermarriage. A study conducted in Moldavia shows that, although 53 percent of Jewish respondents stated that it made no difference whether close relatives married individuals of another nationality (and, implicitly religion), the rate for Russians was 76 percent and for Moldavian respondents 65 percent to 70 percent (Arutiunian, Drobizheva, and Zelenchuk 1980: 202). Comparable ethnic differentials are found in our data: The respondents who are "Jewish only" have the lowest percentage of people with an ethnic preference score of 0 (18 percent), followed by the mixed Jews (25 percent), and then the Russians and others (49 percent). Thus, nationality is significantly associated with the intensity of personal ethnic preference and rejection. Taking account of this, the cross-tabulation between the ethnic attitude score and the ethnic evaluations under study controls for respondent nationality.

As illustrated in Table 10.5, personal ethnic preferences for partners in work and marriage are somewhat associated with differential comments on ethnic policy, but the strength of the association differs according to the question. Compared to comments about discrimination, percentage differentials are smaller between subgroups noting the worsening of ethnic relations in society. In the latter case, there is little variance among the three nationality subgroups, and there is no consistency in the direction

---

[16] This summary score is used in cross-tabulations only; the more detailed score ranging from 0 to 21 is used in regression.

Table 10.5. *Ethnic assessments, by ethnic attitude score and nationality*

Nationality and ethnic attitudes	Percentage citing discrimination	Percentage seeing worsening of ethnic relations	N^a
Jewish only, EA score[b]			
0	37	40	(126)
1	50	50	(300)
2	49	56	(263)
Mixed Jewish, EA score			
0	19	50	(26)
1	42	52	(52)
2	41	48	(27)
Russian and other, EA score			
0	18	44	(63)
1	14	44	(52)
2	33	33	(15)

[a] Indicates total number of respondents on which percentage is based.

[b] A zero indicates that there were no personal ethnic preferences, whereas 1 and 2 indicate a rising intensity of such preferences.

of the association with the ethnic attitude score. Thus, it has just about no effect on the mixed Jewish group's responses, and it deflates the rate of "getting worse" responses among those Russians and others who have the highest preference/rejection score (although the small N makes this finding unreliable). However, among the numerically most reliable group, those who are "Jewish only," the incidence of the perception of a worsening of ethnic group relations increases with an increase in the ethnic preference/rejection score. This is worth noting, although one should beware of causal interpretations; it is equally possible that respondents have a higher preference/rejection score in regard to their partners' ethnicity because of a worsening climate in general ethnic relations, or that they note a worsening of ethnic relations because of their own attitudes. More likely than not, the flow of causation goes both ways or is due to a common underlying factor not identified here.

The most dramatic increase in the frequency of comments about anti-Semitism and ethnic discrimination is notable between Jewish and mixed Jewish respondents with an ethnic attitude score of 1, as compared to members of the same groups who scored 0. In other words, those individuals who said that the ethnicity of their social partners made no difference to them show the lowest rate of comments about discrimination

322   **Rasma Karklins**

they experienced. Again, this can be interpreted several ways. It could mean that people who are indifferent to ethnic distinctions are less likely to experience or perceive discrimination against themselves, or, alternatively, it can be interpreted as a reflection of a social environment that paid little attention to ethnicity.

The other major differential in responses about discrimination concerns the respondents' nationality; it is least often mentioned by "Russians and others," followed by mixed Jews and those who are "Jewish only."

The examination of a multiple regression with all three ethnic profile variables further illuminates their relative effects on the two ethnic evaluation questions. Using a stepwise regression, with the discrimination statement as the dependent variable, "nationality of respondent"[17] enters first in the equation, the ethnic affiliation score enters next, followed by the ethnic attitude score. In contrast, only one variable – the ethnic affiliation score – enters into the equation when the evaluation that relations among non-Jewish nationalities is worsening is taken as the dependent variable. These findings support the thesis that the impact of the various ethnic characteristics differs depending on the questions asked.

Political variables and job satisfaction

Considering the nature of the two ethnic questions under study – the perceptions of ethnic discrimination and the quality of group ethnic relations – it is theoretically reasonable to assume that the political outlook and economic satisfaction of respondents influenced their replies. Thus, both questions relate to politics and are likely to be answered differently by individuals who are involved in politics with specific political views and by individuals who are not. Similarly, both questions have economic implications. Ethnic discrimination frequently refers to a lack of socioeconomic advancement, and the worsening of ethnic relations often is related to group economic competition. Other research has shown that there is a tendency for individual feelings of job satisfaction to be projected onto assessments of micro- and macrolevel ethnic relations.[18]

Two questions are used here to gauge the political profile of respondents.

---

[17] In the regression, a dichotomous version of the "nationality of respondent" variable is used, differentiating between "Jews and mixed Jews" and "Russian or other." Using regression with dichotomous dependent variables is problematic because of violation of the assumptions of regression and because only a small percentage of the variance can be explained. Here, the regression results are examined nevertheless to see if they lend support to the trends seen in the cross-tabulations and to get an indication of the relative ranking of multiple independent variables.

[18] Compare note 10.

Table 10.6. *Ethnic assessments, by political outlook and job satisfaction, controlling for political interest*

	Percentage citing discrimination	Percentage seeing worsening of ethnic relations	Total N
Interested in politics			
Political motive for			
emigration	44	59	(298)
No political motive	48	51	(294)
Dissatisfied with job	54	64	(130)
Satisfied with job	45	54	(355)
Didn't work	41	50	(105)
Not interested in politics			
Political motive for			
emigration	28	45	(76)
No political motive	37	37	(252)
Dissatisfied with job	52	39	(33)
Satisfied with job	31	42	(206)
Didn't work	36	32	(89)

The first is the classic question about "interest in politics" asked in numerous comparative surveys. Cross-tabulation of this variable with our two dependent variables shows that there is a significant association and that it is stronger in the perceptions of worsening ethnic relations ($r = \cdot2047$) than in the statements about discrimination ($r = -.1305$). This differential is not surprising, for the question about the status of overall ethnic relations among non-Jewish nationalities in various union republics is more closely related to general public affairs than is a question about personal experiences of ethnic discrimination.

I also examine a rough indicator of respondents' political attitudes toward the Soviet system: whether they did or did not mention politics as a motive for emigration. Since the emigration question was open-ended and respondents could cite up to three motives, one may assume that people with critical political attitudes toward the regime would have mentioned that here if at all (41 percent of the sample did). This political disenchantment measure also correlates with the two ethnic evaluations, but less strongly than the "interest in politics" variable. Thus, the discrimination statement has an $r = -.0951$ and the "ethnic relations are worsening" variable shows an r of .1246.

Similarly, simultaneous cross-tabulation with both political variables (Table 10.6) indicates that the "interest in politics" variable is unidirectional and the more decisive. A calculation of the relative effects of the interest variable on the two ethnic variables shows an average 14 percent differential in both cases, and in both instances the direction of the influence is toward a higher incidence of statements about ethnic discrimination and about worsening of nationality relations among those respondents who were more interested in public affairs. In contrast, the political disenchantment variable shows weaker and more complex associations. Respondents who are more critical of the system emphasize the worsening of ethnic relations more (average percentage difference is 8), but the direction of the relationship is reversed for individuals mentioning ethnic discrimination (average percentage difference is 6.5). Though the latter may be due partly to the nature of the data (both the statement about discrimination and the statement about political disenchantment are derived from stated emigration motives and thus are, to a minor extent, mutually exclusive), this hardly affects the overall thrust of the finding that political disenchantment does not appear to be a major explanatory variable for statements about ethnic discrimination. In contrast, political disenchantment is partly associated with the perception of a worsening of ethnic relations among the major nationalities.

Turning to the impact of job dissatisfaction, one finds that those respondents who were dissatisfied with their jobs tend to cite the existence of ethnic discrimination more often than those who were satisfied. The association is less pronounced and counterdirectional in the case of comments about a worsening of nationality relations. As Table 10.6 also shows, job dissatisfaction is less influential than interest in politics in the case of a worsening of ethnic relations but is more influential in the case of the discrimination statement.

Summary and multiple regression with all variables

So far, my analysis of correlates of the two ethnic perceptions may be summarized as follows: The three demographic variables – sex, age, and level of education – show no significant association with statements about discrimination, and, except for education, they show only slight associations with the statement that "nationality relations are worsening." The correlation with higher education appears to reflect strained group ethnic relations in more highly educated circles, a finding that is in accord with comparable research on the USSR. It is also found in other multiethnic societies such as Quebec where French-Canadian managerial and professional people show a positive correlation between education and nationalism (Hargrove 1970).

As for the USSR, Soviet ethnosociologists have noted that higher

educational levels tend to go hand in hand with intensified ethnic consciousness (Arutiunian 1969; Susokolov 1976), and the Harvard Project of the
early 1950s found that Ukrainians in white-collar jobs were more hostile to
Russians than were peasants and workers. The analysts related this both to
the more intimate contact between Ukrainian and Russian white-collar
workers and to the higher degree of direct competition for more favored
positions (Inkeles and Bauer 1959: 364–65). Similarly, West German
scholars Kussmann and Schäfer (1982: 175) found that younger and more
highly educated Soviet German emigrants evaluate Kazakh attitudes
toward Russians the most negatively.

Among the three ethnic profile variables, respondent nationality is most
strongly associated with the discrimination statement, followed by the ethnic
affiliation score and then by the ethnic attitude score. In contrast, only
the ethnic affiliation score has a noticeable association with the evaluation
of nationality relations, showing that respondents who tended to associate
more with members of their own nationality mentioned a worsening of
relations more often.

Among the three sociopolitical variables, "interest in politics" generally is
the most influential, followed by job dissatisfaction (in the case of the
discrimination statement) and political disenchantment (in the case of the
perception of nationality relations).

These findings are confirmed by a stepwise multiple regression. Examining the impact of all independent variables at once provides a better notion
of their relative standing.[19] Thus, five variables enter the equation explaining the discrimination statement: Nationality of respondent is first, followed
by interest in public affairs, ethnic affiliation score, ethnic attitude score, and
job satisfaction. In contrast, only four, partly different variables enter the
equation related to the statement about a worsening of group-level
nationality relations. This time interest in public affairs comes in first,
followed by ethnic affiliation score, level of education, and political motive
for emigration. This suggests that the kind of variables associated with
micro- and macrolevel ethnic evaluations do indeed differ.

In the case of macrolevel assessments, interest in politics, general political
outlook, and level of education are among the most significant influences,
together with just one ethnic profile variable: intensity of association with

[19] For the use of this technique, see note 17. For regression, an adjustment was
made in the job satisfaction variable. The "not applicable" category logically
should be excluded from the variable, but this would lead to many missing cases
(22 percent), so part of the latter were recoded by substituting the respective
codes of the "satisfaction with higher education" variable. Although problematic,
this substitution can be legitimized in that it affects mostly individuals whose
"job" it was to study, and by noting that the general pattern of responses to
the two questions is similar.

one's own group. In contrast, microlevel ethnic evaluations are more strongly associated with the three ethnic profile variables analyzed: respondent's nationality, ethnic affiliation pattern, and ethnic attitudes. Among the other variables, interest in public affairs and job satisfaction play an additional role.

Conclusions

This chapter has aimed at presenting the major findings of the SIP General Survey on Soviet nationality policy and ethnic relations and to do so within the context of a discussion of the association between respondent evaluations and the environments and individual characteristics they reflect. I conclude that the latter have a variable impact, depending on the question asked. If an ethnic assessment focuses on the microlevel of personal experiences, the impact of respondent nationality and other ethnic profile variables is considerably more significant than if the question focuses on macrolevel relations among nationalities within entire republics. If the latter is the case, political awareness and outlook, level of education, and the ethnic affiliation pattern are decisive. Responses about the preferential treatment of ethnic groups within individual union republics correlate with political interest, level of education, and job satisfaction.

Furthermore, macrolevel ethnic assessments vary according to the region in which respondents lived. Regional variance remains noticeable even when one controls for other variables that might explain individual statements. There is, thus, every indication that the variance reflects actual regional differences within the USSR rather than idiosyncrasies of the sample or of subgroups within it.

The most significant substantive and theoretical conclusion is that a policy that treats ethnicity as a criterion for socioeconomic and political advancement contributes to ethnic strife. When asked directly about reasons for a worsening of ethnic relations among the major nationalities in their republics, many respondents pointed to increasing competition for jobs and privileges. Moreover, the perception that "nationality relations are worsening" is also indirectly related to responses that republic nationalities are favored: The correlation regarding all three subareas of ethnic privilege is significant at the .002 level or higher. In percentages, we find that of those respondents who saw a worsening of ethnic relations 62 to 66 percent noted the preferential treatment of locals, whereas such favoritism was reported only by 42 to 51 percent of those who saw no change in nationality relations.

What does this mean for Soviet nationality policy and developments? As we are dealing with an ethnically unrepresentative sample, conclusions have to be drawn with caution. At a minimum, one can say that, from the perspective of an extraterritorial nationality such as the Soviet Jews and from the perspective of Russians living in non-Russian union republics to a degree also, a worsening of the ethnic climate is associated with the socioeconomic favoritism of republic nationalities. Other data confirm that socioeconomic competition has increasingly emerged at the forefront of ethnic politics in various regions.[20] Local assertivenesss in these matters is especially high in Central Asia and Kazakhstan, leading to considerable resentment by Russians and other Europeans who have migrated there, who now feel that they are exposed to "reverse discrimination." On the other hand, locals do not appear to be satisfied either, for they judge their gains too small and believe that they are entitled to a dominant position in "their own republic" (Karklins 1986). Thus, a policy of socioeconomic privilege for the locals – or the "nativization" of cadre – appears to have been only partially integrative, at best. Local nationalities have a different perception of the situation and rarely react with gratitude or increased loyalty. More importantly, this policy tends to irritate ethnic groups who do not profit from it, including the Russian nationals. Resentment, as well as a generally increased awareness of nationality as an asset or liability for social mobility, creates new ethnic strains.

Why this is so can be explained both by comparative theories about the instrumental value of ethnicity in competitive situations and by a consideration of the resultant political context. A policy that uses ethnic criteria for socioeconomic and political advancement pits one ethnic group against the other and contributes to ethnic strains, especially if, as usual, available resources are limited. As noted by Teresa Rakowska-Harmstone (1977: 86), members of ethnic elites tend to promote local cadres for positions throughout the republics, squeezing out Russians, and the Russians fight back: "political preference now works both ways, in favor of local candidates as much as immigrants, depending on who controls the hiring, and at what level – a tug of war which is another source of growing ethnic conflict." Although cadre competition has affected Soviet nationality policy from its inception (Connor 1984: 277–86), it accelerated in the 1970s (Zaslavsky and Brym 1983).

Yet, the problem revolves around more than ethnopolitical competition. The political divisiveness of any type of ethnic favoritism is heightened by

---

[20] Besides to previously cited sources giving the same conclusion, see also Popovsky 1979: 130–33 and Simon 1986: 304. Soviet ethnosociological studies have found unusually high rates of negative ethnic attitudes among 18- to 24-year-olds in various parts of the USSR and related this to competition for access to higher education. Drobizheva, *Dukhovnaia obshchnost'*, p. 116; and Russian *samizdat* of the Right has emphasized that Russian nationalism is promoted by the preferential treatment afforded to ethnic minorities. Compare sources cited by Zaslavsky 1980: 73.

each group's reference to different moral and political principles and claims. Thus, members of nonterritorial nationalities who in the contemporary USSR are not favored in any context argue that reference to group identity is discriminatory and that all citizens should be treated equally as individuals. This argument is usually convincing to Western observers, since in the Western political tradition the dominant view of equality is individualistic. In contrast, members of the territorially based non-Russian nations living in their traditional homelands argue in terms of group equality. As is also evident from other multiethnic societies, group equality tends to be defined in many ways, be it the need to "catch up" with other groups or the need to protect native cultures through special privileges.[21] The Russians constitute the third player in this game, and their arguments – if openly expressed – revolve around the special rights due to them as the state-nation that has borne disproportionate sacrifices for everybody else.

In multiethnic societies ethnic groups not only compete with each other but also refer to competing principles and values when evaluating the equity of their standing. Survey research with former citizens of the USSR helps to gauge the sociopsychological reference points of various groups and to gain new insights about the political dynamics of problems such as ethnically differentiated access to socioeconomic and political status. Even if one must assume that there are some distortions in the picture provided here because of sample limitations, these interviews provide a basic outline of the situation. And it shows that various nationalities in the USSR – including the Russians – react negatively if they perceive unequal and unjust treatment of their groups. Politically, this is my most important finding. As has been argued by the proponents of the theory of relative deprivation, what the actual standing of individual groups really is according to various statistical measures is less important politically than how it is perceived and interpreted by the groups themselves. People rebel against their condition not when they are deprived in the absolute sense but when they *feel* deprived.[22]

---

[21] For an excellent analysis of the tension between individual and group rights, see Van Dyke 1977: 343–69; for a synopsis of the American tradition to emphasize the individualistic view of equality, see Verba and Orren 1985: chs. 1 and 2.

[22] For a good summary and new test of the theory, see Guimond and Dube-Simard 1983: 526–35.

References

Arutiunian, Iurii V. 1969. "Konkretno-sotsiologicheskoe issledovanie natsional'nykh otnoshenii," *Voprosy filosofii*, no. 12: 129–39.

Arutiunian, Iurii V., L. M. Drobizheva, and V. S. Zelenchuk. 1980. *Opyt etnosotsiologicheskogo issledovaniia obraza zhizni*. Moscow: Nauka.

Arutiunian, Iu., and Iu. Kakhk. 1979. *Sotsiologicheskie ocherki o Sovetskoi Estonii*. Tallin: Periodika.

Azrael, Jeremy R. (ed.). 1978. *Soviet Nationality Policies and Practices*. New York: Praeger.

Bialer, Seweryn. 1980. *Stalin's Successors: Leadership, Stability, and Change in the Soviet Union*. Cambridge: Cambridge University Press.

Blalock, Hubert, Jr. 1967. *Toward a Theory of Minority-Group Relations*. New York: Wiley.

Connor, Walker. 1984. *The National Question in Marxist-Leninist Theory and Strategy*. Princeton, N.J.: Princeton University Press.

Drobizheva, L. M. 1981. *Dukhovnaia obshchnost' narodov SSSR: istoriko-sotsiologicheskii ocherk mezhnatsional'nykh otnoshenii*. Moscow: Mysl'.

Dzyuba, Ivan. 1968. *Internationalism or Russification? A Study in the Soviet Nationalities Problem*. London: Weidenfeld and Nicolson.

Gitelman, Zvi. 1983. "Are Nations Merging in the USSR?" *Problems of Communism*, 32: 35–47.

Glazer, Nathan, and Daniel P. Moynihan (eds.). 1975. *Ethnicity: Theory and Experience*. Cambridge, Mass.: Harvard University Press.

Giumond, Serge, and Lise Dube-Simard. 1983. "Relative Deprivation Theory and the Quebec Nationalist Movement: The Cognition-Emotion Distinction and the Personal-Group Deprivation Issue," *Journal of Personality and Social Psychology*, 44: 526–35.

Hargrove, Erwin C. 1970. "Nationality, Values, and Change: Young Elites in French Canada." *Comparative Politics*, 2: 473–99.

Hechter, Michael. 1975. *Internal Colonialism*. Berkeley, Calif.: University of California Press.

Hodnett, Grey. 1978. *Leadership in the Soviet National Republics*. Oakville, Ont.: Mosaic Press.

Inkeles, Alex, and Raymond A. Bauer. 1959. *The Soviet Citizen: Daily Life in a Totalitarian Society*. Cambridge, Mass.: Harvard University Press.

Jones, Ellen, and Fred. W. Grupp. 1984. "Modernisation and Ethnic Equalisation in the USSR," *Soviet Studies*, 36: 159–84.

Karklins, Rasma. 1984. "Ethnic Politics and Access to Higher Education: The Soviet Case," *Comparative Politics*, 16: 277–94.

1986. *Ethnic Relations in the USSR: The Perspective from Below*. Boston: Allen and Unwin.

1987. "Determinants of Ethnic Identification in the USSR: The Soviet Jewish Case." *Ethnic and Racial Studies*, 10: 27–47.

Kazlas, Juozas A. 1977. "Social Distance among Ethnic Groups." In Edward

Allworth (ed.), *Nationality Group Survival in Multi-Ethnic States*, pp. 228–55. New York: Praeger.

Kussmann, Thomas, and Bernd Schäfer. 1982. *Nationale identität: Selbstbild und Fremdbilder von deutschen Aussiedlern aus der Sowjetunion*. Cologne: Berichte des Bundesinstituts für ostwissenschaftliche und internationale Studien, 46.

Lapidus, Gail Warshofsky. "Ethnonationalism and Political Stability: The Soviet Case," *World Politics*, 34 (1984): 553–80.

Litvinova, G. I., and B. T. Urlanis. 1982. "Demograficheskaia politika Sovetskogo Soiuza," *Sovetskoe gosudarstvo i pravo*, no. 3: 38–46.

Lubin, Nancy. 1981. "Assimilation and Retention of Ethnic Identity in Uzbekistan," *Asian Affairs*, 12: 277–85.

1984. *Labor and Nationality in Soviet Central Asia: An Uneasy Compromise*. Princeton, N.J.: Princeton University Press.

Misiunas, Romuald J., and Rein Taagepera. 1983. *The Baltic States: Years of Dependence, 1940–1980*. Berkeley: University of California Press.

Ostapenko, L. V., and A. A. Susokolov. 1983. "Etnosotsial'nye osobennosti vosproizvodstva intelligentsii." *Sotsiologicheskie issledovaniia*, no. 1: 10–16.

1985. "Dinamika natsional'nogo sostava studenchestva soiuznykh respublik v poslevoennye gody," *Sovetskaia etnografiia*, no. 2: 46–53.

Popovsky, Mark. 1979. *Manipulated Science*. New York: Doubleday.

Rakowska-Harmstone, Teresa. 1977. "Ethnicity in the Soviet Union," *Annals of the American Academy of Political Social Science*, 433: 73–87.

Rosenberg, Morris. 1968. *The Logic of Survey Analysis*. New York: Basic Books.

Rothschild, Joseph. 1981. *Ethnopolitics: A Conceptual Framework*. New York: Columbia University Press.

Saunders, George (ed.). 1974. *Samizdat: Voices of the Soviet Opposition*. New York: Monad Press.

Shibutani, Tamotsu, and Kian M. Kwan. 1965. *Ethnic Stratification: A Comparative Approach*. New York: Macmillan.

Simon, Gerhard. 1986. *Nationalismus und Nationalitätenpolitik in der Sowjetunion*. Baden-Baden: Nomos.

Solchanyk, Roman. 1982. "Russian Language and Soviet Politics," *Soviet Studies*, 34: 23–42.

Susokolov, A. A. 1973. "Neposredstvennoe mezhetnicheskoe obshchenie i ustanovki na mezhlichnostnye kontakty," *Sovetskaia etnografiia*, no. 5: 73–78.

1976. "Vliianie razlichii v urovne obrazovaniia i chislennosti kontaktiruiushchikh etnicheskikh grupp na mezhetnicheskie otnosheniia (po materialam perepisei naseleniia SSSR 1959 i 1970 gg.)," *Sovetskaia etnografiia*, no. 1: 101–11.

Van Dyke, Vernon. 1977. "The Individual, the State, and Ethnic Communities in Political Theory," *World Politics*, 29: 343–69.

Verba, Sidney, and Gary R. Orren. 1985. *Equality in America: The View from the Top*. Cambridge, Mass.: Harvard University Press.

Young, Crawford. 1983. "The Temple of Ethnicity," *World Politics*, 35: 652–62.

Zaslavsky, Victor. 1980. "The Ethnic Question in the USSR," *Telos*, 45: 45–76.

1982. *The Neo-Stalinist State: Class, Ethnicity, and Consensus in Soviet Society.* Armonk, N.Y.: Sharpe.

Zaslavsky, Victor, and Robert J. Brym. 1983. *Soviet-Jewish Emigration and Soviet Nationality Policy.* New York: St. Martin's Press.

CHAPTER 11

Mobilized participation and the nature of the Soviet dictatorship

WILLIAM ZIMMERMAN

How shall we characterize contemporary regime–society relations in the Soviet Union? In the 1950s Soviet specialists and students of comparative politics more broadly were agreed on the basic outlines of *How the Soviet System Works*, to use the title of the summary volume of the Harvard Project on the Soviet Social System (Bauer, Inkeles, and Kluckhohn 1959). The Soviet Union was a novel dictatorial form in which the regime insisted on, and accomplished, the mobilization to its purposes of the entire society. This pattern of regime–society relations differentiated the Soviet totalitarian system and traditional autocracy, which discourages mobilization of elites and masses and is content with citizen acquiescence.

Changes in the Soviet Union, developments in the social sciences, and improvements in the international climate all served to bring the totalitarian model under severe scrutiny in the 1960s. With the assimilation of the implications of the end of terror as an instrument of political control, there was a newfound sensitivity to the increased social differentiation and articulation of a growingly complex industrial society, along with renewed attention to the persistent impact of traditional Russian culture on the Soviet polity. If the Soviet system under Stalin has been described in Marxian terms as the revenge of the superstructure, the period from the 1960s forward might be described as the rediscovery of the base. Throughout the latter period, however, specialists and generalists alike (cf. Dahl 1971) have continued to describe the Soviet Union in terms that stress, inter alia, the extent to which it is a highly participatory, mobilized, political system. As such, its distinctive attribute is that political participation by the Soviet citizens is not spontaneous but "initiated by the political leaders and supervised by the CPSU" (Barghoorn 1972: 14). Very much at issue, though, is whether and to what extent there have been changes over time in the ability of the regime to harness Soviet citizens to its purposes.

Such is the purpose of this chapter. In particular, I am concerned with two tasks. The first is to examine several domains of the contemporary Soviet citizen's daily life, control over which we associate with an effective

I wish to thank Robert Axelrod, Michael Berbaum, Sandra Gubin, John Kingdon, and Deborah Yarsike for their invaluable assistance and/or advice.

mobilization system. This I do to ascertain which Soviet citizens engage in what kinds of politically relevant behavior, *excluding* efforts by citizens to influence the political process (Di Franceisco and Gitelman 1984: 603–21). Who participates actively in mobilized groups or in the mobilization and agitation that attend elections? Which groups does the regime reach through its control over the media? Are those Soviet citizens most politicized, in the sense of being relatively more interested in politics, also those who are most highly mobilized, in the sense of being most prone to engage in politically affirmative or conformist behavior? I hope in this way to provide an empirical basis for characterizing the contemporary Soviet dictatorship.

Traditional authoritarian dictatorships assume that passivity and quiescence are the norm among all citizens, elites and nonelites alike. A mobilization system, by contrast, is one where at the limit there is high and uniform mobilization across the citizenry, elites and nonelites alike. Variants on the notion of the mobilization system are possible as well. Thus, it might be more descriptive to think of the Soviet dictatorship as an *elite* mobilization system where elites of all stripes are politically mobilized by the regime and engage in politically affirmative behavior whereas nonelites are substantially less participatory. Likewise, only *political* elites – governmental and party workers – might be mobilized by the political system. Both *nonpolitical* elite and *nonelite* behavior would be explained by social and demographic variables or by cognitive or affective dispositions to politics – social mobilization in Karl Deutsch's sense (Deutsch, in Jacobson and Zimmerman 1969: 84) – rather than by regime-induced political mobilization. Such a dictatorship would differ from a traditional authoritarian regime (where passivity and quiescence are the norm), but evidence for regime-dominated mobilized participation throughout the society would be modest.

The second task is longitudinal rather than cross-sectional. Have there been important changes over time in the regime's ability to mobilize the citizenry to its purposes? Is there evidence of significant changes over time in the efforts by citizens to work the system and to avoid mobilization? Addressing this task provides an empirical basis for assessing the evolution over time in the nature of the Soviet dictatorship.

The data for this paper are derived from the Soviet Interview Project, which administered a massive general questionnaire in 1983 to 2,793 former Soviet citizens, most of whom had immigrated to the United States in 1979 or 1980. (Some of the questions were asked of only one-third of those interviewed.) These people are overwhelmingly Jewish, disproportionately urban, and substantially more educated than the general Soviet population. There are also other known and unknown biases: No claim is being made that the survey has yielded a representative sample of the Soviet citizenry or even the Soviet urban population.

Nevertheless, by using the interviewees as informants about behavior, I feel comfortable in making some claims about Soviet society. With respect to some but not all politically relevant behaviors, the behavior of those individuals who subsequently migrated is not likely to have been substantially different from those who did not. Differences across groups in the sample of emigrants, moreover, are often likely to find counterparts in the Soviet Union. (See methodological statement in Chapter 1 herein.)

The contemporary Soviet citizen and mobilization

In order to assess in the survey the contemporary Soviet dictatorship and, specifically, the interaction between regime and citizen in the Soviet Union, it was necessary both to develop a parsimonious scheme for placing Soviet citizens in the social system and to examine responses among various groupings of citizens to a series of questions pertaining to reported behavior relevant to political mobilization in the Soviet Union.

The scheme employed to categorize the Soviet citizen distinguished five categories: political leaders, managers, high-level professionals, low-level professionals and clerical workers, and others (who in this highly urban sample were largely blue-collar workers). Basic occupation was coded according to the official Soviet system of occupations used in the 1970 census and as set out in *Sistematicheskii slovar' zaniatii* [*Systematic Dictionary of Occupations*] (1969). By political leaders I refer to all those persons in the sample whose response to the question about their specialty in the last job occupied during the last normal period in the USSR was subsumed in the *Systematic Dictionary* under the rubrics "leaders of state administration and their structural subdivisions"; "leaders and instructors of party, Komsomol, trade union, cooperative and other social organizations and their structural subdivisions"; and "leaders of enterprises."

I defined as managers those persons who termed themselves engineers and who by the criteria of the *Systematic Dictionary* are categorized as "main specialists," "engineers," or "designers" (categories 16, 17, 18, respectively, of the *Systematic Dictionary*), doctors with medical degrees, leaders of higher educational institutions, "workers in literature and the press," artists and composers, "communications workers," "chiefs of plan, financial, accounting, stations," "managers of cadre sectors, general sectors and offices," directors and chiefs of stores and sections of stores and major eating establishments, or sectors of "supply and markets," "commercial enterprise or everyday services." To be so coded, however, it was also necessary that, along with the respondent's job title, the *dolzhnost'* – the level of the post actually held – clearly identify each as performing substantial administrative tasks. Thus, engineers were coded as administrators only if they had a

Table 11.1. *Respondents' access to official car*

	Occupational grouping					
	Political leaders	Managers	High-level professionals	Low-level professionals	Others	Total
Access to car						
%	26.8	17.3	7.5	5.6	3.2	6.9
N	30	23	63	44	26	186
Total N (100%)	112	133	843	786	823	2,697

dolzhnost' identifying them as head or leading engineers. Doctors and dentists were included only if they were hospital heads of medical divisions or laboratories. Professors were coded as managers if they were heads of faculty or deans; writers, editors, and the like if they were directors or deputy directors of film studios, newspapers, and so on; communications workers, workers in trade, restaurants, financial or accounting "stations" only if they were directors or deputy directors, and so on. Other engineers, doctors (MDs), university faculty, writers, journalists and artists, librarians, lawyers, commodities experts (*tovarovedy*) and economists were treated as high-level specialists.

In like fashion, persons who were technicians, inspectors, bookkeepers, cashiers, communications and postal workers, stenographers and typists were treated as low-level professionals and/or clerical workers. All the remainder were included in the "others" category. These people were largely but not exclusively blue-collar workers. (It will be remembered that there are almost no collective farmers or other rural occupations among these respondents.)

This way of partitioning the data has considerable face validity. With respect to education, for instance, it is noteworthy that of 137 people in the sample with six or fewer years of primary schooling only four were coded as political leaders, managers, or high-level professionals. Seven from the same group were coded as low-level professionals, and the remaining 126 were coded as "others, primarily blue-collar." Similarly, postsecondary education and occupational status are congruent. Privilege as measured by access to an official car and occupational grouping also meshed (Table 11.1).

The method employed was to examine the responses across the five groupings to a series of reported behaviors relevant to the pattern of political mobilization in the Soviet Union. These behaviors represent five categories: (1) those that are election-related; (2) those that involve regime-dominated group behavior; (3) those related to regime-controlled media; (4) those involving access to nonregime media; and (5) those that are testimony to effective mobilization for national security and military preparedness.

Everyone is familiar with the "Ivory Snow" aspects of Soviet voting patterns in which all vote and 99.44 percent of the votes are for the regime candidates. We have known for some time that it is possible to avoid voting in the Soviet Union. Both our notions of regime-induced political mobilization and Deutsch's conception of social mobilization suggest that, if the propensity to vote is not uniform across groups, it should be higher among elites (groups 1, 2, 3 in all tables referring to occupational grouping) than among nonelites (groups 4 and 5) and higher among political (group 1) or politicoadministrative elites (1 and 2) than among other high-status persons (group 3).

The Soviet Interview Project data do not preclude the possibility that Soviet reality meshes with a mobilization system model. The reported voting behavior of those in the sample who played no significant role in the decision to emigrate is compatible with such a model (Table 11.2). From this subset of the sample, nothing can be said with confidence about the political leaders or the managers, and the high-level professionals do not appear to differ from the nonelites in their voting behavior. Nevertheless, if we make the modest assumption that *some* proportion of the Soviet citizens who did not migrate act in their voting behavior in ways parallel to those who emigrated, then Theodore Friedgut is correct when he asserts that it is "exactly the people who should by all criteria, Soviet and non-Soviet alike, be the most active participants in elections" who are relatively prone *not* to vote (Friedgut 1979: 118). If we view the sample as a whole or look separately at those who either made the decision to emigrate or shared in the decision, persons in the SIP sample whose status in the Soviet Union was that of political leader or high-level professional were those most disposed *not* to engage in system affirmation through participation in voting (Table 11.2).

When we turn to participation in elections to soviets, whether as a member of an electoral commission, as a canvasser/agitator or, much less frequently, as a judge or candidate, hypotheses informed by assumptions related to regime-induced political mobilization of more spontaneous social mobilization fare much better. Table 11.3 reports the responses given by those surveyed to the question "Did you ever work in an election to a soviet?" The "others" in our tables (who are almost all blue-collar workers) differ from everyone else (groups 1 through 4). All elites (groups 1, 2, and 3) taken together contrast significantly with others in the sample. Political elites and high-level professionals may not vote as often as others in the USSR. But though political leaders do not contrast significantly with other groups, political leaders and high-level professionals are disproportionately more

Table 11.2. *Voting behavior by role in decision to emigrate: those who "sometimes"*
or "never" voted (%)

	Occupational grouping				
	Political leaders	Managers	High-level professionals	Low-level professionals	Others
Played no substantial role[a]					
%	50.0	33.3	21.5	23.9	21.2
N	3	3	14	16	11
Participated in decision[b]					
%	38.5	28.0	39.5	20.2	19.3
N	25	23	191	100	93
Made decision[c]					
%	60.0	28.9	51.0	29.5	32.4
N	24	11	152	66	90

[a] 100% = 199; chi-square = 8.49; sig. = 0.39.
[b] 100% = 1,606; chi-square = 69.46; sig. = 0.00.
[c] 100% = 887; chi-square = 44.53; sig. = 0.00.

prone to engage in regime-affirming behavior by working in elections to soviets. I suspect that this is so in the Soviet Union as well. It is a relatively easy way to pay dues.

Dues are also paid at the workplace, and some 8 percent of the total sample interviewed stated that they belonged to work committees. There the difference between political and administrative groups and between political leaders on the one hand and managers and high-level professionals taken together on the other is not significant. What is striking is the contrast between elites (groups 1, 2, and 3) and nonelites (4 and 5): Political leaders, managers, and high-level professionals are disproportionately represented among the participators, and the low-level professionals and especially "others" (largely workers) are underrepresented (Table 11.4).

Looking at participation in organs such as the people's militia, people's control, or comrades' courts, however, we do not obtain results indicating that the overall political system should be thought of as a mobilization or as an elite mobilization system. Mobilization seems modest among the respondents: Only a bit more than one-tenth of those surveyed answered that they went regularly to such meetings – which hardly evokes a mobilization system. When we ask the question "How often did you go to the meetings?" we discern an essentially homogeneous distribution across the five

Table 11.3. *Participation in election to soviets, by occupational grouping*

	Occupational grouping					
	Political leaders	Managers	High-level professionals	Low-level professionals	Others	Total
Worked in election						
%	23.2	15.0	26.5	16.7	6.7	16.9
N	26	20	224	132	56	458
Total N (100%)	112	133	846	790	830	2,711

Note: Chi-square = 119.74; sig. = 0.00.

Table 11.4. *Work committee participation, by occupational grouping*

	Occupational grouping					
	Political leaders	Managers	High-level professionals	Low-level professionals	Others	Total
Belonged to committees at work						
%	16.1	15.8	11.0	7.6	4.8	8.6
N	18	21	93	60	40	232
Total N (100%)	112	133	842	788	829	2,704

Note: Chi-square = 39.19; sig. = 0.00.

Model	Estimate	Z	df	L.O.F. G^2
Null Model			4	38.20***
Constant	−1.18302	−34.46***	1	
Contrast Model			2	4.00
Constant	−1.14146	−32.69***	1	
(1, 2, 3) vs. (4, 5)	.45601	5.41***	1	
(4) vs. (5)	.12148	2.30*	1	
Reduction in lack of fit due to contrasts			2	34.20***

  * $p < .05$
  ** $p < .01$
  *** $p < .001$

Table 11.5. *Attendance at meetings of people's militia, people's control, or comrades' courts*

	Occupational grouping					
	Political leaders	Managers	High-level professionals	Low-level professionals	Others	Total
Attended regularly						
%	34.8	47.1	37.6	34.6	38.4	37.6
N	8	8	59	18	28	121
Total N (100%)	23	17	157	52	73	322

Note: Chi-square = 0.94; sig. = 0.92.

Table 11.6. *Newspaper readership in the Soviet Union*

	Occupational grouping					
	Political leaders	Managers	High-level professionals	Low-level professionals	Others	Total
Read Soviet newspaper						
%	95.9	91.1	86.5	87.7	81.8	86.2
N	47	41	237	228	216	769
Total N (100%)	49	45	274	260	264	892

Note: Chi-square = 9.58; sig. = 0.05.

groups – which is incompatible with the conception of elite mobilization. (The *distribution* across groups is itself compatible with a mobilization model, but the *magnitude* is not [Table 11.5].)

Another important domain conventionally associated with the process of political mobilization in modern authoritarian systems is the media. Total control over the means of communications was one of the six elements in the Friedrich and Brzezinski totalitarian syndrome. Newspaper readership in the sample is very high, with political leaders being distinguished as readers from the remaining four groups, and with all elites distinguishable from nonelites (Table 11.6). These differences are more crisply defined in the SIP sample when one focuses upon what it is groups read. Political leaders pay more attention to the news than do others, and the three elite groups taken together are relatively more news-attentive than the remaining two groups.

Table 11.7. *Media content preferences in newspapers, radio, and television*

Content preferences	Occupational grouping					
	Political leaders	Managers	High-level professionals	Low-level professionals	Others	Total
Newspapers[a]						
Variety, %	31.9	46.3	40.1	48.0	51.7	45.5
Variety, N	15	19	93	109	109	345
News, %	68.1	53.7	59.9	52.0	48.3	54.5
News, N	32	22	139	118	102	413
Total N (100%)	47	41	232	227	211	758
Radio[b]						
Variety, %	46.2	59.5	59.7	71.2	71.3	65.9
Variety, N	18	22	126	158	149	473
News, %	53.8	40.5	40.3	28.8	28.7	34.1
News, N	21	15	85	64	60	245
Total N (100%)	39	37	211	222	209	718
Television[c]						
Variety, %	73.9	88.4	86.1	90.8	89.5	87.9
Variety, N	34	38	216	227	221	736
News, %	26.1	11.6	13.9	9.2	10.5	12.1
News, N	12	5	35	23	26	101
Total N (100%)	46	43	251	250	247	837

[a] Chi-square = 10.06; sig. = 0.04.
[b] Chi-square = 16.48; sig. = 0.00.
[c] Chi-square = 11.85; sig. = 0.02.

A similar pattern is observed when we focus on the preferences of television watchers and radio listeners as well, but content preferences by media type are what matter. A hierarchy is evident regarding what Soviet citizens seek in the three media sources: News is sought primarily from newspapers, secondarily from the radio, and residually from television (see Table 11.6). The largely undifferentiated and what must be by international standards relatively high attention by all sectors of Soviet society to news in the papers suggests a rather mobilized population; the preoccupation with variety and musical shows on television may be indicative of a future which is more apolitical and less mobilized as television comes to be the preeminent medium (Table 11.7).

In the pure case, of course, the Soviet regime's monopoly over the media would be complete. It is not. Non-Soviet, Communist, media sources, *samizdat*, and Western sources are available for the diligent and concerned.

Table 11.8. *Overall samizdat readership*

	Occupational grouping					
	Political leaders	Managers	High-level professionals	Low-level professionals	Others	Total
Read samizdat						
%	40.8	26.7	44.7	28.5	14.4	29.9
N	20	12	123	74	38	267
Total N (100%)	49	45	275	260	264	893

Note: Chi-square = 62.40; sig. = 0.00.

Model	Estimate	Z	df	L.O.F. G^2
Null Model			4	64.71***
Constant	−.42605	−11.66**	1	
Contrast Model			2	.32
Constant	−.41237	−10.81***	1	
(1, 2, 3) vs. (4, 5)	.47910	6.15***	1	
(1, 3) vs. (2, 4)	.17477	4.13***	1	
Reduction in lack of fit due to contrasts			1	64.39***

* $p < .05$
** $p < .01$
*** $p < .001$

The regime, with varying degrees of intensity at various junctions, has sought to thwart Soviet citizen efforts to listen to foreign radio and has attempted to deter the reading of *samizdat*. Of the emigrants interviewed who had read *samizdat*, roughly five-sixths answered that it was risky, and roughly two-fifths of them reported they thought it was "very" risky. How risky the reading of *samizdat* actually is may, of course, be questioned: These responses came from people who had read *samizdat*, and only one person in the sample reported having been punished for owning *samizdat*.

Statements about trends in the Soviet Union pertaining to the consumption of *samizdat* need to be made with great care. The proclivity to read *samizdat* was much greater among those who made the decision to emigrate than among those who merely shared in, or were only slightly involved in, the decision. That notwithstanding, the survey data support the common-sense view that, as in the case of vote avoidance, the largely blue-collar "others" are proportionately the least disposed to read *samizdat* (Table 11.8).

Table 11.9. *Foreign radio listenership*

| | Occupational grouping | | | | | |
	Political leaders	Managers	High-level professionals	Low-level professionals	Others	Total
Listened to foreign radio						
%	96.4	93.2	91.0	80.4	76.8	83.9
N	108	124	770	635	636	2,273
Total N (100%)	112	133	846	790	828	2,709

Note: Chi-square = 91.38; sig. = 0.00.

Model	Estimate	Z	df	L.O.F. G^2
Null Model			4	99.95***
Constant	.82561	31.58***	1	
Contrast Model			2	3.82
Constant	1.05984	18.58***	1	
$(1, 2, 3)$ vs. $(4, 5)$	.82145	7.00***	1	
(1) vs. $(2, 3)$	.31426	1.81$^+$	1	
Reduction in lack of fit due to contrasts			2	96.13***

$^*p < .05$
$^{**}p < .01$
$^{***}p < .001$
$^+p < .10$

The same point, with the same caution, pertains to audiences for foreign radio. Overall, those who played no significant role in the decision to emigrate were considerably less prone to listen to foreign radio than were those who shared in the decision or made the decision themselves. At the same time, high-level professionals, managers, and political leaders were considerably more inclined to listen than were the nonelite groupings. At least in the emigrant sample, moreover, if political position translates into being politicized, it is precisely they who are most disposed to listen to foreign radio. We detect this in the marginally more frequent "yes" answers by erstwhile political leaders to the question "Did you listen to foreign radio?" (Table 11.9).

Politicization and attention to non-Soviet media are also related, if politicization is defined as "interest in politics." Dichotomizing the sample into those who are "very interested" or "somewhat interested" in politics and those who were "slightly" interested or professed no interest at all produces a striking result. Persons with high interest in politics from all five

Table 11.10. *Foreign radio listenership, controlling for interest in politics*

| | Occupational grouping | | | | | |
	Political leaders	Managers	High-level professionals	Low-level professionals	Others	Total
Interest in politics[a]						
Foreign radio listener, %	98.9	96.5	95.4	91.8	91.5	93.7
Foreign radio listener, N	89	82	645	424	399	1,639
Total N (100%)	90	85	676	462	436	1,749
Little interest in politics[b]						
Foreign radio listener, %	86.4	87.5	74.1	64.2	60.8	66.2
Foreign radio listener, N	19	42	123	208	236	628
Total N (100%)	22	48	166	324	388	948

[a] Chi-square = 15.03; sig. = 0.00.
[b] Chi-square = 23.96; sig. = 0.00.

groups are more prone to listen to foreign radio than respondents from any of the five groups who have little interest (Table 11.10). Expectations drawn from a regime-induced mobilization perspective would lead us to predict that all the Soviet citizens would be equally disinclined to gain access to nonregime media sources. An elite mobilization model would suggest that although the demographic variables that underly overall media attentiveness ought to drive attention to nonofficial sources as well, the politically active, and especially those whose occupational grouping classify them as political leaders, would be relatively inattentive to such sources in comparison with other elites. Finally, in a conventional modern dictatorship we might well expect all elites to be relatively more attuned to nonregime sources than are nonelites. As it turns out, political interest and political role in the Soviet system dispose persons both in the SIP sample and, we think, in the Soviet Union as well to seek out nonofficial communications channels.

A fifth domain where the regime's capacity to mobilize can be assessed is preparedness and national security. For Stalin, it will be recalled, permanently operating factors gave a Soviet-type mobilization system an inherent advantage vis-à-vis capitalist states regarding waging of nonnuclear wars. Some version of that belief also exists in the Western literature on Soviet studies and on comparative foreign policy. Two areas where this theme has been most pronounced are military service and civil defense. Table 11.11

William Zimmerman

Table 11.11 *Efforts to avoid military service 1965–1980*

| | Occupational grouping | | | | | |
	Political leaders	Managers	High-level professionals	Low-level professionals	Others	Total
Made effort to avoid						
%	28.6	33.3	24.1	12.3	16.7	19.7
N	4	3	32	7	22	68
Total N (100%)	14	9	133	57	132	345

Note: Chi-square = 6.10; sig. = 0.19.

reveals the responses given by those males in the emigrant survey who became eligible to serve after 1964. The cell sizes are small, and the results are not striking. What seems to emerge, though, is a somewhat greater disposition to avoid military service by the three elite groupings and, conversely, somewhat greater conformity by persons in the nonelite groupings. Though this is a hypothesis intuitively plausible and consistent with other findings in the survey, it should, however, be stressed that the data do not permit the use of any stronger term than "suggestive," and they are included here primarily for completeness.

Similar caution for different reasons should guide us in assessing the data generated by the survey of Soviet emigrants concerned with civil defense mobilization. Those who worry about the relative preoccupation with civil defense preparedness in the United States and the USSR will take note that two-fifths of those in the sample who were working (predominantly) or going to school (in a few instances) remembered the location of the civil defense shelter closest to their place of work or school. Similarly, during the last two years before the end of the last normal period in the Soviet Union slightly more than a quarter of the sample that was working or going to school had gone to that shelter, and 8 percent of the respondents reported that there was an evacuation drill in which persons in the respondent's school or workplace had to leave town temporarily. By comparison with experiences in most other countries – though probably not Switzerland and Sweden – these figures are high and an indication of a country more mobilized for national security than the United States (Table 11.12).

Those who are more relaxed about such things will note that three-fifths of the relevant respondents in the SIP sample did not even know the location of the shelter nearest their place of employment; that about three-fourths of these respondents had not been in the shelter for a drill during the last two

Table 11.12. *Civil defense shelter recall*

Do you remember where the civil defense shelter closest to your job/school was located in the end of your last normal period?		
	%	N
Yes	41.3	259
Total	100.0	627
Did you ever leave your job to go to that shelter for a drill in the last two years of your LNP?		
Yes	29.3	76
Total	100.0	259
In the LNP, was there ever an evacuation drill in which people at your (school/workplace) had to leave town temporarily?		
Yes	8.1	51
Total	100.0	627

years of their last normal period in the Soviet Union; and that more than 90 percent of those surveyed reported that their workplace had not had an evacuation drill in which persons left town during the respondent's last normal period. Whichever construction one places on these data, what appears most important for our theoretical concerns is that there is little differentiation across groupings, the only possibly significant distinction being between the largely blue-collar "others" and all the rest (Table 11.13).

Viewed across the five categories of behavior I have described – election-related behavior, behavior involving regime-dominated group participation, behavior related to regime-controlled media, behavior involving access to nonregime media, and behavior related to national security preparedness – the portrait that emerges is one that provides a rather complicated view of political and social mobilization in the contemporary Soviet system. There is little differentiation across groupings in civil defense shelter knowledge, and regular attendance at people's militia and comrades' courts is an instance where rate of participation (or nonparticipation) is basically homogeneous across occupational groups. Nevertheless, there are no domains among those examined where mobilization is both unambiguously high and fundamentally homogeneous across groups.

With respect to elite political mobilization the picture is mixed. On some dimensions, working in elections, for instance, the case can be made that the regime succeeds in inducing the requisite affect from those with high-status positions. When we look at attention to the regime-dominated media, moreover, the data suggest that political leaders are reached disproportion-

Table 11.13.   *Knowledge of nearest civil defense shelter location*

	Occupational grouping					
	Political Leaders	Managers	High-level professionals	Low-level professionals	Others	Total
Recalled location						
%	42.9	48.6	46.4	41.6	32.0	41.1
N	15	17	104	62	56	254
Total N (100%)	35	35	224	149	175	618

Note: Chi-square = 9.48; sig. = 0.05.

ately in ways consonant with a political elite mobilization model. It turns out, though, according to this sample at least, that political elites are mobilized to politics but that they are also more likely than persons in other groupings to engage in behavior incongruent with regime-induced political mobilization. They are less likely to vote, more likely to read *samizdat,* and more prone to listen to foreign radio. As Donna Bahry also demonstrates (Chapter 3, herein), it is those who have jobs that evoke either "red" or "expert" who are most likely to engage in behaviors that suggest they have not been mobilized exclusively by the political system. As Bahry also notes, participation rates in the urban Soviet Union bear striking resemblance to those in West Germany, for example. What we are tapping here seems largely to be the social mobilization that everywhere accompanies industrialization and modernization. It is that which makes the behavior of elite groupings, taken collectively, differ from that of other groups in Soviet society.

Those who most engage in regime-conforming behaviors are the persons whom we have clustered under "other," the largely blue-collar group. They may be less likely than persons from elite groupings to avoid military service. They are less likely to read *samizdat,* less likely to listen to foreign radio, and more likely to vote. They also participate less than others in electioneering. They read Soviet newspapers far less than their counterparts in the other occupational groupings, and they even engage in civil defense drills less. In short, though they conform more, they are mobilized less than are persons in other occupational groupings. For them the Soviet Union is a conventional dictatorship where, in Brezhnev's words, it is possible to "breathe easily, work well, and live tranquilly" (Gruliow 1973: 119, as cited in Breslauer 1982: 192). Theirs, especially, is behavior that corresponds to findings about blue-collar participation in other industrialized states. In terms of assessing the nature of the Soviet system, it is behavior that corresponds much more to an image of a conventional dictatorship than to that of a mobilization system or some variant thereof.

Changes in mobilizational effectiveness over time

A second way of assessing the nature of the Soviet dictatorship is provided by taking a historical perspective. A one-time survey is not the most useful source for efforts to assess change over time. Nevertheless, there are some readily identifiable acts that take place at specific times in a person's life – going to the university, getting a first job, becoming eligible to serve in the military – which occur at more or less the same time for all persons or, in the case of the military, for all males in any given society. Consequently, one can, with caution, examine the pattern of responses to questions about these acts across a sample to ascertain whether there are systematic differences in the pattern at particular time periods. Some of these classes of events involve behaviors that are indicative of the regime's ability to harness the resources of society to its purposes.

Consider, for instance, the areas of education and first job. For a society where education is controlled by the state, an indicator of the regime's ability to utilize its citizens effectively is the extent to which educational experience and training have a bearing on the first job one gets. Although there are many reasons why a citizen may prefer (or the state's decision makers may prefer for its citizens) to take a job that is not connected with his or her training, it seems plausible in general to assert that, if a political system has effectively penetrated society, a substantial proportion of its citizens would work at a specialty that bears on their training. In the USSR, if the experience of the emigrants is indicative, that appears to have been the case (see Table 11.14) throughout the period until 1976 – with exceptions for periods (the first five-year plans and during World War II) that we can readily explain by pressing regime needs. The last five years of the Brezhnev era suggest some change in that pattern. Only half the respondents whose first job occurred in that period worked in the specialty for which they had been trained.

Here we immediately see an example of a possible reasonable objection to extrapolation to the Soviet Union from respondents who left the Soviet Union. An almost visceral reaction to this finding would be: But these people are overwhelmingly Jewish, and they emigrated. Surely those facts are sufficient to account for the discrepant pattern.

Interestingly enough, such is not the case, as Table 11.15 reveals: There is essentially no difference in the response patterns of those whose first job came after 1975, regardless of their role in the decision to emigrate and regardless

Table 11.14. *Utilization of specialty by year of leaving institution of higher education*

	Worked at specialty in first job	Total
1930 or earlier		
%	64.7	
N	11	17
1931–35		
%	47.6	
N	40	84
1936–40		
%	76.1	
N	67	88
1941–45		
%	52.0	
N	38	73
1946–50		
%	70.3	
N	71	101
1951–55		
%	72.5	
N	103	142
1956–60		
%	73.7	
N	151	205
1961–65		
%	72.1	
N	194	269
1966–70		
%	75.7	
N	277	366
1971–75		
%	74.7	
N	333	446
1976–81		
%	50.0	
N	168	336
Total N (100%)	1,453	2,127

Note: Chi-square = 105.53; sig. = 0.00.

Table 11.15. *Work at first job after attending higher educational institution, 1976–1981*

	Proportion saying they worked at specialty
All respondents	
%	50.0
N	168
Those who observed Rosh Hashanah	
%	54.1
N	20
Those who played no significant role in decision to emigrate	
%	50.0
N	13
Those who shared in decision	
%	51.0
N	99
Those who made decision	
%	48.3
N	56

of whether they were highly observant Jews or not. Hence the conclusion stands that in the second half of the 1970s there was an appreciable increase in the incongruence between educational training and first job elected. A somewhat similar indicator – in this instance, control over job selection – provides less evidence of change over time. When respondents were asked whether they had a choice in selecting their first job, somewhat over half indicated that they did (54.9 percent), and no statistically significant trend emerges.

If, by contrast, one thinks of the regime's harnessing of society's forces in the workplace as entailing a situation where working the system through informal influence and protection is precluded, the pattern is quite different. *Blat vyshe chem Stalin* ("Pull is above Stalin") used to be a standard refrain, but Table 11.16 suggests that under Stalin there was little room for *blat*, at least in the initial stages of a career. What one notes, though, is an almost monotonic relationship over time. The closer we get to the present, the more likely is the respondent to have said that he or she used *blat* or influence to get the first job.

Once again, it is perfectly reasonable a priori to wonder about the transferability of this finding to the contemporary urban Soviet Union. I

Table 11.16. *The role of influence in obtaining first job, by year of beginning work*

	Use of *blat* or *protektsiia*	Total
1930 or earlier		
%	6.9	
N	2	29
1931–35		
%	11.7	
N	7	60
1936–40		
%	14.0	
N	7	50
1941–1945		
%	10.6	
N	5	47
1946–50		
%	20.0	
N	13	65
1951–55		
%	25.8	
N	17	66
1956–60		
%	35.5	
N	44	124
1961–65		
%	32.8	
N	38	116
1966–70		
%	31.8	
N	42	132
1971–75		
%	43.6	
N	61	140
1976–81		
%	50.9	
N	29	57
Total N (100%)	265	886

Note: Chi-square = 61.73; sig. = 0.00; tau-B = − .21.

recognize that recall distortions are ubiquitous in survey research. Nevertheless, it strains credulity that the pattern identified in Table 11.16 is solely a product of some kind of systematic longitudinal bias in recall or response disposition. Likewise, one could always hypothesize that persons who emigrated would be particularly likely to be the kind who might have engaged in *blat* or *protektsiia*. Controlling for the respondent's role in the decision to emigrate, however, does not undermine the sense that the proclivity to work the system has increased over time. If we have tapped a trend that transfers to the changing Soviet experience – and the pattern but not the frequencies is the same whether the respondent played no role in the decision to migrate, participated in the decision, or made the decision – we have empirical confirmation of an important developmental change in the Soviet dictatorship, with "developmental" here explicitly not meaning "modernizing." These data constitute empirical support for the argument, advanced most articulately by Ken Jowitt, that neotraditionalism is an increasingly apt characterization of the Soviet Union. Certainly these data are important for the question we are asking: Has the political system's capacity to mobilize changed over time? Absent what Jowitt terms a "social combat" task, and absent the political use of terror, task mobilization has given way substantially to "political capitalism" (cf. Jowitt 1983: 275–97).

If we are witnessing a systemic phenomenon, it should be possible to observe this trend in other domains of Soviet life as well. One area that is amenable to empirical scrutiny through a general survey is that of military service. One critical indicator of a regime's ability to harness its citizens to regime goals is the ability to induce compliance to military conscription. Mobilization in the military sense in this respect is but a dimension of political mobilization. Once again, as in the case of behavior relating to first job, a monotonic relationship over time is discernible in responses to the question "Did you try to avoid having to serve?" (Table 11.17). The proportion of those who served either on active duty or in the reserve has remained basically stable at approximately 80 percent over the years. But the reported incidence of attempts to avoid military service has grown steadily.

The parallelism between the trend with respect to attempted military service avoidance and use of influence and protection in securing one's first job is striking. The implication ought likewise to be similar: Though the efforts at military service avoidance in the recent period are emphatically *not* such as to intimate that the end of Soviet power is imminent, the pattern observed should remind us that there really was a period, in the Stalin era, when by this criterion the Soviet Union was a mobilization system. That period is well behind the contemporary Soviet citizen. Rather, he

William Zimmerman

Table 11.17. *Efforts to avoid military service among Soviet males*

Period	Tried to avoid service	Total
Pre-Stalin (< 1930)		
%	5.6	
N	2	36
Stalin (1930–40)		
%	0.0	
N	0	58
WWII (1941–45)		
%	5.7	
N	7	123
Late Stalin (1946–52)		
%	7.2	
N	6	83
Early Khrushchev (1953–59)		
%	8.7	
N	13	150
Late Khrushchev (1960–64)		
%	14.8	
N	13	88
Brezhnev 1 (1965–69)		
%	16.0	
N	21	131
Brezhnev 2 (1970–75)		
%	26.3	
N	30	114
Brezhnev 3 (1976–80)		
%	29.6	
N	16	54
Missing		
%	31.9	
N	23	72
Total N (100%)	131	909

Note: Chi-square = 68.59; sig. = 0.00.

[handwritten annotation: reveals changing attitudes toward resp? toward state]

has acted increasingly as though there were ways that politically adept people can gain considerable control over the decisions that affect their daily lives. Further, the contemporary Soviet citizen through his behavior, as evidenced in increased efforts at avoiding service, has illustrated the consequences for the Soviet system of the changes in political beliefs reported by Brian Silver (Chapter 4, herein). Judging by the changes in behavior reported here, the mobilization system, propelled by the fuel of social transformation, has been succeeded thus far by a more conventional, albeit dictatorial, political system lubricated by the grease of *blat* and *protektsiia*. It remains to be seen whether a Soviet leader – Mikhail Gorbachev or someone else – can create a Soviet dictatorship with more modern trappings.

References

Barghoorn, Frederick. 1972. *Politics USSR*. Boston: Little, Brown.

Bauer, Raymond A., Alex Inkeles, and Clyde Kluckhohn. 1959. *How the Soviet System Works*. New York: Vintage Books.

Breslauer, George. 1982. *Khrushchev and Brezhnev as Leaders*. Boston: Allen and Unwin.

Dahl, Robert. 1971. *Polyarchy*. New Haven: Yale University Press.

Di Franceisco, Wayne, and Zvi Gitelman. 1984. "Soviet Political Culture and 'Covert Participation' in Policy Implementation," *American Political Science Review*, 78: 603–21.

Friedgut, Theodore. 1979. *Political Participation in the USSR*. Princeton, N.J.: Princeton University Press.

Jacobson, Harold K., and William Zimmerman. 1969. *The Shaping of Foreign Policy*. New York: Atherton.

Jowitt, Ken. 1983. "Soviet Neotraditionalism: The Political Corruption of a Leninist Regime," *Soviet Studies*, 35, no. 3: 275–97.

Sistematicheskii slovar' zaniatii. 1969. Moscow: Statistika.

[handwritten note:] Rely upon family + friendship to provide – Leads to corruption + causes system to break down. Society sees it as "unfair" → explosive situation

The SIP General Survey sample

BARBARA A. ANDERSON and BRIAN D. SILVER

The respondents to the General Survey of the Soviet Interview Project are former Soviet citizens who immigrated to the United States.[1] Surveys of Soviet emigrants have relied on a variety of sampling techniques. Some have used snowball samples in which early respondents to the survey help to recruit later respondents. Others have used quota samples in which a priori target numbers of respondents with certain specified combinations of characteristics are established, and the sampling stops when the targeted number of interviews is completed.

SIP General Survey I used a *stratified random sample*, based on the characteristics of the emigrants when they lived in the Soviet Union. Individual respondents were selected from a list that contained information about all eligible persons, defined by explicit eligibility criteria. The probability that given individuals were selected depended on the educational, regional, nationality, and city-size strata in which they fell. An effort was made to complete an interview with every selected individual. This method of sampling is less susceptible to self-selection by the respondents into the survey than snowball sampling or quota sampling, and it permits greater control over sample composition.

This appendix describes how the SIP General Survey I sampling frame and sample were defined. It analyzes the response rates and describes the basic demographic characteristics of the sample. And it discusses the issue of representativeness of the respondents: To what referent Soviet population can the results of the survey be generalized?[2]

We should like to thank Mike Coble and Amy Hsu for the graphic work, Cynthia Buckley and Victoria Velkoff for research assistance, and Robert Lewis and Michael Swafford for helpful advice.

[1] In this appendix, we describe the sample for the *first* SIP General Survey. A follow-up survey, based on Soviet emigrants who arrived in the United States between May 1, 1982, and December 31, 1985, has also been conducted. When it seems necessary to avoid confusion, we shall refer to the first SIP General Survey as General Survey I.

[2] Several aspects of the question of representativeness and bias are addressed by Bahry (Chapter 3), Millar (Chapter 1), and Silver (Chapter 4) in this volume, as well as in Bahry 1987.

The sampling frame

Designing a sample for the General Survey required the specification of a sampling frame: the set of emigrants from which the sample of prospective survey respondents was to be drawn.[3] The sampling frame was defined as all Soviet emigrants who arrived in the United States between January 1, 1979, and April 30, 1982, and who were between ages 21 and 70, inclusive, at date of arrival. This range of dates of arrival includes the peak emigration year of 1979.

Only recent emigrants were included in the frame in order to minimize problems of recall and because the main purpose of the survey was to study *Soviet* life, not the processes of emigration or adjustment to life in the United States.[4] In addition, most questions in the survey focused on the respondent's "last period of normal life in the USSR" (LNP), a period that ended from a few months to several years before their arrival in the United States.[5] On average, the month of arrival of the actual survey respondents was March 1980, and the end of their last normal period of life in the USSR was December 1978, a difference of 15 months. Because the fieldwork for the survey took place in 1983, with May 1983 the "average" month, the average length of time between the end of the LNP and the interview was 53 months.[6]

To develop the frame, we constructed a list of nearly all adult Soviet emigrants who arrived in the United States during the appropriate period. The list was based on information obtained from family service organizations in the United States and included an abstract of basic biographical information on each individual: date of birth, country of birth, date of arrival in the United States, sex, nationality, religion, education in the USSR, occupation in the USSR, city of last residence in the USSR, and military service and military rank in the USSR.

Biographical abstracts were completed for 37,156 individuals, of whom

---

[3] The sampling frame for the SIP General Survey was also used for developing samples for the specialized or "S" projects, which involved interviews of people with special experiences, such as in economic planning, local government administration, and law.

[4] The survey did contain a large number of questions concerning emigration experience and immigrant adjustment. These were designed primarily as controls for potential response bias.

[5] The "last normal period of life in the USSR" (LNP) was defined operationally in the survey as the five years preceding the major disruption in their lives associated with the decision to emigrate. For most respondents, this disruption was the act of applying for permission to emigrate.

[6] Despite this time lag, the respondents appear to have had excellent recall of life history events. For discussion, see Anderson and Silver 1987.

33,618 met the final eligibility criteria for General Survey I.[7] The biographical abstract data were important not only for sampling but also for defining the makeup of the emigrant population itself. The information the emigrants could give us about the parent population from which they came depended in part on the mix of backgrounds and experiences of the emigrants. Although the predominant ethnic-religious makeup of the respondents, their overall high levels of educational attainment, and their origination predominantly from the European parts of the Soviet Union were known in advance, the number of emigrants with specific combinations of characteristics, such as young persons with less than secondary education or non-Jews from small cities, was not known.

A large size for the sampling frame was desirable to increase the possibility of including in the sample respondents whose backgrounds were relatively rare among the emigrants as a whole. This would increase the diversity of any sample that could be drawn. Also, what *part* of the Soviet population the emigrants could represent depended on the characteristics of the individuals in the frame.

Characteristics of the sampling frame population

We shall now describe the characteristics of the sampling frame and make comparisons among the sampling frame, the sample, the respondents, and the Soviet population.

Column 1 in panel A of Table A.1 reports the distribution of eligible persons by year of arrival in the United States. Normal sampling error and the use of sample stratification criteria that intentionally favored the selection of individuals with particular backgrounds led to differences between the characteristics of people in the sample and people in the frame. The distribution by year of immigration for the sample (column 2) and for the General Survey I respondents (column 3) is less concentrated in the peak immigration year of 1979 than it is for people in the sampling frame (column 1).

The distribution of the frame population by age at arrival in the United States is presented in column 1 of panel B of Table A.1. The overwhelming majority of persons in the frame, and hence also in the sample, had completed their education, and a large majority had considerable employ-

---

[7] Armenian emigrants from the USSR to the United States were excluded from the sampling frame because 60 percent of the Armenians on whom biographical information was gathered were not born in the USSR but instead were individuals who repatriated to the USSR after World War II (primarily from Middle Eastern and Mediterranean countries), and most of the other Armenians were members of their families. Thus, it seemed likely that much of their *Soviet* experience would not be typical even of most Soviet Armenians.

Table A.1. *Comparison of characteristics of sampling frame, final sample, SIP respondents, and referent Soviet population (in percentages)*

	Sampling frame ($N = 33,618$) (1)	Final sample ($N = 3,551$) (2)	Respondents [frame data] ($N = 2,793$) (3)	Respondents [survey data]		Referent Soviet population estimate (6)
				Unweighted ($N = 2,793$) (4)	Weighted ($N = 2,793$) (5)	
A. Arrival year[a]						
1979	55.1	45.2	44.3			
1980	30.3	34.4	33.8			
1981	13.9	19.1	20.5			
1982	0.6	1.3	1.4			
Total	99.9	100.0	100.0			
B. Age at arrival[b]						
21–30	21.2	21.5	21.6	21.6	24.7	24.7
31–40	25.7	25.3	25.7	25.6	25.9	25.9
41–50	21.0	20.3	21.3	21.2	21.5	21.5
51–60	15.9	16.6	15.6	15.7	15.4	15.4
61–70	16.1	16.3	15.7	15.9	12.4	12.4
Total	99.9	100.0	100.0	100.0	99.9	99.9
C. Sex						
Men	45.4	42.6	43.4	43.4	43.2	
Women	54.6	57.4	56.6	56.6	56.8	
Total	100.0	100.0	100.0	100.0	100.0	
D. City size[c]						
500,000 +	88.3	80.8	81.7	80.2	78.8	
100–499,999	9.1	16.8	16.0	17.1	18.0	
< 100,000	2.5	2.4	2.3	2.7	2.2	
Total	99.9	100.0	100.0	100.0	100.0	
E. Region[d]						
RSFSR	24.2	44.3	47.0	46.0	52.7	60.5
West	63.9	34.5	33.6	34.7	25.4	21.0
Baltic	5.2	5.1	5.2	5.6	2.7	2.9
Transcaucasia	2.9	5.3	5.1	5.0	5.1	5.0
Central Asia	3.8	10.8	9.1	8.7	14.1	10.7
Total	100.0	100.0	100.0	100.0	100.0	100.1
F. Education						
Some higher	44.1	33.8	36.8	41.9	27.3	27.3
Comp. sec.	38.5	45.3	44.8	40.7	40.6	40.6
< Comp. sec.	17.4	20.9	18.4	17.4	32.1	32.1
Total	100.0	100.0	100.0	100.0	100.0	100.0

Table A.1. (*contd.*)

	(1)	(2)	(3)	(4)	(5)	(6)
G. *Nationality*[e]						
Jews	98.4	85.7	85.7	82.8	83.1	
Non-Jews	1.6	14.3	14.3	17.2	16.9	
Total	100.0	100.0	100.0	100.0	100.0	

Note: Figures for the sampling frame and sample (columns 1 and 2) are derived from the "frame data" – the biographical abstracts developed for sampling. Figures for the respondents in column 3 are also derived from the presurvey biographical abstracts. Figures for the respondents in columns 4 and 5 are based on the SIP General Survey results, unless otherwise noted. Figures for the referent Soviet population (column 6) are derived from Soviet census data.

[a] All arrivals in 1982 were in the first four months of the year.

[b] Age in columns 1–5 is age at arrival in U.S. The age distribution in column 6 is as estimated for 1979. See Anderson, Silver, and Lewis 1986.

[c] City sizes are based on the population in 1979. The largest size category includes republic capital cities even if they were less than 500,000 population. City size based on the frame data (columns 1–3) refers to size of city in which persons were last employed in the USSR. City size based on the General Survey data (columns 4 and 5) refers to the size of city in which persons lived at end of LNP.

[d] The region categories based on the frame data refer to the region where persons lived when last employed in the USSR. Region based on the General Survey results refers to the region in which persons lived at the end of LNP. Republics included in the multirepublic regions: *West* (Belorussia, Moldavia, Ukraine); *Baltic* (Estonia, Latvia, Lithuania); *Transcaucasia* (Armenia, Azerbaidzhan, Georgia); *Central Asia* (Kazakhstan, Kirgizia, Tadzhikistan, Turkmenistan, Uzbekistan). The figures in column 6 refer to the regional distribution of the Soviet population in cities of 100,000 population or more in 1979.

[e] For columns 4 and 5, persons who were Jewish by self-identified nationality or religion are classified as Jewish; all others are classified as non-Jews. In both columns 4 and 5, if those who were children of Jews (but not self-identified as Jewish by nationality or religion) were counted as Jews, then 87.4 percent of the respondents would be Jews.

ment experience by the time they left the USSR. The distribution by age in the sample and among the actual survey respondents is similar to that for the sampling frame.

Ninety-nine percent of the eligible population were born in the USSR or in territories, such as the Baltic states, that are currently part of the USSR. Of the 168 people reported as born outside the USSR, 114 reported that they were born in Rumania or Poland; it is likely that most of these 114 also were born in parts of Rumania or Poland that were subsequently annexed to the USSR.

The distribution of the sampling frame population by sex (panel C of Table A.1) reflects the numerical superiority of women over men in Soviet society, a product of differential war losses and the higher rates of mortality for men than for women during peacetime.[8] The distribution in the sampling frame also reflects the fact that recent emigrants from the Soviet Union have come primarily as members of families. Seventy-eight percent of the respondents were married in their last period of normal life in the USSR. Of those who were married, 97 percent emigrated with their spouse, and 91 percent of the married couples emigrated with one or more of their children.[9] Eighty-nine percent of the SIP General Survey I respondents emigrated with either their spouse, their children, or their spouse and children. Of the 2,389 respondents who had children at the end of their last normal period in the USSR, 84 percent emigrated with *all* of their children, and only 4 percent emigrated with *none* of their children.

The emigrants came overwhelmingly from cities. The urban origin of the emigrant population is not surprising. At the time of the 1979 Soviet census, 99 percent of Soviet Jews, 74 percent of Soviet Russians, and 62 percent of the entire Soviet population lived in urban areas.[10] Furthermore, compared to the Soviet urban population, the emigrants come primarily from large and medium-sized cities (see column 1 in panel D of Table A.1). Ninety-seven percent come from cities that had populations of 100,000 or more in 1979. By comparison, only 38 percent of the entire Soviet population and 60 percent of the Soviet urban population lived in cities of 100,000 population or more in 1979.

Moreover, 88 percent of the emigrants in the sampling frame came from Soviet cities that had populations of 500,000 or more in 1979.[11] In contrast, only about 20 percent of the total Soviet population, and about 32 percent of the urban Soviet population, lived in cities of 500,000 population or more in 1979.

The big-city origin of the emigrants does not mean that only the Soviet population from large cities can be represented in the survey. There were enough people in the sampling frame from medium-sized cities to permit purposive oversampling of people from medium-sized cities. The proportion of respondents from medium-sized cities is approximately twice as large as

---

[8] For further discussion, see Anderson and Silver 1986b.

[9] The few exceptions when the spouse did not emigrate with the respondent are divided roughly evenly into four categories: (1) Spouse was denied an exit permit (or held a sensitive job); (2) spouse stayed with relatives; (3) spouse was too ill to emigrate; (4) spouse "did not want to go."

[10] Figures that we cite for the Soviet population in 1979 are based on the 1979 Soviet census. We either derive them directly or calculate them from data published in USSR, TsSU 1984.

[11] For purposes of sampling, we included the four republic capitals (Ashkhabad, Dushanbe, Tallin, and Vilnius) that were less than 500,000 in population in 1979 with the cities of 500,000 or more. See Anderson, Silver, and Lewis 1986.

the proportion of persons in the sampling frame who emigrated from medium-sized cities (see panel D of Table A.1).

The emigrants in the sampling frame came primarily from the European parts of the USSR, especially the Soviet West (Ukraine, Belorussia, and Moldavia) and the Russian Republic (RSFSR) (see panel E of Table A.1). For purposes of sample design, however, there was a sufficient number of people in each of five major Soviet regions (groups of republics) to approximate in the sample the distribution by region of the Soviet population that lived in cities with populations of 100,000 or more (column 6 of panel E).

Accordingly, the sample was designed so that the proportion of the people in the sample who originated in the RSFSR would be almost twice as large as the proportion of people in the sampling frame who originated in that republic. The proportion from the Soviet West was reduced correspondingly to about half the proportion of the sampling frame that had come from that region (compare columns 1, 2 and 3 of Panel of Table A.1). Also, to assure adequate regional diversity in the sample, minimum target sample sizes were established for the Baltic and Transcaucasia.

Emigrants from the RSFSR and the West came predominantly from a few cities. The seven cities providing the largest numbers are Kiev (7,384), Odessa (4,881), Moscow (3,718), Leningrad (3,760), Minsk (2,133), Lvov (1,493), and Kishinev (1,286). Those who came from Central Asia, Transcaucasia, and the Baltic came overwhelmingly from the largest cities in those regions – especially the republic capital cities of Riga (1,328), Tashkent (991), Baku (547), Tbilisi (348), Vilnius (240), and Dushanbe (90) (see Anderson and Silver 1986a).

Seventy-five percent of the survey *respondents* came from the republic capitals (including Leningrad). In every region except the Soviet West, over 80 percent of the respondents came from republic capitals. In the West, only 50 percent of the respondents came from republic capitals (Minsk, Kiev, and Kishinev).

Panel F of Table A.1 summarizes the data on educational attainment.[12] Compared to the Soviet urban population, the emigrants as a whole are highly educated, in line with the high average educational levels attained by Soviet Jews. They also have a somewhat higher average educational level than the Soviet population residing in large cities. Forty-four percent of the people in the sampling frame had achieved at least some higher education (column 1). In contrast, in the adult Soviet population in the republic capital cities taken together in 1979, less than 30 percent had attained that level of education. The sample was designed to select people from the frame

---

[12] For further details, see Anderson and Silver 1986a.

in proportions that approximated the estimated distribution by education of the Soviet adult population in large cities in 1979.

Recent Soviet emigrants are primarily Jews or members of families that included Jews. As is shown in panel G of Table A.1, 98.4 percent of all people in the sampling frame were Jews. To maximize the ethnic diversity of the sample, all known non-Jews were included in the sample, so that about 85 percent of the emigrants in the sample were Jews.

The referent Soviet population

Building the sampling frame was one step in identifying a pool of potential survey respondents whose life histories would shed light on Soviet experience. At the same time, the characteristics of the pool of emigrants determined which segment of Soviet society *could* be represented in the sample. For example, since there are almost no people from rural areas in the sampling frame, it is not possible to draw a sample from the emigrants that represents the experiences of the rural sector of Soviet society. Similarly, no sample drawn from this sampling frame could represent the experiences of most of the major non-Russian nationalities, especially the Moslem nationalities.

Recent emigrants are diverse, however, with respect to education, occupational experience, and geographic origins in the USSR, and most of their everyday experiences in the Soviet Union preceding the traumatizing experiences associated with emigration are likely to be reflective of the experiences of an important sector of Soviet society. By using the information about individuals in the sampling frame to select a sample that maximized the diversity of backgrounds of the survey respondents, the sample could approximate some aspects of the demographic composition of "the adult European population in large and medium-sized Soviet cities." We term this the *referent Soviet population*.

The main purpose of identifying the referent population was to clarify the parts of the Soviet population that the survey respondents could *not* represent and to identify a sector of Soviet society that the survey respondents *could* represent if the respondents were appropriately selected from the frame and if the survey instrument provided information to test for various forms of response bias.[13] The concept of a referent population was thus a guide for the sample design and for interpretation of the survey results, not an exact blueprint to be executed in the sample.

---

[13] The main sources of response bias with which we were concerned were the effects of emigrant selection and experience – that is, the fact that most respondents were Jews – and the accuracy of recall.

The sample

Size: The initial sample size was set at 3,750 under the expectation that 80 percent of the individuals in the sample would complete the interviews, yielding 3,000 completed interviews, or respondents. The target of 3,000 respondents was established so that each of the three survey supplements would have 1,000 respondents.[14]

Sampling procedure: The SIP General Survey sample was designed to approximate the educational and regional composition of the referent Soviet population. It was also designed to diversify the sample on the basis of nationality and size of city compared to the distribution in the frame but not to approximate those distributions in the referent Soviet population.

To accomplish these goals, the sample was stratified. Although each person in the frame had a known probability of being selected into the sample, the probability varied with the individual's nationality, education, size of city, and region of origin within the USSR. First, targets were set for the overall educational, regional, and city-size distributions. None of these was modeled to match the referent Soviet population exactly, but they were made to be much more like the referent Soviet population than like the frame population. Second, all eligible non-Jews were selected into the sample.[15] Third, an iterative, random-selection procedure was used to draw the remainder of the sample (the Jews) so that target distributions by education, city size, and region were achieved.[16] The distributions of all these variables in the sample are shown in column 2 of Table A.1.

Had the General Survey I sample been a simple random sample of eligible individuals (the frame), it would have differed much more sharply from the referent Soviet population. By stratifying the sample, persons in the frame whose educational level was "completed secondary education or less" were more likely to be chosen than persons who had attained higher education. Persons in the frame from medium-sized Soviet cities were more likely to be selected than persons from large cities. And persons from the RSFSR, the

---

[14] On the structure of the survey instrument, see Chapter 1 herein. All respondents completed a common set of "core" questions; respondents were then assigned randomly to receive one of the three variant "supplements" so that about one-third of the respondents completed each of the supplements. The actual numbers completing the three supplements, which were designated by the color of their face sheets as orange, blue, and green, were 926, 933, and 922, respectively. Twelve respondents completed no supplement.

[15] The information about the nationality of the persons in the sampling frame was not complete. Based on the data obtained in the survey itself, the nationality of the actual respondents could be determined with greater precision.

[16] See NORC 1985: app. E.

Baltic, and Transcaucasia were more likely to be chosen than persons from the Soviet West (Belorussia, Ukraine, Moldavia) or Central Asia.[17] Minimum sample sizes were established for Transcaucasia and the Baltic – exceeding their relative proportions in the referent Soviet population – to permit multivariate analysis based on the individuals from each of these regions.

Modeling the composition of the sample on the demographic composition of the referent Soviet population reduced the unrepresentativeness of the sample. In two respects, however, no sample of recent Soviet emigrants could match the referent Soviet population. First, any sizable sample had to consist mostly of Jews. Second, for obvious reasons, all persons in the sample were emigrants.

All eligible non-Jews were included in the sample not in order to mimic the referent Soviet population but rather to provide a comparison or control group for assessing the effect of ethnic differences on patterns of survey responses. A similar rationale applies to the effort to increase the number of respondents from medium-sized cities. This permits researchers to test for the effects of city size on response patterns, particularly reports of economic behavior.

The main control for bias linked to the self-selection or to special experiences of the respondents as emigrants was in the design of the questionnaire, not of the sample. For this purpose, a series of questions was included concerning the respondent's motivation for emigration, their role in the decision to emigrate, and their adjustment to life in the United States.[18]

Response rates

The final General Survey I sample was composed of 3,738 individuals selected from the sampling frame.[19] Of these, 187 were subsequently dropped for one of three reasons: (*a*) they were deceased; (*b*) they were too ill to participate in the survey; or (*c*) they were no longer residing in the United States. Because these people did not refuse to participate in the survey, we

---

[17] In addition, *within* the West, a maximum of 100 persons was to be selected from Odessa.

[18] Analysis of the General Survey I data indicates that responses to questions related to religious behavior and to perceptions of discrimination are very sensitive to the ethnic or religious affiliation of the respondent, but responses to questions dealing with most other issues are not sensitive to the respondent's ethnic or religious background. See Bahry 1987 as well as Appendix B herein.

[19] The initial size of 3,750 was reduced to 3,738 when it was discovered that 12 "ineligible" persons had inadvertently been included, before any contacts were made with potential respondents.

interpret them as "ineligibles" rather than as "refusals." Individuals whose addresses were never confirmed are treated as eligible, since some of these individuals may have actively avoided participation in the survey by not responding to letters of inquiry or other efforts by the interviewers or the National Opinion Research Center to contact them.[20]

Of the 3,551 persons remaining in the sample, 2,793 completed the interview, for a response rate of 79 percent. This rate compares favorably with that in most other sample surveys conducted in this country.

Participation in the survey was voluntary, and respondents were assured that both their answers and their participation in the survey would be confidential.[21] Of those who completed the interview, 221 participated only after initially stating that they did not want to participate or after they did not respond to initial inquiries.

Of the 758 persons in the sample (of 3,551) who did not participate in the survey, 647 either "refused" to participate or broke off the interview before completing it. Another 91 persons could not be located. And 20 were not interviewed for some other reason.

Table A.2 shows the response rates for various groups of people. There was no difference in the response rates of Jews and non-Jews. As is true of many surveys, persons with higher education were more likely to agree to participate in the SIP General Survey than the less educated. Although younger people were slightly more likely to complete the interview than older people, the difference in the response rate associated with education is not a function of age. Instead, as is shown in Figure A.1, more highly educated respondents had higher response rates than less-educated respondents in each age group.

Figure A.1 also reveals that the differences in the response rates associated with age are negligible, once differences in education are taken into account. The only sharp deviation is among persons aged 21–30 who had less than complete secondary education, but only 37 persons in the sample (21 of whom completed the interview) were in this category.

Men in the sample were more likely to complete the interview than women (see Table A.2). This difference is not a function of the difference in educational attainment of men and women, for at each educational level men were more likely to complete the interview than women.

In summary, the differences in response rates among educational groups

[20] The effort to obtain current addresses for persons in the sample began only after the sample was drawn. It would have been wasteful and prohibitively expensive to gather this information for all 33,618 persons in the sampling frame. Of the 3,738 persons in the final sample, 91 could not be located.

[21] For a description of the steps taken to assure confidentiality, see NORC 1985: 40–42.

Table A.2. *Percentage of persons in sample completing the survey, by education, age, sex, nationality, and size of city of last employment in USSR*

	Percentage completing survey	Base number in sample ($N = 3{,}551$)	Number completing survey ($N = 2{,}793$)
Education			
Some higher	85.6	1,200	1,027
Comp. sec.	77.8	1,609	1,257
< Comp. sec.	69.3	742	514
Age at arrival in U.S.			
21–30	79.1	764	604
31–40	80.1	898	719
41–50	82.6	720	595
51–60	73.9	590	436
61–70	75.8	579	439
Sex			
Men	80.3	1,511	1,213
Women	77.5	2,040	1,580
Nationality			
Jews	78.7	3,042	2,394
Non-Jews	78.4	509	399
Size of city of last employment in USSR			
500,000 +	79.6	2,868	2,283
100,000–499,999	74.7	598	447
< 100,000	74.1	85	63

Note: The characteristics used in this table are from the presurvey sampling frame data, not the survey results.

had more impact on the composition of the final respondents than differences by age, sex, or nationality. The differential by education moved the composition of the respondents more toward that of the sampling frame and away from that of the referent Soviet population (compare columns 1–3 in Table A.1). Overall, however, the response rates did not vary greatly with social background.

Weighting the cases

Purpose

Weights are used in statistical analyses so that the weighted respondents will resemble more closely the population to which the researcher hopes to

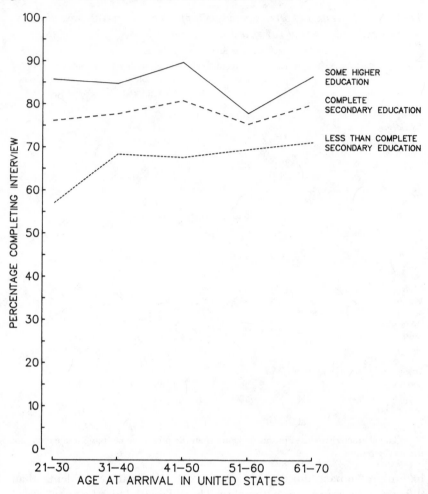

Figure A1. Percentage completing General Survey, by education and age at arrival in the United States

generalize the results than would the unweighted respondents. When a simple random sample is drawn from a population of interest, weights are generally not necessary. Given normal sampling error, the characteristics of the respondents will be identical to those of the population from which the sample is drawn. If the sample is disproportionate, so that individuals in the population do not have an identical probability of being selected into the sample, the characteristics of the unweighted set of respondents will not match those of the population of interest. The use of weights has the effect of counting some cases more heavily than others in the analysis, thus compensating for the initial disproportionate sampling.[22]

Stratifying the sample drawn from the list of eligible emigrants helped to bring the characteristics of the sample more into line with those of the referent Soviet population than would have been true of a simple random sample drawn from that list. For several reasons, however, further adjustments to the composition of the respondents are necessary to make it more similar to the referent population. First, as discussed earlier, the stratification procedure did not bring the sample completely into line with the referent population. Second, information about respondent backgrounds that was known in advance of the survey was less accurate and less complete than information obtained in the survey itself, particularly regarding the respondents' educational attainment. Third, how closely the actual respondents would match the characteristics of the referent population depended on how the response rates varied among different groups of respondents.

Method

Information on the respondents' region (five categories), education (three categories), and age (five categories) was used in devising the weights. As a preliminary step in constructing the weights, we estimated the three-way distribution of age-by-education-by-region in the referent Soviet population – to define the appropriate share that each of the resulting 75 population categories should represent among the weighted survey respondents.

The most formidable problem in estimating the education-by-age distribution of the referent Soviet population is that neither age distributions nor education distributions by age have been published for the most recent Soviet census year, 1979. This census date corresponds most closely to the date of the "last normal period of life" of respondents to the first SIP General Survey. Therefore, we estimated the distributions indirectly using an iterative fitting procedure from 1970 and 1979 Soviet census data, based on the characteristics of the populations in republic capital cities.[23]

The three-way cross-tabulation of the region, education, and age variables defines 75 population categories to which weights were assigned. Each

---

[22] For readers who are not familiar with how weights are applied in practice, it may be useful to note that major statistical software programs, such as SAS and SPSS[x], have built-in routines that automatically weight the cases at the user's option. The user need only designate the name of the variable that is to be used to weight the cases.

[23] A detailed discussion of the method of development of demographic estimates for the weights is given in Anderson, Silver, and Lewis 1986.

category can be represented as a proportion of the total population, so that the sum of the proportions across all 75 categories is 1.000. The weight assigned to survey respondents in any given cell is calculated as the proportion of the referent Soviet population in that cell divided by the proportion of the respondents in that cell.

Thus, if the proportion of respondents in that cell is smaller than the proportion of the referent population in that cell, the weight assigned to respondents in that cell will be greater than unity, thus causing respondents in that cell to count more heavily than they would otherwise. If the proportion of respondents in the cell is larger than the proportion of the referent population in that cell, the weight assigned will be less than 1.00 – to reduce the relative contribution of those respondents to the overall distributions. The actual weights for the first SIP General Survey vary from 6.28 to 0.22. Thus, if analysts choose to use the weights, a respondent with a weight of 6.00 would "count" as six respondents; a respondent with a weight of 0.25 would count as one-fourth of a respondent.

In some of the cells of the age-by-education-by-region distribution, there were very few respondents. No respondents from the Baltic and only one respondent from the RSFSR, for example, fell into the age range 21–30 at date of arrival and had less than complete secondary education. To avoid assigning extraordinarily high weights to young persons with less than complete secondary education for some regions, we collapsed the cells across regions for persons who had less than complete secondary education for each of the three age categories 21–30, 31–40, and 41–50. Had we not done this, no weight could have been assigned to respondents aged 21–30 with less than complete secondary education from the Baltic, and a weight of 57 would be needed for the one respondent from the RSFSR who fell into that age-by-education cell.

The main consequence of collapsing across regions – for those with less than completed secondary education and who were 50 or under at date of arrival – is that the regional distribution of the weighted respondents does not match the estimated regional distribution of the referent Soviet population. This is shown in the distribution in columns 5 and 6 in panel E of Table A.1. But the target distributions for education and age, separately as well as in combination, are matched exactly (see panels B and F).

Average weights for respondents by age and education are shown in Table A.3.[24] Cases that are weighted most heavily are younger persons with less than secondary education. Accordingly (as shown in Table A.3), the 15

[24] These are averages, because they do not reflect the differences in the weights related to the respondents' region of residence in their last period of normal life in the USSR.

Table A.3. *Average weights assigned by educational level and age at arrival in the United States*

Age at arrival	Education			
	Some higher	Complete secondary	Less than comp. sec.	All
21–30	.65	1.34	6.28	1.15
(Unweighted N)	(275)	(312)	(15)	(602)
(Weighted N)	(179)[a]	(417)	(94)	(690)
31–40	.69	.95	5.00	1.01
(Unweighted N)	(371)	(311)	(34)	(716)
(Weighted N)	(258)	(296)	(171)	(724)
41–50	.54	1.09	2.65	1.02
(Unweighted N)	(314)	(194)	(83)	(591)
(Weighted N)	(169)	(211)	(220)	(600)
51–60	.76	.75	1.46	.98
(Unweighted N)	(127)	(170)	(142)	(439)
(Weighted N)	(96)	(128)	(207)	(431)
61–70	.71	.54	.98	.78
(Unweighted N)	(84)	(150)	(211)	(445)
(Weighted N)	(60)	(82)	(206)	(347)
All	.65	1.00	1.85	1.000
(Unweighted N)	(1,171)	(1,137)	(485)	(2,793)
(Weighted N)	(762)	(1,135)	(897)	(2,793)

Note: The weights shown in this table are *averages* because the actual weights vary also according to the region in which the respondent resided in his or her last period of normal life in the USSR. See Anderson, Silver, and Lewis 1986 for the weights by age, education, and region.
[a] Weighted Ns are rounded to the nearest integer.

actual respondents who were 21–30 at date of arrival in the United States and had less than completed secondary education would count as 94 respondents if the data are weighted, and the 84 respondents who were 61–70 at date of arrival and had some higher education would count as 60 respondents in a weighted data analysis.

The *total* number of respondents (the N) is the same for the weighted cases and the unweighted cases. By multiplying the number of actual cases in each cell by the weight applied to each case, the total number of respondents for the weighted cases comes to 2,793.

Weights and the referent population

Most analyses of the SIP General Survey are not likely to use weighted data. This is because most statistical analyses will focus on the *relationships between variables* rather than on either the overall frequency distributions or the "average" score or answer found among all respondents. When the focus is on the relationships between variables, whether one uses the weights will seldom affect analytic results.[25]

If one is interested, for example, in how the level of support for the Soviet regime varies with the respondent's education, it does not matter whether 42 percent of the respondents had some higher education or 27 percent had some higher education (which is the adjustment in the proportion with some higher education that would result if one shifted from using unweighted data to using weighted data). If one were interested however, in measuring the *average* level of support for the regime among *all* respondents, then using weighted data would increase the apparent overall level of regime support because respondents who have higher education are less supportive of regime norms than are respondents with secondary or lower education.[26]

Thus, the weights are an auxiliary tool that may be useful for some types of analysis of the General Survey data. But they are not mandatory for all analyses, particularly those that focus on the relationships between variables rather than on univariate distributions or measures of central tendency for the entire set of respondents.[27]

The question of generalizability

The logic that applies in determining whether or not to weight the responses in analyses applies also to whether it is important that respondents exactly

---

[25] A major exception is when the analysis focuses directly on the relation between age and education – two variables whose relationship is most severely adjusted in the weights – or on the relations among age, education, and another variable that is correlated with both age and education, such as income. See Anderson, Chapter 7 in this volume, for an analysis of the relation between age, education, and income among SIP General Survey respondents.

[26] See Silver, Chapter 4 in this volume.

[27] The main effect of using the weights when one engages in multivariate analysis is on the amount of variance in the dependent and independent variables. Hence, whether one uses the weights will have a much greater effect when one employs correlation coefficients or standardized regression coefficients in statistical analyses than when one uses unstandardized coefficients. For most purposes it is probably preferable to use unstandardized coefficients for analyzing both the weighted and the unweighted SIP data, because the amount of variance among the respondents is substantially affected by a priori, and inevitably somewhat arbitrary, decisions about the composition of the sample.

match the demographic characteristics of the referent Soviet population. The validity of any generalization from the survey to the referent Soviet population requires more than a mechanical matching of the sociodemographic characteristics of the respondents as a whole and the referent population.

It is more important to establish that survey respondents with specific sociodemographic backgrounds are similar to persons with the same background who did not emigrate from the USSR or who were not Jewish. This is not just a sampling issue. Many researchers have compared the distributions on variables of interest in the SIP General Survey with analogous distributions for the Soviet population in official Soviet publications. When these distributions are similar, one can have greater confidence in the results of multivariate analyses using the SIP data.

Diversification of the sample, especially by nationality, coupled with the use of a stratified random sample based on a list of the eligible population, provides another basis for assessing the sensitivity of responses to potential bias. The concept of a referent Soviet population is relevant not because it represents the population from which the sample is drawn and against which the sampling error could be determined in precise statistical terms, but rather because it provides a referent population of Soviet society whose experiences and behavior the SIP General Survey respondents are most likely to represent.

References

Anderson, Barbara A., and Brian D. Silver. 1986a. "Descriptive Statistics for the Sampling Frame Population." *Soviet Interview Project Working Papers*, no. 2, revised.

    1986b. "Sex Differentials in Mortality in the Soviet Union: Regional Differences in Length of Working Life in Comparative Perspective," *Population Studies*, 40: 191–214.

    1987. "The Validity of Survey Responses: Insights from Interviews of Married Couples in a Survey of Soviet Emigrants," *Social Forces*, 66 (forthcoming).

Anderson, Barbara A., Brian D. Silver, and Robert A. Lewis. 1986. "Demographic Estimates for the Post-sampling Weights of the SIP General Survey." *Soviet Interview Project Working Papers*, no. 4, revised.

Bahry, Donna. 1987. "Surveying Soviet Emigrants: Political Attitudes and Ethnic Bias." Manuscript, Department of Politics, New York University.

NORC [National Opinion Research Center]. 1985. *Soviet Interview Project Methodological Report*.

USSR, TsSU [Tsentral'noe statisticheskoe upravlenie]. 1984. *Chislennost' i sostav naseleniia SSSR: Po dannym Vsesoiuznoi perepisi naseleniia 1979 goda*. Moscow: Finansy i statistika.

Response effects in SIP's General Survey of Soviet emigrants

MICHAEL SWAFFORD, CAROL A. ZEISS,
CAROLYN S. BREDA, AND BRADLEY P. BULLOCK

The unintended effects of survey design and interviewer performance threaten the validity of every survey. To minimize the threat to this survey, the research team drew on a great deal of expertise in questionnaire design and put extraordinary effort into interviewer training. Unfortunately, such measures never entirely succeed. We have therefore tested for several potential artifacts that might give rise to unwarranted conclusions.

Four of our tests bear on special features of the Soviet Interview Project (SIP). Briefly, the first one examines the extent to which responses were affected by the time lapse between respondents' departure from the Soviet Union and the date of their interview. Since the survey focused on respondents' last normal period in the Soviet Union,[1] we would like to identify any variables affected by deteriorating recall or contamination by Western experience.

The second test searches for differences between answers from willing and reluctant respondents. Of course, including data from reluctant respondents did not in itself render this survey unique, for all respectable survey organizations endeavor to convert "soft refusals" in the effort to achieve high response rates. Nor were most of the reasons offered by reluctant respondents unusual: that they did not know enough to be worthy of an interview or that they lacked time or interest. A few members of the sample, however, voiced a unique concern: fear that answers might bring reprisals to relatives in their homeland or unforeseen consequences in the United States. Such concerns might have generated misleading answers to some questions. The second test attempts to discover any such questions.

The third test compares answers from Jewish respondents with those from all other respondents. Admittedly, ethnic differences normally count as

---

[1] Respondents were asked to pinpoint the month and year in which they applied to emigrate. They were also asked whether plans to emigrate significantly changed their lives even before that date and, if so, to specify the month and year in which their lives changed. The "last normal period" was defined as the five-year period leading up to the earlier of these two dates.

substantive findings, not as artifacts. However, inasmuch as this survey was designed to support conclusions about the adult, urban European population of the USSR, some people would see the predominance of Jews among respondents as threatening the generality of the study. In this context, then, ethnic differences warrant special attention for reasons that transcend usual substantive concerns.

The fourth test examines the effect of interviewers' country of birth on emigrants' responses. Most of the interviewers were born in the United States or Western Europe. However, 11 percent were naturalized citizens who emigrated from the Soviet Union recently enough so that their origins would likely be detected by respondents. During the planning stage of the project, some team members argued that emigrant interviewers would elicit more valid responses than those who were not intimately acquainted with life in the USSR; others claimed that emigrant interviewers would to some extent impose their own expectations on respondents, or that respondents would not trust emigrant interviewers with whom they were unacquainted. Though interviewer selection and training were designed to minimize the risk of such response effects, only a test can confirm that these efforts succeeded.

In addition to considering these four unusual challenges to SIP's General Survey, we have conducted two conventional tests for sex effects: whether men interviewed by women gave different answers than those interviewed by men; and whether women interviewed by women gave different answers than those interviewed by men. There is no reason to believe that response effects related to interviewers' sex were any different in this survey than in others. However, the results of this test provide a useful backdrop against which to consider the results of the other four tests.

Measuring response disparities

For purposes of this study, we define "response disparities" to be group differences in answers to questions. Thus, for example, when the distribution of answers from willing respondents differs from that of reluctant respondents, we term the difference a "response disparity between willing and reluctant respondents."

We employ "response effects" to refer to those response disparities that are artifacts of study design rather than substantively interesting differences. In other words, we distinguish between "response disparities" and "response effects" – the most common term used to name methodological artifacts in surveys (Sudman and Bradburn 1974: 3). As we point out at the end of this section, many disparities described in this appendix have very plausible substantive or statistical explanations, which lead us to conclude that they are not artifacts.[2] Even though we are ultimately interested in response effects, not disparities, we begin by calculating disparities because response effects are a subset of them.

Analyzing response disparities in this data set has been difficult. First, the sheer quantity of data – more than 1,300 variables – created a burden. To test for five potential response disparities for each variable, we would have had to examine more than 6,500 tables. We could have reduced the burden, of course, by focusing exclusively on variables that seemed most likely to manifest response effects, but by doing so we might have overlooked important unanticipated effects.

Instead, we developed a two-pronged approach to the problem. First, we drew a systematic sample of *variables* by selecting every eighth one in the master sequential list. This reduced the burden while insuring that a wide range of variables throughout the questionnaire would be tested. We then computed five response disparities for each of these variables on the basis of some 1,000 tables.[3] All variables for which at least a modest response disparity was revealed were selected for further scrutiny to determine whether conclusions based on them would be misleading, that is, to determine whether they suffered from true response effects.

Second, from the one-in-eight sample of variables just discussed, two raters independently identified variables that, on a priori grounds, seemed more likely than others to manifest any of the five response effects.[4] For instance, *before any response disparities were calculated*, the raters judged that recent emigrants from the USSR would answer the question about what the United States could learn from the Soviet Union differently than emigrants who had left the USSR earlier. In short, then, our analysis took advantage not only of an exploratory approach, which avoided potentially misleading preconceptions, but also of an approach based on the rigor of hypothesizing in advance of testing.

In addition to the difficulty presented by the quantity of variables at hand, we had to contend with difficulties in *measuring* response disparities. To our

[2] We fully recognize that one person's artifact can serve as another person's key variable. For example, in a study of assimilation, disparities related to time lapse would scarcely be considered artifacts.

[3] Testing sex effects required twice as many tables as testing the other four response effects: one set of tables for male respondents, another for females. Hence, the total number of tables equals six rather than five times the number of variables.

[4] In a few cases, the two raters did not agree on enough problematic variables for a given response effect. They then resorted to the master list of all variables to locate other variables that they both deemed problematic, and they added the few variables identified in this manner to the one-in-eight sample of variables, yielding a total of 169 variables. Since we did not use this sample of variables in making formal statistical inferences to the population of variables, adding cases in this manner created no statistical problems.

knowledge, the relevant literature offers no satisfactory standard procedure for measuring response disparities across the full range of variables in a study such as the SIP. We were obliged to create such a measure by modifying the technique employed by Sudman and Bradburn (1974). For a discussion of our approach, as well as of other technical matters such as significance testing, we refer readers to this chapter's Addendum A. Here, we simply illustrate the manner in which our measure was calculated.

Consider the easiest case: calculating response disparities for variables measured on interval or ratio scales, as exemplified by a question about the value of furniture owned by each respondent's family in the last normal period (VALUFURN: DKCOL 1106).[5] The mean value for the most recent emigrants was 1,634.11 rubles ($N = 501$); for the earlier emigrants, 1,639.64 rubles ($N = 1,917$). Obviously, the difference (5.53 rubles) is minuscule given the monetary sums in question. However, to allow comparisons with other variables, we needed to express the disparity in terms other than rubles. After all, a difference of 5.53 rubles in daily expenditures for, say, food would constitute a substantial disparity, and a difference of 5.53 years of schooling would constitute a monumental disparity. To represent such disparities in terms commensurate with one another, we expressed them as the absolute value of the number of standard deviations between the group means. Thus, since the standard deviation for the early group was 2,811.54 rubles, the response disparity equaled .002 [$|(1,634.1 - 1,639.64)|/2,811.54$]. This small quantity properly represents the minuscule difference in furniture holdings reported by very recent and moderately recent emigrants.

The second illustration is based on a categoric variable: respondents' religious practices during the last normal period (SABBATH2: DKCOL 2541). Among the practices enumerated was lighting Friday night Sabbath candles, a ritual that non-Jews would seldom perform (except perhaps if they were married to a devout Jew). The percentage of Jews reporting that they lit candles was 8.3, while the percentage of non-Jews was 1.8 – a difference of 6.5 percentage points. As is explained in Addendum A, the standard deviation for the non-Jews was calculated to be 13.3 percent. Thus, the response disparity was calculated to be .49 (i.e., $|1.8 - 8.3|/13.3$). In other words, responses from Jews were, on the average, .49 of a standard deviation away from those of non-Jews on this question.

On the basis of these illustrations, our strategy may be described as follows. For each of the 169 variables in our sample, a separate response disparity was calculated for *each* of the five potential sources of bias: time lapse, reluctance to

---

[5] The variable names and locations (deck and column numbers) are included as a service to readers who use the data; other readers are not expected to find them useful.

participate, ethnicity, country of interviewer's birth, and sex correspondence between interviewer and respondent. If the response disparity exceeded a low level – .30 of a standard deviation – the variable was tagged for further examination. In the above illustrations, then, the first variable was not tagged for problems related to time lapse since the response disparity was only .002; the second one, however, *was* tagged for problems related to ethnicity because the response disparity (.49) was greater than .30 of a standard deviation (henceforth: .30 s.d.).

We must emphasize that response disparities above .30 s.d. do not necessarily indicate that results are biased. Consider SABBATH2 again. After we identified the variable as potentially problematic, we readily concluded that there was a compelling substantive reason for the disparity between answers from Jews and non-Jews on lighting Sabbath candles. Indeed, had there been no disparity, we would have wondered about the quality of the questionnaire, the respondents, or the measure of response disparity.

Readers should also bear in mind a second reason why large response disparities do not necessarily indicate that a variable is problematic. As statisticians well know, even when there are actually *no* response disparities whatsoever in the population about which one wishes to make inferences, a few disparities can be expected to appear large (due to normal sampling error) when many response disparities are calculated on the basis of a sample. There is no valid substantive explanation for such disparities since they would disappear (and be replaced by a different set) if a different sample were drawn. Given that we calculated more than 1,000 response disparities, it was inevitable that some would appear large, but it would be statistically naive to contrive an a posteriori nonstatistical explanation for every one of them. If a disparity constitutes a true response effect, a similar disparity should manifest itself in similar variables throughout the data set. Fortunately, the large number of variables included in our sample allows us to look for such patterns.

One other consideration must be taken into account in assessing response disparities. Our measures are based on bivariate relationships, for example, the relationship between reluctance to participate and value of furniture holdings. Without due concern for intervening or antecedent variables, bivariate relationships can be misleading. For example, suppose that willing respondents were found to give different answers than reluctant respondents. Of course, this might reveal a response effect, suggesting that reluctant respondents were trying to hide something. However, it might merely reflect the fact that reluctant respondents on the average had lower levels of education and that differences in education were generating legitimate differences in answers.

To reiterate, once our procedure identified response disparities above .30

s.d., we could not assume that the variables were in fact problematic. Instead, we merely treated the procedure as a means by which to identify potentially problematic variables among the hundreds at our disposal. We then had to examine the potentially problematic variables on a case-by-case basis to assess the true magnitude of the problem.

Overview of findings

The response disparities calculated on the basis of some 700 tables are presented in Addendum B. An approximate English translation of the question on which each variable in the sample is based may be found in the right-hand column; variable names and tape locations, in the two left-hand columns.[6] Asterisks have been inserted wherever a lack of cases, due to normal branching within the questionnaire, rendered the calculated response disparity unreliable.[7]

The findings in Addendum B are summarized in Table B.1. As the first line indicates, the median response disparity in all five tests was very low, ranging from .08 to .11 s.d. Likewise, the last line shows that the percentage of disparities exceeding .30 s.d. was particularly low (1 to 4 percent) in the tests of time-lapse, interviewer, and sex disparities. The percentage exceeding .30 s.d. in the tests of reluctance was somewhat higher than this (11 percent), as it was in the tests of ethnic disparities. However, as will be demonstrated below, many of these disparities can be easily explained on legitimate substantive grounds.

Though the response disparities in Addendum B are generally small, they are actually somewhat exaggerated, in part because sampling by nature generates some spurious large disparities (see above) and in part because our measure of disparity necessarily overstates the effect in certain variables (see Addendum A). In sum, then, the results give us considerable confidence that response effects generally do not contaminate the validity of the SIP survey.

Response disparities related to time lapse

Despite the small number of substantial response disparities observed above, some isolated variables may nevertheless suffer from substantial response

---

[6] We have occasionally used approximate translations so that we could add words to help readers understand questions outside the context of the questionnaire while keeping the table as short as possible.

[7] Twenty-two variables for which none of the five response disparities could be reliably calculated have been omitted from Addendum B to reduce its length. This, as well as the asterisks in Addendum B, accounts for the discrepancy between the 700 tables mentioned in this paragraph and the 1,000 mentioned above.

Table B.1. *Summary of response disparities in Addendum B*

	OUT	REL	JEW	INT	INTSEX	
					Men	Wom
Median response disparity	.09	.11	.10	.11	.08	.09
S.d. of response disparities	.08	.17	.35	.09	.07	.15
Number of disparities > .30	4	12	18	2	1	6
Number of disparities calculated	145	110	139	49	140	134
Percentage of disparities > .30	3	11	14	4	1	4

Note: OUT = time lapse; REL = reluctant to participate; JEW = Jewish; INT = interviewer's country of origin; INTSEX = interviewer's sex (Men = men respondents, Wom = women respondents).

effects, and these effects might well figure heavily in some analyses. We therefore turn now to a more detailed examination of all variables for which the calculated response disparity exceeds .30 s.d., as well as of those variables hypothesized in advance to be unusually susceptible to such effects.

First, consider disparities related to the time lapse between emigration and interview. These interest us for two reasons: Time lapse may have affected respondents' recall of events and attitudes in the Soviet Union; and experience in the West may have affected respondents' retrospective evaluations of their lives in the USSR.

Obviously, the only way to test time-lapse disparities definitively is to compare retrospective answers with independently verified information to which the questions refer. Fortunately, a number of methodological surveys permit such tests (Sudman and Bradburn 1974; Hindelang 1976; Powers, Goudy, and Keith 1978; Cherlin and Horiuchi 1980; Smith 1984). The results of such studies do indicate that the lapse of time may have detrimental effects on the accuracy of the reports. Although memory decay and forward telescoping may counteract each other to some extent, the general direction of errors appears to be toward underreporting events. Even with events we would consider highly salient, such as crimes that were reported to the police, there is underreporting. For retrospective reports of attitudes and simple demographic information, it is also clear that errors should be expected. However, the analysis of relationships between variables and estimates of values for the sample as a whole need not be drastically affected by such errors if the errors are randomly distributed.

Of course, the vast majority of surveys do not permit rigorous methodological tests of time-lapse effects because there is no possibility of comparing retrospective answers with answers given earlier or with independently verifiable facts; the SIP General Survey is no exception. Nevertheless, considerable confidence in the reliability of SIP respondents' recall has already been generated by Anderson and Silver (forthcoming), who compared the answers given by 163 married couples whose answers should have matched one another on certain questions.[8] They found a gratifyingly high level of agreement between spouses.

In this study, we have compared the answers given by the most recent emigrants (those whose interviews occurred less than 30 months from the time they emigrated) with those given by the earlier emigrants. The top five items in Table B.2 were designated in advance as items that might well suffer from time-lapse effects. They cover the respondents' evaluation of what is good about the USSR, how difficult it is to make American friends, the nature of super power relations, and the cause of productivity problems in the USSR. The entries in column 4 indicate that the response disparities turned out to be small. Columns 2 and 3 contain percentages from the tables on which the response disparities were calculated so that readers may judge for themselves how negligible the disparities were.

As was explained earlier, our analysis was not confined to variables that were hypothesized in advance to be particularly susceptible to response effects. In our sample of 169 variables, we also identified all variables for which the disparity exceeded .30 s.d. in the effort to find unexpected problematic variables. Only four variables (3 percent) did exceed this level. They are listed at the bottom of Table B.2 (items 6 through 9). The response disparity for living in the RSFSR (item 6) might be explained by changes in emigration trends from the various republics. We shall not offer explanations for the disparities in items 7 though 9. As was explained above, sampling by nature generates some disparities that would disappear with a different sample. Given the absence of several similar items generating similar response disparities, attempts to come up with an a posteriori explanation for items 7 through 9 would doubtless be unjustified.

Response disparities related to reluctance to participate

Respectable survey organizations endeavor to convert "soft refusals" to achieve a respectable response rate. However, in doing so they risk degrading the validity of the data with respondents who may give the appearance of cooperating when in fact they are providing misleading answers. Given that our respondents sometimes raised concerns about

---

[8] For example, spouses' estimates of living space in the USSR should match one another, and a husband's estimate of a wife's earnings should match the wife's own report.

Table B.2. *Disparities related to time lapse between emigration and interview*

(1)	(2)	(3)	(4)	(5)
	Time lapse		Response	
No.	Moderate	Short	disparity	Question (variable name; deck & column)
1##	61.3%	60.5%	.02	R disappointed in difficulty in making American friends. (DISFRDS; DKCOL:2273; *N*s:2,158 & 542)
2##			.10#	First way in which U.S. could learn from USSR. (USLEARN1; DKCOL:2347; *N*s: 2,044 and 510)
	15.0%	13.1%		SYSTEM OF EDUCATION
	22.4%	20.0%		CRIME; LEGAL SYSTEM
	5.9%	5.9%		MILITARY READINESS
3##			.07	R's LNP opinion on friendliness between the USSR and the United States. (HOSUSA; DKCOL:3753; *N*s:651 & 173)
	2.2%	1.7%		VERY FRIENDLY
	31.0%	29.5%		SOMEWHAT FRIENDLY
	18.4%	15.6%		NEUTRAL
	41.3%	43.9%		SOMEWHAT HOSTILE
	7.1%	9.2%		VERY HOSTILE
4##			.14#	What things in the present Soviet system should be kept? (KEEP1; DKCOL:3805; *N*s:650 & 158)
	25.1%	24.7%		HEALTH CARE
	21.4%	17.1%		KEEP NOTHING
	.9%	.0%		KEEP EVERYTHING
5##			.04#	Why was the productivity of labor declining? (YDOWN1; DKCOL:4150; *N*s:457 & 112)
	58.0%	58.0%		LACK INCENTIVES
	8.5%	7.1%		ALCOHOLISM
	9.0%	9.8%		APATHY
6	62.0%	80.4%	.38	R lived in RSFSR at least 6 months. (RSFSR6Mo; DKCOL:0413; *N*s:2,233 & 557)
7	17.5%	4.3%	.35	Warnings did discourage R from drinking. (DISCDRIN; DKCOL:3158; *N*s:656 & 161)
8			.34#	What was the second friend's religion? (BRELIGQ; DKCOL:2615; *N*s: 109 & 31)
	58.7%	41.9%		JEWISH
	35.8%	51.6%		ORTHODOX
	5.5%	6.4%		ALL OTHER
9	29.9%	14.3%	.34	R went to place of work for more housing space. (WORKPLC; DKCOL:2615; *N*s: 109 & 31)

Notes to Table B.2. (*contd.*)

Note: # indicates that the entries in columns 2 and 3 are abbreviated.
indicates that we considered these variables susceptible to response effects in advance of calculating them.
Caution: The percentages in these tables often *cannot* be properly interpreted as percentages of all respondents because only certain subsets of the respondents answered some questions.

possible repercussions to themselves or to family members in the USSR, we wanted to compare the results from willing and reluctant respondents, where the latter were defined as those who initially firmly declined to participate but who later agreed to do so, for example, after receiving a letter attesting to the legitimacy of the study.[9]

Again, our comparisons involved two kinds of variables: those we designated in advance as particularly susceptible to response effects (items 1, 2, 3, and 5 in Table B.3), and those that actually manifested disparities above .30 s.d. (items 4, 6 through 15). The first group includes items about avoiding the KGB, abortions, whether the respondent became angry at any point during the three-hour interview, and the respondents' willingness to be interviewed again. Only the question about being interviewed again manifested a response disparity above .30 s.d., and it is quite understandable that answers to that question would correlate with respondents' initial willingness to participate.

The largest disparity in the second group (item 4) is for the month of interview. This merely indicates that reluctant respondents were usually interviewed later than others. The large disparity for item 5 has already been discussed. The remaining 10 response disparities above .30 s.d., however, cannot be easily disregarded. We initially believed that differences in the age and education distributions of willing and reluctant respondents had generated the disparities; however, those differences turned out to be minimal, and controlling on education made little difference in the size of the disparities.

Although the disparities cannot be explained with antecedent or intervening variables, we are reassured by the fact that they also do not suggest a pattern of misleading answers to sensitive questions. Furthermore, these disparities do not necessarily indicate that answers from reluctant respondents are biased. Approximately 90 percent of their answers revealed very low disparities. Moreover, the whole point in attempting to convert refusals was to make sure that all viewpoints were represented properly. People who initially declined to participate might well have held different opinions than

[9] This implies that participants are not treated as reluctant in this analysis if they at first declined but were relatively easily persuaded to participate in a follow-up request.

Table B.3. *Disparities related to respondents' reluctance to be interviewed*

(1)	(2)	(3)	(4)	(5)
	R's reluctance		Response	
No.	Willing	Reluctant	disparity	Question (variable name; deck & column)
1##			.17	How easy/difficult was it to avoid the KGB? (AVOIDKGB; DKCOL: 1442; *N*s: 2,018 & 140)
	15.1%	24.3%		VERY EASY
	34.7%	33.6%		FAIRLY EASY
	28.6%	17.1%		FAIRLY DIFFICULT
	21.6%	25.0%		DIFFICULT
2##	3.4 times	3.4 times	.01	How many times did R have an abortion? (ABORTNO; DKCOL: 4328; *N*s: 310 & 32)
3##	15.9%	21.5%	.15	Did R become angry during the interview? (INTANGRY; DKCOL: 2418; *N*s: 2,530 & 214)
4			1.20#	Month of interview (INTMO; DKCOL: 2467; *N*s: 2,571 & 221)
	25.2%	0.0%		MARCH AND APRIL
	3.3%	26.2%		NOVEMBER AND DECEMBER
5##	88.8%	53.5%	1.12	R willing to be interviewed again. (RECONTCT; DKCOL: 2361; *N*s: 2,524 & 213)
6	52.9%	29.1%	.48	R didn't read *samizdat* because it wasn't available. (NOAVLSMZ; DKCOL: 2952; *N*s: 537 & 55)
7			.43	How often did R listen to BBC? (BBCFRE; DKCOL: 2510; *N*s: 535 & 37)
	33.5%	21.6%		ALMOST EVERY DAY
	49.0%	37.8%		AT LEAST ONCE A WEEK
	17.6%	40.5%		LESS THAN ONCE A WEEK
8	25.8%	42.5%	.38	R read books about Soviet culture. (SOVCULT; DKCOL: 2805; *N*s: 492 & 40)
9			.38	How satisfied was R with courtesy of medical personnel? (MEDCOURT; DKCOL: 3362; *N*s: 733 & 58)
	21.6%	36.2%		VERY SATISFIED
	48.0%	51.7%		SOMEWHAT SATISFIED
	20.1%	12.1%		SOMEWHAT DISSATISFIED
	10.4%	0.0%		VERY DISSATISFIED
10	68.3%	50.8%	.37	R had applied to a daytime university or institute. (DAYVUZAP; DKCOL: 0205; *N*s: 1,421 & 118)
11	30.0%	13.9%	.35	R listened to Radio Israel. (ISRLRAD2; DKCOL: 2521; *N*s: 842 & 79)

Table B.3. (*contd.*)

12	64.9%	48.9%	.34	R wanted to read more nonfiction but could not. (WANTNONF; DKCOL: 2821; *N*s: 522 & 45)
13			.34	How closely did R follow scientific achievements? (SCIENCE; DKCOL: 3105; *N*s: 836 & 77)
	7.7%	3.9%		VERY CLOSELY
	26.1%	19.5%		FAIRLY CLOSELY
	44.6%	36.4%		NOT TOO CLOSELY
	21.7%	40.3%		NOT AT ALL
14	50.4%	34.8%	.31	R read modern fiction. (MODFICT; DKCOL: 2815; *N*s: 716 & 69)
15			.31	Should nationality be included on internal passport? (NATPASS; DKCOL: 2629; *N*s: 828 & 74)
	8.3%	12.2%		INCLUDED
	79.0%	66.2%		OMITTED
	12.7%	21.6%		INDIFFERENT

Note: # indicates that the entries in columns 2 and 3 are abbreviated.
indicates that we considered these variables susceptible to response effects in advance of calculating them.
Caution: The percentages in these tables often *cannot* be properly interpreted as percentages of all respondents because only certain subsets of the respondents answered some questions.

others – opinions that correlated with their willingness to participate. Securing their participation has contributed to the validity of the study.

Response disparities related to ethnicity

Perhaps the most common question about the methodology underlying the Soviet Interview Project is this: "But aren't the emigrants mostly Jews?" The answer, of course, is yes. Soviet regulations permit applications for emigration from members of ethnic groups for which a homeland exists outside the USSR.[10] Hence, more than 200,000 Soviet Jews and Germans have emigrated since 1967. The Germans have for the most part settled in Germany; roughly half of the Jews have settled in the United States rather than in Israel.

From a statistical standpoint, the sampling in any survey affects results when the criteria on which selection is based correlate with processes under

[10] They also permit applications from Soviet citizens who have close relatives outside the USSR. It is on this basis that most Armenians apply to emigrate. Of course, many who apply to emigrate are denied exit visas.

study. Thus, to the extent that we study topics affected by ethnicity in the USSR, our results naturally differ from those that would otherwise be obtained. But by the same token, to the extent that we study topics that are unrelated to ethnicity per se in the USSR, the Jewishness of our sample should not bias findings.

Table B.4 confirms this expectation. Consider, first, the 18 variables for which the response disparity exceeds .30 s.d. (items 4 through 21). Of these, 11 have clear ethnic content (items 4 through 12, 15, and 17). Another three disparities were generated by the fact that Jews in our sample were, on the average, somewhat older than non-Jews (items 14, 18, and 19). Yet another two disparities were generated by the fact that non-Jews in our sample were, on the average, somewhat better educated than Jews (items 13 and 21).[11] Only two of the 18 items remain unexplained. These both pertain to the reading tastes of respondents (items 16 and 20).

Many of the variables just discussed were identified in advance as susceptible to ethnic response disparities (items 5, 7, 8, 11, 12, 15, and 17). Three such variables that did not yield large disparities are listed at the top of Table B.4.

To sum up, discounting questions that bear directly on ethnicity – which *ought* to manifest disparities of the sort we observed – we found virtually no problematic variables. These findings complement those of another detailed study of ethnic bias in our data, conducted by Donna Bahry (1987).

Response disparities related to interviewers' countries of origin

The majority of interviews were conducted by Westerners who were fluent in Russian. However, 85 interviews were conducted by 11 former Soviet citizens (now naturalized U.S. citizens) who immigrated to the United States during the late 1960s and early 1970s. Although the SIP team and NORC went to great lengths to insure that all interviewers were trained to minimize interviewer effects, it nevertheless seemed interesting and advisable to test for effects. Unfortunately, the small number of interviews conducted by these 11 interviewers rendered an ideal test impossible to execute. For instance, none of the questions from the three questionnaire supplements could be tested because only a third of the 85 interviews included any one of the three supplements. Likewise, even normal branching within the core questionnaire sometimes reduced the case base to a level so small as to render comparisons unreliable.

[11] The correlation between education and ethnicity results from the stratification of our sample. It does not necessarily reflect conditions in the USSR or among Soviet emigrants in the United States.

Table B.4. *Disparities related to respondents' ethnicity*

(1)	(2)	(3)	(4)	(5)
	R's ethnicity		Response	
No.	Non-Jew	Jew	disparity	Question (variable name; deck & column)
1##	30.9%	21.6%	.20	Was friend *A* religious? (ABELIEV; DKCOL: 2571; *N*s: 123 & 685)
2##	66.3%	72.3%	.13	Stalin's actions were contrary to Marx. (JOEMARX; DKCOL: 3721; *N*s: 104 & 639)
3##	11.4%	11.6%	.01	R practiced Soviet rituals when child was born. (CIVILRIT; DKCOL: 2531; *N*s: 114 & 674)
4	93.0%	14.7%	3.07	R attended a church (as opposed to a synagogue, unsanctioned prayer house, etc.); asked only of those who said they attended religious services. (GOCHURCH; DKCOL: 925; *N*s: 171 & 756)
5##	5.2%	44.9%	1.79	R observed Rosh Hashanah (ROSHHASH; DKCOL: 854; *N*s: 135 & 786)
6	10.5%	60.4%	1.62#	R considers marriage between relative and Ukrainian undesirable (WEDUKR1; DKCOL: 2640; *N*s: 133 & 775)
7##	21.2%	65.4%	1.08#	What was religion of R's second friend? (BRELIGQ; DKCOL: 2615; *N*s: 33 & 107)
8##			1.06	How would R view Jews as coworkers? (WEDJEW2; DKCOL: 2648; *N*s: 134 & 782)
	4.5%	25.7%		DESIRABLE
	94.0%	72.8%		INDIFFERENT
	1.5%	1.5%		UNDESIRABLE
9	16.8%	38.4%	.58	R listened to Radio Israel. (ISRLRAD; DKCOL: 1859; *N*s: 346 & 1,986)
10	9.3%	23.7%	.50	R treated [differently] by work supervisor because of nationality. (TREATNAT; DKCOL: 742; *N*s: 97 & 514)
11##	14.2%	31.1%	.49	R listened to Radio Israel (asked of a different group than answered ISRLRAD above). (ISRLRAD 2; DKCOL: 2521; *N*s: 134 & 787)
12##	1.8%	8.3%	.49	R lit Friday night Sabbath candles. (SABBTH2; DKCOL: 2541; *N*s: 395 & 2397)
13	81.3%	64.2%	.44	R applied to a daytime university (VUZ) (asked of those who said they applied somewhere). (DAYVUZAP; DKCOL: 205; *N*s: 246 & 1,293)

Table B.4. (*contd.*)

(1)	(2)	(3)	(4)	(5)
14	11.5%	25.6%	.44	R received pension or grant. (RECVPENS; DKCOL: 4231; *N*s:130 & 802)
15##			.40	Should nationality be included on internal Soviet passport? (NATPASS; DKCOL: 2629; *N*s: 131 & 771)
	11.5%	8.2%		INCLUDED
	61.1%	80.8%		OMITTED
	27.5%	11.0%		INDIFFERENT
16	40.6%	20.8%	.40	R read samizdat and tamizdat on international politics. (INTPOLIT; DKCOL: 2968; *N*s: 64 & 216)
17##	44.3%	62.7%	.37#	How important is nationality in joining the Communist party? VERY IMPORTANT (INFNAT; DKCOL: 3609; *N*s: 97 & 617)
18	34.5%	45.3%	.34#	R is currently retired. (OTHCURR; DKCOL: 2314; *N*s: 58 & 470)
19	38.3 years	43.1 years	.34	R's age at end of LNP. (AGEELNP; DKCOL: 962; *N*s: 395 & 2,397)
20	75.3%	61.4%	.32	R wanted to read nonfiction, which was unavailable. (WANTNONF; DKCOL: 2821; *N*s: 93 & 474)
21			.30	Spouse's educational level. (SPEDUCQ; DKCOL: 1666; *N*s: 308 & 1,854)
	.6%	.6%		NO FORMAL SCHOOLING
	2.3%	4.4%		ELEMENTARY
	4.2%	9.4%		INCOMPLETE SECONDARY
	2.9%	3.8%		VOCATIONAL-TECHNICAL
	14.0%	14.7%		COMPLETE SECONDARY
	15.3%	22.2%		SECONDARY SPECIALIZED
	54.5%	42.3%		HIGHER EDUCATION
	6.2%	2.6%		ADVANCED DEGREE

Note: # indicates that the entries in columns 2 and 3 are abbreviated.
indicates that we considered these variables susceptible to response effects in advance of calculating them.
Caution: The percentages in these tables often *cannot* be properly interpreted as percentages of all respondents because only certain subsets of the respondents answered some questions.

Nevertheless, we can offer some conclusions on the basis of 49 variables that *did* have large enough case bases. As Table B.5 indicates, only two of the 49 variables manifested response disparities greater than .30 s.d. The first of those (month of interview) has utterly no substantive import: It merely reflects the fact that the former Soviet citizens who conducted interviews started work later than other interviewers. We cannot readily explain the second large disparity (whether the respondent applied to a daytime

Table B.5. *Disparities related to interviewers' origins*

(1)	(2)	(3)	(4)	(5)
	Interviewer origin		Response	Question (variable name; deck &
No.	Russian	Western	disparity	column)
1##			.03	How easy/difficult was it to avoid the KGB? (AVOIDKGB; DKCOL: 1442; *N*s: 74 & 1,834)
	14.9%	15.3%		VERY EASY
	35.1%	34.7%		FAIRLY EASY
	29.7%	27.8%		FAIRLY DIFFICULT
	20.3%	22.2%		VERY DIFFICULT
2##	13.3%	11.2%	.06	R discussed black market clothing purchases with coworkers or classmates. (BLACKCOW; DKCOL: 3729; *N*s: 83 & 2,357)
3##	9.5%	8.3%	.04	R criticized government officials to relative. (CRITREL; DKCOL: 3737; *N*s: 84 & 2,368)
4##	40.0%	27.7%	.25	USSR's foreign policy would be the same even with a different government. (FORPOLIC; DKCOL: 3745; *N*s: 30 & 676)
5	24.7%	12.6%	.48#	Month of interview (INTMO; DKCOL: 2467; *N*s: 85 & 2,391)
6	50.9%	69.0%	.36	R applied to a daytime university (VUZ); asked only of those who indicated that they had applied somewhere. (DAYVUZAP; DKCOL: 205; *N*s: 55 & 1,318)

Note: # indicates that the entries in columns 2 and 3 are abbreviated.
indicates that we considered these variables susceptible to response effects in advance of calculating them.
Caution: The percentages in these tables often *cannot* be properly interpreted as percentages of all respondents because only certain subsets of the respondents answered some questions.

university). More interesting are the variables we hypothesized to be susceptible to this response effect in advance of calculating the disparities. Items 1 through 4 include potentially sensitive questions to which respondents might have changed answers when confronted with an interviewer who had emigrated from the USSR. As the table indicates, no appreciable differences materialized in the questions pertaining to the KGB, the black market, or criticism of Soviet government officials. The apparent disparity on answers to the question about foreign policy was somewhat greater, though still only .25 s.d.

These results do not prove that, in general, using ex-Soviet citizens as interviewers would have a negative or positive effect on surveys of emigrants, because only a very select group of ex-Soviets served as interviewers in the project. The results do seem to indicate that the Soviet interviewers we employed introduced no substantial biases in the data.

Disparities related to the sex of interviewers and respondents

In analyzing disparities related to the correspondence between interviewer's and respondent's sex, we made separate calculations for men and women respondents. This approach allowed for the possibility that response disparities among male respondents would differ from those observed among female respondents. For example, "macho" males might have inflated their reported earnings or alcohol consumption to impress a female interviewer, but female respondents probably would not have done so. Hence, Addendum B contains two columns related to sex disparities; corresponding to those two columns, Tables B.6 and B.7 report separate results from male and female respondents.

For men respondents, none of the eight variables deemed most susceptible to response disparities revealed a disparity over .30 s.d.; in fact, no disparity even exceeded .17 s.d. Of particular interest are the responses to questions about birth control and about the good life in the USSR (items 1 and 2). As the entries in columns 2 and 3 (Table B.6) indicate, men differed very little in answering interviewers of either sex. Indeed, only one response disparity out of 140 exceeded .30 s.d.

Table B.7 gives much the same impression about women respondents. Again, their answers to questions about birth control and about the good life in the USSR differed little between male and female interviewers (items 1 and 2, Table B.7). Of the five variables deemed susceptible to response disparities (items 1 through 4 and 8), only one actually yielded a response disparity above .30 s.d. Though we expected differences in reports of rape, the differences turned up in reports of robbery (item 8). We see no noteworthy pattern among the variables that did manifest response disparities exceeding .30 s.d. (items 5 through 10).

Conclusions

Let us return to the issue raised at the beginning of this appendix: To what extent do the unintended effects of questionnaire design and interviewer performance threaten the validity of this survey? We would be too bold if we claimed that our analysis entirely rules out the possibility of significant

Table B.6. *Disparities related to interviewers' sex: men respondents only*

(1)	(2)	(3)	(4)	(5)
	Interviewer's sex		Response	
No.	Male	Female	disparity	Question (variable name; deck; column)
1##	3.6%	2.3%	.07	Couple used IUD for birth control. (IUD; DKCOL: 4313; Ns: 555 & 647)
2##			.05	Who has the good life in the USSR? (GOODLIFE; DKCOL: 1623; Ns: 551 & 639)
	70.2%	67.9%		MEN
	26.9%	29.0%		EQUAL
	2.9%	3.1%		WOMEN
3##	10.4%	15.4%	.17#	Warnings did not discourage R from drinking. (DISCDRIN; DKCOL: 3158; Ns: 164 & 214)
4##	9.0%	5.9%	.11	Did not serve in military because of family hardship (NOMILFAM; DKCOL: 1869; Ns: 111 & 169)
5##	16.9%	21.1%	.07#	R did not follow scientific achievements at all. (SCIENCE; DKCOL: 3105; Ns: 172 & 232)
6##	58.1%	54.7%	.07	Did you limit your alcohol intake for health reasons? (NOTDRINK; DKCOL: 3150; Ns: 172 & 232)
7##	1.7 times	2.1 times	.16	Number of times unemployed for more than 30 days in five years. (NOUNEMP; DKCOL: 1142; Ns: 33 & 54)
8##	139.4 rubles	138.5 rubles	.01	Gross monthly income before first move. (GROSMOV1; DKCOL: 4365; Ns: 63 & 63)
9	99.3%	96.5%	.35	Did R ever read any fiction? (READFICT; DKCOL: 2836; Ns: 151 & 200)

Note: # indicates that the entries in columns 2 and 3 are abbreviated.
indicates that we considered these variables susceptible to response effects in advance of calculating them.
Caution: The percentage in these tables often *cannot* be properly interpreted as percentages of all respondents because only certain subsets of the respondents answered some questions.

response effects. In the first place, some types of variables might have been poorly represented in our one-in-eight sample, thereby escaping detection.

Table B.7. *Disparities related to interviewers' sex: women respondents only*

(1)	(2)	(3)	(4)	(5)
	Interviewer's sex		Response	
No.	Male	Female	disparity	Question (variable name; deck & column)
1##	5.4%	3.8%	.07	Couple used IUD for birth control. (IUD; DKCOL: 4313; Ns: 624 & 939)
2##			.04	Who has the good life in the USSR? (GOODLIFE; DKCOL: 1623; Ns: 551 & 639)
	71.3%	69.4%		MEN
	25.8%	28.6%		EQUAL
	2.9%	1.9%		WOMEN
3##	19.9%	14.3%	.14#	Warnings did not discourage R from drinking. (DISCDRIN; DKCOL: 3158; Ns: 166 & 272)
4##	3.6 abortions	3.2 abortions	.13	How many abortions did R have in USSR? (Asked only of women who reported that they had had an abortion.) (ABORTNO; DKCOL: 4328; Ns: 151 & 191)
5			1.53	Why didn't R smoke? (YNOCIGAR; DKCOL: 3168; Ns: 150 & 236)
	10.0%	14.8%		MORAL REASONS
6	15.0%	30.1%	.42	R treated differently by supervisor because of nationality. (TREATNAT; DKCOL: 742; Ns: 120 & 193)
7	65.6%	45.8%	.42#	Rs second friend was Jewish. (BRELIGQ: DKCOL: 2615; Ns: 32 & 48)
8##			.38#	R or R's family a victim of what crime? (CRIVIC; DKCOL: 3449; Ns: 36 & 58)
	8.3%	27.6%		ROBBERY
	2.8%	3.4%		ATTEMPTED RAPE
9	1.7 times	1.3 times	.37	Number of times unemployed for more than 30 days in five years. (NOUNEMP; DKCOL: 1142; Ns: 34 & 50)
10	43.4%	30.7%	.33#	Pension decreased income a lot. (PENSINC; DKCOL: 4259; Ns: 53 & 88)

Note: # indicates that the entries in columns 2 and 3 are abbreviated.
indicates that we considered these variables susceptible to response effects in advance of calculating them.
Caution: The percentages in these tables often *cannot* be properly interpreted as percentages of all respondents because only certain subsets of the respondents answered some questions.

Second, other analysts may see problematic patterns where we saw none. Indeed, in reporting the percentage distributions for variables whose response disparities exceeded .30 s.d., we were intentionally making it feasible for others to search for patterns.

Nevertheless, by normal survey standards, we have forced a wide range of variables through an extraordinarily large filter, testing for possible disparities in time lapse, reluctance to participate, ethnicity, interviewer's country of origin, and sex correspondence between interviewers and respondents. Discounting the large disparities that could be dismissed for valid substantive reasons, the results proved quite reassuring.

Addendum A

Method for calculating response disparities

Our method for calculating response disparities for quantitative variables (variables based on interval or ratio scales) is outlined in the text. It seems so straightforward as to require no further explanation except as regards the calculation of standard deviations. Note that the standard deviation was calculated on the basis of the early emigrant group.[12] If the standard deviation had been calculated on the basis of the later emigrant group, the response disparity would doubtless have turned out to be different than .002. This rather arbitrary element in the calculation of the response disparity could have been avoided by using the standard deviation for the pooled observations from both groups. To determine how much difference using the pooled observations would have made, we recalculated the response disparities for one of the five factors: time lapse between emigration and interview (Addendum B, column "out" and Table B.2). The response disparities based on pooled-observation standard deviations correlated $r = .99$ with those reported in this chapter, and none differed from our reported values by more than two percentage points. We conclude, therefore, that our choice of one base group rather than the other exerted no appreciable effect on our results.

As for the categoric variable illustrated in the text, its standard deviation was calculated with the well-known formula for the standard deviation of a dichotomous variable: the square root of $P \cdot (1 - P)$. The square root of $(.018) \cdot (1 - .018)$ is .133, the standard deviation given in the text and used in the calculation of the response disparity between Jewish and non-Jewish respondents.

Unfortunately, calculating response disparities for variables based on

---

[12] The base groups for the other factors were as follows: willing participants, non-Jews, ex-Soviet interviewers, and male interviewers.

ordinal or nominal scales is considerably less straightforward than for variables based on ratio or interval scales. Consider the variable AVOIDKGB (DKCOL 1442), which contains answers to a question about how easy it was to avoid trouble with the KGB. Responses were distributed as follows:

	Time lapse	
	moderate	short
Very easy to avoid (1)	16.4%	12.6%
Fairly easy (2)	34.1	36.7
Fairly difficult (3)	27.7	28.8
Very difficult (4)	21.8	21.8
	100.0%	99.9%
N	1,712	444

Since this table contains three degrees of freedom, no single index can uniquely represent all the differences between the distributions in the two columns (unless one treats the ordinal variable like an interval one). Since response disparities would most likely affect the percentages in the extreme cells, we calculated a response effect for the top and bottom rows,[13] then averaged their values to arrive at a single index for the table. In the top row, the percentage difference is 3.8; the standard deviation of AVOIDKGB for people in the left-hand column is 37.0 percent. Thus, for the top row, the response disparity is .102; for the bottom row, it is obviously .0, since the two percentages are identical. The overall index of response disparity is the average of the absolute values of these two quantities: .05 of one standard deviation. This small amount, in our opinion, correctly reflects the substantively inconsequential differences between the two distributions. Our approach, by basing calculations on the extreme rows, tended to enlarge the estimates in comparison to those which would have been obtained had we used all rows. In other words, any problems with response disparities would have seemed even less than we reported had we chosen to base our measure on all rows in the tables.

In a few cases, we were faced with tables based on polytomous variables. In these cases, we based calculations on the first and last rows in the table,

---

[13] When a top (or bottom) row contained less than 10 percent of all the cases, we took enough adjacent rows so that the estimate would be based on a relatively large number of cases—as long as doing so did not create an overlap in the rows being used at the top and bottom of the table.

making certain that at least 10 percent of the cases were in each set of rows. Since our objective was to apply a filter that would pick up problematic variables, this approach sufficed. Had we been calculating a unique index for the table, this would have been unsatisfactory because there was no basis for ordering the rows.

The cutoff point of .30 s.d. was unavoidably somewhat arbitrary. Everybody would no doubt agree than 1.0 s.d. should be considered sizable; most people would consider .50 s.d. worth talking about. To put our data to a more stringent test, we chose an even lower cutoff point. In examining tables for which the response disparity was .30, we usually found the differences barely worth exploring. This, however, ultimately amounts to a matter of taste. On the basis of Addendum B, those who disagree should be able to pursue their investigation to lower cutoff points.

It should perhaps be emphasized that statistical significance would not have constituted a valid alternative criterion by which to assess response effects in this methodological study. For questions answered by a large number of respondents, we naturally found some very small disparities that were statistically significant (assuming that tests of significance are warranted under these circumstances).[14] However, the statistical significance of these small disparities did not render them worthy of discussion. Given that response disparities were used primarily to identify potentially problematic variables in this study, we decided that the information contained in the standard errors did not warrant doubling the quantity of numbers reported in this appendix. Suffice it to say, virtually all response disparities greater than .30 s.d. *were* statistically significant.

---

[14] Technically speaking, the standard tests of significance produced by such statistical packages as SAS or SPSS-X require adjustments for the lack of independence among the observations (e.g., the 85 interviews conducted by naturalized recent Soviet emigrants were conducted by 11 people, not by 85) and for the lack of a simple probability sample.

Addendum B: *Response disparities in the SIP General Survey*

VARIABLE	DKCOL	OUT	REL	JEW	INT	INTSEX		Question
						men	wom	
DADBORNQ	133	.07	.04	.21	.07	.02	.01	In what year was your father born?
DADBELV	149	.09	.01	.29	.01	.03	.06	Is/was he [your father] religious?
MOMYRSCH	167	.05	.09	.13	.04	.01	.07	Altogether, how many years of schooling did she [your mother] complete?
DAYVUZAP	205	.13	.37	.44	.36	.00	.04	Which of these did you ever apply to in the Soviet Union? [university or institute – daytime]
DATEKYRS	221	.11	.18	.11	*	.04	.08	For how many years did you ever attend a daytime *tekhnikum* or other secondary specialized school?
NOGRADAP	237	.13	*	*	*	.00	*	How many graduate schools did you ever apply to?
OCCTRAIN	252	.15	.03	.19	.15	.01	.06	Which of the reasons on this card was important in your decision to attend that [last] school?
MILINST	269	.12	.21	.03	.03	.00	.02	Did you receive any kind of military instructions there? [last school]
REACHLEV	321	.03	.02	.17	.07	.00	.01	Did you reach the level of education that you wanted to in the Soviet Union?
AGEJOBI	357	.09	.20	.11	.19	.01	.02	How old were you when you started that job? [first job after highest education]
RSFSR6MO	413	.38	.29	.28	.20	.06	.04	Which Soviet republics did you ever live in for at least six months? [RSFSR]
TADZH6MO	429	.03	.00	.02	.10	.01	.02	Which Soviet republics did you ever live in for at least six months?

Note: * = No measure computed; *N* of small group < 30; DKCOL = deck & column; OUT = time lapse; REL = reluctant to participate; JEW = Jewish; INT = interviewer's country of origin INTSEX = interviewer's sex (men = men respondents, wom = women respondents).

Variable	ID							Question
YRSMOVED	445	.17	.08	.12	.10	.15	.09	I would like to know the years in which you changed your place of residence in the Soviet Union?
WKBEFLNP	659	.05	.05	.10	*	.26	.04	Did you ever have a job in a state or cooperative enterprise or organization before (end of LNP)?
PRTYAPPQ	724	.04	*	.01	*	.13	.10	What level of the party apparatus was responsible for this position?
TREATNAT	742	.06	.14	.50	*	.06	.42	Why were you treated (better/worse)? [by the supervisor at your job]
WKENDLNP	758	.08	.22	.05	.01	.08	.07	Did respondent work in end of LNP?
JPRVOCCQ	805	.03	*	.13	*	.14	.06	What kind of private work did you do?
ROSHHASH	854	.15	.02	1.79	*	.05	.07	What religious practices did you observe during your last normal period? [Rosh Hashanah]
GORELIG	870	.15	.06	.25	.28	.01	.08	Did you ever attend or take part in any kind of religious services then? [during LNP]
GOCHURCH	925	.15	.24	3.07	.06	.04	.04	Was that in a synagogue, church, unsanctioned prayer house, informal gathering, such as in a home?
AGEELNP	962	.10	.06	.34	.12	.05	.02	Subtract B from A. [year of birth subtracted from end of LNP]
VALUFURN	1106	.00	.08	.01	.08	.06	.05	What was the value of the furniture? (That is, what could you have sold it for in end of LNP?)
HAVHOUSE	1126	.05	.06	.00	.06	.01	.10	In (end of LNP), did (you/your family) own a house or cooperative apartment?
NOUNEMP	1142	.09	*	.19	*	.16	.37	How many such times were there during those five years? [when R was unemployed for 30 days or more]
SATEDUC	1166	.02	.19	.22	.07	.10	.09	In (end of LNP), how satisfied or dissatisfied were you with opportunities for higher education?
CHGINJOB	1174	.15	.09	.09	.05	.02	.05	Comparing (LNP) with (5 yrs. earlier), how much of a change (better or worse) was there in your job?

Addendum B (contd.)

VARIABLE	DKCOL	OUT	REL	JEW	INT	INTSEX men	INTSEX wom	Question
ACT1GPQ	1216	.24	*	.22	*	.07	*	What action was taken? (First action) [in response to contacting govt. official about problem]
CONMEDNO	1233	.05	*	*	*	*	*	About how many times did you write such a letter or make such a call during that time? [media contact]
ELECTYPE	1315	.13	*	.07	*	.07	.08	Was this a local, union republic, or all-union election? [last election R worked in]
LEADWKCO	1339	.22	*	*	*	.14	.22	Were you a leader, an organizer, or an officer? [in committee at work]
LEADART	1348	.09	*	.12	*	.21		During your last normal period, did you ever take a leading role in the (art show/reading/concerts)?
PROTEST	1371	.23	.04	.20		.10	.02	During your last normal period, did you ever take part in an open protest against some Soviet policy?
AVOIDKGB	1442	.05	.17	.06	.03	.02	.03	During LNP, was it easy to avoid trouble with KGB, fairly easy, fairly difficult, or very difficult?
CLOSSHOP	1573	.17	.07	.10	.07	.03	.02	Between T1 and end of LNP, did you receive legal access to special rations, or closed shops?
NATHIED	1614	.09	.12	.23	*	.16	.08	[Which nationality treated best in] access to higher education?
GOODLIFE	1623	.08	.28	.10	.24	.05	.04	Taking everything into account, who has the better life in the Soviet Union – men or women?
SPEMIG	1639	.09	.01	.06	.14	.06	.01	Did (he/she) [spouse] emigrate from the Soviet Union?
SPEDUCQ	1666	.19	.22	.30	.22	.05	.17	What was your (husband's/wife's) highest level of education in (end of LNP)?

Variable	ID	1	2	3	4	5	6	Question
JSPOCCQ	1710	.02	.07	.15	.06	.18	.12	What was his/her specialty on that job (in end of LNP)/just before he/she left it)? [spouse's job]
MANAGHON	1743	.03	.11	.22	.04	.10	.05	How many of the people in charge of the management of industry were honest?
MANAGCOM	1751	.29	.06	.10	.06	.06	.04	How many of the people in charge of the management of industry were competent?
PROFINF	1759	.08	.05	.17	.11	.07	.05	Influence of a professor at Moscow State University
DOCINF	1775	.07	.04	.13	.04	.07	.10	Influence of a medical doctor
KGBPRIV	1819	.13	.07	.13	.09	.10	.03	Privilege of a colonel in the KGB
COLEARN	1829	.03	.01	.22	.03	.03	.05	How much did a colonel in the army earn?
INDRIGHT	1840	.13	.17	.14	.20	.05	.13	Rights of accused versus rights of society in crimes in the Soviet Union.
FUNDCRIM	1851	.06	.04	.08	.06	.30	.08	Reducing the crime rate... were they spending too much, too little, or the right amount on that?
ISRLRAD	1859	.12	.13	.19	.58	.19	.11	[Hand card.] Which of these [radio stations] did you listen to during that year? [last year of LNP]
NOMILFAM	1869	*	.11	*	.21	*	.09	Why not? [never served in the military]
YRRESVQ	1918	*	.17	*	.20	*	.02	When did you leave the reserves? (Year)
MILEMER	2068	.03	.02	*	.12	*	.18	Did you ever engage in civil emergencies, such as fires, or civilian clean-up maintenance?
GODUTY	2230	*	.12	*	*	*	.05	Did you (always) go? [when called to the reserves or to active duty]
CHGJOB	2241	.04	.03	.04	.02	.09	.14	Did you change, lose, or quit your job or your place in school because of leaving Soviet Union?
FAMLOSTS	2257	.01	.23	.05	.09	.00	.14	Did anyone living with you change, lose, or quit a job or place in school due to your leaving USSR?
DISFRDS	2273	.03	.06	.19	.07	.08	.02	Would he/she be disappointed by the difficulty of making close American friends?
OTHCURR	2314	.05	.14	*	.34	.11	.06	What is that? [what is R currently doing?]
FAMFRODT	2328	.03	.01	.06	.05			From which of these sources do you get this news? [news of the USSR]

Addendum B (*contd.*)

VARIABLE	DKCOL	OUT	REL	JEW	INT	INTSEX		Question
						men	*wom*	
USLEARN1	2347	.10	.02	.06	.10	.07	.02	In what ways do you think the United States could learn from the Soviet Union? (first way)
RECONTCT	2361	.17	1.12	.07	.13	06	.02	That's all the questions. Would you mind if we got in touch with you again?
OTHHELP	2406	.00	.15	.10	.23	.06	.11	Did the respondent ever ask anyone else for help with any of the questions?
INTANGRY	2418	.04	.15	.03	.20	.12	.10	Did the respondent ever become angry or impatient during the interview?
INTMO	2467	.26	1.20	.09	.48	.07	.01	Date of interview (month)
BBCFRE	2510	.16	.43	.13	*	.13	.24	Did you listen to the BBC almost every day, at least once a week, or less often than that?
ISRLRAD2	2521	.13	.35	.49	*	.18	.10	Did R listen to Radio Israel?
CIVILRIT	2531	.17	.10	.01	*	.01	.04	Did you practice any New Soviet rituals when your child was born, such as naming ceremony or christening?
SABBATH2	2541	.03	.09	.49	.14	.06	.06	[*Hand card.*] Which, if any, of these religious practices do you engage in now? [Friday night Sabbath candles]
VARDAN2	2557	.02	.02			.06		[*Hand card.*] Which, if any, of these religious practices do you engage in now? [celebrate Vardanats]
ABELIEV	2571	.04	.19	.20	*	.06	.07	Was he/she [closest friend] religious?
BRELIGQ	2615	.34	*	1.08	*	*	.42	What was (his/her) [second closest friend's] religion?
NATPASS	2629	.21	.31	.40	*	.02	.17	Did you think during your LNP that nationality should be kept in the internal passport?

Variable		Question						
WEDUKR1	2640	– During LNP if relative had married a Ukrainian, would you have regarded it as desirable or undesirable?	.06	.03	*	1.62	.08	.03
WEDJEW2	2648	During LNP, if coworker were Jewish, would you regard this as desirable, undesirable, or no diff.?	.05	.02	*	1.06	.15	.03
WEDBURI3	2656	During LNP, if supervisor at work were a Buriat, would that be desirable, undesirable, or no diff.?	.06	.13	*	.13	.10	.08
WORSPOLI	2668	In which of these times was Soviet policy the worst for nationalities?	.04	.16	*	.11	.18	.06
PAPER1	2711	What newspaper did you read most often?	.11	.13	*	.21	.27	.09
PAPER3MO	2730	How many times per month did you read (newspaper)?	*	*	*	.69	*	*
CONCERTS	2753	During your last normal period in the Soviet Union, did you go to music concerts?	.06	.05	*	.09	.02	.06
YNOTI	2761	Why couldn't you do more of that? (first reason) [cultural activities R could not do as often as wanted]	.04	.10	*	.24	*	.27
SOVCULT	2805	I'd like to know what kinds of nonfiction you read during that year. Which of these kinds of books?	.14	.04	*	.01	.38	.05
WANTNONF	2821	Are there any books listed on that card that you would have liked to read more of, but could not?	.12	.01	*	.32	.34	.18
READFICT	2836	Did R read any fiction (Q. 31)?	.13	.35	*	.13	.13	.04
MODFICT	2851	[Hand card.] Which of these kinds of books did you read? [modern foreign fiction]	.06	.12	*	.25	.31	.26
WANTWW2	2912	Which ones (did you want to read more of, but couldn't)? [novels about the Great Patriotic War]	.19	.08	*	.01	*	.13
RUSAUTH2	2929	Who were your favorite Russian or Soviet authors of fiction? (second one)	.20	.11	*	.15	.13	.06
NOAVLSMZ	2952	Was that because they were not available where you lived? [samizdat or tamizdat]	.06	.04	*	.00	.48	.17

399

Addendum B (*contd.*)

VARIABLE	DKCOL	OUT	REL	JEW	INT	INTSEX men	INTSEX wom	Question
INTPOLIT	2968	.04	*	.40	*	.04	.19	Which of these did you read during your last normal period? [*samizdat* or *tamizdat* – internat'l politics]
PAYSAMZ	3022	.05	*	.06	*	.25	.14	When receiving *samizdat*, did you pay for, borrow, exchange something, or was it given to you?
FOLKMUSI	3034	.10	.04	.15	*	.01	.00	Which of these kinds of musical performances did you attend – folk/ethnic music concerts?
WESTFILM	3048	.01	.03	.07	*	.13	.09	What kind of foreign films were shown in (hometown) – West European or American movies?
PRINTS	3060	.11	.01	.05	*	.06	.02	Which of these kinds of art did you enjoy? [prints and drawings]
AUTOSTR1	3071	.14	.26	.08	*	.04	.18	Would you have tried to get more information about that or not? [strike at an auto plant]
SCIENCE	3105	.10	.34	.08	*	.07	.04	During your LNP, did you follow scientific achievement closely, fairly closely, not closely, or not at all?
SOLVCRME	3113	.15	.19	.07	*	.16	.16	Did you believe Soviet technology could solve most, some, or none of the problems in the field of crime?
LEASTBAN	3121	.09	.18	.27	*	.08	.02	In which of these times was there the least censorship?
MEATFRE	3134	.05	.03	.09	*	.09	.16	About how often did you eat meat? [during last year of LNP]
EGGSFRE	3142	.08	.01	.04	*	.13	.12	About how often did you eat eggs? [during last year of LNP]

Variable	ID							Question
NOTDRINK	3150	.10	.03	.04	*	.07	.16	Did you avoid or limit your intake of beer, wine vodka, or cognac for health reasons?
DISCDRIN	3158	.35	.07	.12	*	.17	.14	In your experience, did these warnings discourage you personally, or people you know, from drinking?
YNOCIGAR	3168	.16	.17	.10	*	.18	1.53	What was your main reason for (not smoking/giving up smoking)?
WORKELNP	3205	.05	.05	.05	*	.05	.16	Did R work or go to school in (end of LNP)?
SHELTLOG	3213	.02	.16	.04	*	.10	.13	Do you remember the location of the civil defense shelter closest to where you lived in (end of LNP)?
WORKPLC	3312	.34	*	.07		.26	.13	Did you go to the housing dept. of local govt., housing committee or another org. or inst.? [for living space]
REPACT	3339	*	*	*	*	*	.19	How satisfied or dissatisfied were you with treatment you received from (answer #5)? [apt. maintenance]
MEDCOURT	3362	.05	.38	.29	*	.10	.01	How satisfied or dissatisfied were you with the courtesy and helpfulness of medical personnel?
MEDPROT1	3406	.08	*	.13	*	.06	.10	What did you do? (first thing) [when used protektsiia or znakomstva to get better medical treatment]
PRIVWAIT	3421	.10	*	.06	*	.08	.06	How satisfied or dissatisfied were you with the amount of time you had to wait for treatment?
PARTICIP	3432	.13	.19	.11	*	.14	.12	People should be able to participate in any org. even if org. opposes govt. laws. [agree or disagree]
FEWLEAD	3440	.10	.15	.09	*	.10	.02	It will always be necessary to have a few strong, able people actually running everything. [agree or disagree]
CRIVIC	3449	.26	*	.05	*	.14	.38	What was that crime? What actually happened? [most recent criminal victimization]
TELLCRI1	3460	.07	*	.24	*	.21	*	Did you report this crime to the militsiia, to some other official, or to a comrades' court?

Addendum B (*contd.*)

VARIABLE	DKCOL	OUT	REL	JEW	INT	men	wom	Question
						INTSEX		
OFFDIDIT	3507	.06	*	.25	*	.01	*	Was the person an official in a responsible position? [person who committed crime]
INFNAT	3609	.00	.06	.37	*	.01	.19	Was nationality very important, somewhat important, or not important in being asked to join the party?
WORKJOIN	3617	.23	*	.11	*	.14	.11	Which social class, stratum, or group was most likely to be recruited into the party?
FRDJOIN	3628	.09	.22	.07	*	.04	.23	Would you advise friend of the same skill and social level to join the party or not?
CPSUMEMB	3643	.04	*	.25	*	.13	*	About how many people belonged to the party in (end of LNP)?
YPUNISH2	3655	.00	.04	.09	*	.08	.08	And which was the next most important? [second reason for punishing criminals]
VUZBENE1	3705	.02	.03	.03	.15	.02	.03	Who benefited most from the Soviet Union's system of higher education, or did no one benefit?
AGRBENE2	3713	.03	.05	.08	.02	.07	.09	At that time, who did you think benefited the most from the collectivization of agriculture?
JOEMARX	3721	.04	.25	.13	*	.21	.08	Stalin's actions were contrary to the ideals of Marx and Lenin. [agree or disagree]
BLACKCOW	3729	.02	.13	.15	.06	.09	.02	Tell me with which people you would have talked during LNP about where to buy clothes on black market.
CRITREL	3737	.02	.14	.04	.04	.09	.07	With which of these people would you have talked during LNP about criticizing government officials?

Variable	ID							Question
FORPOLIC	3745	.24	.16	.25	.08	.14	.03	Do you think the Soviet Union's foreign policy would be the same regardless of Communist government?
HOSUSA	3753	.13	.06	*	.14	.21	.07	What about the United States? [how hostile was it toward the USSR?]
POWYUGO	3761	.18	.12	*	.04	.24	.02	What about Yugoslavia? [how powerful was it in relation to the USSR?]
KEEP1	3805	15	.05	*	.09	.13	.14	If you created a new system of government in the Soviet Union, would it be different or the same?
POVERTY	3820	.02	.04	*	.01	.20	.06	A significant number of Soviet citizens live in poverty. [agree or disagree]
ASSIGNMO	3907	.05	.19	*	.10	*	.19	How long was that assignment supposed to last? [job assignment after completed level of educ.]
ADVERTJ1	3920	.06	.12	*	.04	.08	.05	How did you find out about that vacancy? [job vacancy advertised at school]
FRDJ2	3937	.09	.03	*	.01	.15	.13	How did you find out about that vacancy? [told about job vacancy by friend]
BUSINO	3952	.15	.12	*	.10	*	.08	How many times a week did you do that? [use work time for personal business]
JOBADV1	3963	.14	.07	*	.12	.04	.09	What was the most important factor, in your opinion, that helped to advance your career?
FEWER2O	4008	.28	.23	*	.18	*	.02	On your job, could you have met the targets with 20% fewer workers?
MONEYREL	4029	.04	.01	*	.22	.19	.05	Did you receive money from relatives or friends that year that you were not expected to pay back?
YDOWN1	4150	.13	.09	*	.03	.01	.04	In your opinion, why was the productivity of labor declining? (first reason)
YNOMEAT	4165	.21	.21	*	.20	*	.08	Which of these would you have said was the main reason? [for a shortage of meat]
NOGOODS2	4216	.23	.09	*	.18	*	.13	Why did you think this happened? (second reason) [shortages of other goods like cars & furniture]

Addendum B (contd.)

VARIABLE	DKCOL	OUT	REL	JEW	INT	INT SEX		Question
						men	wom	
RECVPENS	4231	.16	.02	.44	*	.01	.12	Between T1 and end of LNP, did you receive any kind of pension or grant?
PENSINC	4259	.08	*	*	*	*	.33	Did your total income decrease a great deal, somewhat, or increase after receiving a pension?
IUD	4313	.01	.04	.00	.03	.07	.07	Which of these methods did you (or your partner) use? [birth control, IUD]
ABORTNO	4328	.04	.01	.18	*	*	.13	How many times did you have an abortion or terminate a pregnancy when you were in the Soviet Union?
NEIGHBOR	4343	.27	.08	.04	*	.12	*	When your children were three years old or younger, who took care of them while you were at work?
GROSMOV1	4365	*	*	.41	*	.01	.02	What was your own gross monthly income from all sources just before you moved from there?
CITYCULT	4429	.15	*	.15	*	.19	.13	Were cultural opportunities better in (place in Q. 55) or (place in Q. 58) or about the same?
CENSHOME	4437	.05	.03	.16	*	.00	.05	Was the census conducted in your home, or in some other place?
RCENSUS	4452	.02	.25	.03	*	.14	.23	Refer to Q. 62C. Did R answer census questions?
ANSW4KID	4522	.01	*	.07	*	.11	.14	For whom did you answer [census] questions? [child/children]

References

Anderson, Barbara A., and Brian D. Silver. Forthcoming. "The Validity of Survey Responses: Insights from Interviews of Married Couples in a Survey of Soviet Emigrants," *Social Forces.*

Bahry, Donna, 1987. "Surveying Soviet Emigrants: Political Attitudes and Ethnic Bias." Manuscript, Department of Politics, New York University.

Cherlin, Andrew, and Shiro Horiuchi. 1980. "Retrospective Reports of Family Structure: A Methdological Assessment," *Sociological Methods and Research,* 8: 454–69.

Hindelang, Michael J. 1976. *Criminal Victimization in Eight American Cities.* Cambridge, Mass.: Ballinger.

Powers, Edward A., Willis J. Goudy, and Pat M. Keith. 1978. "Congruence between Panel and Recall Data in Longitudinal Research," *Public Opinion Quarterly,* 42: 380–89.

Smith, Tom. 1984. "Recalling Attitudes: An Analysis of Retrospective Questions on the 1982 GSS," *Public Opinion Quarterly,* 48: 639–49.

Sudman, Seymour, and Norman Bradburn. 1974. *Response Effects in Surveys.* Chicago: Aldine.

Glossary

Active household: Family with at least one member employed in the public sector.

Active population: Those who were employed and received wages in the public sector at the end of the LNP.

Attestat: School completion certificate.

Blat: Connections or influence (used to avoid undesirable activities or to gain advantages).

Closed (medical) clinics: Clinics available only to those with special privileges.

Closed shops: The network of shops closed to all but specially designated shoppers.

COMPH: Variable name for "completed higher education."

COMPSEC: Variable name for "completed secondary education."

Core questionnaire: The common component of the questionnaire that was administered to all respondents.

CPSU: Communist Party of the Soviet Union.

Druzhinniki: People's patrols composed of volunteers assigned to help maintain public order, for example, at sports events, on the streets, or at official public demonstrations.

GRADST: Variable name for "at least some graduate study."

HH income: Household income.

ISIP: A family budget survey conducted in Israel by Gur Ofer and Aaron Vinokur with a sample of 1,250 families that emigrated from the Soviet Union to Israel during the mid-1970s.

KGB (*Komitet gosudarstvennoi bezopasnosti*): Soviet secret police.

Kolkhoznik: Worker on a collective farm.

Komsomol: Young Communist League.

Last normal period (LNP): Respondents were asked to pinpoint the month and year in which they applied to emigrate. They were also asked whether plans to emigrate significantly changed their lives even before that date and, if so, to specify the month and year in which their lives changed. The "last normal period" was defined as the five-year period leading up to the earlier of these two dates.

Life history chart: Chart used in conjunction with the SIP questionnaire, on which one space appears for every year since the early twentieth century. The respondent marked those years in which a move from one city, town, or village to another took place and those years (since reaching age 18) in which he or she did not have a paying job for at least six months. A column was similarly marked for spouse's unemployment.

Na levo: Under-the-table or other quasi-legal economic transaction.

Natsional'nost': Nationality.

NCSEER: National Council for Soviet and East European Research.

Nomenklatura: Category of jobs directly under the party's or a higher agency's control.

NORC: National Opinion Research Center, University of Chicago.

Obshchestvennaia rabota: Community service/public affairs work; participation in community/public affairs.

OVIR (*Otdel viz i registratsii inostrannykh grazhdan*): Visa and registration department.

Praktika: The practical application of scientific research.

Protektsiia: Protection or influence, used to obtain advantageous position or avoid something.

Psychological weighting: A subjective tendency to romanticize or denigrate conditions to which one cannot return.

Rabochie: Manual workers.

Referent population: The adult European population of large and medium-sized cities of the USSR.

Rynok: A legal private market.

Samizdat: Illegal, underground literature.

Sample for the General Survey: 3,738 individuals selected from the sample frame according to stratified sampling procedures. Each individual in the sample frame had a known probability of being selected, which varied with the individual's nationality, education, size of city, and region of origin within the USSR.

Sample frame: All Soviet emigrants who arrived in the United States between January 1, 1979, and April 30, 1982, and who were between ages 21 and 70, inclusive, at date of arrival, totaling 33, 618.

SATGOODS: Variable name for "satisfaction with availability of consumer goods."

SATHOUSE: Variable name for "satisfaction with housing."

SATJOB: Variable name for "satisfaction with job."

SATMEDC: Variable name for "satisfaction with public medical care."

SATSOL: Variable name for "satisfaction with standard of living."

SIP: Soviet Interview Project.

SIP Data Management Center (DMC): Located at Vanderbilt University; under the direction of Professor Michael Swafford.

Sloi: Stratum.

SOMEH: Variable name for "at least some higher education."

SPECSEC: Variable name for "specialized secondary schools."

Supplements to the core questionnaire: Three one-hour questionnaires, randomly assigned to one-third of the respondents. These were called the blue, green, and orange supplements.

Tamizdat: Unauthorized manuscripts by Soviet authors published abroad only.

Tekhnikum: Technical school

VUZy (*vysshie uchebnye zavedeniia*): Institutions of higher education; can be either a university or an institute. (Singular, VUZ.)

Znakomstvo: Acquaintance.

General bibliography of Soviet Interview Project publications

Anderson, Barbara A. "The Life Course of Soviet Women Born 1905–1960." University of Illinois SIP Working Paper Series, #11, February 1986.

Anderson, Barbara A., and Brian D. Silver, "Descriptive Statistics for the Sampling Frame Population: The Eligible Population for the Soviet Interview Project General Survey," University of Illinois SIP Working Paper Series, #2, revised January 1986.

"The SIP General Survey Sample," University of Illinois SIP Working Paper Series, #21, July 1986.

"The Validity of Survey Responses: Insights from Interviews of Married Couples in a Survey of Soviet Emigrants," *Social Forces* (forthcoming in 1987).

"Attitudes and Values of Migrants and Natives of Moscow, Leningrad, and Kiev." University of Illinois SIP Working Paper Series (forthcoming in 1987).

Anderson, Barbara A., Brian D. Silver, and Robert A. Lewis. "Demographic Estimates for the Post-sampling Weights of the SIP General Survey." University of Illinois SIP Working Paper Series, #4, revised June 1986.

Bahry, Donna. "Politics, Generations, and Change in the USSR." University of Illinois SIP Working Papers Series, #20, April 1986.

Bahry, Donna, and Brian D. Silver. "The Intimidation Factor: The Symbolic Uses of Terror." University of Illinois SIP Working Paper Series, #31, February 1987.

Balzer, Marjorie Mandelstam. "Guide to Materials for the Project on the Soviet Social System (Harvard Project/Soviet Refugee Interview and Questionnaire Data, 1950–53)." University of Illinois SIP Working Paper Series, #1, August, 1980.

Edwards, W. Sherman. "Interviewer Training for the Soviet Interview Project General Survey." University of Illinois SIP Working Paper Series, #3, June 1983.

Garrard, John. "Soviet Book Hunger." *Problems of Communism*, 34, no. 5 (1985): 72–81.

"Hunger nach Büchern in der Sowjetunion: Okonomishe und ideologische Hindernisse," *Beiträge zur Konflikt Forschung*, 3 (1986): 79–97.

"Shta chitaju Soviet," *Nedeljne Informativne Novine* (Belgrade), September 21, 1986.

Garrard, John, and Carol Garrard. "The Organizational Weapon: Russian Literature and the Union of Soviet Writers." University of Illinois SIP Working Paper Series, #17, April 1986.

Gray, Kenneth. "Insights from the Soviet Interview Project: The Soviet Food Complex." University of Illinois SIP Working Paper Series, #26, October 1986.

"Soviet Utilization of Food: Meat and Milk Industries." University of Illinois SIP Working Paper Series, #34, April 1987.

409

Gregory, Paul R. "Productivity, Slack, and Time Theft in the Soviet Economy: Evidence from the Soviet Interview Project." University of Illinois SIP Working Paper Series, #15, February 1986.

Gregory, Paul R. and Irwin Collier. "Soviet Unemployment: Evidence from the Soviet Interview Project." University of Illinois Working Paper Series, #35, March 1987.

Gregory, Paul R., and Janet Kohlhase. "The Earnings of Soviet Workers: Human Capital, Loyalty, and Privilege" (Evidence from the Soviet Interview Project). University of Illinois SIP Working Paper Series, #13, revised June 1986.

"Soviet Regional Wages: Evidence from the Soviet Interview Project." University of Illinois Working Paper Series (forthcoming in 1987).

Karklins, Rasma. "Soviet Elections Revisited: The Significance of Voter Abstention in Non-competitive Balloting." *American Political Science Review*, 80 (June 1986).

"Nationality Policy and Ethnic Relations in the USSR." University of Illinois SIP Working Paper Series, #10, January 1986.

"Determinants of Ethnic Identification in the USSR: The Soviet Jewish Case." *Ethnic and Racial Studies*, 10, no. 1 (1987): 27–47.

Linz, Susan J. "Managerial Autonomy in Soviet Firms." University of Illinois SIP Working Paper Series, #18, April 1986.

Lubrano, Linda L. "The Attentive Public for Soviet Science and Technology." University of Illinois SIP Working Paper Series, #32, January 1987.

Millar, James R. "Emigrants as Sources of Information about the Mother Country: The Soviet Interview Project." University of Illinois SIP Working Paper Series, #5, December 1983.

"The Soviet Interview Project: History, Method, and the Problem of Bias." University of Illinois SIP Working Paper Series, #22, September 1986.

Millar, James R., and Elizabeth Clayton, "Quality of Life: Subjective Measures of Relative Satisfaction." University of Illinois SIP Working Paper Series, #9, February 1986.

"Education, Job Experience, and the Gap between Male and Female Wages in the USSR: Evidence from the Soviet Interview Project." University of Illinois SIP Working Paper Series, forthcoming in 1987.

Millar, James R., and Peter Donhowe. "Poll of Soviet Emigres: It's No Workers' Paradise." *Washington Post*, February 2, 1986, pp. C1-4.

"Trouble in the Workers' Paradise?" *Houston Chronicle*, February 9, 1986, sec. 6, p. 4.

"The Classless Society Has a Wide Gap between Rich and Poor." *The Global Pulse* (*Washington Post* national weekly edition), February 17, 1986.

"An Overview of First Findings of the Soviet Interview Project," University of Illinois SIP Working Paper Series, #16, March 1986.

"Emigres Cite Soviet Problems: 'Living Archive' Recalls Discontent, Inequities." *Dallas Times Herald*, March 9, 1986.

"Life, Work, and Politics in Soviet Cities: Results of the Soviet Interview Project." *Problems of Communism*, 36, no. 1 (1987).

Shenfield, Stephen, "The Functioning of the Soviet System of State Statistics

(Findings from Interviews with former Soviet Statistical Personnel)." University of Illinois SIP Working Paper Series, #23, June 1986.

"How Reliable Are Published Soviet Statistics on Kolkhoz Trade?" *Journal of Official Statistics* (Stockholm), forthcoming.

Silver, Brian D. "Political Beliefs of the Soviet Citizen: Sources of Support for Regime Norms." University of Illinois SIP Working Paper Series, #6, December 1985.

Solomon, Peter. "The Case of the Vanishing Acquittal: Informal Norms and the Practice of Soviet Criminal Justice." University of Illinois SIP Working Paper Series, #28, January 1987.

"Soviet Politicians and Criminal Prosecutions: The Logic of Party Intervention." University of Illinois SIP Working Paper Series, #33, March 1987.

Swafford, Michael, "Perceptions of Social Status in the USSR." University of Illinois SIP Working Paper Series, #12, March 1986.

"Perceptions of Distributive Justice in the USSR." University of Illinois SIP Working Paper Series, forthcoming in 1987.

Swafford, Michael, Carol A. Zeiss, Carolyn S. Breda, and Bradley P. Bullock. "Response Effects in SIP's General Survey of Soviet Emigrants." University of Illinois SIP Working Paper Series, #29, January 1987.

Vinokur, Aaron, and Gur Ofer. "Inequality of Earnings, Household Income, and Wealth in the Soviet Union in the 70s." University of Illinois SIP Working Paper Series, #25, June 1986.

Zimmerman, William. "Mobilized Participation and the Nature of the Soviet Dictatorship." University of Illinois SIP Working Paper Series, #19, April 1986.

Zimmerman, William, and Deborah Yarsike. "Inter-generational Change and Soviet Foreign Policy." University of Illinois SIP Working Paper Series, #24, September 1984.

Index

Abdolali, Nasrin, 61
abortion, 213–14; response disparities, 381
Abramson, Paul R., 75, 100
absenteeism: frequency, 246, 263, 273; by occupation, 265–66; perception of, 241–43, 248–50; and productivity, 253–59
absorption: survey focus on, 11, validation of survey results, 3
Academy of Sciences: confidence in, 156–60
active population, 174; income, 184–89
age: and abortion, 213–14; and attentiveness to science, 145; and career continuity, 227–28; and childbearing, 207, 212f; and collective–individual rights, 117–23; and compliant behavior, 83; and education, 208–10; and employment, 222–25; and ethnic relations, 316–17; and fertility, 216–17; and health care satisfaction, 49–51; and income, 236–37; and job satisfaction, 45; and labor-force participation, 205f; and marital status, 207, 210–11; and material satisfaction, 130–32; and political interest, 88; and political participation, 73, 76–81; and productivity, 251–54; and reason for emigration, 107–08; and regime support, xi, 26–27, 125; of respondents, 358; and response rates, 364–66; and sample frame, 356–58; and sample selection, 355; and satisfaction with quality of life, 33–36, 51–53, 55–56; and scientific attentiveness, 153–55, 166; of scientists, 151; and second job, 271; and state–private control, 117–19, 122, 125; and social values, x; and support for regime norms, 118–22; and time theft, 268; and wage, 199, 225t, 232–34; weights, 367–69; see also generation
agriculture: confidence in scientific improvement of, 161–65; support for private, 22
alcoholism: extent of, 246, 263, 272–73; by occupation, 265–66; and productivity, 248–50, 253–59; at the workplace, 241–43
Aleksandrova, A., 177
Andropov, Iuri: influence of KGB, 91
arrest: and unconventional behavior, 86–87
artifacts: testing, 372–73, 374n
attentiveness: methodology, 145–46; see also scientific attentiveness
attentive public: defined, 142–43
Australia: distribution of wealth, 193
Axelrod, Robert, 322
Azrael, Jeremy, 4n, 72, 82, 100, 101

Bauer, Raymond, 4, 91, 95, 114, 281–82, 286, 299
Belgium: fertility, 215
Berbaum, Michael, 322
Bergson, Abram, 171–72, 177, 181, 190, 192, 194, 242
Berliner, Joseph, 26, 61, 171, 241–42, 279
Bialer, Seweryn, 72, 100, 102, 302
bias, 18–25, 388; detection, 139; emigrant, 19–20, 104, 108, 138–39, 173, 297; ethnic, 104, 173, 303, 376, 384, 388; interviewer country, 373, 376–77; interviewer sex, 376–77; memory decay, 22–23, 104, 351; and the referent population, 371; reluctant participants, 375–76; response, 361, 361n; and sample selection, 371; sample stratification, 23–24; structural, 173; time lapse, 375–79
Big Deal, 102; success of, 128
birth control: response disparities, 388; see also abortion, fertility
black market, see na levo
blat: and career advancement, 48; and employment, 349–53; increase of, 28; job advancement, 48

412

87; sample reliability, 64–65; by sex, 86

union republics: and ethnic privilege, 326–28; and ethnic relations, 303, 314

United Kingdom: distribution of wealth, 193; financial assets, 196t; wage distribution, 182

United States, 56, 373; civil defense, 344; distribution of wealth, 193–94; and emigrant bias, 138–39; female labor-force participation, 203–05; financial assets, 196t: health care, 49; income of women, 237t; perception of, 20, 28, 53, 114; and reluctant respondents, 372; scientific attentiveness, 145–50, 153–55; social stratification, 236–37, 279, 283; wage distribution, 182

University of Illinois, 7; archive, 30; Institutional Review Board, 18

U.S. Air Force: Harvard Project funding, 4, 6

U.S. Department of Defense: SIP funding, 6, 9

U.S. State Department: SIP funding, 9

Velkoff, Victoria, 100, 203, 354

Verba, Sidney, 75

Volkov, Iu. E., 73

voting behavior, 62–63, 69; and conventional behavior, 83; by decision to emigrate, 336–37; by generation, 83–84; mobilization, 333–38, 345–46; by occupation, 84f, 336, 346; participation, 62–63, 236–37; and regime support, 133, 133n

wages: by age, 225t, 232–34; and childbearing, 232; deciles, 176–77, 180, 197–98; distribution, 175–77, 180–82; and distribution of wealth, 172–74, 197; by education, 176–77, 182, 232–

34; and material incentives, 258–59; methodology, 199; by occupation, 179t, 259; by participation, 232–34; and productivity, 273; public sector, 183; questions asked, 173; by sex, 176–77, 232–34; source of, 174–75; Soviet studies, 185

wartime generation: defined, 74; KGB power, 92f; Komsomol membership, 79f; political activity, 77f; political risk, 90f; privilege gap, 93f; voting behavior, 83–84

Weber, Max: social stratification, 25

weights: and multivariate analysis, 370n; purpose of, 365–69; research implications, 370–71

Western Europe, 72; interviewer's country, 373

West Germany: mobilization, 346; political activity, 69–70

Wiles, Peter, 171–72, 190

women: childbearing age, 207, 212f; education, 208–10; income, 236–37; labor-force participation, 203–08; marital status, 207; see also sex

work committees: membership, 337–38

worker efficiency: and productivity, 253–58

working class: prestige, 25; and social stratification, 284–86, 300

working conditions: descriptive statistics, 249–50t; questions asked, 246–47

work slack: by occupation, 261

World War II, 61, 68, 102, 281, 286; effect on labor force, 203; as a formative experience, 72; generational effects, 71

Yarsike, Deborah, 332

Young, Crawford, 301

Zaslavsky, Victor, 302

Zeiss, Carol, 142